PUBLISHED ON
THE FOUNDATION ESTABLISHED IN MEMORY OF
OLIVER BATY CUNNINGHAM
OF THE CLASS OF 1917, YALE COLLEGE

N'EN CROYEZ PAS NI LES DIATRIBES
VIRULENTES DE SES DÉTRACTEURS NI
L'ENTHOUSIASME NON MOINS RIDICULE
DE SES PARTISANS!
CE N'EST PAS UN DIEU
CE N'EST PAS UN DIABLE
C'EST UN HOMME
ET C'EST L'HOMME QUE NOUS AIMERIONS
À METTRE À NU DEVANT LES YEUX DE
NOS LECTEURS

JOURNAL FRANÇAIS 16 NOVEMBRE 1792

DANTON

BY HERMANN WENDEL

TRANSLATED FROM THE GERMAN

NEW HAVEN · YALE UNIVERSITY PRESS · 1935

TO

THE *MANES* OF GEORG BÜCHNER

———

THE dedication to the German poet Georg Büchner might
lead some people to the conclusion that this book belongs
among works of the imagination. It does not. It is history,
which I have attempted to shape, that is, as far as I could to
bring to life. Without disdaining the methods of the artist
it nevertheless keeps straitly to the rules of the historian.

For, without inner visions, the very mandarin of historical
science, in spite of buttons and peacock feathers, remains a
bungler.

HERMANN WENDEL

INTRODUCTION TO THE AMERICAN EDITION

I AM very glad that DANTON, after having been published in German, French, Italian, Dutch, and Portuguese should now be presented to the nation which in the eighteenth century provided the model for the *Déclaration des droits de l'homme* and in the twentieth century studied the Great Revolution more ardently than any other country, with the exception of course of France.

During the few years since the appearance of my book in German, research on Danton has not been dormant. In 1932 Louis Barthou brought out his monograph in which the Minister of Justice of the Third Republic speaks with both competence and elegance of the Minister of Justice of the First Republic. Along with Mirabeau, Danton seems to him the greatest man of the Revolution. He praises not only Danton's truly revolutionary gift of oratory and the steadfastness of his policy, but also his wise moderation that was evident in spite of his unruly impulses, his political instinct and astuteness and his well-developed diplomatic sense of the necessities of a government, although his tactics were not based on any elaborate theory, and he refers repeatedly to Jaurès, who said of Danton that he bore the revolution in the center of his being. Quite obviously Barthou enjoys this colorful, rough, impetuous, abundantly rich, Rabelaisian nature which with all its contradictions is more attractive than any pale, anæmic, rectangular abstraction. This year in addition there will go to press Pierre Caron's thorough study, *Danton et les massacres de septembre*, which promises to give the definitive answer to a much contested and still disputed question.

The dispute over Danton's morals and integrity is by no means done with, and, even for a number of non-specialists, it is linked with the names of Alphonse Aulard and Albert Mathiez. By their investigations and work both alike have been of eminent service to the French Revolution. Aulard was born

July 19, 1849, in Montbron (Charente). After completing his
studies at a Gymnasium, he attended from 1867 to 1870 the
École Normale Supérieure, from which so many enlightened
minds have emerged, and he then taught first as professor at
the Gymnasiums in Nimes and Nice and later at the universities
in Aix, Montpellier, Dijon, and Poitiers. In 1885 a professorship in the history of the French Revolution was created for
him at the Sorbonne which he held until he reached the retiring
age in 1922. His chief work is a voluminous and profound
Political History of the French Revolution, but the three volumes of his *Orateurs de la Révolution* and a quantity of shorter
studies, collected in the *Études et leçons sur la Révolution Française,* also confirm his proud but modest words: "I have served
the Revolution through truth." And in a separate book he unmasked Taine as a frivolous, thoroughly unreliable, and partisan
historian of the Great Revolution. But with all his scientific
zeal, all his thoroughness, all his inclination to neutrality, Aulard
did not have toward the subject to which he had devoted his
life the cool detachment of an entomologist toward the beetle
he impales. He never made a secret of his spiritual relationship
to the Revolution. He rightly insisted that to describe a fire
objectively while it is still burning our fingers is an ideal beyond
reality. He stressed the fact that so far every history of the
Revolution has betrayed its author's political conviction. He
referred to Michelet who "wanted to teach the Republic by
telling of the Revolution," and confessed that in his own work
he had to reveal himself as an enthusiast for the democratic lay
republic.

So this savant was to be found wherever there was a fight for
a more republican republic, for a more democratic democracy.
It was not merely during the days of the Dreyfus scandal that
his was one of the loudest voices in the battle for human rights;
and instead of confining his knowledge to lecture hall and study
he proclaimed in innumerable articles of the Leftist press his
republican, democratic, anticlerical, and humanitarian convictions. Furthermore, during the World War he deduced from the
principles of the years 1789 to 1793 the necessity for a true
league of nations, and was later one of the sturdiest pioneers of

the Franco-German conciliation. Happy and deeply moved he presided in the Reichstag in Berlin at the "International Congress of the Federated Leagues of Nations in 1927," and he was still actively interested in the problems of the day when he died on October 23, 1928, at the age of almost eighty.

Mathiez' career was similar. He was born in 1874, of a farmer family of the Department Haute-Saône. Like Aulard, he, too, graduated from the École Normale and first had to earn his living as a gymnasium teacher in small towns such as Montauban and La Roche-sur-Yon before he attained, in 1926 by way of the universities of Caen, Nancy, Besançon, and Dijon, the professorship at the Sorbonne which had been created for Aulard. A long series of works is evidence of the passionate earnestness with which he went at his task, and of the unusual knowledge of facts which he acquired in studies such as *Les Origines des cultes révolutionnaires, Le Club des Cordeliers pendant la crise de Varennes, Les Grandes journées de la constituante, La Victoire en l'An II, Études Robespierristes, Robespierre terroriste, Autour de Robespierre, La Révolution Française, L'Affaire de la Compagnie des Indes, La Vie chère et le mouvement social sous la Terreur.* What the *Société de l'histoire de la Révolution Française* with its publication, *La Révolution Française,* was to Aulard, the *Société des Études Robespierristes* with its review, *Annales historiques de la Révolution Française,* was to Mathiez. Like Aulard, Mathiez had an enormous interest in the political problems of the present day. Everything that smacked of surfeit and greed repelled this fiery and pure character; his development, therefore, led him, after the war, as far left as the Communists, but he stayed there no longer than did Anatole France. In contrast to Aulard he was still at the age of productive energy when, on February 26, 1932, he died in his classroom at the Sorbonne in the middle of a lecture; hopes were buried with him.

Mathiez could almost call himself a disciple of Aulard since at his start as a historian he was advised and sponsored by his older and maturer colleague. But over Danton they quarreled, and although Mathiez attacked Aulard, while Aulard never attacked Mathiez, the difference as to Danton's worth and character remained the dividing line that irreconcilably separated

those two great historians of the Revolution. And yet neither of
them got around to writing a monumental work about Danton.
What they had to say about him is to be found in a series of
shorter studies, which Aulard incorporated in his *Études et
leçons*, and Mathiez gathered in such reference books as *Autour
de Danton* and *Danton et la paix*.

Whatever attitude one may himself take toward the problem
of Danton, it must be recognized that Aulard treated it with
more calm, circumspection, and restraint than Mathiez. Without neglecting the moral aspect he concentrated chiefly on the
political, demonstrating what a driving power of political energy
Danton was to the Revolution. Mathiez, on the other hand, concentrated chiefly on morals and fired his opinions of the tribune
like shells. The deeper he got into the subject the grimmer his
attitude became, and eventually he hated Danton as one hates
a personal enemy; in the last years of his life he no longer even
called him by name, but referred to him only as "the rascal"
and "the bandit." To Mathiez the man whose monument rises
in Paris on the Boulevard Saint-Germain was "a cynical gambler," "a soldier of fortune of the Revolution" who used the
Revolution to fill his own pockets, "a pleasure-seeking demagogue who sold himself to all who wanted to buy him: to the
court as well as to the Lameth brothers, to the purveyors of supplies as well as to the counterrevolutionaries; a bad Frenchman
who doubted of victory and secretly prepared a shameful peace
treaty with the enemy; a deceitful revolutionary who became
the last hope of the Royalists." Therefore: a bandit! Therefore:
a rascal!

To support this conception Mathiez sagaciously collected evidence from everywhere—even one of his collaborators and followers, Professor Georges Lefebvres, is compelled to admit
"just like the chief of police of the Committee of Public Safety."
Quite obviously Mathiez was, however, in error when he set
down the "hero worship" of Danton as the belated work of the
sons of the tribune or of the Third Republic. Already Stendhal
had numbered Danton among the *"fondateurs de la France
actuelle"*; Victor Hugo in his inaugural speech before the Académie Française in 1840 had called Danton *"un homme de premier*

ordre," and as early as 1835 when the German poet Georg Büchner selected a hero for the symbolic and dramatic personification of the Revolution, he chose Danton.

To what extent the accusations against Danton can be reconciled with the facts I have tried to show in my biography; I have treated this subject in still greater detail in an essay, "Danton and Robespierre," published in the December, 1932, issue of *Die Gesellschaft*. In the meantime the material damaging to Danton has decreased rather than increased. His friends and enemies alike have had to admit that the strongest argument against him was the sentence in Mirabeau's letter of March 10, 1791, to Count de la Marck, which is mentioned in this book on p. 78. The Mirabeau–La Marck correspondence was published by Adolphe Bacourt. As early as 1891 it was pointed out that where it was possible to make comparisons, the printed text deviated considerably from the original manuscript; however, there have not been many opportunities of comparing, as the Arenberg family keeps the papers of La Marck hidden even from historical investigation. The same Bacourt also published the memoirs of Talleyrand in five volumes and their authenticity was immediately and vigorously challenged. Now Lacour-Gayet in the fourth volume of his monumental Talleyrand monograph is making very sensational revelations. After the accidental discovery of a manuscript of Talleyrand's permitted him to check, it developed that Bacourt had not only deleted and arbitrarily altered Talleyrand's original, but had also added to the memoirs whole long paragraphs of his own manufacture! If Bacourt was so much the opposite of a conscientious editor of the memoirs of the Prince of Benevent—the term "forger" almost suggests itself—what guarantee is there that he has not also corrected the letters of Mirabeau according to his whims? Who can prove that the famous sentence, "Danton received thirty thousand livres yesterday," is actually Mirabeau's and not Bacourt's? At all events the question remains open.

I have known both Aulard and Mathiez personally, although not intimately. Aulard resided on the Place de l'École, close to the spot where the Café du Parnasse once stood and where Danton met his Gabrielle. I sat opposite him in his study, which was crammed with books and decorated with engravings of the time of the Revolution. The old gentleman straightened up at his desk and looked younger when the conversation turned to the days of the Convention. I made the acquaintance of his savage opponent at a dinner at the house of M. André Moczow, professor of Slavonics at the Collège de France. Mathiez' outward appearance was as I had imagined it: shoulders like hewn stone, chest like a battering-ram, legs like pile drivers, a roughly hewn head, a somewhat aggressive face with a foil-like pointed blond moustache, and behind a *pince-nez* vivid eyes which now flamed angrily. For the host, inclined to be humorous, had touched off the mine at the very introduction: "Monsieur Mathiez, Robespierrist!" "Monsieur Wendel, Dantonist!" At once Mathiez exploded, hurled flashes of lightning, erupted fire and lava, and even after he had begun to eat his soup, the volcano continued to smolder. Soon he sent me an English copy of his *Révolution Française* with a threatening dedication which impressed upon me—*"que la réhabilitation de Danton n'est pas seulement un outrage à la vérité, mais l'indice d'une politique équivoque et dangereuse pour la démocratie."*

Aulard and Mathiez are dead, leaving behind the work of a lifetime, but Danton lives on, and not solely in the dissension of their disciples who fight over him as once Greeks and Trojans fought over the dead body of Patroclus.

HERMANN WENDEL

Neuilly-sur-Seine, May, 1935.

I
Rise
1759—1789

· DANTON ·

RCIS-SUR-AUBE is a town in the center of Champagne—
la Champagne pouilleuse, barren Champagne—an arid,
gently undulating region which stretches endlessly north
and south, east and west, one of the barest and most deserted
districts of France. In recent years the country has been re-
forested and the region produces props for use in coal and iron
pits. Here and there an isolated dwelling may be seen, crouching
away from the wind; but beyond these there is nothing but the
vast expanse of chalky plain. The town in the midst of this
desolation is not in a position to draw much strength or pleasure
or beauty from its surroundings. It once possessed a sub-prefec-
ture, but this has now been abolished; it still has a stocking factory and the customary war memorial; and when, after the arrival of the local train, the omnibuses of the Mulet Hotel and of
the Pomme d'Or make their way back from the station to the
town, many a passer-by pauses for a moment, and everyone
turns around, to see whether they will afford the spectacle of a
passenger. Such a metropolis is Arcis-sur-Aube.

In the second half of the eighteenth century, cut off from all
the world, the modest hamlet lay in the cocoon of its isolation,
surrounded by almost audible silence. No main road passed
through it; no diligence stopping for a moment to change relays
brought the noise and breath of the outside world. The express
mail to Paris left Troyes every Sunday; on Fridays the mail
from Basle to Paris stopped there before jingling on to the capital; but Troyes was three and a half hours distant and the mail
did not disturb Arcis in its slumbers. With a population nearer
one thousand than two, with unpaved streets which every rain-
fall changed into a morass, with wooden houses of which only
the most pretentious boasted a plaster front in place of stone—
since stone was hard to come by in this region of chalk—with
rudiments of a stocking industry based on a system intermediate between cottage industry and pure sweating, the little town
existed in a peace as profound as it was lethargic.

At the same time, in a desert where scanty stalks of buck-

wheat were dried and preserved for fuel, Arcis was an oasis if
only because it was built on a river. Trees and bushes grew on
the banks of the Aube; black cows grazed in the deep grass, a
wooden bridge crossed the stream, and some distance above a
weir had been built, providing water for a mill belonging to the
neighboring castle. These were so many elements of life in a
landscape of death, and if a peasant of this district ever
dreamed that his sons might rise from their low estate, it was of
Arcis that he thought as the first stage in their career.

Père Danton, who in his day had ploughed the stiff soil of
Plancy, a few hours down stream, and watched the flowers
growing gayly on the roof of his hovel, would have had reason
to be proud had he lived longer. For his son Jacques prospered
as advocate before the local feudal court at Arcis; and though
an attorney was not one of the gentry, still he had no calluses
on his hands, never wore his cloth next his bare skin like the
poor devils in the village, and owned a good house in the Rue de
Vilette. It was not for nothing that his second wife had been
Jeanne-Madeleine Camut, the daughter of a builder who had
silver coins in his pockets. When, on a holiday, he would pay
his mother a visit in his native village—his father had died in
1733—arrayed in his coat of royal blue, yellow waistcoat with
silver buttons, velvet breeches, and cocked hat with silver lace
elegantly under his arm, there was only one opinion in Plancy:
young Danton had got on in the world.

Mère Danton too had been dead and buried for many a long
year when, on October 26, 1759, a son was born to the attorney
—a new rung on the ladder. That an insuperable barrier separated the classes; that peasants and bourgeois sweated and
toiled and paid their due of corvée and of tax while the privileged
classes of nobility and clergy lived on the fat of the land—such
was the law of France which altered not. Yet for the individual
there were loopholes. The grandfather had drudged as a peasant
at Plancy, the father had been a member of the bar at Arcis, and
the son, who had been baptized Georges-Jacques, would have a
practice in Troyes and might yet go to Paris. As for the son's
son—who could tell? There had been cases of a man's wearing
a "de" before his name and a sword at his side in the sun of

Versailles and the court of His Majesty, when his great-grand-
father had carted manure.

———————◆———————

The object of such hopes grew up in the sheltered compla-
cency of small people, but his early education was left a good
deal to himself and to nature, with the result that his childhood
was full of adventures. According to the custom in Champagne,
his first nurse was a cow. One day when he was drinking at her
udder a bull dashed up in a jealous rage and flung the child aside,
slitting his lip with its horn. With the scar there remained an
angry desire for revenge. At seven young Danton attacked a
grazing bull with his stick; the huge beast knocked him down
easily and crushed his nose with its hoof. Another time he was
trampled by a herd of pigs which he had tried to subdue with a
whip; finally smallpox, in those days as common as a cold, left
on his broad face traces as of hail.

But such misfortunes could do no harm to the descendant of
a red-cheeked and virile line of ancestors; his grandfather had
begotten eight children, his father, who was married twice,
eleven. As the grandfather had died at forty-three and the father
at forty, it seemed as though Danton had inherited their stored
marrow and sap; broad shouldered and bull necked, he over-
flowed with exuberant vitality. His mother, a widow since February, 1762, could not always control his impetuosity, nor did
things improve after she had contracted a second marriage with
a respectable cloth merchant named Recordain. The best results
were obtained when young Georges sat on his grandfather's knee
and the old man would say to him: "This is A; say A." But at
the school of an elderly spinster where he was sent to pursue
further the study of reading and writing, his behavior was de-
plorable, and more than once the exasperated woman laid him
across her knee. Young Rousseau had experienced secret trans-
ports of delight under the rod of Mademoiselle Lambercier;
young Danton, already very different from him, kicked violently against the whip and bolted. Again, when a tutor was
engaged to introduce him into the mysteries of *mensa, mensae,*
he often preferred to go roaming with other urchins, to climb

the park railings or to indulge in a game of cards behind a bush in defiance of his elders.

But it was the Aube which exerted the greatest attraction upon him. Although its waters were so shallow that the weeds at the bottom could be plainly seen squirming like fishes, there was a deeper pool below the weir, and for young Danton it was an unparalleled delight to dive into the depths, to split the water with vigorous strokes, or to fill his lungs and stay below the surface until his companions on the banks began to feel half frightened.

At thirteen young Danton was sent to Troyes where it was hoped that he would acquire more seemly manners. How the lad from Arcis opened eyes, mouth, and nose when for the first time he drove through one of the six gates of the capital of Champagne. What a vast city! True, the chalky soil provided no building materials and most of the houses here too were of wood; but though they were weathered, blackened by smoke, and gloomy they were of an imposing height and there were so many of them, so many. What great long streets, some of them actually paved, and all of them full of people hurrying past each other without concern for their neighbors and without time to stop and talk. True, war, famine, and taxes had done much to reduce the splendor of the town; the number of its inhabitants was not what it had been; yet thirty thousand people gathered in one spot were enough to impress and confuse a native of Arcis. And there was plenty on which to feast the eye: the costumes of women and magistrates, cassocks, the frocks of monks and the uniforms of soldiers; the proverb said truly that you could not go through a street in Troyes without meeting a priest or a garde-du-corps.

The town was divided into two parts by the Cru Cordé, a tributary of the Seine. The clerical quarter on the right bank, with its monasteries and churches which centered around the Gothic cathedral, was less important than the bourgeois quarter which centered around the town hall, where the streets were more numerous and the gardens fewer. The prosperity of Troyes derived from its trade in cloth and stuffs and so the city was

Danton's Mother

thoroughly bourgeois. Even its nobility were descended not from crusading squires but from successful tradesmen who had bought the title of Secretary to the King or Treasurer of France, and if it was possible at all for a boy to appreciate such matters, some breath of civic liberty must have touched young Danton in this environment. Of course, there was no lack of piety under the grave sound of the bells of Sainte-Madeleine, Saint-Urbain, Saint-Remy, Saint-Jean-au-Marché; but still the city had vigorously and successfully held off a Jesuit settlement for over a century, while even Louis XIII and Louis XIV attempted in vain to break the liberal spirit of its citizens; and when François Pithou, dying in 1621, left estates, buildings, and capital for the founding of a college, he did so under the express condition that the school must never fall into the hands of the disciples of Loyola.

Instead of the Jesuits it was the Oratorians who had charge of the *Collegium Trecense,* in whose *Catalogus scolasticorum* young Danton was entered after one or two years of training in the lower Seminary. A body of secular clerics, they were much less subject to that blind obedience which made the inferior the helpless instrument of the superior than were the cloistered monks, and they had a constitution that delegated supreme authority to a parliament of the Order. So their government bore no resemblance to that of the State. For since 1614, the period of the rise of the Oratorians, the States-General had not been assembled and the royal autocracy had been continually increasing in scope. The doctrine of *"L'état c'est moi"* muzzled the nation, which had no voice to protest against entanglement in disastrous wars, impoverishment through harsh taxes, and the waste of public money. "It was at this time," a later historian of the Order wrote, "that the Oratorians acquired a constitution which meticulously safeguarded the rights of all, requiring superiors to take into account the opinion of subordinates, and compelling those in authority to give account periodically of their actions, abandoning their powers in favor of a higher authority which was that of the congregation itself as represented by its deputies." Thus the statutes of *Oratorii Christi Domini Nostri Congregatio* were a democratic training ground, provided that Danton in those happy unpolitical years had eyes for politics.

The college was situated in the bourgeois quarter, in the shadow of the church of Saint-Remy and in the quadrangle formed by the streets of L'Eltville, Des Buchettes, Maupeigné, and Du Bois. Although at the beginning of lessons teachers and pupils alike knelt down and prayed *Veni, sancte spiritus,* while on Sundays and holidays mass was compulsory and the confessional had to be attended once a month, the college was free from pious obscurantism. After all, was not the founder of the Order, Father Bérulle, on intimate terms with Descartes, whose principles were condemned by church and monarchy alike? The Order boasted of being a champion of Jansenism, whose religious and political assaults upon traditional authority were a preliminary to the full blast of the Revolution. It was an Oratorian, Father Quesnel, who was the author of "Moral Considerations on the New Testament"—a Jansenist manifesto so bold that the papal *curia* found itself compelled to intervene with the Bull Unigenitus. Again in 1743 the bishop of Troyes, poncest de la Rivière, took severe measures against the Oratorians because they declined to conceal their Jansenist leanings. Finally, it was precisely in the second half of the century, after the expulsion of their ancient foes, the Jesuits, had brought the Oratorians a resounding triumph, that repeated charges were brought against them urging that the spirit of revolt and heresy was at home under their roof tree.

Inspired by the progressive spirit of Jansenism, the Oratorian plan of studies did full justice to the spirit of the new age. Danton was by no means spared Latin and Greek; but greater importance was attached by the Fathers to French and history; and it was an eloquent and almost heretical concession to the spirit of the century of enlightenment that instruction was given in experimental physics, cosmography, mathematics, mechanics, and anatomy. Both masters and scholars took especial pleasure in publicly performing a homemade comedy or tragedy at the end of each scholastic year; an old tradition which, owing to the choice or treatment of subjects, had led on more than one occasion to conflict with the authorities.

Danton's days at the college were happy. He was not one of the few boarders whose daily work was minutely regulated from the moment when they rose at half-past five until half-past eight when they went to bed. Danton was a day boy, boarding with a certain Monsieur Richard, and out of school hours he was at liberty to do practically as he liked. Whether or not the seventeen-year-old lad, as a companion of his youth tells, really set off in June, 1775, to tramp to Rheims and gaze with wonder at the anointing of Louis XVI in the ancient cathedral, it is certain that, led by a lively curiosity, he explored every corner of Troyes, fought with boys of his own age, and gaped with admiration when Bishop Claude-Mathias-Joseph de Barral went in pomp to the cathedral, arrayed in robes of gold, surrounded by venerable vicars-general and canon and clouds of incense.

There were occasions when he showed a certain lack of industry, although he picked up some knowledge of English and Italian in his spare time. But every trace of laziness vanished when it came to exploring the various streams which run through Troyes in every direction. According to the rules of the college, bathing in the open was prohibited, and the comment *doctus in aquis ludere* after the name of a scholar implied disapproval. But this did not worry Danton, who dived and swam to his heart's content.

The September holidays, however, brought still greater joys, when Homer and Suetonius, Pindar and Theocritus were flung aside and he could lie in the grass on the banks of the Aube, drink in the smell of his native soil, and stare up at the sky. The clouds drifted. A jay screamed. There was the sound of the weir.

A question which deeply exercised the whole family—mother, stepfather, grandfather, and the uncle who was post-master at Troyes—was what to do with the boy. His other uncle, the curé of Baberey, described the dignities and prospects of an ecclesiastical life alluringly, but he failed to convince; clearly the stubborn head of young Danton was not meant for a tonsure.

The law, on the other hand, was a profitable trade for its disciples, especially at Paris, and so it was decided that Georges should study law in the capital. Georges had no objection, packed his knapsack, and was off—"God keep you, Mother. Good-by, Father!" Monsieur Recordain drew a long face and talked about the bad times and the lack of business. Young Danton, with a grand and careless gesture, told him to take his future inheritance and use that to make good his losses. What did money matter when his heart was full of the future? In any case, thirty livres and some sous had just been saved, for he had managed through some friends to get a place in the mail for nothing.

And so on a fine day in the year of our Lord 1780 Georges Danton drove off. His age was twenty, his baggage light, and his appetite considerable; but he had vigorous jaws and sharp teeth and was consumed with a curiosity about the morrow that sent shivers down his spine. The driver cracked his whip and clicked his tongue; Troyes, Nogent, Provins, Nangis, Brie Comte-Robert were left behind; the coach rattled, the driver cursed; for the road was one of the busiest and consequently one of the most badly worn in the kingdom. Danton never noticed the jolts and the potholes and hardly had eyes for the towns they passed. But he itched to stretch out his hand and to seize Paris,

P A R I S,

as soon as it should appear above the horizon.

In other days it had been the provincial nobility which the great magnet of Versailles drew from their distant fastnesses to the center of France. Scions of the nobility, young and not so young, they came riding on their nags to catch in their cocked hats the rain of ducats that fell from the Roi Soleil. Now times had changed and different figures were on the way. Every day and week from every district and corner of France they converged on the capital, commoners, the grandsons of peasants and the sons of bourgeois, all in the hope of making their fortunes in Paris, not as parasites but by honest brain work. The restlessness in their hearts added to the restlessness in the metropolis—so many drops falling into a brimming vessel which some day must surely overflow.

When Danton, tired and half intoxicated by all the novelties he had seen, rolled through the Porte Saint-Antoine, his breath nearly stopped: before him there were twenty-five thousand houses and seven hundred thousand inhabitants, a sea of roofs and an ocean of men foaming and roaring; but he had a broad chest and strong arms and the reputation of being a good swimmer.

———————

He felt among friends at the Black Horse in the Rue Geoffroy-l'Asnier, the regular stopping place of all those who came from Champagne. Sounds of home filled his ears, the wind swept over the chalky plains, the Aube babbled.

Next day he knocked at the offices of Maître Vinot, *procureur du parlement*, firmly resolved to obtain a job.

"Well, sit down and copy this page."

After a look at the first few lines the lawyer exclaimed aghast, "Good God, man, what a fist!"

"Maître, I did not come here to do your copying."

Such impudence was disarming. In the old hotel where Vinot lived on the Island of Saint Louis in a street of the same name, Danton found dinner at noon and a bed at night; and here he began to devour the lore of jurisprudence, the youngest and merriest member of the Basoche, that guild of youthful law students which had a judicature of its own, was organized into companies and regiments, and every year, after planting its Maypole in the court of the Palais-de-Justice, marched through the city with drums and fifes. These clerks of the procureurs du parlement were a lawless crew and always ready for their amusements, although they had a rhymed lament which gave a piteous account of their hard day's labor:

> *Un pauvre clerc du Parlement,*
> *Arraché à son lit brusquement,*
> *Comme il dormait profondément,*
> *Gagne l'étude tristement,*
> *Qu'il ose interrompre un moment*
> *Pour déjeuner sommairement,*
> *En revanche écrit longuement,*
> *Dîne a trois heures sobrement,*

Sort au dessert discrètement,
Reprend sa plume promptement,
Lors va souper légèrement,
Grimpe et se couche froidement
Dans un lit fait négligemment,
Dort, et n'est heureux qu'en dormant,
Ah! pauvre clerc du Parlement!

Since his illegible hand made Danton useless for clerical work, he "did the Palais-de-Justice," in the jargon of the clerks. Soon he was at home in the rambling old palace on the Île de la Cité, with its towers and courts, its halls and waiting rooms, its passages and galleries. When once the day's business was over and the last document safely delivered, free time was left which might be spent with other Basochiens in the taverns, passing an arm round the generous hips of tavern wenches and arranging a rendezvous in quick whispers. At other times rapiers would clash in fencing matches, or again he would persuade his friends to come down to the banks of the Seine where he displayed his skill at swimming. Before them lay the jagged outline of the city, and across the river, behind walls and roofs, a heavy mass of stones surrounded by towers—six, seven, or eight of them— rose into the air. Danton threw a questioning look at his companions. "The Bastille," one said. But Danton was already in the water.

Maître Vinot's clerk absorbed Paris with all his sensitive faculties, a monstrous and marvelous town beside which Troyes shrank to a nutshell as Arcis did beside Troyes. A native of treeless Champagne, he was amazed to see whole forests floated down the Seine, piled on the banks, hastily sawed to pieces, and sold for fuel. When he recalled the labor it took at home to gather the building materials for a single stone house, he was astounded at the headlong enterprise which conjured out of nothing long rows of houses and whole streets—and all of stone! Remembering the dark streets of his native town, he stopped full of curiosity the first time he saw a lamplighter wind down one of the new oil lamps, fill it, light it, and finally wind it up again. He gazed thoughtfully up at the gibbet arm where the lamp swayed with a light tinkle of glass and iron.

Then again, what hustling and bustling on the Pont-Neuf, the bridge through which the entire traffic of the city pumped as blood pumps through the heart. True, the recruiting sergeant who swaggered up and down, hand on hip, only threw encouraging glances at the athletic youth and said nothing; and the public scribe who for five sous wrote fine letters for embarrassed clients sat mute in his box. But the street sellers whose goods were spread on the parapet cried their wares in a babel of voices —gingerbread, lace, and leather. And there were second-hand books—he stopped—in boxes and baskets, each and every volume two sous. Fishmongers, oystermen, and greengrocers shouted. The cries of old clothes men and rag dealers mingled with those of the vinegar merchant who pushed a barrel on wheels before him—sounds ranging from bass to falsetto. To draw attention some quacked, some rasped, some miaowed. A long-drawn melancholy cry made Danton turn: the sooty face of a chimney sweep gave him a friendly white-toothed grin. A throng of porters, waterbearers, coal-carriers. A street singer accompanied himself on a squeaking fiddle, a charlatan recommended polar bear's fat for falling hair, and a pretty flower girl stuck a bunch of violets under Danton's nose—"Cheaper than at the Palais-Royal, sir, they're six livres there."

The Palais-Royal? The rendezvous of the idle world, where the Swiss Guard had been posted to keep away "servants in livery, housemaids, school boys, street boys, workmen, and dogs"—here, too, Danton would stroll under the arcades, examining the elegant displays: a collection of waxworks, a mechanical billiard table, a puppet show, a giantess from Prussia— a world of wonders. He feasted on cheese cakes washed down with cider; it was not lack of appetite which kept him from dining at Beauvilliers or La Barrière, but how should he dare to go where the soup was twelve sous, a dish of beans twice that, and a wing of chicken two livres and five sous!

With empty pockets, and hence platonically, the young clerk sauntered through the Tuileries and their terraces until he reached the Place Louis XV on the Seine with its avenue, where beautifully dressed ladies in hats à la Tartare or à l'Espagnole sat on the double row of chairs, inviting admiration. He heard a beauty with a monster muff beseech a toy dog: "Come here, Zémire, come here." He smiled at an *élégant* whose silk waist-coat was embroidered with hunting scenes and from each of whose lower pockets dangled a watch chain with multifarious charms. Splashes of sunlight trembled on the sand and from the boughs of the trees poured lovely music. In the wider streets, the vigorous arteries of the Rue Saint-Denis and Rue Saint-Honoré, the newcomer was overwhelmed by the thunder of vehicles which at the busiest time of the day drowned even the church bells. Wagons, carts, hacks, cabriolets, stagecoaches, a fashion-able English Whiskey rolled and rumbled and sped past. Way, there, way! Preceded by outriders on spirited horses; followed by a master of the horse, posting easily in the saddle, in a state coach all glass and gold with glittering lackeys on each foot-board, a brother of the King's passed and was gone. Danton pressed against the wall to avoid being crushed under the wheels and stared after the noise and glitter with a frown. Clearly in Paris the people were of no account; no one paid any attention to the man on foot, there were no sidewalks for him.

Danton wandered observantly through the suburbs, too; through Saint-Marceau where everything smelt of tanner's bark and the river Bièvre was stained red, blue, and green with the wastage of the dye works, and Saint-Antoine, where the rhythm of saws and planes sounded from the carpenters' shops. Once, at four in the morning, he met a somber cart drawn by twelve men in which yesterday's corpses were being conveyed from the Hôtel-Dieu, the poorhouse, to the Cemetery of Clamart; before it hurried a boy with a bell and another with a tall crucifix and lastly a priest in a greasy cassock. After meeting such a ghost in the dawn, the soul as well as the body needed warming with hot café-au-lait from the tin can of the itinerant vendor who poured it at two sous a cup for the workmen.

So the years passed and a morning came when Monsieur Danton stood in his Sunday best in the anteroom of Maître Vinot ready to say good-by to his master. In his pocket he had the diploma of the *Licencié-en-Droit;* the black attorney's gown had already been ordered. The diploma had not cost him great intellectual labor; after all, what was Rheims for?—a university with the reputation of giving away, nay, of selling its *brevets.* It was an open secret that anyone who wished to become an avocat du parlement could buy the authorization for five hundred livres in the metropolis of Champagne. In any case, Danton had attended lectures at Rheims from April to September, 1784, and was now one of the six hundred attorneys who were either earning their living in Paris or merely rejoicing in the possession of a title. He had an office of his own in the Rue des Mauvaises-Paroles, a narrow alley where the houses were irregular, squat, sooty, and damp, in an ill-smelling, gloomy quarter of the right bank. If he opened the window he looked out over a fantastic landscape of roofs and chimneys. As a beginner he could not be too demanding, and although he had won his first case, the suit of a poor shepherd against the lord of the village, there were not so many clients that they pulled off his door knob. Remittances from home were scanty, and his meals at the Hôtel de la Modestie were of the most frugal. To eat for once to his heart's content he had to make a trip to Arcis and his mother's fleshpots.

On the other hand, he had plenty of time for reflection. He had never taken anything for granted, or any institution for unalterable; and the ferment of the time worked powerfully in him. The child of peasants who had narrowed their eyes to see far and well against the winds of Champagne had inherited an unerring sight; it was impossible for him not to see how disastrously affairs were out of joint in France. He was a child of the soil, he had felt the net of feudal exploitation which enmeshed the peasantry. True, each year the number of landed proprietors grew and they were exempt from the pressure of feudalism. But the peasants still suffered under the weight of medieval imposts. For the fish in the river, the wine in the press, the fire in the oven, and the wind that drove the mill, for everything they paid tithes to the nobleman.

Yet a single walk through the streets sufficed to show how the new class, the bourgeoisie, was elbowing its way ahead. Despite the Louvre, the Tuileries, the Palais-Royal, the Luxembourg and Palais-Bourbon, despite the splendid hotels of the Conti, La Trémoille, Périgord, Mailly, Montmorency, and the palaces of La Rochefoucauld, Harcourt, Luynes, and Croy, Paris was a bourgeois city. The bourgeoisie owned the houses, the land on which they stood, and the cellars which stretched for miles underground. Caravans of merchandise on the road, merchant fleets on the seas, toiling hands in factories and slave labor in tropical colonies all served to fill their pockets. And since the bonds of the huge national debt crackled in their strong-boxes; the bourgeoisie as a financial power already ruled the State.

Politically, however, like the peasants, they had no standing at all. Bourgeois and peasant alike were burdened with heavy taxes for the benefit of the tax-exempt nobility and clergy; and for reward they were without all political rights. Civic rights? The phrase was unknown in France. Mercier wrote in his *Tableau de Paris:* "If I were to appeal to my rights as a citizen, everybody down to the municipal officials would laugh at me."

Unrecognized, but wealthy, self-confident, eager for power and thirsting for change, the bourgeoisie planned for itself a world in its own image. When Danton fell sick of a fever a pile of thick books collected at his bed, among them the *Encyclopédie ou Dictionnaire raisonné des sciences, des arts et des métiers,* published by Messrs. Diderot and D'Alembert, a summary of all knowledge arranged in alphabetical order. Danton impatiently turned the pages. "Acapulco, town and harbor in Mexico . . ." No good. "Acmella, this plant, which is found in Ceylon . . ." No use. "Agrotea. A name of Diana derived from the fact that . . ." No! "Authority . . ." That's better. What does it say about political authority? "No man possesses the natural right to command others. Freedom is the gift of heaven and all individuals of the same species have an equal right to enjoy it if they possess reason."

The reader drew a deep breath.

Again: "Power acquired by force is usurpation. It lasts so long as those who command are stronger than those who obey. When the latter in turn acquire force and cast off the yoke, they have the same right to do so as those who imposed it upon them."

Right again. The important thing was to grow stronger. Danton smiled, his temples throbbed, he read on eagerly. Many a harmless heading contained a sting which went home. "Unpunished" —in itself a harmless and meaningless participle. But: "Crimes remain unpunished because . . . or because the guilty party can evade the law, either by means of . . . or . . . ."—The very case of France! The very case of France!—"through the unhappy privileges of his rank, authority, privilege, money, patronage, or birth." Again, "Legislator": "The person who makes and abolishes laws. In France the king is legislator, at Geneva the people." Impossible not to stop reading and with a clouded brow draw conclusions. Yet again, "Deputy": "In a despotic state the head of the nation is everything and the nation itself nothing. The will of one individual makes the laws and the people are not represented. Such is the constitution of"— France, Danton read, before he had seen the next word. The next word in fact was—in order to confound the censor and no one else—"Asia."

Thus the seed was sown in a receptive mind. Indeed the Encyclopedia was an unrivaled compendium of clear and bold, critical and aggressive philosophy, preaching the gospel of revolution against heavenly and earthly authority with tongues of fire.

Subversive ideas of this kind were in the air wherever Danton went. He had no entrée to those polite salons where victorious reason sat in judgment over every tradition; but in the taverns and streets too traditional authority, far from being held in proper awe by the populace, was the object of impudent mockery. Houses insured against fire were inscribed MACL: *maison assurée contre l'incendie;* and Danton's roar of laughter caused people to turn around in the street when somebody whispered to him the more recent interpretation: *Marie-Antoinette cocufie Louis!* And indeed since the affair of the necklace the *"Autrichienne"* had ceased to be an asset, and the monarchistic principle itself had suffered a blow.

Many of the conversations in the Café du Parnasse were not meant for the ears of informers. The café was situated at the corner of the Place de l'École and the quay and near enough to

the Palais and the Châtelet to become the regular rendezvous of
all the denizens of the courts, the place where prosecutors and
counsel for the defense, ushers, clerks, and young lawyers were
wont to call before and after the sittings. Here Danton would
often sip his coffee and play dominoes. The proprietor, François-
Jérôme Charpentier, was an amiable middle-aged man with a
little round wig and a gray suit; with his napkin tucked under
his arm, he liked to stand behind the young lawyer's chair and
watch his game. Finally the giant would fling the bones clashing
into their box, slap the *patron* on the shoulder, and go to the till
where the ladies Charpentier, mother and daughter, were smiling at him. There, resting on his elbow, Monsieur Danton would
talk of this and that and his powerful voice would take on a
milder accent when he began to speak of the beloved valley of
the Aube. The dark and gentle eyes of Antoinette-Gabrielle
gazed at him with secret admiration; but when his eyes looked
deep into hers with unmistakable meaning, a swift blush spread
over the girl's fresh young face.

Danton was a direct young man. His mind was unspoilt; and
he believed that honorable love must lead to an honorable end.
He was weary of a gypsy life in stuffy attics; he would come
knocking all the more gladly at the door of the father of his
chosen one because Père Charpentier was known to be successful. He did some tax farming and already had a fortune amounting to one hundred and twenty thousand livres, besides the café
and its furniture which were worth another forty thousand.
(Wherever one looked, the bourgeoisie were coming up!)

To further his suit Danton held out the prospective dignity
of an *avocat aux conseils du roi*. Charpentier nodded; after
many years of acquaintance with lawyers he was in a position to appreciate this office: the avocats aux conseils, a body
of seventy-three in number, were the élite of the profession. In
their capacity of attorneys before the various courts, supreme
or otherwise, they had closer access to ministers, and even to
the crown, than other members of the profession. An avocat aux
conseils—as a member of the King's table, and a court official
possessing numerous privileges—was an eligible son-in-law and
worth a certain outlay. Fifty years earlier the title could be ac-

quired for four thousand livres; today it cost ten thousand; then
a practice had to be bought, and there were admission fees and
perquisites—all of which added up—not to mention four pounds
of candles and twelve pounds of sugar which were the traditional gift of a newly elected avocat to every member of the
guild.

It so happened that early in 1787 Maître Huet de Paisy
thought of retiring; this offered a favorable opportunity, and in
March of that year Monsieur Charpentier advanced Danton
fifteen thousand livres. Another thirty-six thousand livres were
put up by a certain Mademoiselle Françoise-Julie Duhauttoir,
while an aunt and uncle in Arcis, together with the uncle at
Troyes, gave their guarantee for these amounts. Of the seventy-
eight thousand livres required Danton found fifty-six thousand,
and these sufficed to insure the desired title and office. There
remained only a few formalities, a petition, visits, and a certificate testifying that the candidate was a good Catholic—the latter applied for by the disciple of Diderot not without feelings of
inner irony. In a solemn meeting Danton was admitted to his
guild. At a later date he claimed that his address "on the moral
and political state of the country, in its relation to the practice
of the law" contained revolutionary thunderbolts; *motus popu-
lorum, ira gentium, salus populi suprema lex;* and he would describe the panic it caused among the old wigs.

On June 12, 1787, the royal letters patent, duly sealed, were
his; and two days later the bells of Saint-Germain-l'Auxerrois—
the same which had given the signal for Saint Bartholomew's
night—rang for the wedding of Monsieur Georges-Jacques Danton, avocat ez conseils (as he spelt it) and Demoiselle Antoinette-Gabrielle Charpentier. All the relatives had come from
Arcis; and his mother watched with emotion when the sand
finally blotted the marriage contract. It was a proud moment
for her, for the witnesses and guests were procurators, counsel-
lors, lawyers, notaries, bankers, and merchants—the élite of the
bourgeoisie, the leaders of the future. All were merry, as men
are when the future is theirs, and toasted the young couple, their
children, and the day of their golden wedding—their golden
wedding, which would be in 1837. It was June in Paris, the sky

was blue, and the grandson of the striving old peasant of Plancy was radiant: he had arrived.

But the climax was reached when he left the offices of his predecessor in the Rue de la Tixeranderie, on the right bank close to his first rooms in the Rue Geoffroy-l'Asnier, and with his father-in-law's assistance set up his own establishment on the left bank, a comfortable residence on the first floor. The study faced the Cour du Commerce which had lately taken the place of an ancient mass of dwellings, and the windows of the dining room faced in the same direction. It was bliss to stretch his feet under the table, on which a chicken steamed in its rich juice, where the white bread tempted, and the red wine glowed and where the table cloth was still a bit damp from the last washing. An inviting room, adorned by a delightful wife. His hand would caress her firm white neck; sweet Gabrielle! Night after night he would have the delight of lying next to her in the alcove of the bedroom facing the Rue des Cordeliers.

———————

His genial manner made the young avocat aux conseils popular among his colleagues; his two clerks, too, were devoted to him. Both Jules Paré and François Desforgues—the one from the Marne, the other from Normandy—were to pass into history with and through their employer. Even after Danton had become avocat au parlement, Paré remained his head clerk. Another colleague of Danton's who held a similar title occasionally drafted pleas for him. Of meager figure, with a short, retreating chin, long, knife-edged nose, and piercing eyes, Jacques-Nicolas Billaud—de Varenne he called himself, after a village near his native La Rochelle—had a chilly and reserved manner which did not attract; but he was industrious, and of discreet behavior. His wife, Anna Angelika, née Doye, came from Osnabrück, and had all the buxom charm of Westphalia. Danton, aware that his colleague had taught as lay master at the famous Oratorian College of Juilly, looked at him with a certain curiosity when, in a moment of confidence, Billaud confessed his literary ambitions. His life lay under a shadow; the little lawyer was tormented because he could not be a great poet; but un-

Antoinette-Gabrielle Danton

fortunately all his plays shared the fate of his piece, *"La femme comme il n'y en a plus,"* which had been a resounding failure in 1781.

In far and near districts of France there was more than one servant of jurisprudence at work whose future significance in his life Danton little suspected.

In Paris the son of a far from affluent but respectable family of Guise pursued a somewhat bohemian existence. Filled with the classical spirit through his schooling at the Lycée Louis-le-Grand, Camille Desmoulins, whose dark eyes sparkled with intelligence and wit, had been avocat au parlement since 1785. A slight impediment in his speech made forensic triumphs impossible, and he preferred to scribble poetry in his garret, waiting, susceptible and gay, until his star should rise. At the opposite social end of the legal scale was a young gentleman who was born almost the same day as Danton, blue blooded, a cousin of the Polignacs and Contades, who wore the scarlet robe of an advocate-general of the criminal and civil court of the Châtelet. Prepossessing in mind and body, a master of the art of living, his leisure hours in his bachelor quarters in the Rue Basse-du-Rempart were equally divided between the library whose four thousand volumes covered every branch of knowledge, and the shaded, yellow-hung boudoir, whose bed and vast mirror might tell of more than one lady of the great and of the lesser world. At other times the master of these premises hunted in Epone, his country seat near Nantes, or perhaps composed epigrams in the woods; but the chief pride of Marie-Jean Hérault de Séchelles was that he had heard the living voice of Diderot. Jean-François Delacroix was a tall, handsome man at whose passing by the women of Anet near Dreux would turn their heads. Danton's senior by six years, with the bearing of a cavalry officer, he had actually served in the gendarmery before he took up the study of law.

François-Joseph Westermann, born in 1752 at Molsheim, the son of a surgeon, had likewise carried a sword before he took to the pen. From the Esterhazy Hussars he transferred into the *Petite Gendarmerie,* received his discharge as corporal, and in 1775 found his way back to Alsace as advocate in the *Conseil*

Supérieur. But an obscure affair savoring of embezzlement or theft made it imperative for him to discard the gown, and this time the Royal Dragoons afforded him a welcome shelter. Of very different stuff from this scapegrace was Pierre Philippeaux, who had the gravity proper to one who since 1785 had been attorney at the Présidial, the Lower Court at Le Mans. Deeply read in Rousseau, Helvetius, and Mably, he had been guided in the choice of his profession by a desire for independence. As *avocat des gueux,* the "beggars' pleader," he was revered by the poor, and brooded over the causes of the people's miseries.

At Grenoble Antoine-Pierre-Joseph-Marie Barnave was beginning to attract attention. The son of an advocate, he had himself become avocat au parlement at nineteen; although polished, elegant, tactful, handsome, and a beguiling talker, he was not satisfied with external graces and greedily pursued knowledge in every form. He had inherited from his Protestant ancestors a tendency toward opposition to His Most Christian Majesty. Jérôme Pétion, though less brilliantly gifted, was successful in the courts of Chartres through his golden mediocrity; pleasant looking, honest, straightforward, and amiable, he won people by unheroic virtues. Sparks of genius, on the other hand, lay hidden under a complacent exterior in Pierre-Victurnien Vergniaud, who did not wait in vain at Bordeaux for the case that was to make him famous. Tall, powerful, deep chested and broad shouldered, with brown hair, broad nose, lively black eyes, sensual lips, and a pock-marked face, he was not only an Epicurean who appreciated "Limoges chestnuts and the wine of Saint-Emilion," but also a littérateur, who, while not neglecting the erotic department of his library, read Seneca and knew Winckelmann. The literary society at Bordeaux had classified one of his pieces beginning:

Voir l'eau couler, quel plaisir délectable!

as one of the great poems of the world.

With equal ardor Bertrand Barère pursued the easy laurels of the provincial academies. Appointed avocat au parlement at Toulouse in 1775 at the age of twenty, tall, slim, with delicate features, narrow eyebrows, ironic mouth, and gently caressing eyes, he had been born to please. He was a Gascon; his hand was light, his tongue ready, and his talk like a gavotte, but he did not know the meaning of principles. To give the impression of gentility he attached "de Vieuzac," the name of an estate of his father's, to his own name; and when in 1785 his marriage with Elizabeth de Monde, a child of twelve, allied him with the lesser nobility, he was gratified to see at the ceremony the Prince de Rohan-Rochefort, lieutenant general of the King's armies, and his wife, the Princess.

At Arras another lawyer of about Danton's age spent his spare time on the banks of the Scarpe, singing of wine and love with a more bucolic than expert note. A member of the literary society of the Rosati, Monsieur Maximilien de Robespierre timidly offered a day's hunting spoils to the lady of his affections in delicate rococo strains:

> *Trouvant le don mesquin et l'épître imparfaite*
> *Vous allez sûrement dire d'un ton moqueur*
> *Cette chasse est bien d'un poète,*
> *Les vers-la sont bien d'un chasseur!*

At the same time at Clermont-Ferrand another colleague, a man in the thirties with a broad forehead and frank eyes, was winning men through his kindness and strength of character; all Auvergne knew *"le bon Monsieur Couthon."* Jean-Pierre Amar, too, was known, though less favorably, in his native town of Grenoble. He came of a wealthy family, had begun as avocat au parlement, and later paid two hundred thousand livres for appointment as one of the Treasurers of France for Dauphiné, which brought with it the equivalent of a knighthood. Nice rumors were circulated about him: he was supposed to have seduced the niece of a priest and compelled the uncle at the pistol's point to give the fair sinner absolution; more recently, engaged in the pursuit of a pious Marguerite, he tripped in processions, candle in hand, to lure her into his bed.

Lastly, at Pamiers, at the foot of the Pyrenees, the president of the Présidial indulged in idyllic plans for the future. In his early fifties, his temples already graying, Marc-Guillaume Vadier had a fortune of three hundred thousand livres; soon he would retire to one of his properties, to Bordenave, Peyroutet, or Nikol, to grow roses and read his beloved Voltaire under the ancient walnut trees.

Desmoulins, Hérault de Séchelles, Delacroix, Westermann, Philippeaux, Barnave, Pétion, Vergniaud, Barère, Robespierre, Couthon, Amar, Vadier—none of them knew the other; none of them knew Danton. And yet Danton was destined to meet all of them on his road through life, and some of them on his way to the grave.

———————————◆———————————

HE did not have to insert an apostrophe between the first two letters of his name to attract a throng of clients. Danton or D'Anton, it did not matter—his asset was his legal skill at getting at the roots of problems instead of obscuring and befogging his cases. Success came, documents multiplied on his shelves, and his clerks had no time to idle. Again and again the cases with which he dealt afforded him profound insight into the State and society. High and low laid their affairs before him: De Paul de Barentin, the president of the Tax Tribunal, the Marquis de Clerc de la Devèze, and the brothers Annet de Langlade du Chayla de Montgros, as well as the tailor Accassat, the café owner Boudray, and the goldsmith's apprentice Gauthier. Danton's everyday practice showed him more clearly than the most beautiful theory the wounds and sores of the body of France— the nobles' monopoly of military rank, the burden of traditional privileges that lay on the land, the insane restrictions of the Guilds.

But it was the great events of the day rather than the petty experience of his office that turned Danton's attention from law to politics. The notables, convoked in the hour of need, had long ago dispersed without doing anything. The avalanche of national bankruptcy, long impending, began to move, and compelled the rulers to convoke the States-General for May 1, 1789. For the first time in one hundred and seventy-five years —elections! Forthwith the sky was black with *cahiers de doléance,* twenty thousand, forty thousand or more, voicing the complaints of twenty-five millions of Frenchmen: Down with despotism, down with confusion and chaos, down with the feudal barbarity which puts the peasant's field under grass in order to spare the partridges for the lord of the manor! Down with the purchase of offices, down with privileges, prerogatives, and abuses! Down with the unchecked waste of public monies! Down with the confusion of tax legislation, down with the inland customs which goods coming from Artois to Provence have to pay seven times over! But louder than all was the cry for protection of property, safety of trade and freedom to develop. For the sake of these things millions of voices demanded a constitution like the British or the American as the foundation of the monarchy. A plea for order, civic order in the midst of anarchy!

There was a wave of enthusiasm when the States-General assembled, the Third Estate seized power and the National Assembly opened the way for a new era. But Danton's name was not mentioned when his district drew up the list of its complaints and the valley of the Aube elected deputies. During the decisive period he was engrossed by private troubles; on April 25, 1789, he lost his year-old son. He was distracted with grief; what was a family without an heir?

But although he stayed in the background, Danton remained attentive and waited his hour. He had an animal's instinct for the imminent earthquake. The nobility were wont to refer contemptuously to the Paris populace as frogs; but Danton suspected that the frogs could do more than croak, and every nerve tingled when he learned on the twelfth of July that the King had dismissed Necker, his Minister of Finance. The populace, ignorant that Necker was a windbag, were attached to him: his dismissal is the sign that the court party is preparing to strike! Alien troops, the Royal Allemand, the Royal Croate, the Swiss Salis-Samade Regiment, and other mercenaries are under arms ready to fire on Frenchmen.

On the thirteenth of July there is a new power, the Committee of Electors, in the Hôtel-de-Ville; it is decided to form a civic militia. All Paris is in the streets, the suburbs are on the march, shouts of "To arms!" on every tongue. Shops are looted for guns, pikes hastily manufactured, the barriers flaming. And suddenly: Long live the Gardes Françaises! The most famous regiment of the kingdom has joined the popular cause. Victory is assured. At every corner and square unknown orators, suddenly inspired, leap on chairs, are raised on men's shoulders, and shout: Forward! Courage! Strike! Forward!

In the library of the monastery which gave its name to the Rue des Cordeliers a man stands on a table with outstretched arms and clenched fists, his pock-marked face inflamed; his voice is a tocsin: "To arms, citizens! Fifteen thousand ruffians have gathered at Montmartre, there is an army of thirty thousand at Versailles ready to descend on Paris, to butcher us and to plunder your houses. To arms! To arms!" The audience is carried away; "To arms! To arms! Long live Danton!"

On Tuesday, July 14, 1789, the Bastille falls.

On Wednesday night Danton straps on a big sword and at the head of the newly formed civic militia of his district marches on the state prison, now rendered harmless. Soulès, the warden, put in charge of the empty fortress by the new ruler, Lafayette, refuses to open when the rifle butts pound on the gates. He is seized by the collar and dragged through the district to the Hôtel-de-Ville, the militia forcing their way through mobs yelling, "Hang him! Hang him!" The whole performance is an empty farce—for everyone except the poor devil who suffers in anticipation all the pangs of death; nobody knows this is a comedy better than Danton, but he has need to test his lungs, his popularity, and his control of the crowd. And it works!

Meanwhile, Gabrielle lies awake in the dark, the lashes of her lovely brown eyes wet with tears. If she but knew that this is only the first of many nights she will lie sleepless with beating heart while outside is a silence more terrifying than the most sinister uproar—than footsteps or distant shots—her tears would flow faster, and more uncontrollably.

II

Integration and Fulfilment
1789–1792

PARIS was the white hot core of revolutionary France, the District of the Cordeliers the white hot core of Paris, and Danton was the white hot soul of his district. This was the result of the Fourteenth of July, 1789.

Danton plunged into the political turmoil with the same boisterous abandon with which he plunged into deep water, attacked a saddle of mutton, or embraced his wife. If he was no Nazarene, with tears flowing at the thought of the happiness of mankind, he was all the more profoundly convinced that the volcano which had erupted in July was the true element for his volcanic nature. In the fresh, keen air he could develop as he could never have done in the lukewarm temperature of the courts, under the square advocate's cap. One of the driving forces of the Revolution, Danton was himself driven by the Revolution; never were a man and his task more utterly one.

He had tested the compelling power of his words the day before the fall of the Bastille. A born orator, he required touch with others to bring out what he had in him. Withdrawn within the cell of his ego, he was little or nothing; at his desk he was a nonentity; but the warmth of his family circle, the applause of friends, the resistance of enemies made him luminous.

But the qualities which swayed the multitude were not those which most appealed to shrewd observers. Within the mind of the skilled advocate, who continued to plead until the reorganization of the judiciary put an end to his practice in 1791, the events of the Revolution soon appeared in the light of new legal ideas and forms; he had the gift of disentangling things so that what had yesterday been criminal and revolutionary today appeared legal and legitimate. He developed into the reverse of a crown counsel and became a masterly jurist of the Revolution, just such a pleader of the revolutionary cause as the Revolution was urgently demanding.

No one could fail to be impressed with the unbridled energy he radiated when, filling his lungs and clenching his fists, he began to speak. With his towering figure, broad shoulders, great limbs, irregular and mobile features, with hair swept back from a high forehead and a ruddy complexion that mocked the indoors air, and with small, glittering eyes that could stare from under shaggy eyebrows into the face of friend and foe alike—he stood, a peasant's son, sinewy, red blooded, a lover of life and of the Revolution precisely because it was an intenser and more vital life. He knew his strength and the impression it made, and would boast that he was not the pale offspring of privileged and enervated bastard races: "Nature has given me as dowry the athletic frame and the rough features of freedom." This sense of power was a perilous source of weakness, for it led him to underestimate danger; but it also lent him victorious strength. It gave the man of the people that security which had lamentably deserted the late ruling classes, from the King to the youngest ensign of the Guards. The careless giant had no feeling of inferiority to overcome before an appearance in public; the cause he pleaded was not the revolt of trembling slaves but of rulers claiming their due.

A blind man hearing Danton on the platform could have told the nature of the speaker from the manner of his speech. It had no architectural structure, none of the 1A, 2B taught in the schools of rhetoric. While the deputies brought their speeches into the National Assembly set down in black and white, Danton scorned preparation; no sheet of paper stood between him and the rush of his words. The thought of the moment burst from him like fluid lava, not in continued periods and lengthy sequences, but in swift phrases like hammer blows.

In an age which looted the whole ancient world for its finery and named ladies' fashions after Rome and Corinth, Sappho and Cleopatra, Danton did not harass the classical world for his similes more than was absolutely necessary. His plastic images were therefore all the more impressive, whether he called the Commune "the first sentinel of freedom," or, speaking of the Constituent Assembly, urged that the temple of liberty must not become the sanctuary of the supporters of despotism, or threatened the satellites of tyranny with annihilation by the avenging angel of freedom.

Few could resist the ring of this strong, vibrant voice, the harsh fascination of his whole personality. The educated were charmed by the robust animal nature, by the earthy smell of this man of the people who yet was one of them by training and rank, and whose Latin and Greek were no worse than theirs; the masses were flattered to think that a man with their muscles, their appetites, and their voice, and, if necessary, their language, was a scholar and a gentleman wearing a fine coat and breeches, an embroidered waistcoat and linen underwear. And every audience, high or low, that listened to his rude eloquence felt, at times, something like the startled tremor of the female scenting, in the mating season, the victorious male.

———◆———

THE Palais-Royal afforded a vigorous speaker the greatest field. It was still the bright and glittering haunt of pleasure; for Paris, having drunk of the cup of liberty, had redoubled its gayety, its dancing and singing, and exerted a magnetic attraction on provincials and foreigners. Blue, white, and red were gay, joyous colors beside the snowy chill of the banner of the lilies. Once the grain shortage of the autumn of 1789 was past, and a pound of bread no longer cost a sixth of a man's wages, and lines no longer stood outside the bakers' shops, the capital slid like a ship of flowers into the all but unruffled waters of festive rejoicing, the center of which was the Palais-Royal. Whether you desired to admire paintings and engravings, to hear music, to buy a partridge, a dress, or a saddle, or one of those costly new clocks which indicated the seconds and the phases of the moon, to swallow fresh oysters, to partake of a choice meal, to pass the time with chess or the popular Italian game of chance called Biribi, to climb into a hot perfumed bath or to dally with one of those charmers whose names were contained in a special directory, the *Calendrier des plaisirs*—the Palais-Royal was the place for all: market, rendezvous, inn, opportunity.

However, since July 12, 1789, when Camille Desmoulins, standing on a table before the Café de Foy with a pistol in each hand, had called the citizens to arms, a political tradition too attached to these arcades. For the elections to the National Assembly Paris had been divided into sixty political units or districts; the Palais-Royal was considered a sixty-first district. Each breath of rumor blew every hothead in the town here, and particularly those who came from outside and had no vote or domicile in any district. On disturbed days a continuous meeting of the populace would boil and bubble here; and those whom the spirit seized would climb on tables or chairs and wave their arms and address the crowd. Threatening resolutions were passed and hurried deputations despatched to the Commune or the National Assembly; from here emanated electric shocks which the new rulers felt like shooting pains in every limb. Those who jumped up to speak or stood by to listen had to be prepared at any moment to feel the rifle butt of the National Guards against their ribs. This did not prevent Danton from using the Palais-Royal on occasion as his tribune for stirring up those without district or organization, and he was treated as one of the presidents of the tribunal which the people had established in this place. No student of logotachygraphy—the new invention for rapid writing—took down his words, and no news sheet presented them to its readers next morning, but for all that they were not scattered by the wind. They were for the masses an elixir of resolution, which, far from expelling their fever, heightened it to the point of action.

If the street parliament of the Palais-Royal resembled a popular commotion rather than a regular meeting duly called, with regulations and an order of the day, the *Société des amis de la Constitution, séants aux Jacobins* was at the opposite pole. "Jacobin" had been a nickname in the mouths of opponents until, following the example of the Gueuses, the "Friends of the Constitution" proudly adopted it themselves. The enemies of the Revolution painted the club as a band of regicides; it was rumored that its members had sworn a terrible oath upon the dagger which the Dominican, Jacques Clément, had plunged into the breast of Henri III to destroy the monarchy. Such libels gradually fostered the illusion in countries unacquainted with the state of France that Jacobins were red-capped ruffians waving bare and hairy arms in dens full of tobacco fumes while gin flowed together with bloodthirsty speeches. The truth was that the society, which had taken the place of the Breton Club, a body composed solely of parliamentarians, included the élite of an educated and prosperous bourgeoisie, deputies of the National Assembly, writers, scientists, merchants, physicians, artists, and lawyers; among its presidents, who ruled in turn for a fortnight, were the Baron de Menou, the Duke of Aiguillon, the Vicomte de Noailles, the Prince de Broglie, and the Vicomte de Beauharnais; the impecunious were debarred if only by the entrance fee of twelve livres and the yearly subscription of twenty-four. The meetings, held originally in the refectory, later in the library, and after May, 1791, in the chapel of the Jacobin monastery in the Rue Saint-Honoré, were conducted on parliamentary lines, and although there were times when political feeling ran high, the president, supported by the secretary and attendants, endeavored to keep out of the most heated exchanges expressions which would not have been admitted to the columns of the famous dictionary of the Academy.

The meetings usually began at six in the evening with an attendance of between four hundred and five hundred, which would grow to one thousand by eight o'clock and then decline until, about ten o'clock, the meeting closed. Even in externals parliamentary practice was followed. The president's chair was in the middle of one of the two longer sides of the oblong chamber, faced by the speaker's platform, while seats for members were arranged in ascending tiers; the house had a bar and a public gallery. The rules had been drawn up by Barnave, who wore the motto of the club even on the metal buttons of his suit: *"Vivre libre ou mourir!"* "Love of equality" and a "profound sense of the rights of man" were requisites for admission to the society. In a nation that was unable to overcome centuries of enslavement in a moment, the Jacobins made it their task, "as priests and missionaries of liberty," to promote a civic sense, to form a public spirit, and to give flesh and blood to the paper constitution by forming a "constitutional man." They sowed the new ideas broadcast when they circulated the *Almanach du Père Gérard* for 1792, a collection of simple dialogues composed by Collot d'Herbois which made the meaning of the great changes within the state intelligible to the dullest mind. Often, like an academy of philosophers and economists, they discussed ques-

tions of taxation, debated the advantages or disadvantages of
the factory system, studied problems of education, investigated
the position of the bill brokers, or looked into complaints of
violations of the Constitution; their chief occupation, however,
consisted in preparing the raw material of legislation for the
National Assembly. By the spring of 1792 they had no less than
406 affiliated societies spread over the whole of France from
Brest to Toulon and from Lille to Bayonne. The "Friends of the
Constitution" thus exerted considerable influence; addresses,
petitions, and denunciations were piled high in their offices and
deputations thronged their bar from far and near. For simple
souls the Jacobins were the last court of appeal in all human
affairs, and even wives who had been roughly treated would
bring their complaints to the Rue Saint-Honoré.

It was some time before Danton too lifted his right hand in
this assembly and declared: "I swear to live or die free, to remain faithful to the principles of the Constitution, to obey the
laws and enforce their respect, to contribute to their perfection
to the best of my ability and to comply with the rules and customs of the society." His appearances, once he had been elected,
were infrequent, and he did not often speak. When, on May 30,
1790, he sprang onto the platform for the first time to address a
few words to the assembly, their violence caused murmurs of
disapproval from a large part of the gathering. Those who applauded were few. Yet it was as impossible not to listen to his
words as to ignore his figure; both were too forceful.

Danton was in constant touch with other lawyers among the
"Friends of the Constitution" besides his former colleague Billaud-Varenne. There were Pétion of Chartres, Merlin of Metz,
Vergniaud of Bordeaux, Le Chapelier of Rennes, Louvet of
Paris, and Réal of Grenoble; Reubell of Colmar, who caused
astonishment in the National Assembly when he objected to
civic rights for Jews; Prieur de la Marne, whose righteousness
had become so proverbial that the people of Châlons said "*probe
comme Prieur*"; and Couthon of Clermont-Ferrand, who, with
legs paralyzed by a disease of the nervous system, had to be
supported by two friends, but whose logic flashed clear, inexorable, and keen. Another ex-lawyer was Anthoine, deputy for

Saargemünd in the Constituent Assembly until he assumed the office of lieutenant general for civil and criminal cases at the Bailli court at Bolchen in 1788. Roederer and Adrien Duport were parliamentary counsels; and there was Hérault de Séchelles, an elegant figure for whom the Revolution was a matter of faith as well as a sensuous stimulus.

Jacques-Pierre Brissot, too, had begun with the law; a rolling stone, he had nearly joined the Benedictines in his youth merely in order to have something to read and to eat; he was author of a work, *On Truth or Considerations on a Method for Reaching the Truth in All Human Sciences,* a Faustulus whose love of learning had brought him to the Bastille for a couple of months under the despotism. Intellectually restless, often pedantic and often confused, he had been editor of the *Patriote français* since July, 1789, and fought eloquently for the liberation of the Negroes in the French colonies.

Menou and Choderlos de Laclos were soldiers, the latter captain of artillery at Toul and author of *Dangerous Passions,* a ruthless work which reflected all the cold viciousness of a decaying society. Alexandre de Lameth, the youngest of four brothers who were much in the public eye, had been an officer in the King's army before he joined the American rebels to fight the British. Dubois-Crancé enjoyed reputation and popularity as one of the authors of the Tennis Court Oath. His military career had begun at fourteen in the famous company of the *Mousquetaires du Roi.*

About Claude Basire there was something of the cloistered student, for although he was a deputy in the Legislative Assembly, his real interests, apart from women, were physics and geology, and his most precious possession in his house at Dijon was a small private museum, containing an infant's skeleton, fossils, and minerals. From the world of business came the brewer Santerre, a man of education, already known for his charities before 1789 as the "Father of the Faubourg Saint-Antoine" and decorated with the evergreen laurels of the stormers of the Bastille; Cambon of Montpellier, a cloth merchant whose wholesale trade had acquainted him with financial matters; and Isnard, the proprietor of a silk and soap factory in the Alpes Maritimes, who found time to indulge in youthful rhapsodies about liberty and equality.

Among the foreign members of the Jacobin Club the most striking figure was Jean-Baptiste Clootz, who in accordance with the prevailing taste for antiquity adopted the name of Anacharsis; the descendant of Dutch merchants who had settled in Cleve and had become barons of the Empire, he had attended an ecclesiastical college in Paris and learned to doubt the saving grace of the church. At the military academy in Berlin he had come to despise military despotism. In the salons and cafés of the French capital in the years before the Revolution, he attracted the attention of the police. As he shook the dust of Paris from his feet, he swore to return when the Bastille was no more, and he kept his word. A person whose enthusiasm knew no bounds, he was continually bubbling over with ideas, projects, plans, suggestions, proposals, and dreamt not only of democracy in France, but of the brotherhood of mankind. He appeared at the bar of the National Assembly June 19, 1790, with thirty-six foreigners in his train, including Prussians, Dutch, British, Russians, Poles, Italians, Spanish, Swedes, and Swiss, and even some dubious Turks, Arabs, and Chaldeans, and pleaded their cause in fiery and ecstatic words, as spokesman of the human race.

Among the Jacobins many a liberal and generous mind greeted the new era. But darker figures had slipped in too, like François Chabot, an ex-Capuchin monk who made an unpleasant impression in this company of well-brushed coats and orderly periwigs when he started to play the revolutionary ruffian by showing himself in dirty linen which laid bare his neck and chest.

At first Honoré-Gabriel-Victor Riquetti, Marquis de Mirabeau, had towered among his companions like an oak above the undergrowth, because of his diabolical will power and concentrated intellectual energy. But the tempest of passion shook the branches, and the core of the tree was decaying. Mirabeau died April 2, 1791. And now Maximilien Robespierre held the center of the stage in the debates of the club. Devoted to the cause, dividing his time only between the Jacobins and the Constituent

Assembly, compelling conviction by the soundness and logic of his arguments, the zealous disciple of Rousseau came to the front, if only through his persistence in rising to speak and his reluctance to stop. When called on to yield the floor he would squabble pettishly and obstinately with the president.

Danton could not fail to recognize in Robespierre a tower of strength for democracy and a politician who could plan a Revolution without sentimentality. Occasionally they exchanged courtesies publicly in the club, and once Danton even took up the cudgels on behalf of the much attacked lawyer from Arras, praising his "sovereignty of reason" and "virtue which the whole Revolution confirms." Yet it may be suspected that the obstinate despotism of this somewhat over-rigorous reason and the emphatic insistence on revolutionary virtue may have proved at times irritating to Danton. When he looked into those pale green wide-set eyes, or watched that thin-lipped mouth which smiled graciously or sarcastically but never opened in honest laughter, even his careless vigor experienced a feeling of insecurity. No, it was impossible to feel warmly toward this milk addict, who was always correct and never youthful, who indulged only in the consumption of oranges, and could scarcely know the meaning of Horace's *desipere in loco*.

Danton, firmly rooted in his native soil and deeply attached to his family, liked the scene of his public activities to lie where he could still sniff the smoke of his own hearth. It happened that his house was in the district named after the Cordeliers, whose monastery with its wide courts and gardens was within a few minutes of the Cour du Commerce. When in the early summer of 1790 the capital was reorganized in forty-eight sections, Danton's district became part of the Théâtre-Français; the name of Cordeliers, however, survived, and the *Société des amis des droits de l'homme et du citoyen*, which cherished the traditions of the district, was popularly called the "Club of the Cordeliers." Whether Danton appeared at a meeting of district, section or club, it was among the Cordeliers that he felt most secure. Here his love for the concrete could have full play and the grandson of peasants strode out like a ploughman to plough his field.

Some districts, like that of the Filles Saint-Thomas or that of the Butte des Moulins felt distrust and hesitation in embracing the new order. But the Cordeliers had vigorously assumed the leadership of the Paris movement, aided by the fact that the Théâtre-Français had belonged to the district since 1782, and the actors, now for the first time enjoying civic rights, introduced a more unrestrained note into the political meetings. The majority of the members of this theater openly regretted the days when the aristocracy delighted to shower gold upon the actors and still more upon the actresses. Although recently the name of the theater had been changed to Théâtre de la Nation, it required external pressure in 1790 before a revolutionary play like *Charles IX* could be revived. On July 24, when the first revival took place, one of the usual squabbles arose in the stalls between the supporters of the old and the new regime, the former following the practice of the court and removing their cocked hats while the latter with civic pride retained their round hats. Danton, challenged to uncover, crammed his hat down with his fist and boasted: "It's as firm as the hat of Servandony"— Servandony being one of the towers of Saint-Sulpice. An uproar arose, the police were called, and Danton was carried off to the Hôtel-de-Ville. A few months later Talma and all his colleagues who wore the red, white, and blue cockade with conviction emigrated to the right bank.

It was not so much the theater as the social structure of the population which made the district the feverish brain of revolutionary Paris. The working population was densest, not in the faubourgs of revolutionary fame—Saint-Antoine and Saint-Marceau—but in the northeast suburbs. According to the census of those years the Théâtre-Français was one of the eight sections containing more than two thousand laborers; at the same time it had a character of its own. More than half the Paris proletariat was employed in various branches of the building industry; and the next greatest number in ribbon, cloth, and lace factories. The section of the Théâtre-Français was unique in that

Camille Desmoulins

a class of workmen preponderated who were directly engaged in molding public opinion, in political propaganda; out of 2,200, no less than 700 were employed in twenty-one printing firms, of which that belonging to Momoro, "the first printer of liberty," was the best known. More lively spirits could hardly be imagined than these disciples of the "black arts"; well-paid, mentally active, and avid readers, considering themselves artists rather than workers, they were a yeast that leavened the whole district.

Their influence was seconded by the newspapers, which found their way from this active center to every quarter of the town. Among these the *Révolutions de Paris* had won by its clear style and lucid argument a circulation of fifteen thousand which presently rose to twenty thousand. The editor, Elisée Loustalot, was an ardent and altruistic warrior, known among his friends as the "Evangelist" because of the purity and strength of his convictions; he died at the age of twenty-seven before the first magnanimous illusions of 1789 had had time to fade. A neighbor of his was Stanislas Fréron, the son of a father whom Voltaire had damned to everlasting fame, a dandy and mentally no great light, who read and translated Petrarch and printed the *Orateur du peuple*, spending no little energy and spirit on its production. In the immediate neighborhood of Danton's residence Guillaume Brune, author of *A Picturesque and Sentimental Journey through Diverse Provinces of Western France*, edited his *Journal de la cour et de la ville*, little suspecting that he was destined to receive a marshal's baton and to die suddenly at the hands of Royalist assassins after the Battle of Waterloo.

Camille Desmoulins was inevitably drawn into the District of the Cordeliers. A mixture of genius and gamin, he had already made a name for himself as editor of the weekly *Révolutions de France et de Brabant*, and the intelligentsia devoured his articles which sparkled like dry champagne and sometimes left, like it, a flat after-taste. With somewhat savage wit he called himself the Administrator of the Gibbet; but what then should one call Dr. Jean-Paul Marat, whose forty-seven years made him the oldest and most experienced among these turbulent youths? A Genevese Calvinist, he had lived in France and England, had been for eight years physician of the bodyguard of the Comte d'Artois, was the author of works on philosophy and physics as well as of novels, and had labored on inventions and discoveries without ever winning recognition. Now his daily political paroxysm filled the columns of the *Ami du peuple*. The brutal candor with which he called a spade a spade and Rollin a scoundrel caused him to be threatened and persecuted by the authorities, so that he considered it advisable to pitch his tent among the Cordeliers, and since November, 1789, his presses had been established in the Rue des Fossés-Saint-Germain, hardly a stone's throw from Danton's house.

Marat was not alone in praising the District of the Cordeliers as "one of the firmest pillars of the country, whose sons will be forever worshiped in the annals of the Revolution"; Fréron too referred to the district as the "terror of the aristocrats and the sanctuary of the victims of political oppression in the capital." Desmoulins, who had deliberately migrated into the "incomparable District of the Cordeliers," wrote enthusiastically: "If the seven sages of Greece were members of the district and if it embraced the schools of all the philosophers, Plato's Academy, the Gardens of Epicurus, the Lyceum of Aristotle, and the Stoa, its logic could not be sounder." At the corner of every street in the region between the Quai des Augustins, the Rue de Condé, Rue de la Harpe, and Rue de Vaugirard, his mind's eye could read in invisible letters *Via Sacra*. The Cordeliers themselves, cherishing their reputation like a tattered battle flag, would sometimes refer to the "section of the Théâtre-Français, formerly known by the famous and terrible name of the District of the Cordeliers."

Through the calumnies of its foes the meetings of the club, which the municipal authorities had compelled in May, 1791, to move from the *Aula Theologica* of the monastery of the Cordeliers into the rooms of a scientific society, the *Musée de Paris*, in the Rue Dauphine, were painted in even more sinister colors than the meetings of the Jacobins. Roussel d'Epinal compared the three hundred members who sat on benches arranged in ascending tiers to a collection of beggars, so ragged and unclean was their appearance; while Chateaubriand, recollecting that he had attended the Cordeliers on three or four occasions between his American period and his emigration—in other words in 1791 —described their meetings a good thirty years later with more imagination than accuracy as a gathering of dirty, drunk, and sweaty vagabonds, sitting on old logs, broken-down benches, dilapidated choir stalls and mutilated images of saints, in ragged coats, with pikes on their shoulders or bare arms crossed over their chests.

Actually the "Friends of the Rights of Man" did admit "passive" citizens, and while the district and section meetings were confined to active citizens; that is, to those whose income tax amounted to at least three days' wages, the yearly annual subscription of one livre and four sous was within the means of all but the poorest. But although the Cordeliers consisted partly of artisans, tradesmen, and respectable members of the lower middle classes generally, of people without breeches (in other words, sansculottes), who made an efficient chorus, but were not different from the Jacobins, it was the bourgeoisie and their intellectual forerunners, the educated classes, who made the Cordeliers what they were. The backbone of the club was made up of merchants, printers, goldsmiths, engineers, scientists, more than a few lawyers—among them Buirette de Verrières, the venomous hunchback who was reputed to write the *Ami du peuple* when Marat's pen flagged—officials, and judges, one of whom, Garran de Coulon, was to end as president of the Court of Cassation. A comparatively large percentage of writers, actors, and artists gave the society a somewhat Bohemian flavor and Danton himself liked to choose a cravat in bold contrast to his sober cloth coat.

One of the few in Danton's immediate circle unacquainted with classical lore was Louis Legendre, a substantial man, a master butcher who had his stand in the Rue des Boucheries-Saint-Germain and drove briskly in his own cabriolet to the cattle market at Poissy. A colossus with a tremendous chest and a booming voice, little book-learning but plenty of mother wit and hot blood, he had played his part bravely at the storming of the Bastille. The funeral oration he delivered over Loustalot was so magnificent that Desmoulins compared Legendre with

Demosthenes; and, since Legendre had a bulldog attachment to Danton, there was a note of tenderness in Danton's references to his lieutenant. The story went that the two had sworn that if either saw the other's patriotism waning, it should be his duty to slay him.

Besides Desmoulins, who clung somewhat passively to Danton, and such old friends as Paré and Billaud-Varenne, Brune, Fréron, and Momoro, the large Pierre-François Robert was one of those who always found the door open on the first floor of the house in the Cour du Commerce. A writer himself, he had married a writer, Louise-Félicité Guinement de Kéralio, who had become a member of the Arras Academy in 1787 under Robespierre's presidency on the strength of a history of Queen Elizabeth and some mediocre novels. Now the couple were publishing the *Mercure national*. Another member of Danton's circle was Fabre d'Eglantine, actor and dramatist. Whence the aristocratic surname? According to his tale, a poem of his had been awarded the gold eglantine at the floral games at Toulouse. But this was idle boasting, merely a sign of Gascon imagination in a native of Carcassonne. Still, there was no doubt about the success of his later plays like *Philinte* and *L'Aristocrate*, although the only piece which was destined to survive him was a careless rococo song dashed off hastily years ago at Maestricht—"*Il pleut, il pleut, bergère.*" Collot d'Herbois was another actor and dramatist whose latest play, *La famille patriote,* unlike earlier ones in which he had copied Calderon or Shakespeare, pleased the public taste and achieved a popularity at least equal to that of Fabre's comedies. Both, however, were dwarfed by Marie-Joseph de Chénier, the brother of the inspired André. Born in Constantinople, the son of the French ambassador, Marie-Joseph began his military career in the dragoons, and had produced a number of complete failures before his *Charles IX,* "the work of a free man dedicated to a free people," became an enormous success in the year of the capture of the Bastille, and he could boast:

> *J'ai voulu rappeler la Melpomène antique*
> *Et dans les premiers jours de notre liberté*
> *J'attachai sur son front, avec quelque fierté,*
>   *La cocarde patriotique.*

Unlike these three, Dr. Chévetel could approach the stage only by back alleys: his mistress Mademoiselle Fleury was a star of the Théâtre-Français.

Pierre-Louis Manuel, the son of a potter, was of a less refined clay. Nursed with divinity, he had begun as prefect of studies with the fathers of the Ordre des Frères Chrétiens at Nogers, later became a tutor, and, at Paris, a bookseller's assistant. Although early failures had embittered him, he was straightforward and honest, with interests beyond his daily round. In 1792 he published the *Letters of Mirabeau to Sophie*, with a preface of his own. François-Nicolas Vincent had taken up the study of law, being ambitious to rise higher than his father, who was a turnkey; while Antoine-François Sergent, the pupil of Saint-Aubin, was a painter, and had just begun on a gallery of famous personalities in French history when he was seized by the Revolution, flung for awhile upon the president's chair of the Cordeliers, and thus became himself an historic personage.

There was an exotic air about Claude Fournier l'Héritier, nicknamed the "American," who since 1760 had spent many years at San Domingo distilling brandy from sugar cane. Since his concern had gone up in flames, allegedly through the ill will of neighbors, he had cooled his heels for years in the anterooms of the Admiralty, complaining and demanding compensation. He saw in the Revolution a heaven-sent chance to settle a private score. A more genuine foundation supported the revolutionary enthusiasm of Gaspard—or Anaxagoras—Chaumette, the son of a sabot-maker of Nevers, who had been a cabin-boy, and then studied surgery, physics, and botany before he turned up in Paris in 1790; with long, ill-kept hair, and a scarf instead of a tie knotted round his neck, he looked like a school teacher. But in spite of his eternal immaturity, he knew the people and the language that touched the heart of the masses.

When in October, 1791, the Legislative took the place of the Constituent Assembly, two of its deputies were new to office. Edmé-Bonaventure Courtois of Troyes had been tax collector at Arcis-sur-Aube before his department elected him deputy. Danton welcomed him as a compatriot; but he was selfish, grasping, and given to drink—and not altogether the best of companions. Jean-François Delacroix was more pleasing. He had risen to the post of procurator general syndic of the Eure-et-Loir and deputy judge in the Court of Cassation, and was hampered in politics by only one fault—his inability to express himself.

In all this lively group there was not one who was not attracted by Danton's noisy joviality and held by the strength of his will. Often a group of these leading Cordeliers, leaving the beer of Santerre's Brasserie Hortense, would burst into the Café Procope in the Rue Neuve-des-Fossés-Saint-Germain-des-Prés, an unpretentious place, yet requiring no grand mirrors or rich gilding; the glory of its past sufficed. Here Voltaire had sipped his coffee; Diderot had conversed with fellow encyclopedists; and Beaumarchais had waited for the result of the first performance of *The Marriage of Figaro*. Desmoulins celebrated it as "the only spot where liberty has not been violated." At the Procope Danton would play dominoes with his friends; his boisterous laughter would burst out. "Bravo!" he shouted across seven tables when Zoppi, the Italian proprietor, set up a bust of Mucius Scaevola as an example to the coffee-drinking friends of liberty. Often the dominoes were left in the middle of a game when a messenger entered and murmured something in the ear of the leader, and voices, noisy a moment ago, were lowered to a whisper. And sometimes when delay seemed dangerous they made a hasty exit, leaving behind a glass of sticky Dijon Casis trickling on the table or a half-empty bottle of Bavaroise, a favorite brand of lemonade.

Danton often welcomed his friends under his own roof. He loved his home, his library with its Plutarch and Lucretius, its Rabelais and Voltaire, and its Shakespeare, Ariosto, and complete Encyclopedia, and the alcove with its flowered cretonne curtains. He would seize a companion by the arm saying: "Come and have supper with us. There's chicken for dinner." Or late at night he would sometimes bring guests home from a meeting of the Cordeliers or Jacobins: important discussions could not be broken off short, and it was not for nothing that his cellar, along with bottles of Burgundy and Bordeaux, had barrels of red wine from Bourgogne and a keg of white wine from

Auvergne. They would talk and drink and laugh and forget the present in recollections. Collot d'Herbois had been brought up by the Oratorians and Billaud-Varenne had been a teacher at the Collège Juilly. With both Danton could exchange comparisons and reminiscences of school days. An excellent institution! Only this year the Collège had staged for the customary autumn performance at Troyes such revolutionary plays as *The Tricolor Cockade* and *Paris Saved, or the Conquest of Freedom.*

Fréron, dainty, frail, with delicate, inscrutable features, would talk of his childhood. He would tell how, at the age of six, he recited a poem at Versailles in honor of his godfather, Stanislas Leszynski, King of Poland and sovereign of the duchies of Lorraine and Bar, and how the daughters of Louis XV, Adelaide, Victoire, and Louise, had petted him. Or he would recall his Bohemian days, when complaisant beauties thronged the mansion of his patron Bertin, the financier, and the whim took him to leave the arms of Irma Laborde, versatile mistress of ten lovers, and visit the nunnery where his sister Teresa was being brought up in Catholic chastity. Legendre had served ten years as a mate and had tales and jests and wonderful yarns to spin. Fabre d'Eglantine had been a strolling player at Grenoble, Chalon-sur-Saône, Beauvais, Liége, Arras, Douai, Geneva, and Lyons, and was full of names and stories. Collot d'Herbois could tell similar tales. Something that had happened fifteen or sixteen years ago at Angers had deeply impressed him. During one of the numerous conflicts between the military and civil authority, forty soldiers with loaded muskets were ordered by arrogant officers to break into the Opéra-Comique. There was confusion, shots, and a girl of fourteen with fair curls lay white in a pool of blood. Things like this could not be forgotten or forgiven; but while the company sat shaken, Desmoulins would make some joke and at last they would disperse only because the candles had burnt out.

Gabrielle, *"Dame épouse du sieur Danton,"* was respected by all of them. But these informal symposia sometimes caused her astonishment; and looking from Fréron, who, with feminine love of finery, was always dressed to the nines, to Collot, who affected a studied shabbiness and disorder in his dress, she would shake

her head. But the good housewife listened anxiously and timidly
to the resounding tread of history. Danton had never taken
much pleasure in women who tried to play a part in politics.
Théroigne de Méricourt, "the Amazon of Freedom," got applause from the Cordeliers by appearing in a short blue dress, a
hat with a feather, and a complete outfit of riding crop, pistols,
and sword. But when she instituted a patriotic woman's club in
the faubourg Saint-Antoine, Santerre, addressing the "Friends
of the Constitution," was one mind with Danton: "The men of
the faubourg prefer to find their homes in order when they come
back from their work rather than see their wives returning from
meetings which do not always teach them sweetness of manner."
Gabrielle radiated sweetness of manner; and the fact that she
gave him a comfortable home, always conjured up appetizing
dishes, and bore him two sons—Antoine on June 18, 1790, and
François-Georges on February 2, 1792—gave her greater claims
on his affection and gratitude than if she had imitated Mademoiselle Chevallot, the sister of the postmaster at Varennes,
who, in her patriotic fervor, begged the Jacobins to provide her
with a pike.

For a while Desmoulins lived in the same house as Danton in
the Cour du Commerce, and Gabrielle naturally came to know
his young wife. Lucile, née Duplessis, a dainty little blonde, less
domestic and more romantic than Madame Danton, poured out
her heart in her secret diary and loved to walk in the gardens of
the Luxembourg at hours when they were deserted. It had not
been easy to persuade her wealthy father to consent to her
marrying a journalist; at the ceremony Pétion and Robespierre
were the witnesses. Gabrielle would smile tenderly when Desmoulins rushed into the room where the two women were chat-
ting, and embraced Lucile with cries of *Ma Lolotte! Mon rou-
leau!* When in July, 1792, a baby boy was born, little Horace-
Camille and the youngest Danton were sent to the same wet
nurse in the country.

But best of all were visits from Arcis; Danton's mother or his
sister Anne-Madeleine, Mme. Menuel by marriage, brought a
breath of the valley of the Aube into the room in the Cour du
Commerce. How was the other sister, Marie-Nicole-Cécile, who

Lucile Desmoulins

had taken the veil under the name of Thérèse-Amédée in the nunnery of the Visitation at Troyes? How was Anne herself? And the little Menuels, the nephews and nieces of Uncle Danton? Could seven-year-old Georges-Marie read yet? And Georges-Martin? Like his elder brother, he had been named after Danton. And how was Antoinette-Gabrielle? She was four years old now, and had been named for her aunt. And what about the baby, Marie-Elizabeth?

And what of beloved Arcis? Sometimes the feeling of home-sickness was so strong that Danton rushed off to Arcis with or without Gabrielle, with Desmoulins, or Delacroix, or by him-self. There was a different smell about his native soil; his blood flowed more calmly, the politician dropped away from him, and the man remained, a peasant of Champagne, possessed by the same hunger for the land that his ancestors had felt. Thus it came about that in April, 1791, a big house was built at the northern end of the town, in the Place du Pont. Although it had only one story, it had a front of nine windows and a park, to which he kept adding with true peasant acquisitiveness. He would buy from a neighbor a meadow, a plot, or a copse, regis-tering each new purchase with the notary until his property amounted to twenty-seven and a half acres.

The farm of Nuisement, 180 acres acquired from the abbey of Anceny in March, 1791, was a good thing, too. But what af-forded him the most pleasure was the house at Arcis where he installed his mother and brother-in-law. Danton himself, when he was drawn irresistibly to his native town, would sleep in the alcove of a little room on the first floor through whose single window he could see meadows, hedges, and clumps of alders— all his own! Looking out on the other side, he could hear across the road the weir of his childhood, which must have murmured sometimes in his Paris dreams.

When he wished, a few dozen steps took him to the banks of his beloved river, where his boat awaited him with fishing tackle lying ready. There were days when the Cordeliers or the Jaco-bins would whisper anxiously, "Where is Danton? He has been gone for weeks," and all the while Danton was drifting in his boat on the Aube in heavenly comfort, with no thought but for his rod and not a wish in the world. For Danton was given to spells of grandiose indolence, akin to the peasant's idleness during the winter months by the fireside; and at the bottom of his ambitious soul there dwelt the conviction that it was more worthy of a human being to lie by a stream under the willows and wait for the fish to bite, than to spend the twenty-four hours on the treadmill of duty, or to pursue mirages of wealth and fame. If his house at Paris was a bulwark behind which he could take refuge from the nerve-racking drudgery of public life, the perfect peace of Arcis gave him new strength. Antaeus touched the earth.

DANTON was loved and admired by his fellow townsmen; but it was inevitable that so challenging and powerful a personality should elsewhere be the object of feelings the very reverse of popularity. No name was too bad for him. According to Mercier he combined the language of a coal heaver with the logic of a brigand. To others he was the "ruffian Danton, whose face alone is enough to hang him." But the loyalty of his own party was all the more unswerving; while presidents changed in other districts, Danton remained. The Club of the Cordeliers offered to make him honorary president in perpetuity, and *"Vive Danton!"* was the constant cry heard at their banquets through the clinking of glasses and the rolling of drums. When his son Antoine Danton was christened in June, 1790, at Saint-Sulpice, he was saluted in the court style of the district as heir apparent of the Revolution: "Let the tyrants tremble. A new Danton has been born who will follow in the footsteps of his father. The mighty Danton has said that his first lisping words shall be, 'We must live free or die.' Madame Danton forgot her pains in decorating the child with the national cockade."

Danton was universally regarded as "the man of the Cordeliers." When he was absent his supporters saw to it that the meetings of the district, of the section, of the club, were carried on in his spirit, and that the resolutions passed showed the marks of the lion's claws. Even the hypercritical Marat could not say of Danton as of Robespierre that he turned pale at the sight of naked steel. His supporters had the greatest expectations of him. In the *Orateur du peuple,* Fréron appealed to the sections: "I predict that Danton will save the country if you give him the chance to save it. You need men of character who will grow with the danger they have to face and will cause your foes to tremble. You need men to watch the steps of your enemies, capable of penetrating their intrigues and eager to frustrate them. Who has fulfilled this hard and difficult task better than Danton?" When the municipal tolls were abolished, May 1, 1791, and the barriers raised, and long trains of cheap meat, cheap wine, beer, and tobacco rolled down the streets, the people, in a carnival of liberty inspired by freely flowing wine, sang:

> *Voulez-vous de sûrs moyens*
> *Pour que cela dure?*
> *Formez de bons citoyens*
> *La législature!*
> *Ne prenez que des Dantons*
> *Et toujours nous chanterons:*
> *La bonne aventure au gué*
> *La bonne aventure.*

If they chose Danton, all would be well. . . . And his popularity reached beyond Paris and Arcis. By the spring of 1791, his name and the part he played in the capital were known in the more distant provinces.

In an age without political traditions, parties, or programs, when even the elections for the Legislative Assembly were carried through practically without political speeches or pamphlets, everyone had to go through a more or less difficult process of self-orientation. Danton refused to take over a political opinion ready made from anyone. From his master, Diderot, he had learned that sovereignty could be embodied in one person, when it was called monarchy, or that it could be embodied in the people, when its name was democracy. And Danton was a democrat. If he said sovereign, he meant the sovereign people, and "the majesty of the people," "the religion of the people," or "our sacred Revolution" were not trite phrases on his lips; they took on the solemnity of a confession of faith.

The manner in which Danton reached his political conviction was different from that of the aristocracy, who left a collapsing caste to take refuge in the Third Estate. The son of humble parents whose ancestors could be traced back for centuries without finding a single great or illustrious name could not but believe passionately in an era which, as Mirabeau said, judged men by the contents of the little space between their eyebrows. Danton was not willing to cede a finger's breadth of the principle: "No office within the kingdom can be the privilege of any one man; it must be open to every citizen fit to fill it and elected to it by a free people." He was a bourgeois; but he was a bourgeois at a turning point of history, where to be one hundred per cent bourgeois meant to be ninety per cent a revolutionary. For this reason he refused to subscribe to Duport's announcement in the National Assembly: "The Revolution is achieved." No, a thousand times no! It still remained to be achieved; as Danton insisted among the Jacobins, it must still be completed, perfected.

Like a sculptor before a lump of wet clay, ready to mold it with sinewy hands according to his inward vision, Danton surveyed the State. Robespierre's political abstractions made him smile, and he shrugged his shoulders at Marat, who took politics for a science that could be mastered over midnight oil. What really mattered was a sure instinct for the demands of the moment, an infallible sense of the available possibilities; as a descendant of peasants Danton knew instinctively that calculations or incantations would not turn the soil at the sowing; the hand upon the plough alone could drive the share through the soil. Facts, not laws, make revolutions.

The fall of the Bastille had taught the nation that nothing accomplishes nothing. The castles and seats of the feudal lords had to go up in flames before the infamous feudal right was abolished which compelled the peasants to beat the ponds at night with poles lest the croaking of the frogs disturb the master's slumbers; before concrete results could be achieved, the masses must rise. But the masses were fickle. In these sultry months of agitation they were easily inflamed; with the chain marks of the past still on their souls, they were incalculable in their rage. Woe betided when the hoarse cry rose: *"A la lanterne!"* In the autumn of 1789 the mob had seized an honest baker on the vague suspicion of complicity with the grain profiteers, had dragged him to the Place de Grève and promptly hanged him. His young wife, who was pregnant, rushed from the house to look for him; meeting the mob on the bridge of Notre Dame, and recognizing above them a bloody head stuck on a pike, she had swooned and died, and the child in her womb too had died. But sudden outbursts were followed by exhaustion and indifference, which furnished cause for much complaint among the Jacobins and the Cordeliers. Many lighthearted Parisians were far too eager to enjoy their short lives to wish to endure the Sisyphean labors of politics. Others who could not read or write met events dully and indifferently. Only a fraction—on an average not more than one tenth—of the registered electors would trouble to vote; in October, 1790, when the department officers, judges, and priests were due to be elected, only about two thousand votes were recorded in the forty-eight sections of Paris out of a possible seventy-eight thousand.

Differences which slowly emerged within the Third Estate did their share to quench political enthusiasm. The eulogists of the old order constantly represented the Revolution as the war of the "Haves" against the "Have nots," and Pétion, in February, 1792, complained in a letter to the deputy Buzot, that "the large and wealthy class of the bourgeoisie" had split off from the people. He preached: "The bourgeoisie and the people together have made the Revolution, and their union alone can preserve it." Danton, too, did not have to puzzle it out, but felt in every fiber that the driving force of the Fourteenth of July was derived from the unity of purpose of bourgeois, peasant, and worker. Therefore in moments of crisis he would hold that the elimination of conflicts on the revolutionary front would suffice to save the country.

But although common sense controlled his passion, although he was moved by a sense of realities, political wisdom, and even

a certain peasant cunning, as well as by revolutionary impetuosity, yet in his moments of exultation, when wife and child,
hearth and home, and all the ties of private existence were left
behind, something like a mystic flame burned in the man of
reason: a faith in the destiny of France, a faith that the plots
of its enemies were destined to work for the advancement of.
liberty.

———————

DANTON's taste for the concrete led him to direct his campaign
first against the two new rulers of Paris, Bailly and Lafayette.
Both were easy to reach, both were within rifle shot.

Insurgent Paris had torn Jean-Sylvain Bailly from the privacy of his study to thrust him into the mayor's seat. His fame
as a mathematician and astronomer had made him member of
three great academies in France and of many learned societies
in Bologna, Goettingen, Haarlem, Stockholm, Saint Petersburg,
Florence, and London. Tragedies and comedies, the relics of an
earlier period, lay fading in his desk. Always moderate and restrained, he had shunned telltale collaboration with the encyclopedists, and received a title and pension from the court as a
reward for good conduct; once the new dignity had been conferred, he laid bare the weakness and vanity of his character.
Yielding where he should have resisted, aggressive where moderation would have been in place, and always perfectly satisfied
with himself, his foresight, generosity, and conciliatoriness;
with an exaggerated sense of gravity and a weakness for display,
he discovered that it was easier to write the history of astronomy
than decently fill a few pages of earthly history.

Thirty-two years old, more than twenty years the junior of
the elderly and withered mayor, Marie-Joseph-Paul-Yves-Roch
Gilbert du Motier, Marquis de Lafayette, was commander in
chief of the newly formed civic militia. As a boy he had a yearly
income of one hundred and twenty thousand livres; a young
officer, he rode out with the Noailles Regiment of Horse through
the fortress gates of Metz; a grown man, he wedded the daughter of the Duke of Ayen. But despite the ties which bound him
to the old regime, the Marquis had laid the foundation of his

popularity by taking part, like a number of French nobles, in the American War of Independence on the side of the rebels; the lovely eyes of the Countess Simiane were not unconnected with this, his most profitable adventure. As founder of the National Guard, Lafayette played the bourgeois general skilfully and repeated at every street corner that the military must be subordinated to the civic authority. But ambition was stirring hopes of power in the slender aristocrat.

Further, Bailly and Lafayette, though not untouched by a reflection of the dawning liberty, and ready to welcome the constitutional State, were agreed that the Fourteenth of July which had given them power must be the aim and end of the Revolution. At the historic crossroads they planted a board: "Halt! Those who pass will be shot."

The instruments by which they intended to institute and safeguard the new order, if order it might be called, were far from inspiring. As only active citizens paying a minimum tax rate of six livres had the municipal franchise, so that one hundred and fifty thousand Parisians were debarred from control in their own civic affairs, the three hundred municipal representatives—the Council General of the Commune—consisted of wealthy citizens and scholars, lovers of a fixed income and tranquillity; it was no accident that among merchants, bankers, notaries, lawyers, professors, and writers, the inventor of a fire engine held a seat. To extinguish and not to add fuel to the revolutionary flames was the self-imposed task of this smug and portly assembly.

The National Guard, too, with two cannon and a section of gunners, was well interspersed with aristocratic officers. It was a militia of property owners, organized for the defense of property. Active citizens alone could be enrolled, and the four *louis d'ors* which were the price of a uniform were a sufficient deterrent for the penniless. Then there were the paid troops, who lived in barracks and were mainly recruited from former Gardes Françaises.

But though Bailly was lukewarm and Lafayette apathetic, their espousal of the revolutionary cause had won them such general esteem that they had no need to husband their popularity. Even in the section of the Théâtre-Français 478 out of 580 votes were cast in favor of Bailly when he was reëlected in May, 1790, while it was forever remembered that Lafayette had added the royal white to the red and blue of Paris, creating the national cockade which he foretold would make its way round the world. When, at the head of his staff, the preserver of the public order rode through the streets on a white horse whose obvious function it was to pass into legend, romantic young men thronged in girlish ardor to kiss at least the animal.

Danton declined to be impressed by the general's horse any more than by the state coach which, with outriders in front, and lackeys in rich livery on the footboards, conveyed the mayor to the Hôtel-de-Ville. Lafayette he dismissed as the "eunuch of the Revolution," and his opinion of Bailly was much the same. This bloated official could not be taken seriously. His pomposity demanded ridicule—and got it on December 26, 1789, when Danton headed a deputation of his district to the town council. Speaking rapidly with quick gestures, he complained of the commission granted to the officers of the National Guard, which contained a reference to *"Monseigneur le Maire."* There were interruptions, cries of "Impossible!" "Shame!" and "Show it!" at which Danton apologized with well-feigned alarm, saying he had misread. But his shaft had hit the mark.

Danton's campaign was based on the districts' greed for power. Created as electoral bodies in April, 1789, they had a tendency from the beginning to act as highly independent communities, especially serving the interests of the Revolution. For the districts were better guardians and depositories of the revolutionary ardor of the populace than the town council, whose polite and select deliberations were guarded from the streets by padded doors. By the appointment of special committees, by the insistence on rights which it did not have, and by a jealous disregard of inconvenient instructions emanating from the Hôtel-de-Ville, the District of the Cordeliers set a shining example to the other districts. It was the germ of a state within the State, and the title, "Republic of the Cordeliers," was no longer a joke.

The first conflict between Hôtel-de-Ville and district arose in the autumn of 1789 on the fundamental question of democracy;

that is, whether a deputy is tied to his electors, bears their mandate, and can be recalled by them. Danton refused to budge; his slogan, "the new aristocracy of mandataries," roused the people; but Bailly stuck to his guns and the National Assembly confirmed his attitude. Yet it was Danton who laughed last. Three of the five representatives of the district who had resigned because of the refusal to accept the principle of the mandate did not venture into the Commune even when the Constituent Assembly had given its decision; and in the end the Commune willy-nilly had to recognize the deputies.

After the preliminary skirmishes came the battle. In the autumn of 1789 the National Assembly decreed the appointment by each parish and district of *notables-adjoints,* whose function it was to safeguard the rights of arrested persons. The Cordeliers immediately went a long step further, and, in January, 1790, appointed five *conservateurs de la liberté,* whose countersignature was to be essential to make valid any warrant against a resident of the district. It might be that the Châtelet court, on the strength of a decree of the previous October, would attempt to arrest Marat, who had taken timely refuge in the District of the Cordeliers.

In many respects the editor of the *Ami du peuple,* with his dingy and untidy dress, leaden complexion, and greenish eyes, could not but be repulsive to Danton, who looked down with a kind of pitying amazement on his short-necked and short-legged figure. A subterranean life among cellar rats had given him scab and shingles, and when the overheated fanatic raised a somewhat oily voice to demand an ascetic manner of life and unmitigated earnestness in a revolutionary writer, Danton smiled sarcastically. An honest admission that he disliked Marat the man. But Marat the politician he esteemed because he kept the fires of democracy burning, and Danton extended his protection all the more readily because such a course allowed him to quarrel with Bailly and Lafayette.

At the Hôtel-de-Ville it was known that the Cordeliers were not to be trifled with and steps were taken accordingly.

January 22, 1790: In the grayness of a winter morning, the National Guard make a splash of color with their blue tunics,

green collars, and white facings—three thousand strong. Guns
—by each a gunner with a lighted fuse—are turned upon the
Rue des Fossés-Saint-Germain, where Marat is reputed to be
living. All this to catch one insignificant journalist. Yet the
Council for the Châtelet, followed by two bailiffs, is reluctant to
enter the Hôtel de la Fautrière, where the "People's Friend"
lodges. On the ground floor the expedition blunders into the district guard room. The guards, playing cards in clouds of tobacco
smoke, greet them scornfully.

Arrest? By authority of the *conservateurs de la liberté?* Next
floor, please! Whose deal?

Warrant in hand, the councilors make their way up the stair,
and run into a giant in the uniform of the National Guard, who
flings up his head belligerently.

"Your business, gentlemen?"

In the street the din of voices grows. The whole neighborhood
gathers to see why the "foreign soldiers" have come. Legendre
hastens up with bloodstained apron straight from his butcher's
block: "Butchers out! Shut up shop! To arms!" The troops find
themselves surrounded; the gunners with their fuses feel uncomfortable.

Danton is everywhere, threatening Lafayette's troops, calm-
ing his men, explaining to the jurists with convincing logic that
the warrant, drawn up in accordance with the practice of the
old regime, is both out of date and invalid. Eventually the district assembly decides to send a deputation to the commander of
the National Guard, and another to the National Assembly. Late
in the afternoon, however, comes an appeal from the Constituent
Assembly to the patriotism of the district, urging them not to
obstruct the agents of the law. The tumult dies away, excited
faces become calm. Legendre disappears, and Danton, with sudden, overwhelming politeness, points out that the road is clear;
please make what arrests you see fit. For Marat is by now well
away; and council, bailiffs, National Guard, and guns retreat,
tired, hungry, and ashamed.

Danton's superior tactics had inflicted a humiliating defeat on
those in power, for which they intended to repay him. The next
Friday he roused the indignation of the district assembly. "If

LEGENDRE.

Louis Legendre

we were to consult only our outraged feelings we would take arms and meet force with force. We would appeal to the laws of war and clear our district of soldiers who have come solely to seize it and mock us." Applause followed, indicating a dangerous readiness to obey—but a gesture stayed it. "Those soldiers are our brothers. Their only fault is a too blind obedience to the orders of our chief. Armed like us for the cause of freedom they do not suspect that they are the servants of tyranny. Tomorrow when they see clearly like true patriots, they will regret it." If the district were in arms it would surely provoke civil war, which was just what the counterrevolutionaries wanted. So the danger of a bloody conflict was averted, and the magic words *"La Loi!"* quieted excited spirits.

Spies, however, swore to hearing Danton proclaim thunderingly: "What do these troops want? We have but to sound the tocsin, to raise the whole faubourg Saint-Antoine and have more than twenty thousand men, before whom these soldiers would turn pale." Although the district repudiated this slander upon "sieur d'Anton," the Châtelet issued a warrant against him on March 17. The district assembly promptly countered with a resolution, doubtless originated by Danton, urging an appeal to the National Assembly on the ground that the action of the Châtelet "threatened to substitute tyrannical despotism for liberty," and urging the other districts to resist. For a fortnight the Danton affair kept all Paris stirred up. Since Anthoine, the judge-advocate of the parliamentary committee, advised against prosecution and the Constituent Assembly hesitated to stir up a wasps' nest, the agitation gradually died down and the matter ended with the abolition of the jurisdiction of the Châtelet. However, a satire entitled *Great Account of the Great Misdemeanor of the Great Monsieur Danton, Committed in the Great District of the Great Cordeliers; with an Account of the Great Consequences of the Same* described with much wit and relish how in order to arrest the leader of the Cordeliers, eighty guns, thirty mortars, and two thousand men were raised, and the inhabitants of the district were not permitted to sup or dine or even speak, and how all around the house of the agitator sappers sat on the roofs ready, in case of an attempt at escape by air, to cut the ropes of the gondola of his balloon with their axes. Danton had grown considerably in authority and popularity; the laugh was with him and many who knew his robust Gallic humor suspected him of being the author of the *Great Account*.

———◆———

In the same January in which *l'affaire* Marat gave birth to *l'affaire* Danton, Danton was elected to the provisional Commune and so gained a foothold in the enemy camp. However, when the section of the Théâtre-Français sent him on August 11 into the first constitutional Commune, it appeared that forty-two sections had been stirred up against him through certain baleful machinations; these sections refused the necessary confirmation, and Danton alone of ninety-six elected deputies became the victim of this ostracism. In compensation for this defeat he gained admission in October to the electoral college, which appointed him one of the thirty-six administrators of the Department of Paris. Fréron celebrated this "triumph of patriotism" enthusiastically: "Our only wish now is to see Monsieur Danton appointed procurator general of the department. His high intelligence and resolution call him to this post." In the Commune, in spite of the stimulus of Bailly's presence, he kept in the background, probably for lack of response, confining himself to a vigorous attack upon a resolution moved in June to vote the mayor a civic crown. In the department, a body composed of public figures and fat bourgeois, he felt out of place and dumb, and declared laughingly that he had got no recruits among "the asses of the department."

It was in Lafayette, who had bayonets at his back, that he saw his most dangerous opponent. He did not share the morbid suspicions of Marat, who suspected the snuff boxes decorated with the portrait of the "hero of two worlds," which the vain general lavishly distributed, of containing secret instructions for counterrevolutionary conspirators. Nor did he share the blood lust which made Marat swear to rip Motier's "fiendish heart" out of his breast although he were surrounded by "battalions of slaves." But he was always ready to make any move that might checkmate the commander in chief of the National Guard.

When in May, 1790, the District of Saint-Germain-l'Auxerrois, alarmed by rumors of Lafayette's resignation, passed a resolution: "He has been given us by providence; may providence preserve him for us," the Cordeliers replied claiming that their district had a better insight into the designs of providence, holding the general's retirement no irreparable loss and gently pointing out to the citizens of Saint-Germain-l'Auxerrois that in their blind enthusiasm for Lafayette they were forgetting the principle of the new age, which recognized no authority save that conferred by the people. Danton's hand again. He was always thinking it well to recall Frenchmen to a sense of their dignity as men and as citizens. "A truly great people," he said on another occasion, "must know no consideration for so-called great men."

On the twentieth of June, 1791, the Jacobins were debating a reactionary declaration in support of which Sieyès had managed to procure a number of signatures from the "Friends of the Constitution." Danton seized this opportunity of bringing up the name of Lafayette, who, a year before, had tried to talk him into a similar thing: "He reminded me that I, who had devoted all my powers to the cause of freedom, had been banished from public office by a kind of ostracism of the sections, while Bailly had been reëlected. He was sure that he would soon succeed in checkmating the society of the 'Friends of the Constitution.' I replied"—here we can see Danton fling back his head and stretch out his arm—"that the people would sweep away its enemies with one gesture."

At eleven that night, after the meeting, Danton and Desmoulins walked home together, through the Rue Saint-Honoré, past the Tuileries, and across the Pont-Neuf. Paris slept; the streets were deserted. They met only a patrol of the National Guard which scrutinized them as they passed.

The next morning about eight Danton started up in bed. These are not the ordinary street sounds, the shouts of news vendors and the wheels of vegetable carts. Instead there is a sullen surge of noise with screams rising above it like the cries of storm birds, and the fast roll of a drum.

"What is it, Gabrielle?"

Windows are thrown open, someone shouts across the street: "The King has gone! The King has gone!"

The thought flashes through Danton's mind: Now I have him! He means Lafayette.

Passion made Danton blind. At court the marquis commander of the Civic Guard was detested as a renegade who had thrown in his lot with the canaille, and it is certain that he had no hand in the flight of the royal family. On the previous evening, while Madame de Tourzel, one of the court ladies, was waiting in the Rue d'Echelle with the Dauphin and his sister, Madame Royale, for the other fugitives, Lafayette drove past. The terrified watchers recognized him by the mounted torch-bearers surrounding his coach, and Madame de Tourzel hid the Dauphin under her skirts.

But Danton's voice was the voice of the people: The morning of June 21, when news of the disaster sent the general hurrying to the National Assembly, he was met with cries of "Traitor!" and the same evening he found at the Jacobins' perplexed faces, whispers, distrust, uncertainty. It was said that the ministers and deputies would wait on the "Friends of the Constitution." Danton rose in the uniform of the National Guard, with a sword at his side: "Gentlemen, if the traitors come to this place, I pledge myself either to go to the scaffold or to prove that those who have betrayed the nation should lie there."

The doors fly open and a body of deputies enters led by Lafayette, pale, redhaired, and somewhat embarrassed. Danton, from the tribune, opens fire: Will you be good enough to explain, sir? Gentlemen, let us be under no delusion: the King's flight is a widespread plot contrived by leading public officials. "And you, Monsieur de Lafayette, who pledged your person that the King should not escape—do you think that you are meeting your obligations by appearing at this meeting?" Flashes of lightning: "You have sworn that the King would not go. Either you have sold your country, or you were a fool to go surety for a person you were unable to answer for." Cuttingly: "At best you have demonstrated your unfitness to command us." Quietly: "Still, I am ready to believe that you are guilty only of blundering." Loudly: "If the liberty of France depended on one man alone, the nation would deserve slavery and humiliation." With a flourish of trumpets: "France can be free without you!" Finally, driving his nail into the cross-grained wood: "Your power is a burden upon the eighty-three departments. Your fame has traveled from pole to pole. If you would be truly great, become a simple citizen, and cease to give cause for the justifiable mistrust of a great part of the nation."

Lafayette merely shrugs his shoulders with their heavy gold epaulettes, and tosses a few disdainful words like alms; but they are enough to win him the support of the meeting, and he retires covered with applause, so blinding is his popularity. In vain the Jacobins resolve next day that the general shall be required to answer Danton's charges; he excuses himself in writing with a "Later!" which means "Never!"

But a time came when Bailly ceased to be first magistrate and Lafayette no longer commanded the National Guard, and Danton was in the ascendant. On December 6, 1791, he was elected deputy procurator syndic of the Commune by 1162 votes against 654 for Collot d'Herbois. Pétion was mayor, and Manuel procurator; both of them old acquaintances, and, for the time being, of similar political views. With these men coöperation was possible. But the new post with its annual salary of six thousand livres did not permit him to make much use of the power of his personality: Danton had only one real chance to come before the public. This was in April, 1792, when, in the face of vituperative opposition, he strenuously supported a motion of Manuel's for the removal from the Hôtel-de-Ville of the busts of Bailly and Lafayette. Danton had been decorated with the tricolor sash and invested with his office on January 20. Now, in a rhetorical masterpiece, he made a powerful confession of his political and personal faith.

Remembering the ostracism, which, a year and a quarter before, had caused him to be struck from the list of representatives of the Commune, he did not lose the opportunity of triumphantly emphasizing that he had now been drawn from his obscurity by a genuine and irresistible wave of public opinion, "which knows no amnesty for traitors and whose supreme court quashes the judgments of fools and the decrees of judges bribed by the tyrants." Decline the office? Unthinkable; it was an advance post in time of danger. But—and his searching eyes fixed in turn on each of his colleagues—since his coworkers had the right to know his political convictions, here they were: Paris, like the rest of France, was divided into three classes. First, the sworn foes of all liberty, equality, and a constitution: "I have no words for these; I will fight them to the death." Next, the fervent adherents and supporters of the sacred Revolution. It was to these he owed his presence here, and for these, too, he had no words: "They have passed their judgment upon me and I shall never disappoint their hopes." The third class, equally numerous and well meaning, also desired liberty but feared the cost. They did not hate the defenders of liberty and would even, in times of danger, support them; but they frequently condemned their resoluteness which they considered out of place or dangerous.

There followed a skilful appeal for the support of this lukewarm and straddling class, an appeal necessary for political and personal reasons. Danton, freely maligned as a street demagogue, was not afraid of liberal self-praise. He described himself "as a man who knew how to combine the cold blood of reason with a fiery soul and a firm character," and introduced himself as a cautious tactician who had indulged in occasional strong language only in order not to appear weak. But now? Let us have legality at all costs, nothing but legality, legality above everything!

Then, with drums and trumpets and flying banners, came the impassioned climax culminating in an oath to the people whose will was the supreme law: "My whole life has been devoted to the people and no man shall attack and betray them unpunished. If necessary I am ready to die in their defense; my last wishes are for them and to them I give all credit. Their enlightenment and courage have raised them from humiliation and insignificance and their enlightenment and courage will make them immortal." The whole meeting was carried away, and amid shouts of "We will die with you!" bowed in awe before the storm of this oratory.

All this was a tactical maneuver to conciliate irresolute members of the moderate bourgeoisie, with whom he hoped to fill a gap on the revolutionary front. It was good tactics, too, to observe silence during the following months, not only to avoid causing offense but also to gather strength until his hour had come. He felt it drawing near. His eyes were open, and Gracchus Babeuf's admonition of the previous year—"Brutus, you sleep while Rome lies in chains"—was beside the mark.

THE Cordeliers favored direct legislation by the people, and so Danton did not share the popular awe for the National Assembly. His sense of realities showed him in what respects it was great and in what respects it was insignificant. The Constituent Assembly was all too frequently short of fiery revolutionary breath, and since the Fourteenth of July its membership had become completely out of date. With 291 representatives of the clergy and 250 representatives of the nobility as against the 577 deputies of the Third Estate, it had ceased to represent the nation. The fact that the fall of the Bastille had stirred the existing society to its depths and flung to the surface all the houseless and propertyless members of the submerged classes was a source of anxiety to the propertied classes and damped the revolutionary ardor of the Assembly. It shrank from a great historical gesture like that of liberating the peasants without indemnity, and in June, 1791, it timidly recalled that when the nation and its representatives felled the tree of feudalism on August 4, 1789, they had not intended to "impair the sacred and inviolable rights of property." Tithes, sales taxes, duties on fields, vineyards, and dwellings, and other burdens such as *agrier, arrage, reliefs, svètes,* and *tierce* were declared to be not extinct but only redeemable. But the peasants were by now thoroughly roused and took no notice of such decrees.

The Assembly made a more vigorous attack on the question of church property, which had to be turned into money somehow in order to cover the fatal deficit. The bulk of the enormous property of the Dead Hand, worth three billion livres and more, went to the monied bourgeoisie; only one sixth was parceled out to the peasants. This gigantic transfer of property, one of the most important in history, caused the Revolution to strike innumerable roots in the economic soil. All those who had acquired national property, together with their descendants to the fourth and fifth generation, were now the fervent adherents of the Revolution, for if once the old regime returned, good-by to castles, towers, and parks, yellow wheat fields, and even tiniest pastures. The small printed papers called *assignats,* drafts on national assets, whose rapid liquidation they had really started, bound innumerable people to the Revolution with the firmest of all ties, that of interest. All owners of assignats fought tooth and nail against a counterrevolution whose success would make their money good for nothing but lighting a pipe.

Soon after the Fourteenth of July obscure forces began to work for a constitution which would divide the power between the King and a bourgeois oligarchy. The intention was to create two chambers and to give the monarch an absolute veto against objectionable laws. These plans failed, and in their place the Constituent Assembly attempted to base the new order on a solid body of middle-class citizens, peasants, and better-paid workers, by enfranchising all persons who paid taxes amounting to three days' wages and making eligible for election all those paying taxes of fifty livres and owning real property; for according to the theory of the Abbé Sieyès, the State was a joint-stock company and the taxpayers the shareholders. Even Robespierre at first was not unduly troubled by the fact that the distinction made between active and passive citizens deprived more than three million adult Frenchmen of the most elementary political rights. Danton, on the other hand, belonged to a class of brainworkers at whose expense the privileges of the upper bourgeoisie could alone exist, and he clenched his fists as soon as talk arose of a bi-cameral system. Opposing such machinations and supporting the Revolution, which he wished to see develop according to laws of classic tragedy, he proclaimed to the Jacobins in June, 1791: "No! The unity of time, place, and action will always remain, and the play will continue."

In their great hours the members of the National Assembly could rise to the heights of mankind, and then they found a response in Danton; the *Déclaration des droits de l'homme,* which proclaimed that men were born free and with equal rights and must so remain, lit a torch that was seen beyond the confines of one country. When the Constituent Assembly adjourned in the autumn of 1791, it could boast of its achievements: it had dealt a death blow at feudalism, had declared the popular will to be the law, and the law to be supreme. The work of two centuries had been compressed into two years.

The Legislative Assembly, which Danton had demanded as early as April to complete the work of the Constituent Assembly, included among its 749 deputies a bare dozen nobles and another dozen landed proprietors; the overwhelming majority were representatives of the middle class and of the small bourgeoisie, jurists, and officials of the autonomous revolutionary administrative bodies. But although it was a parliament of youth, most of the deputies being under forty, many under thirty, and sixty under twenty-six, it had been out of touch with popular wishes from the beginning; most of the electors had been appointed before the great event of the King's flight. Fear of street risings, a desire for moderation at any price, and fear of what Danton called "great means" usually characterized the Legislative Assembly.

Danton frequently attended the sessions, either in the public gallery or in a special box which he might use as administrator of the department; and sometimes he appeared at the bar of the House with a deputation. So he had a more than superficial acquaintance with the parliamentary practice in the royal riding academy where Louis XV had learned to sit a horse. On the left near Robespierre there sat Buzot, Dubois-Crancé, Prieur, Roederer, and others, most of whom he had already met at the Jacobins' and the Cordeliers'. Among them too sat a grave man with gentle, benevolent manner; an apostle of humanity indeed, Dr. Guillotin by name.

Danton had personal relations also with the brothers Alexandre and Charles de Lameth, who, with Barnave and Duport, formed a single group. Although nobles by birth, they had decided to follow the fortunes of the Third Estate, and despite a somewhat frivolous elegance, they displayed such revolutionary intransigence that they won the favor of labor as rapidly as the hate of the court. To their right sat Le Chapelier, Thouret, and Rabaut Saint-Etienne, stout champions in the fight against feudal oppression and religious intolerance, and members of the Left; while the waverers, the "ifs and buts," began with Mounier in the center.

On the right sat the great Mirabeau's younger brother, the Vicomte, known as Mirabeau-Tonneau for his amazing Falstaffian capacities; Cazalès, who fascinated men with his stirring southern eloquence; and that hotspur of fanatical Royalism, the Abbé Maury, the cobbler's son, who caused repeated scandals. Under his cassock he carried two pistols which he was fond of brandishing under his adversary's nose; he spat after a speaker: "The hound has lived on his wife's immoral earnings!" and he actually attacked Barnave on the speaker's stand.

For Danton the will of the people did not cease to be the supreme law when the parliament was concerned. The nation in sending the deputies to the riding school had sent them to a post of danger; woe to all deserters! Guy d'Arsy, infuriated by the conferring of civic rights on the children of free colored parents in the colonies, laid down his mandate together with the other deputies from San Domingo. When he appeared unsuspectingly among the Jacobins, Danton called down fire and brimstone upon him for his treachery to the nation; one who turned his back upon the Constituent Assembly would find no place among the "Friends of the Constitution."

And indeed the National Assembly as a body stood above the individual members. Will of the nation, good! Sanctity of deputies, good! Yet Danton unhesitatingly conceded to the National Assembly the dangerous right to expel and to hand over to justice deputies who promoted civil war by signing declarations against the Constitution. His "lieutenant," Legendre, only appeared to go a step further when, at this time, he pointed out to a deputy that the people were but too eager to whip the time-servers out of the Manège, as Jesus had scourged the money changers from the Temple; for at decisive moments Danton himself did not hesitate to threaten to loose Acheron: "Let the National Assembly tremble!"

As Danton put the nation above the National Assembly, he put the National Assembly above the ministers. Even two years after the fall of the Bastille the members of the cabinet acted primarily as deputies of the King, since they did not belong to the parliamentary majority and were not dependent on its votes. Consequently Danton was not the only one who considered them the natural enemies of the people's cause; suspicion was generally sown between deputies and ministers; the "man of the Cordeliers" said everything when he bluntly retorted to a eulogy by Collot d'Herbois in honor of a member of the Jacobins who had been appointed ambassador and minister plenipotentiary: Those who lend their support to the enemy forces—the executive power—are no longer "Friends of Freedom."

From the hypothesis that the nation was sovereign, and the Assembly the expression of the national will and sharer of its sovereignty, the revolutionary conclusions were drawn when on November 10, 1790, Danton headed a deputation of the Commune, urging the Constituent Assembly to overthrow the ministers. Reluctantly enough Bailly introduced his bitterest enemy at the bar. Forthwith Danton, casting fear of God and men to the wind, insisted on the right of the National Assembly to demand the resignation of members of the government at any time, and claimed in the name of the people "the immediate and prompt dismissal" of three: Champion de Cicé, Guignard de Saint-Priest, and La Tour du Pin, the ministers respectively of Justice, of Internal Affairs, and of War. In vain the Right tried to shout down the unabashed speaker, and the pistol-bearing Abbé Maury exploded with rage. Danton's lungs were stronger than all this; he enumerated the sins of the three ministers: falsification of documents, dilatory execution of the laws, appointment of enemies of the new regime, unconstitutional actions, and support of counterrevolutionary activities. Away with such servants of the counterrevolution! Proofs? Revolutionary logic did not require proofs. "The nation has a right to say to those functionaries whom it mistrusts: 'You are unworthy of public confidence if only because you still claim to be the depositories of my interests while I am bringing forward my case against you.' " A call for a national court of justice which would try crimes against the majesty of the people brought this threatening speech to a threatening close.

Danton's keen eye did not fail to perceive the various hotbeds of counterrevolutionary activity. Immediately after the Fourteenth of July all those aristocrats whose delicate constitutions could not bear the fresh air of freedom fled the country with the King's brother, the Comte d'Artois. The Prince de Hénin, the Comte de Vaudreuil, the Marquis de Blignac, and various scions of the families of d'Harcourt, Duras, Villequier, Beauvau, Cambis, and Lauzun, the most ancient of the kingdom, fled before the distant thunder of the approaching nineteenth century and crossed the Rhine into the Middle Ages. Under the benevolent protection of the electors of Mayence and Treves they pitched their tents at Coblenz and proceeded to plot against their perverted country. Obviously such a contrary state of things could not last—where the bluest blood of France was put on a level with the blood of any tailor; it was a state of national fever, delirium, intoxication, and must pass.

Danton did not pay overmuch attention to these emigrants who, at a safe distance, were fonder of talk than action. He was too confident of his own and the people's native strength to be frightened by the goblins of Coblenz. Except where foreign policy was concerned, the laws which threatened the emigrants with the penalty of death and confiscated their property were sufficient.

The first group of those who turned their backs indignantly upon France was not without its share of priests; the secularization of church property made a large part of the clergy overnight into bitter enemies of the Revolution. Fields, meadows, vine-yards, and forests, the finest in the kingdom, gone at a stroke—who could preserve Christian meekness in such circumstances! But Rome was too cunning to weaken its position by a defense of temporal goods, and concentrated its opposition on the civil constitution of the clergy which affirmed the sovereignty of the State over the Church. Out of a hundred and forty-three bishops, all of them nobles without exception, only two, Talleyrand and Gobel, swore the requisite civic oath; the Pope himself rashly interfered; and since the aristocratic enemies of the new order, although most of them were themselves mockers of the Vol-tairian school, took good care to see that the pious masses should share the dissatisfaction of the clergy, dangerous fires soon be-gan to burn beneath the surface. All religious devotees stormed against the constitutional priests; and in the Vendée, when a priest who had profaned himself by taking the civic oath was celebrating mass, the devil in shape of a black cat had been observed escaping from the High Altar.

Danton, though unobtrusively without faith and not violently anticlerical, could not always resist the temptation to please his Jacobin audience by irritating those of his political enemies who were members of the clergy, as on June 21, 1791, when he de-nounced "the priest Sieyès who defended tithes, the priest Sieyès who objected to the secularization of church property, the priest Sieyès who has drafted a law to dilute the freedom of the press." Essentially, however, Danton treated the whole move-ment as a part of politics and would not let others take it lightly.

In the spring of 1791 a priest gave the Jacobins a very black picture of the maleficent activities in the Department of the Meurthe: "Among the priests who refused the oath there is not one who would not in cold blood rend the vitals of his country, and among those who have taken it are many without faith or loyalty who would break it at the least excuse." Some peace-maker suggested that the affair should be handed over to the proper ecclesiastical committee of the National Assembly. Dan-ton sprang to his feet, waving away objections with a movement of his hand: "Nothing that concerns the common weal goes be-

yond the competence of this society." Only this clear, cutting
phrase—but the "Friends of the Constitution" appointed commissioners to investigate the case.

More malignantly still the counterrevolution was boring its
way into the structure of the State itself. The law courts had
not been reconstructed immediately, and the sentences of the
Châtelet and of the other criminal courts were like a slap in the
face to the now-awakened populace. Revolution? We'll show
them! On October 5, 1789, when the people escorted the royal
family from Versailles to Paris, a plucky fruit peddler, Reine-
Louise Audu, had put herself at the head of eight hundred
women and, defying the sabers of the guards, had forced her
way into Louis' presence. For this crime she was thrown into
prison, put on bread and water, and lay long months on straw
in the dungeon of the Châtelet. She was not released until September, 1791. And this was one case out of hundreds. It was
not without reason that the "Friends of the Constitution" called
the courts of justice the "most dreadful of all aristocracies"
which weighed upon every form of our "moral, material, civic,
and political existence"; nor were the Jacobins of Vic the only
ones who complained of the *"incivisme,"* the lack of civic sense,
in the administration of justice. Danton stigmatized the prerevolutionary system as a source of abuses even in the petitions
he drew up for clients. And he did not spare the Justice which
tried to shut out the glare of the Fourteenth of July by covering
the windows with its robes. Speaking at the bar of the National
Assembly on behalf of the Council General of the Commune he
told the Minister of Justice to his face that he was in the habit
of appointing as public prosecutors the declared enemies of the
new order. This same minister had been charged in a Jacobin
circular with infecting a large number of courts with aristocratic
elements.

The firmest bulwark of the counterrevolution, however, was
the army. As early as December, 1789, Dubois-Crancé had told
the National Assembly that every soldier must be a citizen and
every citizen a soldier. Yet the Assembly retained the old system
of mercenaries commanded mostly by nobles. These young
aristocrats made no secret of their hostility to the Constitution

and the Assembly, and the champions of freedom saw with growing anxiety the sword of the State turning against the heart of the State. It was a counterrevolutionary orgy of the Flanders Regiment and of the Gardes du Corps at Versailles which, in October, 1789, made the people set off to bring back the King; the officers cursed the Revolution, sang the King's anthem, and trampled on the tricolor cockade. Again and again reports were received from the provinces that officers, and frequently men instigated by them, had insulted the principles, symbols, and representatives of constitutional France. The general staff and the War Office were full of militarists who yearned for things as they were before the fall of the Bastille. The Naval Minister Bertrand de Moleville, an inveterate counterrevolutionary, suggested to his best officers that they resign their commissions in order to paralyze the fleet; and after the King's flight had failed, the officers of entire regiments followed the example of the emigrants and fled the country. The Jacobins frequently debated methods to "de-aristocratize" the army and to introduce a new spirit together with new officers. Robespierre complained that the aristocracy had been abolished but that it continued to flourish undisturbed in the army, and Bécourt affirmed: "There are in the army twelve hundred aristocrats, all junior and senior officers and generals, and all of them of the old school, appointed by the despots. . . . The officers should be dismissed or their position should be adjusted by a process similar to the secularization of the clergy. Otherwise, the Revolution will go to the devil."

The troops, on the whole, favored the cause of liberty more than did the officers, among whom only those belonging to such technical branches as the artillery and the engineers were reliable. On the other hand, in August, 1790, the Swiss Regiment of the Château-Vieux mutinied at Nancy because the officers met the men's requests for arrears of pay with acts of brutality. The Marquis de Bouillé, commander in chief at Metz, led three thousand infantry and fourteen hundred cavalry—mainly German troops—against the insurgents, entered Nancy, and created a carnage. Twenty-one men were hanged as ringleaders and forty-one were sent to the galleys for thirty years; while the terrified

National Assembly voted its admiration of the resourceful general. But the Paris of the Cordeliers and the faubourgs raged, and for long Château-Vieux was the battle cry of those who witnessed with fury and despair the Revolution coming to nothing through the timidity of the wealthy bourgeoisie.

As early as May, 1790, Danton brandished the torch of his wild eloquence at the Jacobin Club against the counterrevolution in the army. Soldiers were dishonorably discharged for their patriotism; ha! if he, Danton, had been in their place, he would have washed away such a stain with the blood of ministers. In the case of the Château-Vieux Regiment he shared the opinion of the Cordeliers; Bouillé was a traitor and the mutineers had deserved well of their country. A pardon granted to the forty-one in the spring of 1792, which set them free from the galleys of Brest, was made the occasion of public festivities by the populace of Paris, and Danton took his part. The chains of the unfortunates were hung up in the debating hall of the Jacobins as trophies of the triumph of Justice.

In January of the same year the "Friends of the Constitution" considered the case of the former Gardes Françaises who had been incorporated with the paid and garrisoned companies of the National Guard, and were now dismissed and persecuted for their attachment to the revolutionary cause and left destitute. They were not even used in the line in spite of the lack of troops. A deputation of the guards appeared before the "Friends of the Constitution," and the president, in memory of their share in the success of the Fourteenth of July, welcomed them with: "Never on returning from battle did you bear more honorable scars; they are the scars of liberty." Danton suggested to the sections a petition to rouse the enthusiasm of well-disposed citizens in their behalf.

The following day the society debated a motion to form a bodyguard of the Gardes Françaises for the protection of the Assembly, although the Assembly could call upon the Paris garrison and had to give its sanction if other troops were to come within thirty miles of the capital. Danton opposed the motion and pointed to the example of England, where no bayonets were to be seen save at the seat of the executive, the king. "A time will come when bayonets will cease to dazzle the eyes of citizens. . . . For such is the power of freedom that every citizen can command in the name of freedom without arms; this is the aim of freedom." Danton had in mind something similar to Dubois-Crancé's identification of soldier and citizen. When in February, 1792, a deputation waited upon the "Friends of the Constitution" and President Basire requested them to hand in their pikes at the Secretariat, Danton pointed to the tricolor behind the president's seat, to which, as symbol of the "unity of the free peoples of the earth," the Union Jack and the Stars and Stripes had recently been added, and exclaimed: "I move that in token of the indissoluble union between army and people, that is, between citizens carrying bayonets and citizens carrying pikes, a pike be added to each of these flags." This was done.

THOUGH emigrants, clergy, courts, and army hated the Revolution, the focus of animosity was the court.

A tough sponge which even the hammering of fate could not mold, Louis XVI was perfectly indifferent to everything outside his favorite occupations—his hunting and his work as a locksmith. His diary for the Fourteenth of July, 1789, said quite simply, "Nothing." At meetings of the cabinet he read the English papers, wrote letters and drew figures, talked of traveling when European politics were discussed, of national customs when questions of diplomacy were debated, and of agriculture and cattle breeding when the internal situation was brought up. His minister, Montmorin, admitted despairingly that even when the King's most immediate interests were at stake one might just as well be talking of the affairs of the Emperor of China. This monarch was devoid of all sense of dignity. When brought back to the Tuileries after his attempted escape in June, 1791, he nodded familiarly to the officers of the National Guard: "Yes, yes, I made a fool of myself." He greeted his valet with, "You back again? I'm back again, too"; then, pulling himself together: "Get me a roast fowl, quick." If he stood in the way of the Revolution, this weakling who allowed the reins to drag was equally an obstacle in the way of counterrevolution.

Mirabeau had long ago observed that the King had only one man near him, "his wife." The young archduchess had tied her husband to her apron strings when he was still the dauphin. Pretty and coquettish, amiable and haughty, incredibly ignorant, intent on pleasure, devoting her entire time to trifles and confusing the court with the world, the Queen could take a hand at faro, play the harp, drive a cabriolet, and look after the flower beds. She seldom touched a book; but she perceived her power over her husband, and being of quick apprehension, she soon ruled the country as the Du Barry had ruled it under Louis XV. She flung millions about like confetti, controlled the appointment of ministers and marshals, and under the guidance of the Imperial ambassador, Count Mercy-Argenteau, became the tool of Hapsburg policy at the court of the Bourbons, though not of Austrian policy in France. When the fall of the Bastille with its consequences threatened the privileges of the crown, royal pride was stirred in the daughter of Maria Theresa; and since she was of a passionate nature, not merely by comparison with the flour bag of a king, she soon gave the signal for the war against the new order.

Louis and Marie-Antoinette shared an abysmal ignorance of the significance of this new order. Revolution, freedom, justice, law, and constitution—these were all confusion of mind on the part of otherwise loyal citizens, probably caused by British gold. Hence the only course was to remain firm. In vain Mirabeau, who was both Royalist and Democrat, begged the King to accept the Revolution for the sake both of the Revolution and of the crown, and explained that he need only become a constitutional king in order to block the Revolution and insure the safety of the dynasty. His words went in one ear and out the other. For the court all those who wished to rise were *canaille:* Marat, who was whetting his dagger on the Left, as well as Lafayette who on the Right was trying to mix a soft revolutionary drink of milk, honey, and lime flowers. The difference between Feuillants or moderate constitutionalists and Jacobins or pronounced constitutionalists was that between thieves and murderers. The gallows awaited both once the Royalists were again on top.

When the Queen unburdened her heart to her intimate

friends, she described the Constitution as an abomination and considered herself surrounded by monsters; and when Louis returned on September 21, 1791, after solemnly swearing adherence to the Constitution, he sank heavily into a chair: "Alas, Madame, all is lost." For even when the court bowed to the Revolution and the King put on the mask of constitutional hypocrisy, the aim was to gain time, to take no irrevocable step, and to avoid accomplished facts.

At the same time the Tuileries were well aware that there was as much danger from within as without. For if there was animosity between Marie-Antoinette and the King's brothers, the Comte de Provence and the Comte d'Artois, between her and the head of the younger line, Louis-Philippe-Joseph, Duke of Orléans, there was nothing but deadly hatred. With a yearly income of three million livres, the corpulent Bourbon was the wealthiest man in France and was reputed a man of the world and a *roué*. He was an Anglophile who adored tail coats, clubs, and horse racing; curiosity led him to dabble in alchemy, to go down into mines and up in balloons. An equally cunning and contemptible statecraft on the oriental pattern had introduced him at fifteen to dissipations that might quench the ardor of his ambition, so that, surfeited at fifty, he had recourse for the stimulation and satisfaction of his senses to means unknown even to the Marquis de Sade. Weak-willed, indolent and incapable of concentrating even for a few minutes on serious matters, the Duke of Orléans nevertheless was considered a source of danger at court; for he loved popularity and was mellow wax in the hands of two advisers. The brilliant Comtesse de Genlis, Marquise de Sillery—harpist and novelist, possessed of a thousand dazzling gifts, and yet, at bottom, meant by nature to conduct an academy for young ladies—had such influence as the duke's mistress that contrary to precedent he even intrusted her with the education of his sons. Still firmer was the control exerted by that outwardly cold and inscrutable analyst, Choderlos de Laclos.

And Danton—what more appropriate place for him than among twenty-four members of the Commune who proceeded in a deputation to the Tuileries on February 20, 1790, to present their humble thanks to the King for the gift of his marble bust? While Bailly drawled solemn commonplaces: "Lineaments which are engraved in our hearts . . ." "Beloved image . . ." "Father of the fatherland . . ." Danton had time to observe the King's dull fleshy features, his heavy person and sleepy gestures, and his private comment was not respectful.

But had Danton the right to look His Majesty freely and un-concernedly in the face? In the chorus of hostility which had raged around him since he had begun to make a name, the charge of bribery was brought most constantly and shrilly. Danton! that fellow is bought! Some said that he received vast sums from the secret fund of the civil list, others that he was in the pay of the Duke of Orléans, while others thought he drew from both.

Indeed, in the period between 1789 and 1792, greater sums were spent for bribery than perhaps at any other time in history. Under the illusion that the Revolution was not a natural movement but the work of British gold, the court saw the most effective antidote in French gold, with the result that the *atelier d'influence* was a gayly flowing fountain of corruption whence millions poured into pockets that were opened only too readily. Mirabeau was the first whose vast debts were paid, and he pock-eted six thousand livres monthly besides, and was only cheated by his untimely death of a full million that was to have rewarded the conclusion of his work in the National Assembly. Among the "Friends of the Constitution" Carra claimed in February, 1792, that not less than 230 deputies of the Legislative Assembly were taken care of by the royal purse. In order to buy even the visitors in the public galleries of the National Assembly, three million livres were thrown away during the period of the Con-stituent Assembly; and a petty rogue like Durand, who had been lawyer, consul, and director of the Senegal Company, had but to whisper to Montmorin that thirty-four thousand livres monthly would be enough to assure the support of the National Guard by keeping free table for twenty officers and men, and the gold clinked on the table.

As such practices were well known, charges of corruption were readily made in the political struggle. Even the halo of in-corruptibility which surrounded Robespierre in the eyes of his admirers amounted only to a reply to suspicions—else the emphasis on it would have been unnecessary—and even Robespierre was not safe. An aristocratic lampoon on Santerre ran thus:

> *Il faut ajouter à cela*
> *Robespierre, Danton, et Marat*
> *Pour ruiner la France sans resource*
> *Et tous quatre remplir leur bourse.*

The same Santerre was accused of having withdrawn a much discussed libel action against Lafayette for a consideration. The *Révolutions de Paris* charged that Isnard received money from the court. A similar charge was brought by Marat against Vadier, who had made a violent attack upon the King in the Legislative Assembly and withdrawn it a few days later; but Marat himself, who had as few personal needs as a mendicant friar and was thus above temptation, had to defend himself repeatedly in the *Ami du peuple* against the accusation that he had sold his pen to the Duke of Orléans, the aristocrats, the judges, the Protestants, and the priests. Who stood high enough above the tumult to be out of range of mudslingers?

Certainly not Danton. One of those powerful men who, aware of their own strength and security, are not afraid of bad appearances, he loved to startle his hearers with vigorous cynicisms: "Public opinion is a whore and posterity nonsense!" Or he would pat some admiring innocent on the shoulder, remarking ironically: "While you are in Rome, do as the Romans do. Once you have made your pile, you can do as you like." Such remarks, made *pour épater le bourgeois,* were taken literally, exaggerated and spread, and supported the rumors of Danton's corruptibility. Thus Lafayette claimed that the court had paid Danton one hundred thousand livres for his office of *avocat aux conseils;* in other words, had made him a present of ninety thousand livres. But this bitter enemy in a letter of April, 1792, mentioned Robespierre, as well as Danton, and Desmoulins, as being in the pay of the court; while the post of advocate, which had cost seventy-eight thousand livres, was redeemed in a perfectly legal manner by the competent authority for the sum of 79,031 livres in September, 1791. Bertrand de Moleville, minister of Louis XVI, related that his colleague Montmorin had shown him the written voucher for a payment of one hundred thousand écus to Danton; but no other mortal eye ever saw this document, and Montmorin, that spiteful minimizer of the Revolution, also spread the rumor that Brissot, Condorcet, Pétion, and others had been heavily bribed by the mulattoes to oppose negro slavery. Brissot, again, held that Danton was in the pay of the Duke of Orléans; but he said the same also of Robespierre and Marat.

Danton's private fortune was altogether incompatible with the idea that he pocketed hundreds of thousands of livres, still less of écus. The Marquis de Sémonville and M. Talon, a deputy of the Constituent Assembly, both of whom were known as agents of Montmorin and received pensions from the royal purse, acquired real estate to the value of eight hundred thousand and one million five hundred thousand livres, respectively, while Danton never enjoyed more than a modest prosperity which might very well have been the result of his lucrative practice. On the other hand, one who might have known wrote on March 10, 1791, to one who must have known—Mirabeau to the Count de la Marck, an intimate of the court—a letter with the bare statement: "Yesterday Danton received thirty thousand livres." This assertion, though somewhat vague and telling nothing about the source and purpose, throws Danton's figure at this important junction into an uncertain twilight. The great leader of men was not only "a good son, good father, good husband, good friend, and good citizen"—according to the testimonial of his countryman Courtois in the *Orateur français*—other impulses were dormant in Danton; in any case he took lightly things which others took seriously, and to snatch at the banknotes fluttering like butterflies around the court he would have had to overcome fewer scruples than many of his political friends. But if Lafayette urged on behalf of Mirabeau that he had taken money only to express opinions which were his own and if even Jaurès did not regard him as venal, at the worst the same might be said for Danton. The incriminating letter complained of the waste of money, as the attacks on Mirabeau in the latest issue of the *Révolutions de France* were due to Danton, and those who like d'Annonville suspected the "man of the Cordeliers" asserted bluntly that Danton had used the sums received from the court against the court and even to bring about the fall of the throne. Cheated cheaters—those who tried to buy Danton. He was not overscrupulous, and he may well have laughed to himself: If the counterrevolution wants to get rid of its good money, it is better for it to flow into the coffers of the Revolution and the pockets of the revolutionaries! But he was no more corruptible than a river into which pieces of gold are flung; he did not change his direction.

IN July, 1789, Desmoulins could find hardly ten Republicans in Paris; certainly Marat, who considered a strictly limited monarchy the best form of government, was not among them, nor Robespierre, who allowed the first article of the Constitution— "The Constitution of France is monarchic"—to pass uncontested. Danton too, although his friend Robert had been shouting loudly for a republic in the *Mercure national* since the end of 1790, was satisfied with a government in which the monarch as "first public functionary" was dependent on the popular will. Desmoulins said more acidly that the French nation had done Louis the honor of appointing him its first police official with a salary of twenty-five million.

What eventually made the monarchy collapse was not the spread of Republican opinions and catchwords but its own conduct. And yet even the obvious fact that the court was unable or unwilling to adapt itself to the new state of affairs suggested recourse to the younger line of Orléans rather than to a republic, which, according to Rousseau, was suitable only for small states. The Orléanist tendency was welcomed by Choderlos de Laclos' puppet, who was courting popular favor. As representative of the Paris nobility Orléans had gone over to the Third Estate; the Comtesse de Genlis sparkled for the benefit of revolutionaries like Pétion and Desmoulins in the salon of the Orléans castle of Bellechasse and created a sensation at the Academy Exhibit of 1791 by appearing, with the daughter of the duke, in

a Phrygian cap; her complacent husband, the Marquis de Sillery, worked with Laclos in the interests of Orléanism among the
Jacobins. Even the Duke of Chartres, the seventeen-year-old
son of the Duke of Orléans, who with adolescent fervor idolized
his governess the Comtesse, thirty years his senior, joined the
"Friends of the Constitution" in October, 1790; and immediately after the flight of the King the Duke of Orléans himself
was a Jacobin among Jacobins.

Rightly or wrongly, the Cordeliers had the reputation among
their enemies of being Orléanists. If Danton really considered
the scheme to replace Louis by Philippe, there were sufficient
good and politic reasons for such a course. This Masonic dignitary, every inch a mediocrity, weak willed and open to control
for good and evil, appeared to have been born to be a constitutional monarch. Since he had thrown in his lot with the Revolution and was celebrated even by Marat as a patriot with the
soul of a simple citizen and as the irreproachable champion of
the people, it might be worth while at least to try him.

But Danton's approval of the Duke of Orléans never equaled
his hate of Louis XVI. When, in October, 1789, the King hesitated to sanction the Declaration of the Rights of Man, and the
challenge of the counterrevolutionary banquet at Versailles infuriated the masses, the District of the Cordeliers issued an
insurrectionary summons—Danton's handiwork; Danton's impetuosity was in the stride of these men and women who set out
with pikes, guns, and rifles, to the sound of drums and tocsins,
compelled the Bourbon to sign, and fetched the whole royal
family back to Paris to be under the people's eye—a second victory for the Revolution as great as the taking of the Bastille!

The year 1790 passed in tolerable quiet. The first trouble
came when the King, who was very sensitive in religious matters,
began to extend undue consideration to the priests who objected
to the civic oath. On April 17, 1791, the Cordeliers sent their
congratulations to a grenadier of the National Guard in the
Barracks de l'Estrapade because, when on duty at the Chapel
Royal, he had berated the King for going to hear mass read by

a bishop who had refused to take the oath—"Bravo, bravo,
Dupas!" The next day the populace suspected a rehearsal for
a flight in an intended visit of the royal family to Saint-Cloud.
The National Guards refused to open the gates, there was a
tumult, commotion, cries of: "Fat swine!" "Damned aristocrat!" and "Long live the Duke of Orléans!" and some of the
grenadiers were already biting off their cartridges to pour
powder down their rifle barrels. Was Danton behind this? In any
case, he stormed into the general assembly of the department,
stopped Lafayette and Bailly, who were about to declare a state
of siege, and insisted on a manly and honest address to the King.
"Announce to foreign nations that there has been a glorious
Revolution in France, that you are now King of a free people,
and intrust with the working out of the new order such ministers
as are not unworthy of so exalted an office!"

When the King's flight on June 21 created an accomplished
fact the Republican enthusiasm of the Cordeliers crackled like
fire in dry underbrush. They declared that their society "con-
tains as many tyrannicides as members, each of whom has sworn
to slay the tyrants who dare to attack our frontiers, or to make
an assault on our freedom and our Constitution." They carried
an address to the bar of the Jacobin Club demanding the abolition of the monarchy. Here a fanatical devotion to the Constitution had produced a similar devotion to the monarchy, but when
an indignant member described the document as criminal, Danton casually motioned him to silence. Next day he thundered in
the Rue Saint-Honoré against "that individual known as King
of France." There were but two choices: This individual was
either a criminal or, at best, a fool; and a fool could not be King;
but there was no need of a regency, only of an interim committee
of ten to twelve members, to be appointed by the departments.

Was this a pronunciamento in favor of Orléans? Never! for
him a regency would have been the first step to the throne, and
on July 3 Danton repeated: "We need no regent, but a responsible administration of the former kingdom." Now came the
turn of the Orléanist "kingmakers"; Laclos proposed to the
Jacobins a mass petition for Louis' deposition. Many had their
hearts in their mouths, but Danton himself, who only two days

before had again firmly proclaimed that "anyone who wants to restore the King is a fool or a traitor," supported this suggestion on July 15, and boldly forged far into unknown regions whose frontiers began with the deposition of the King. "Those who have not the courage to act as free men," he remarked contemptuously, "need not sign our petition. Do we not need a vote to purge our society—*un scrutin épuratoire?* There it is!"

Already a deputation from the Palais-Royal was at the bar, presenting a resolution declining to recognize Louis XVI as King any longer; five commissars, including Brissot, Laclos, and Danton, were to draft a petition to this effect for the departments. By the next morning it had been drawn up by Laclos and written down by Brissot. "The National Assembly is called upon to take note in the name of the nation that Louis XVI on June 21 resigned the crown intrusted to him, and it is requested to find a substitute." The clause "with all constitutional means" betokened the Orléanist cloven hoof, for it opened a way to the regency of the duke.

On July 16, Danton, dressed in gray, read out the document in a resounding voice before the Altar of the Country on the Champ-de-Mars; the Cordeliers were drawn up under the banner "Liberty or death!" each wearing in his buttonhole his member's badge, an eye surrounded with rays, symbol of watchfulness. There were many signatures.

The next day a new petition drew the populace to the Champ-de-Mars. Composed by Robert, this had a stronger Republican flavor, for, while the word itself was avoided, it demanded, besides the deposition of the King, "the calling of a new constituent power to sentence the guilty and more especially to set up a new executive."

But the Constituent Assembly, alarmed by so much restlessness and ferment, had had enough. The time had come to take drastic steps against agitators. There was no longer any wavering and thoughts of abolishing the throne were dropped when Barnave explained: "If the Revolution proceeds one step further, the pursuit of liberty will mean the destruction of the throne, and the pursuit of equality the destruction of property. For God's sake, do something!" Even Robespierre himself cautiously protested against republicanism, claiming that he detested a government ruled by agitators.

In the gray dawn of July 17, two poor devils were pulled out from under the Altar of the Country. They were a couple of peeping Toms, harmless enough politically, who had drilled a hole in the steps in order to get a view under the wide skirts of the women who signed the petition. There was an outcry: "They are trying to blow up the signers!" and in an access of fury they were torn to pieces. Now it was easy for the malcontents in the National Assembly to convince the credulous of a popular uprising. The president, Treilhard, exhorted the Hôtel-de-Ville to action, Bailly unfurled the red flag, the official token of a state of siege, and Lafayette led the National Guard to the Champ-de-Mars and opened fire on unarmed petitioners, harmless spectators, peaceful vendors of gingerbread, and innocent pedestrians. Marat exaggerated when he said that four hundred bodies were thrown into the Seine; but the dead were numbered by dozens.

On the evening of this "Saint Bartholomew's night of the patriots" Alexandre de Lameth, whose personal relations with Danton were friendly, sent him urgent warning that measures were impending against himself and the other leaders of the Cordeliers. Danton first took refuge on some land of his father-in-law's near Fontenay-sous-Bois, and then proceeded to Troyes and Arcis. He was pursued by a warrant because of having stirred up an already excited populace on June 21, while on his way to the department, with such incendiary speeches as: "You are right, all your leaders are traitors and deceive you!" The Jacobins of his native town, however, declared in the press that in order to break into Danton's place of refuge all the man power of the Arcis district would first have to be crushed. Nevertheless when his stepfather went to England to buy modern mechanical looms, Danton seized the opportunity of accompanying him as interpreter and watching the flames of liberty burn in England.

In the *Patriote français*, Brissot regretted that Danton had

left Paris: "Was he afraid of a warrant and of prison? To be
a great example he must lead the way. Danton in chains dragged
before a judge could easily smash the petty upstarts, whom he
perhaps supported and who now persecute him! Great would
have been his service to the cause of liberty!" It was not fear of
prison that kept Danton from coming to the rescue, but his clear
appreciation of realities. The prevailing wind would have flung
the boldest sailor on the rocks. It was easy for the Abbé Fauchet
to say, as he had done weeks ago, "The tyrants are ripe!" The
people were not yet ripe.

Indeed, not one opposing voice, not even Robespierre's, was
raised against the raging counterrevolutionary storm. On the
day of the massacre, paid troops of the National Guard proceeded to the Jacobin monastery with artillery to level the debating hall to the ground; the National Assembly passed an
emergency decree punishing instigation to murder, plundering,
and arson. The investigating committee of the Constituent Assembly made indiscriminate arrests, and before the Tribunal of
the Sixth Arrondissement, the Minister of Justice himself encouraged the public prosecutor, who was only too ready to find
the kernel of the so-called conspiracy in the report that Danton
and Fréron were to have been proclaimed tribunes of the people
on the Champ-de-Mars.

Everyone drew in his head. The "Friends of the Constitution" disclaimed responsibility for the petition on the Champ-
de-Mars, but could not prevent the majority of the deputies with
the other adherents of Lafayette and of the brothers Lameth
from turning their backs on them and forming the society of the
Feuillants. The club of the Cordeliers saluted the Constitution
with ill grace. The *Révolutions de Paris,* and the *Orateur du
peuple* stopped their presses. Fabre d'Eglantine denied that he
had ever crossed the threshold of the Cordeliers or played a part
among the Jacobins or advocated a democracy for France. He
and Legendre went into hiding, while Brune and Momoro were
imprisoned. Like Danton—Desmoulins, Marat, Santerre, Fréron, and Robert took to flight. Only the amnesty of September
13 brought an end of the persecution. Danton, who had returned

from London a few days before, was to have been arrested in the electoral club, of which he was a member; but this attempt of petty officials to vent their rage on the object of their hate and fear turned instead into a triumph for Danton.

In his speech of January 20, 1792, Danton outlined a rather moderate program in which he insisted on the Constitution and nothing but the Constitution, and hinted that the constitutional monarchy might enjoy a longer life than the despotic monarchy had. Such moderation had the appearance of wisdom learned from flight and persecution; but a big "if" was attached to Danton's admission. "Should the monarchy finally prove itself a friend to that liberty which is its sovereign," he flared, then and only then did his picture of the future prospects for the monarchy hold good. Only four days later, speaking at the Jacobins', he referred contemptuously to the executive power which asked for guards when it could only claim lackeys.

In March a deputation gave the "Friends of the Constitution" 1445 livres, the result of a collection made in the section of the Tuileries on behalf of the condemned men of the Château-Vieux Regiment. The court too had contributed 110 livres. The president expressed his thanks: "The society will record the sacrifice of the Civil List in its annals"; and everyone was radiant with pleasure until Danton sprang on the tribune. Remembering perhaps that the Cordeliers had rejected a contribution of 208 livres "for needy patriots" which had been made by declared enemies of the Revolution, he hurled at the meeting: "How dare the royal family offer such alms, and how dare you accept such an insult? Gentlemen, the entire nation proclaimed the innocence of the men of the Château-Vieux; the entire nation clamored for justice. The inclusion of these soldiers in the general amnesty had to be wrested from the National Assembly and the executive power, and it took long enough. Are we now to express our thanks for alms of 110 livres? My motion is— Rejection!" But the speech of the trouble maker met with disapproval, not alone because many of the moderates who had broken away the previous year had found their way back from the Feuillants to the Jacobins; at the request of Robespierre

himself, who observed that the private action of the royal family
did not concern anyone, the House moved to proceed to the
order of the day.

Indeed, despite restrictions and humiliations, the monarchy
still asserted itself as a power. According to the *Almanach royal*
of 1792, it had been 4422 years from the creation of the world
to the beginning of the French monarchy; 1422 years had
passed since then, and the House of Capet had ruled for more
than eight hundred years. In what stars was it written that the
illustrious dynasty was not to reign for many centuries to come
and that no further kings should be added to its line of thirty-two
monarchs?

Then the war came and started on its downward path what
was destined to fall.

AFTER the unsuccessful flight of the King the number of emi-
grant princes, nobles, priests, and their followers grew rapidly.
The King's two brothers—"Monsieur" or the Comte de Provence and the Comte d'Artois resided at Coblenz with their mis-
tresses, court officials, pages, ministers, diplomats, and armies.
At this second Versailles the whole military masquerade which
the Revolution had scattered out of the Tuileries revived with
musketeers, Chevaux-légers, mounted grenadiers, Knights of the
Crown, guards and companies of Saint-Louis. Since they were
armed, these Furies of yesterday fumed and chafed; but despite
their boasts that the entire Revolution would collapse at the first
cannon shot, they knew their weakness and rested all their hopes
upon those states on whose financial support they existed.

As early as October, 1789, the Comte d'Artois adjured Joseph
II in his capacity as head of the Holy Roman Empire not to
suffer the fairest monarchy of the world to turn into the most
shameful of democracies: "The cause of the King of France is
the cause of every sovereign who needs must fear a similar
fate"; and in the following year, in his capacity as secret ambassador of Louis XVI to the Powers, the Baron de Breteuil

warned the Emperor Leopold II in a memorandum: "If the swift and dreadful march of democracy is not stopped, not a throne will stand firm!"

Rulers of Europe, quick, put out the conflagration before the flying sparks set fire to your own houses!

At court many of the follies of the emigrants were disapproved of, the more so since those who hated the Queen and despised the King were their spokesmen. But the court and Coblenz were united in the conviction that only foreign aid could restore the crown of the Bourbons to its former splendor. The Swedish Count Axel Fersen, who possessed the heart of the Queen and the confidence of the King, compressed the contents of a hundred confidential talks into one sentence: "The King will never be king through the French and without foreign help."

But Fersen's lord and master, Gustavus III, was the only crowned Don Quixote to experience any desire to unsheathe his sword on behalf of the Dulcinea of monarchism. Unhappily, Sweden was distant and insignificant, and what was the use of his suggesting to the King and Queen what they would have been only too ready to do—escape from the capital, declare the National Assembly illegal and its members outlawed, restore the prerevolutionary state and allow the "Paris den of murderers" to perish by forgetting its existence! Catherine of Russia, who considered two thousand Cossacks and six thousand Croats enough to tame the revolutionary monster, was engrossed by Polish and Oriental questions and took good care not to provide a single Cossack. Charles IV of Spain would have liked to put the whole of France in quarantine, but lacked the sinews of war, money. The Court of St. James's hoped to acquire long-coveted colonies like San Domingo without bloodshed by keeping out of continental quarrels. Prussia was not sorry to see France weakened by internal troubles, and even the house of Hapsburg, which was bound by the closest ties of blood to the lady in the Tuileries, could not suppress a secret feeling of malicious political joy. Thus the agreement signed at Pillnitz in August, 1791, by Leopold II and Frederick William II could hardly be taken as the prelude to a war against the Revolution

inasmuch as it was assumed that France, weakened and paralyzed, was sure to give way as soon as the saber was earnestly
rattled.

But there were forces at work in Paris which did not shrink
from war. The feeling that the Revolution was an event of European significance grew to a restless yearning to break the bondage of other peoples. In August, 1790, Carra indulged among the
"Friends of the Constitution" in reveries about the French as
the chosen people, "the messianic people which all others look
to as savior. Instead of the torch of war and discord we must
bring them that of wisdom and freedom." The next summer the
Cordeliers appealed to all the nations of the world to cast off the
yoke of slavery, to break their chains and be free. Not much
later an address of the Jacobins urged the neighboring peoples
not to suffer the emigrants in their midst: "To you we declare
peace, trust, unity, fraternity. English, Germans, Belgians,
Swiss, Savoyards, Piedmontese, and Spaniards, soldiers of all
nations—henceforward France and you are a single nation in
which disharmony is no longer possible."

It was unthinkable that the despots would dare to meddle
with the free people of France. At the Jacobins' in July, 1791,
Brissot jeered: "The Powers must avoid war to preserve their
peoples from contagion with revolutionary France. . . . The
French Revolution will become the sacred hearth from which
sparks will set afire the nations whose masters dare to approach
too closely." Vergniaud assured the Legislative Assembly that
the kings trembled lest the day of battle unite the two enemy
armies into one people of brothers. And by December Brissot
had progressed so far as to preach in his paper the "holy war,"
the war of atonement which was to alter the face of the world
and plant the standard of liberty on the palaces of kings, the
seraglios of sultans, and the castles of petty feudal tyrants.
Isnard sounded the call for a "war of peoples against kings"—
"the French have become the chosen people of the universe, and
must show themselves worthy of their new destiny"—while a
circular letter addressed by the Jacobins to the affiliated societies in February, 1792, spoke of the neighboring nations:
"Let us hasten to succor these victims of despotism; let us im-

plant freedom in all the peoples around us, and set up a bulwark of free peoples between ourselves and the tyrants!"

But while Brissot, Vergniaud, and Isnard wreathed their
swords with the red roses of freedom, the question of war was
for them a sober problem of internal politics as well. After the
reaction which followed the massacre on the Champ-de-Mars,
the Revolution, badly hampered by the ball and chain of business stagnation, inflation, and the high cost of food, was barely
dragging along; the bourgeoisie was weary, the masses sullen.
In October, 1791, Desmoulins complained uneasily among the
"Friends of the Constitution" of the cooling zeal of the patriots: "There was less slackness under the old regime." But
war!—let war be declared and at a stroke uneasiness, laxity, and
enervation would be mastered. With war the passion of the great
fateful days would give momentum to the movement. With war
the work of the Revolution would be completed. "The safety of
the country," so a Jacobin circular reiterated, "depends on one
single and drastic measure—war! We need it to assure the Constitution and our existence as a nation. We need it in order to
impress on our Revolution the imposing character becoming to
the actions of a great nation."

Yes, might not war also win to Brissot those behind Lafayette? Why not? And it might well be the means of introducing
discipline into the demoralized army. When the new Minister
of War, Comte de Narbonne—a dashing gentleman, spoilt by
easy boudoir victories, of late lover of Necker's blue-stocking
daughter, Madame de Staël—announced (at the Legislative Assembly, December 14, 1791) the formation of three armies of
fifty thousand men under Rochambeau, Lückner, and Lafayette,
he added complacently that if the call to arms sounded, "it will
be for us the longed-for signal of order and justice," that order
and justice against which the dead of the Champ-de-Mars bore
hideous witness. With luck—who knows—there was a chance
of returning at the head of victorious and seasoned troops, to—
let us say—"straighten out" the Revolution.

Eventually even the court no longer found fault with Brissot's
plan. It meant tacking and so gaining time; and the court nursed
the wicked hope, too, that the defeat, the sure and inevitable

defeat of France, would force a humble and contrite people to their knees at the foot of a throne made absolute once more. For this reason the King, speaking at the Manège on December 14 against the pro-emigrant governments, could lay his false hand on his false heart and proclaim the joy of being the ruler of a free nation. A sea of applause roared around a small island of silence at the extreme Left.

For apart from the moderates around the Lameths and Barnave, who had forebodings that the war would devour them, Robespierre turned from Brissot's plans with suspicion and disgust; the mere fact that Lafayette commanded an army and that the court sanctioned a policy of war was enough to arouse his suspicions. When Brissot explained that the country needed war in order to insure peace at home—"the malcontents depend only on Coblenz, refer only to Coblenz, are insolent only because Coblenz exists"—the lawyer from Arras replied: "The real Coblenz is in Paris!" and he continued to urge peace with the Powers. However, ten days after April 20, when Louis declared war on the King of Bohemia and Hungary—a war resolved on by the Legislative Assembly almost without a dissenting voice —Robespierre exculpated himself by explaining that he had never objected to war but had only said that internal foes must be dealt with first.

Danton's section, like most of the others, was eager for war. In December, 1791, his friend Legendre declaimed at the bar of the Legislative Assembly: "Representatives of the people, I ask you to decree! The eagle of victory and the fame of the centuries are poised above your heads and ours! When the cannon of the enemy are heard, the lightning of freedom will shake the earth, illuminate the universe, and strike the tyrants." Such grandiloquence was not Danton's style. Five days later when the question of declaring war was before the Jacobins, he slapped Brissot genially on the back with a "good champion of liberty," praising him as a man of whom great things were expected and one who would not disappoint the hopes reposed in him; but as a matter of fact he inclined toward Robespierre. In the back of his mind he may have been convinced that the conflict was unavoidable, that the sudden bursting of the bour-

Front View

Rear View

Danton's House at Arcis-sur-Aube

geoisie through the rotten crust of the old order would spread over the whole of Europe, that democratic France and the feudal-absolute rest of the world could not live peacefully side by side. Yet chiefly he pondered the When and How of this war: "I want war; it is inevitable; we must have war. But first all means of averting it ought to be exhausted." Why, for instance, was the "executive" planning war? Was it not strange that the King was now up in arms against the emigrants—when he would formerly not have had a hair of their heads touched? What of Lafayette? What of the ministers, and the party which hoped to exploit a general war in order to give France a British constitution—with an Upper House—in the hope of soon replacing it with some thing Turkish? In grave words he pointed out the inner and outer dangers of the venture, and urged the need of first testing, investigating, and weighing all the facts.

However, as late as January the Brissot-Madame Staël-Narbonne group hoped to win him over to their side and Danton, feeling that the watchword "No war!" left the masses unresponsive, grew silent, shrugged his shoulders and stood by.

THE giant bellows of war fanned the revolutionary fervor until Paris became one white-hot smelting furnace—from which modern France emerged.

But the party whose cry was war was too short winded to keep pace with events. Brissot laid bare the most secret and daring parts of his policy when he explained to the Jacobins that great treacheries were needed to bring salvation, that France still had a strong dose of poison in her veins and required violent discharges in order to eliminate it. But was the cabinet of Brissot's friends to which the court had recourse in March really equal to such a purge? Its head, Jean-Marie Roland de la Platière— a sere and sorry man, a wily and suspicious bureaucrat and sober Puritan who hoped to preserve his civic dignity by going to court with laced instead of buckled shoes, and was the creature, politically and otherwise, of his wife Manon, his junior by twenty years—was anything but a leader at a time that demanded the sowing of an iron crop. Of a very different caliber was General Dumouriez, the Foreign Minister, who also had the portfolio for War. With the bearing of a cavalier of the old regime, of dazzling appearance, enterprising, ambitious, and full of youthful vigor at fifty-five, charming everyone by the ease of his manner, he was unhampered in his egoism by prejudice or conviction: he served neither the Revolution nor the monarchy but only himself. To the troops he spoke in the language of liberty, and caused rejoicing among the "Friends of the Constitution" by appearing on the tribune of the Rue Saint-Honoré after his appointment and clasping Robespierre in a fraternal embrace. But privately among his peers he would call the National Assembly an old courtesan who must soon be got rid of.

Military operations against the Austrian Netherlands began with advances against Mons and Tournai at the end of April; in May there were engagements on the Sambre and in June an advance upon Courtrai. But this activity soon slackened, and Marshal Lückner retired irresolutely and timidly to his starting point, Lille. These disappointments infuriated the masses. What was responsible for the failures? The conspiracy of the "Aristos." Treason, yes, treason! "The court conspires," Réal exclaimed at the Jacobins', "the general staff conspires, the departments conspire, in short, everyone conspires!" Gensonné pointed to the source of the evil: "This war is a sham; our military leaders are controlled by the House of Austria!"

They were not seeing ghosts. In perfect innocence—since divine dispensation had given France to the Bourbons, the court did everything to hasten the humiliation of the country, which meant the exaltation of the throne. High treason? How so? The Revolution was high treason against the principle of legitimacy, therefore every means of stifling the Revolution was legitimate. And so code messages were continually passing by secret channels from the Queen informing the enemy with complete accuracy of the strength of the French battalions and the plans of the French high command: "The troops," they were encouraged, "are without supplies and utterly confused." For months the *"Autrichienne"* had been like a deer at bay with not a soul on earth except Fersen to support and protect her; for the King counted for nothing and the court temporized. But, entangled in dynastic pride and religious delusions, she willingly deceived herself about the impending danger; her eyes brightened when she read the reassuring letters from the Swedish Count at Brussels: Courage! The Prussians are on the way!

The French setbacks at the front caused the Royalists to become more impudent daily. Danton's lieutenant, Legendre, found that out: he was dragged from his carriage by grenadiers of the National Guard who held him at the bayonet's point because he did not take off his hat when a religious procession passed; when the pious crowd learned his name cries of *"A la lanterne!"* were heard and a woman shrieked: "Give me a stone and I'll break open the tin box where they keep the lantern rope! What a pleasure to hang the scoundrel!"

But a searing fever—Treason! Treason!—racked the patriotic masses. The pike which since October, 1789, had almost vanished was restored; there were instructions for their manufacture: length of stem, 6 feet; iron point, 10 inches.

Because Louis put off signing the decree banishing those priests who refused to take the oath, in the middle of June he received a letter from Roland earnestly warning him that the prevalent unrest would burst into flame unless he regained popular confidence by strictly constitutional behavior. Result: the dismissal of Roland and two other ministers—a triumph of the counterrevolution which relied on bayonets, and a proof that the court would not tolerate even a tame revolutionary cabinet that ultimately revolution and monarchy were as fire and water.

Excitement grew. Robespierre, to be sure, in lengthy periods minimized the significance of this step taken by the crown: the public weal depended not on a few ministers but on the cherishing of principles, the fostering of public spirit, the wisdom of the laws, the incorruptible virtue of the representatives of the people, the power of the nation itself, and so forth. Not so Danton. Already in December, 1791, when to the "Friends of the Constitution" war seemed certain, Mirabeau's secretary, Pellenc, a man with intuitions, wrote the Count de la Marck: "It looks as though Danton will play a big part in it." Danton himself, his finger on the pulse of events, felt that his hour had come, that it was time to strike. Open the sluice gates and the force of the people will carry away the throne. The Paris bourgeoisie, among whose twenty-three deputies to the Legislative Assembly there were only five convinced Jacobins, was certainly not entirely or even predominantly Republican; but one of those moments had come when a resolute minority can carry the cause of a hesitating majority to victory. On June 13, the order of the day at the "Friends of the Constitution" was the dismissal of the ministers. Danton arose: "The executive has become bold only because we have been weak. I pledge myself to carry terror into the corrupt court." The next day he demanded in a brief and pregnant speech two important though not yet Republican measures: a system of taxation shifting the bulk of the burden from the poorer to the wealthy classes, and the passing of a law by the National Assembly compelling the King to separate from his wife and send her back to Vienna.

A few days later the masses felt another crack of the whip. From his camp at Maubeuge Lafayette indited an impudent letter to the Assembly opposing the "Jacobitic" party, and supporting the "sanctity of the kingly power." One saber-rattling phrase —"in the midst of my brave army"—made the Jacobins on June 18 brim over with indignation. Desmoulins, Robespierre, and Collot d'Herbois spoke, and finally Danton stood on the tribune, gloating to see his old enemy cast off the mask at last. He moved to summon the general before the bar of the National Assembly; noncompliance would mean that he had gone over to the enemy, compliance would put him at the mercy of the Legislative Assembly and all the patriots.

Then Danton unfolded his own plan: He wanted, not an irregular, accidental uprising, but a blow struck by the organized force of the people of Paris, by the sections. Accordingly he supported a motion of Fabre d'Eglantine to invite the sections to appear before the Legislative Assembly. We do not want to seem a handful of agitators. Bring out the people. Let the masses appear before the National Assembly.

The answer came on June 20. Ten thousand men with pikes,

rifles, sticks, and green branches passed before the tribune of the Assembly, and their bearing and resolute looks proclaimed: We are sick of it! This demonstration carried terror into the court; it surged into the inner chambers of the Tuileries and roared around the helpless and humiliated monarchy. "Choose between Coblenz and Paris!" they cried to the King; and Louis, adding one more to his many insincerities, put on a red cap while a red, white, and blue cockade was fixed on Marie-Antoinette's breast. But the court refused to learn. The next day, when the mayor waited upon the King, the latter shouted down his objections with an imperious: "That is not true! Be silent! Withdraw!" Pétion and his two companions bowed themselves out, then looked at each other and burst into laughter.

True, fear of anarchy inspired in the moderate bourgeoisie a desire to see such unmannerly demonstrators punished by "the sword of the law"; it was in vain, however, that Lafayette came to Paris surrounded by gunners and grenadiers and on June 28 appeared menacingly at the bar of the National Assembly. Although the majority were with him, finding himself between the two fires of revolution and monarchy, he saw the uselessness of his coming and hurried back to camp pursued by Jacobin demands for proceedings against him.

Betrayed by the court and deserted by the army leaders, the nation had to rely upon itself. Vergniaud delivered an inspired oration, in which he exposed the King's responsibility for the foreign menace to liberty, and concluded by asking that the country be declared in danger. A week later Hérault de Séchelles laid before the National Assembly the report of an investigating committee on the same subject; here once more the banner of the holy war was unfurled: "The war which we have undertaken does not in any way resemble the usual wars which so often have brought grief and destruction into the world; it is the war of liberty, equality, and the Constitution against a coalition of powers which are all the more eager to alter the French Constitution because they fear that our philosophy and the light of our principles may break upon them. This war is the last war of all between them and us."

After this speech the Assembly resolved: *"La patrie est en danger!"*

At six in the morning of July 23 the signal gun in the Artillery Park on the Pont-Neuf fired three shots which were repeated each hour. The assembly was sounded in the streets. At eight two columns of troops began to move: cavalry with trumpeters, sappers, drummers, band, National Guards, six guns, more trumpeters followed by four mounted bailiffs of the municipality bearing standards embroidered with "Liberty," "Equality," "Constitution," and "Fatherland"; twelve municipal officials with tricolor sashes, notables, mounted representatives of the Commune; then, alone, a mounted guardsman bearing a large tricolor inscribed *"Citoyens, la patrie est en danger!"* Six guns, National Guards and cavalry were at the end of the column. The procession stopped here and there and each time, after a roll of drums, an official read out the resolution proclaiming the country in danger. Every heart and mind was impressed.

At the Place Royale, the Parvis-Notre-Dame, the Place Dauphine, the Théâtre-Français, and at four other points tents had been erected; boards laid across a couple of drums formed tables at which volunteers enrolled—fifteen thousand of them in a week.

On July 11, Robespierre prophesied: "If within a month the country is still in danger and the situation has not greatly altered, we shall have to say not: The country is in danger! but: The country is lost!" Still he continued to plead for legal methods, caution, and a policy of "wait and see." Although he did not go so far as Brissot, who, faithlessly denying his former policy, began suddenly to proclaim a change of constitution inopportune during the war, Robespierre now had in mind only a Convention to be elected by equal and universal suffrage, and declined to commit himself on the delicate question of the monarchy.

But already Danton was taking steps to effect a radical change. He shared the opinion of Legendre, whose slogan among the Jacobins was: Deeds, not words! A general uprising will save the country! Danton prepared for deeds in more ways than one. Pétion and Manuel had been deprived of their important posts by the reactionaries in the directorate of the departments. Immediately Danton was in arms, and it was another triumph for him when the Legislative Assembly canceled the decree in spite of the royal confirmation. Another move: Check!

And immediately afterwards, on July 17, the Commune set up a central office of communications for the sections at the Hôtel-de-Ville; it would be child's play now to embrace in one great unit the forty-eight revolutionary fragments of Paris.

Danton's calculating look also turned upon another organized force of the people, the federates. Ever since the various cities and communes had united under the sign of the new liberty at the beginning of the Revolution, the anniversary of the Federation had been celebrated at Paris each Fourteenth of July. In 1792 the third celebration was about to take place, attended by National Guards from all over France. On the evening of July 13, the Jacobins were buzzing with the wildest rumors; Lafayette was in Paris—no, it was Lückner—there had been a massacre of the patriots—no, a plan to abduct the King—mysterious wagons loaded with weapons and ammunition had been observed at Meudon. After Desmoulins, Robespierre, and Anthoine, Danton raised his old warning cry: "People, you are being betrayed; you cannot deal with tyrants. The presence of our brethren from the departments must establish the rule of liberty forever or liberty is lost! The right of petition has not yet been buried with the corpses of those who died on the Champ-de-Mars. So let us send a petition to the departments to decide the fate of the executive power—the deposition of the King—and let the federates swear not to disperse before they have received the answer of the sovereign people."

This proposal preserved the appearance of legality, but its aim was to produce a plain state of revolution.

The federates, having once assembled in the capital, decided to remain there and this resolve in itself advanced things. A directorate of their central committee was formed with forty-three members. These were no proletarians, men from the faubourgs. There were Vaugeois, vicar general of the bishop of Blois, Professor Guillaume of Caen, Deberre, departmental official from the Drôme, Simond, the Strasbourg publisher, Anthoine, deputy from Metz, and Santerre. Danton was connected with them through Fournier, nicknamed the "American," of the section of the Théâtre-Français. This revolutionary committee, which met secretly in an inn in the faubourg Saint-Antoine, worked out a detailed plan of insurrection. But the federates were only five or six thousand strong, and powerless without Paris.

On July 18, a sansculotte gardener handed a huge bouquet to the president of the Jacobins at the beginning of the session.

Every day and every hour excitement grew. The people were haunted by nightmares; in the streets they formed clusters and shouted each other down with hysterical gestures. On the Rhine and the Moselle an Austro-Prussian invading army was concentrating for a blow at the heart of France, under the command of Duke Charles William Ferdinand of Brunswick, notorious seller of his soldiers and persecutor of Lessing. He boasted that he would be in Paris on the day of Saint-Louis, August 15.

Every rumor found a crowd of listeners and panic spread rapidly. On July 28 the proclamation which the Duke of Brunswick addressed to the French people from his headquarters at Coblenz was published. It snarled in the arrogant tone of the Junkers and emigrants: ". . . Anarchy in France must cease, the King must have the security and freedom and legitimate authority to which he is entitled." . . . "National Guardsmen fighting against the troops of the Allied Courts and taken under arms will be punished as rebels against their King and disturbers of public peace" . . . "Inhabitants of towns, villages, and hamlets daring to defend themselves against the troops of Their Imperial and Royal Majesties and firing upon them will be dealt with immediately by martial law, their houses destroyed and burnt down" . . . "The city of Paris shall surrender to the King forthwith and without delay" . . . "Their Imperial and Royal Majesties make every member of the National Assembly, the district, the municipality and the National Guard of Paris responsible, personally and without pardon, for all disorders" . . . "If the Tuileries should be attacked and taken by violence, unparalleled and eternally memorable vengeance will be taken;

the city of Paris will be handed over to the military and razed to the ground." WE, by the Grace of God!

This manifesto, designed to cause paralyzing terror, provoked instead boiling rage. The foreign monarchs, by insulting the liberty of the French people, signed the death warrant of the monarchy in France.

True, not all the French were lions. When the drum sounded the alarm on July 30, and the Jacobins rushed from the debating hall, a sceptic remarked that this was what always happened: they pretended to hurry to the parade ground of their battalion and in fact they barricaded themselves at home. But if anger does not make a man a hero, fear turns him into a wild beast.

On July 30, the battalion of Marseilles Volunteers were enthusiastically greeted as they entered Paris: two guns and five hundred men burnt a deep brown by their twenty-eight days' march through the fairest cantons of France, with red Phrygian caps, daggers and pistols in their belts, and shouldered rifles. They marched without hindrance across the leveled square where the threatening Bastille stood less than three years ago, and—yes, they were singing a new tune that made eyes flash and fists clench: "The Battle Song of the Army of the Rhine."

> *Allons enfants de la Patrie,*
> *Le jour de gloire est arrivé.*
> *Contre nous de la tyrannie*
> *L'étendard sanglant est levé.*

It resounded from the walls and echoed in every heart. The Parisians joined in the chorus that was destined to grow wings.

> *Aux armes, citoyens! Formons nos bataillons!*
> *Marchons, qu'un sang impur abreuve nos sillons!*

That same day the barrier between active and passive citizens was torn down by the Cordeliers. A resolution was passed by the section of the Théâtre-Français and signed by Danton as president beginning: "In view of the fact that no one class of citizens can claim the exclusive right of saving the country," and welcoming those citizens "who have hitherto been styled in the aristocratic manner 'passive citizens.'" It was the first incursion of the poorer classes into the world of political rights; the masses began to move; the man in shirt sleeves ceased to be only cannon fodder.

———————◆———————

MEANWHILE the insolence of the aristocrats reached a climax. At Coblenz dukes and vicomtes divided the posts in the new ministry and brooded over long lists of revolutionaries to be broken on the wheel or merely to be hanged after the victory.

"La patrie est en danger!"

Marie-Antoinette, proud and unshakable, had rejected the idea of flight by the royal family, which was possible under the protection of dependable troops. A premonition told her that the triumph of the lily over the Jacobin cap was not far. There must be fighting—the blood of the *canaille* must be spilled.

"La patrie est en danger!"

The Tuileries were turned into a fortress, the Swiss regiments were drawn from their barracks at Courbevoie and Rueil and there were even a few hundred nobles willing to fight for the King's cause and their own.

"La patrie est en danger!"

A cloud of visions and rumors darkened the city. The enemy was approaching, annihilation threatening. Anthoine exclaimed: "The Austrians are in Thionville; tomorrow they may be in Metz!"

"La patrie est en danger!"

———————◆———————

WHERE to find help or security? By deposing the King, whose allies proclaimed the destruction of Paris.

On August 3, forty-seven of the forty-eight sections clamored at the bar of the National Assembly for deposition. "Louis has separated his interests from those of the nation; we do as he does." But they talked in vain; for even the most democratic deputies, who for the first time in French history enjoyed the shade and protection of a constitution, hesitated to cut down the tree they had planted. Accordingly next day the section of the Gravilliers gave an ultimatum: "If the Legislative Assembly will not depose Louis, the people will."

For now it was the people and not Cæsar that made history. No single individual, however strong willed, controls events. But if Merlin of Thionville, Chabot, and Basire continued to incite the sections, Danton, too, inspired them. His confidence and strength imparted themselves to others, begetting fresh strength and confidence.

Panis and Danton's friend Sergent, both administrators of police in the Commune, took upon themselves the responsibility of issuing cartridges to the Marseilles battalion. On the night of August 4–5, the battalion secretly moved from the faubourg Poissonière to the monastery of the Cordeliers. In this section, which was electric with revolutionary ardor, it took up its quarters, and became the center of the storm troops.

On August 5 Danton had vanished from the scene. Before starting the great play of which no one could know the issue, he threw himself once more into the arms of his native village. With the roar of the seething capital in his ears he drove through the provincial summer peace of the Champagne, embraced his mother and sister, took his little nephew in his arms, fed his niece lumps of sugar, arranged with the notary for the Recordains and Menuels to have the lasting use of his house, walked once more through the familiar streets, stood on the bridge and watched the flowing Aube, and gave them all a long look of farewell.

On August 9 he is back in revolutionary Paris. The first news he hears is that yesterday the Legislative Assembly rejected the charge brought against Lafayette. This knocks the bung out of the cask, and liquid fire spurts.

The day is oppressive, sultry; the narrow streets are filled with bad smells which further irritate already tense nerves. But night comes quiet and starry.

This evening, for the first time since the Bourbons possessed a court ceremonial, the solemn *"coucher du roi"* is omitted.

This evening the sections elect commissioners to be sent to the Hôtel-de-Ville on a prearranged signal: there will be a revolutionary Commune by the grace of the people!

This evening Lucile Desmoulins, who has entertained the Marseilles leaders at dinner, flees with a strange uneasiness in her heart to the Dantons'.

Gabrielle is in tears, little Antoine clings bewildered to her skirt. The women embrace with deep emotion, then, to regain their calm, escort Gabrielle's mother, Madame Charpentier, home—only a ten minutes' walk.

Returning, they find hurried men with resolute faces moving in the Cour du Commerce. Camille enters carrying a rifle; Lucile falls on his breast with a sob. Gabrielle watches her Georges anxiously. She who knows and reads every movement of his brows, sees his inward fever. To the others he seems calm, unmoved, a collected force, muscles tensed to strike. He leaves the house with the usual parting words and goes to the neighboring meeting of the section, perhaps to inflame the men of Marseilles once more with the torch of his speech.

Gabrielle weeps silently. But Lucile feels as on that day when Camille at last persuaded her purse-proud father to give his consent to their wedding and, overwhelmed with joy, fell before her on his knees! She laughs shrill, wild bursts of laughter while tears course down her pale cheeks.

Danton returns and nods to new visitors. Little Madame Robert pours out a flood of incoherent speech. Elegant Fréron, nicknamed "the Rabbit" in this circle, in love with Lucile as he had been with her fair, coquettish mother, murmurs with pathos, "I am weary of life." Danton, with a casual look of surprise at him, flings his great body on his bed, and falls asleep; messengers come and go, tap his shoulder; he hears them in a drowse, mutters something, and falls asleep again.

A little after one in the morning the expected call comes from the Hôtel-de-Ville. Wide awake, he is up and off. His firm, resolute steps die away in the night.

Gabrielle and Lucile are left alone. It must be nearly three—the first vague light of morning filters through the open window.

Then: Dong! Dong! Dong! The deep bell of the Cordeliers begins to sound the alarm. The shriller note of Saint-André-des-Arts joins in. Dong! Dong! Dong! Other bells follow. A swarm of hurried notes hangs jangling over Paris.

The night becomes strangely alive. The stirring roll of the assembly sounds near and far, doors are flung open, there are cries of *"Vive la nation!"* The clash of arms, marching feet. The sections are on the march.

On the march, the sections of the Théâtre-Français, Gravilliers, Montreuil, Quinze-Vingts, Bonne-Nouvelle, Innocents, Gobelins, Lombards, Mauconseil, Croix-Rouge; almost all of them are marching, and the men of Marseilles, and the other federates.

This time the people unfurl the red flag, a sign: Now we are law and authority, we proclaim a state of siege, we shall crush the King who rebels against us!

For the first time the red flag waves above an insurrection.

On his arrival at the Hôtel-de-Ville, Danton finds the position uncertain and full of dangers. The Tuileries are garrisoned with Swiss Guards, gendarmes, nobles, and even National Guards. Their new commander, Jean-Antoine Galliot, Marquis de Mandat, has, besides those companies that will immediately go over to the people, a number of dependable grenadier companies, in bearskin caps. He is resolved to strike. Cannon on the Pont-Neuf guard the right bank, the side of the Tuileries, against troops on the left.

At the Hôtel-de-Ville the legitimate and the revolutionary Communes meet side by side. Danton frightens the former by a harsh statement of the situation and encourages the latter. His participation as deputy procurator in their deliberations gives this body an appearance of legality. Because of pressure he exerts, the old Commune adopts two important resolutions: to withdraw the guns from the bridge and instruct Mandat to give a personal report from the palace. At the Hôtel-de-Ville a gigantic figure looms before the commander and says: "To the

Commune, give your account!" It is Danton. The Marquis replies somewhat contemptuously, "I am responsible only to the genuine Commune, consisting of honest persons." Danton, with a wolfish sparkle in his small eyes, all but leaps at his throat: "Traitor, you will be taught to obey by the Commune which saves the people that you betray—you who conspire against them with the tyrant." Dragged before the insurrectionary Commune, Mandat after a brief examination is deprived of his office and put under arrest. Outside he is swallowed up by the masses, torn from the hands of his guards; a cross is put beside his name; Mandat is finished. Santerre takes over the command of the National Guard.

The backbone of the defense of the Tuileries is broken.

———— ◆ ————

LUCILE kneels at the open window of her house, her face hidden in her handkerchief. She feels Gabrielle's hand on her hair. Both are listening.

It has long been broad day. Listen! A crackle like the tearing of a great piece of silk. They start; Lucile lifts her head. Musket fire! The attack on the Tuileries has begun.

Rolling salvos, and then heavy single reports—my God! Cannon! A volley of grape shot.

The two women have grown pale. Closing their eyes, they see the slaughter on the steps and terraces, in corridors and chambers; they hear the cries of the wounded and the gasps of the dying.

Where is Camille? Where is Georges? Gabrielle sinks in a faint.

———— ◆ ————

BEFORE the fighting began the royal family fled across an avenue full of dry leaves to the Manège, and claimed the protection of the Legislative Assembly. The latter, irresolute and frightened, would not take sides. Not until the victory of the people had been achieved did it arouse itself and under strong pressure from the Commune issue its decrees. Suspension of the King, calling of a National Convention, proclamation of universal and equal franchise. Louis Capet, lately His Most Christian Majesty, listens benumbed, from the tachygraphers' box.

Democracy! Democracy!

———————◆———————

THAT evening Danton climbs the stairs in the Cour du Commerce with heavy steps. He has spent the whole day in action at the new focus of power, the Hôtel-de-Ville; has deliberated, decided, and given orders. He is dog tired, staggers to his bed, and sleeps.

At three in the morning someone shakes his arm. He starts up, leaning on the pillow. Desmoulins and Fabre are at his bedside. "Get up, Danton, you are minister."

Minister?

Yes, minister.

The power and the fate of France are in his hands.

He rises, dresses, and goes with his two friends.

But Gabrielle, who has heard the message half incredulously, wanders troubled in the early dawn through the house where she has been so happy and which now she is to leave. She looks into the gold-framed mirror over the fireplace. She follows with her eyes the arabesque on the wall paper, straightens the hand-painted porcelain cups on their tray, caresses the mahogany console table—the edging of gilt copper is cool to the touch—and pats tenderly one of the six green satin arm chairs which are the pride of her housewifely heart. Here all is warmth and home-like comfort; how will it be in the great chilly mansion of the Place Vendôme?

Gabrielle feels chilled; she shivers and sighs deeply.

III

Heights

1792—1793

THE *huissiers* in the Hôtel de la Chancellerie, powdered and pig-tailed, noiseless, well-trained servants, schooled by association with reserved, unapproachable and silent dignitaries, were startled by the entry of France's new Keeper of the Seals and his staff, as loud and noisy as though the Ministry of Justice were the Café Procope. Hallo Camille! Hallo Fabre! Hallo Robert!

In the minister's office Danton, taking possession, flung himself heavily into a chair, stretched out his legs, and glancing round the lofty paneled chamber, with its silken hangings, its gilt-framed mirrors and French windows, noticed a rococo clock on the mantelpiece. He went up to it. It had stopped either for lack of winding or because of the explosions of yesterday's street battle. Its hand was in the shape of a lily. With a smile half pitying, half contemptuous, Danton flicked the dial lightly with thumb and index finger, and the hand flew off into the room. Bourbon hand, you will never show the hour again!

Indeed, the first shot fired in the battle at the Tuileries had inaugurated a new era, a new century. The unsentimental victors brushed aside more than a thousand years of rule by God's grace as indifferently as if it had been yesterday's newspaper. They did not talk of reconciling the past with the present; they whistled at tradition, and dated the history of France from July 14, 1789, its modern history from August 10, 1792. A grand purge began. The statues of the last of the Louis tumbled from their pedestals, even that of Henri IV on the Pont-Neuf, who, on the threshold of the Revolution, had been the most popular of all. The coats of arms disappeared from houses, and the court purveyor plates from the shops. The streets were Republicanized overnight: the Quai d'Orléans became the Quai d'Egalité, the Rue Saint-Louis the Rue Révolutionaire, the Rue de Madame the Rue des Citoyennes; and the Ministry of Justice no longer was in the Place Vendôme but in the Place des Piques. Well aware of the part played in every revolution by form, externals, and symbols, Danton lost no time in reminding the president of the National Assembly of the necessity of altering the State seal and the formula used in pronouncing sentence. It was resolved that the seal was to represent a Goddess of Liberty, armed with a pike and crowned with a Phrygian cap, while judgment was to be delivered in the name of the French nation.

Nobody was less inclined than Danton to stop with externals. He had a high conception of his office: it must be no superintendent's office in a document factory but an organ of truth called on to enlighten the nation. His predecessors had antagonized the courts against the peoples' associations, those "strongest bulwarks of liberty," and the bench had conspired to instil into the masses the belief that Louis XVI was a lover of freedom and the Constitution. Here there was work for new brooms. Fabre d'Eglantine was appointed Secretary General of the Ministry, Desmoulins, Secretary of the Seal, and Robert, Chief Secretary, while Paré, Barère, and Collot d'Herbois were made members of the Judiciary Committee—Robespierre sullenly declining to serve; it was not so much that Danton, having reached the top, wished to hold out the ladder for his friends as that he wanted the collaboration of men who had stood on his side of the barricades.

Danton's cleansing of the courts had to be extended to the smallest villages. A circular of August 19 vigorously reproved many judges for their lack of public spirit; those of the Sixth Arrondissement, who, after the Massacre of the Champ-de-Mars, had persecuted the friends of liberty, himself included, he dragged out by their ears; their example had so infected the departments that the call for a reform in the administration of justice had become universal. The first essential step in that direction was the summary dismissal of all royal commissars or public prosecutors; reliable prosecuting attorneys were needed in order to assure the rule of liberty and equality. The graybeards who had spent their lives prosecuting and judging in the King's name could serve no good purpose—the seal of the lilies was engraved in their hearts; and Danton, though his bulk made him look forty, was young, not yet thirty-three, and convinced that the age of arterio sclerosis is ill suited to revolutions. A stream of youth was to cleanse the Augean stables of the law.

"The love of liberty can only penetrate ardent souls," he wrote the National Assembly, demanding the reduction of the minimum age for public prosecutors to twenty-five.

On September 22, the National Convention resolved on the renovation of the administrative and judicial bodies. On this occasion one of the youngest members, Tallien, moved the admission of others than jurists to the office of judge. An official of the revolutionary Commune, he had been clerk to notaries and procurators and so acquired a smattering of the law; his motion brought the men of law to their feet. Chasset, a former lawyer of Villefranche and now judge at the Court of Cassation of Rhône-et-Loire, shook his head: "To appoint others than experts would be to substitute the judge's whims for the law. . . . A person desiring to become judge without a knowledge of Roman Law, Canon Law, the numerous rescripts, and the judicial decisions of the National Assemblies would be an enemy of the people and a rascal. . . . An excessive love of liberty might lead to the gravest confusion. . . . If ever the judges neglected the law to trust only their own whims and caprices, the very safeguards of life and property would be shaken." He was supported by Goupilleau, a lawyer from the Vendée; Mathieu, formerly one of the Paris avocats du parlement, wished to restrict the lay element to criminal cases, where the law was comparatively simple, and Thuriot, an acquaintance of Danton's who had been a lawyer and now was a judge, held that at least for the president of any tribunal an examination in law should be compulsory. Lanjuinais, a Breton who had got his degree of doctor of laws at seventeen, acquired considerable reputation and practiced at Rennes, and was already known under the old regime for a pamphlet against the feudal "dovecot rights," suggested referring the question to a commission; he was supported by Vergniaud and Kersaint, former count and rear admiral. Sergent, however, supported Tallien; and Osselin, who had not been admitted as notary in spite of his legal studies, clamored for the extinction of the "Robinocracy." What of Danton?

Danton was Minister of Justice, a legal expert and not to be frightened by technicalities; but it was a Champagne peasant, descended from Champagne peasants and deeply imbued with mistrust of legal quibbles, who seemed to speak when he opposed the men "tarred with the brush of jurisprudence," and demanded an administration of the law according to the simple rules of common sense. Chasset had pointed out that in his capacity as judge of the Court of Cassation he received many cases full of technical flaws: but these cases were certainly the work of the experts. Those who really knew their way about the codes were few, and the courts were full of subalterns who understood the jargon of the law but not its spirit. So away with those abuses and good riddance!

But above all it was the revolutionary in Danton that rebelled against the "monstrous aristocracy" of the jurists. To a man they were counterrevolutionaries and supporters of the old regime and the archives of the ministry were full of the proof of their infamy. If anybody was to be excluded from the administration of justice it was the jurists and not the laymen; the privilege which the former had arrogated was the disease of mankind. But here Danton stopped. Let the people elect as judges also those "*hommes de loi*" they trusted—and anybody else too.

The tearful objection that in the course of such a precipitate parliamentary procedure a strong pair of lungs could carry the meeting to rash decisions was ignored by the Convention which followed Danton.

Eager to make a clean sweep of the whole legal system, Danton took detailed work and trifles easily. It was the custom for the presidents of the civil courts to meet weekly at the Chancellery under the chairmanship of the minister. But on August 16 Danton remained invisible and on the twenty-third he appeared for a few moments, cordial and jovial, and then closed the meeting. Documents? Signatures? "Fabre, you attend to them." Danton masked his distaste for writing as an aversion to spilling ink when the times demanded action: "Revolutions are not the time for writing." He had intrusted the stamp with his signature to Fabre d'Eglantine, who largely deputized for the Keeper of the Seals.

In fact, Danton's portfolio was to him merely incidental. The servants were aware of this and went on tiptoe when Robespierre, Marat, Sergent, and Panis walked informally into the

minister's office and voices in heated debate could be heard growing louder and louder in the antechambers.

IT was not accident that Danton at the outset seized the first
fiddle in the concert of ministers. When the Legislative Assembly had reinstated by a simple show of hands the ministers
dismissed in June, Danton, among those newly elected, received
the most votes—222 out of 284—and thus held a clear lead over
the others. The Assembly still remained cautious, and the majority surely listened to many of his utterances with coughs of
embarrassment: what decided them to elect Danton has been
set forth by the least corrupt of his contemporaries, a thinker of
distinction, for whom politics meant unselfish service in the interest of mankind. Condorcet has explained: "The ministry required a man commanding the confidence of the same people
whose action had overthrown the monarchy; a man whose influence was strong enough to control the contemptible tools of a
useful, glorious and necessary Revolution. He must be a man
possessed of enough eloquence, intellect, and character not to
humiliate the ministry or the members of the National Assembly
who had to deal with him. Danton alone possessed these qualities: I voted for him, and I do not regret it." Brissot, too, having
been informed of Danton's impending election by Fabre d'Eglantine, gladly agreed: "He will seal our reconciliation."

According to the will of the Legislative Assembly, Danton
indeed personified the tenth of August in the Provisional Executive Council: he was the representative plenipotentiary of this
Second Revolution and he was a bridge with the street. He
proudly referred to the "ever memorable revolt of August 10,
this sacred and a thousand times blessed insurrection" which
had ripped off every mask, had cleared all eyes, and formed "the
necessary supplement to July 14." He felt himself to be the
minister of the people and the "Minister of the Revolution," and
he emphasized that his office had been conferred on him to the
thunder of the guns with which the citizens had destroyed the
despotism. His colleagues cast sidelong looks to see if the stains

of gunpowder still stuck to the hand which added this assurance
to the circular to the courts: "In an office conferred on me by the
glorious decision of the nation and reached through the breach
struck in the Tuileries, at a moment when guns had become the
ultima ratio of the people, you will find me steadfast and un-
changeable, just as when I was president of this section of the
Théâtre-Français which, under the name of the District of the
Cordeliers, contributed so much to the Revolution of July 14,
1789, and under the name of the section of Marseilles so much
to the Revolution of August 10, 1792."

And the masses unreservedly acknowledged Danton as their
own. When on Friday, August 11, he took the oath on the tribune of the Legislative Assembly, he was vehemently cheered by
an armed crowd in the gallery, in bloodstained clothes and with
the light of battle still in their eyes: revolutionary Paris render-
ing homage to its captain. In these weeks his oratory reached
the loftiest and noblest heights, and it was no mere phrase when
he said that in these times there should be room in every soul
only for exalted emotions, whole-hearted devotion, and every
virtue. But that he could also speak the language of the gutter
was not the least important factor in his power over the common
people. Once he encountered some women of the faubourgs—
poor starving wretches with drooping breasts, red eyes, disheveled hair; not arrayed, God knows, in silks and satins or
smelling of musk. And before them strutted this fine gentleman
with good coat, buckled shoes, and full belly—the man responsible for the war. Curses, abuses: meager arms stretched, fingers
bent claw-like. Whereupon Danton turned coolly, scanned them
from head to foot, and thundered: "You cows, you dirty bitches,
you harlots!" Hypnotized, cringing, they heard the familiar
words. And suddenly flames burst forth: Danton spoke to them
of the common cause for which all, do you hear, must sacrifice;
there they stood listening open mouthed, shaken, stirred, those
poor women, convinced that everyone must give his country the
most precious thing he has—and they their husbands and sons.
Tears were wiped with the hems of bedraggled skirts. Long live
Danton!

It was the street that conferred authority on him, not the

Legislative Assembly; it resembled the waning moon in its daily decrease—on August 8, 680 deputies had voted on the charge against Lafayette; three days later the Executive Council was elected by only 384 members; and on September 2 the president was elected by no more than 257 out of 745 members. It had become a rump parliament without respect or dignity, vacillating and irresolute, which had allowed itself to be set at nought in the moment of crisis. The people grudgingly gave it a minimum of confidence—just enough to finish current business pending the election and assembly of the National Convention.

Two of Danton's five colleagues in the Provisional Executive Council were foreigners. Clavières had come to power in his native town of Geneva as leader of the Democrats in 1781, had fallen in 1782, and had fled to France, where he enjoyed the protection of Mirabeau, who said of him: "I do nothing without consulting my baldheaded friend." An industrious and expert Minister of Finance, tenacious and stubborn, often hypercritical and choleric, this man of ledgers was not made of the stuff a revolution requires. Instead of perceiving great historic relationships his eyes remained fixed on Geneva, where he hoped to return in triumph some day. Nine years after him Lebrun had come to Paris with a deputation of patriots from Liége, had been drawn into Brissot's circle, and shoved into a place in the Foreign Office by Dumouriez. Now that he held the portfolio himself, he continued to despatch business with efficiency; but his fundamentally subaltern character needed a master and found one in Danton.

Completely helpless, timid, and clumsy, the Minister of Marine, Monge, groped about the world which lay outside the realm of the Pythagorean proposition: a master in geometry, in politics a child. Joseph Servan was in command of the One Hundred and Fourth Regiment after a generation of army service when he was given the post of Minister of War in the first Roland cabinet. In earlier days he did not belie the influence of his brother who had been attracted by the encyclopedists while advocate general at Grenoble; his work on national defense, published in 1780 under the title of *Le Soldat citoyen*, was full of bold suggestions for the democratization of the army. But, although learned and assiduous, Servan was deprived by ill health of the steady nerves and *sang-froid* required to master a crisis; instead of spurring him on, difficulties intimidated him.

Finally the minister who gave his name to the cabinet, Jean-Marie Roland de la Platière, was a dour Quaker with long, unpowdered hair, bald forehead, and jaundiced complexion who ruled the lines in the ledger of the Revolution like a conscientious clerk; he was self-opinionated because he knew Austria, Switzerland, England, and Germany as far as Berlin, and had contributed to a *Dictionnaire des manufactures*. He paraded his probity like a best Sunday coat; whenever he talked unctuously of his virtue and again of his virtue, Danton was sorely tempted to cut him short with some obscene oath of the faubourgs.

By the side of Clavières, Lebrun, Monge, Servan, and Roland, Danton was wholly devoid of those qualities which are the ornament of a minister in normal times. Perseverance, assiduity, punctuality, a sense for regular hours, and pleasure in red tape were lacking in him. To handle papers, to sort papers, to swallow the dust of papers, quickly bored him; he would think longingly of a river, a boat, and a rod. But as a revolutionary minister in abnormal times he was in his element where the others were nonplussed. Almost all the others were theoreticians who had Systems and created Literature. Danton, detesting theories and systems, had learned a thousand times more from life than from books and was the one practical man among them; and with his discernment, discrimination, sense of realities, scent for the way out, sureness of aim, and knowledge of men, he was the born statesman needed in a year when events were hopelessly confused, a figure in stature and character equal to this great Revolution. Qualities usually allotted to different individuals—the power to see, to grasp, to will, and to act—were fused in him into an irresistible whole.

Thus equipped, Danton easily pushed his colleagues aside. It was a recognition of his supremacy that the Executive Council met for the first time at the Ministry of Justice—on August 13, at 2 P.M. True, three days later Roland succeeded in changing the scene of the meeting to the Tuileries, and having each of the six ministers preside in turn for a week; but even so, Danton, whose turn did not come until September 9, remained the real leader of the cabinet. Monge tried to justify his invariable acquiescence in Danton's wishes with a stammering: "He will have me hanged if I object," and the remaining four were equally pliant to his will, his voice, and what Roederer called his bull dog face that showed bared teeth at the first hint of opposition. But there was hardly ever any opposition. Madame Roland's description of a single instance—"little questioning, no discussion, rapid signature"—was universally true, and her awed husband described Danton's "terrible predominance" over "the limited minds and timid souls" of his colleagues. It was Danton who suggested, decided, issued appeals and decrees, appointed commissars for the departments, instructed them, fixed their expenses and provided them with the necessary money. He interfered recklessly in every department—home and foreign affairs, war, navy, finance. All appealed to and took their orders from him.

When Marat suggested the transfer of unlimited powers to Danton, he was lagging behind events. Made Minister of Justice on August 11, Danton had hardly turned around in his chair before he was the unchallenged Dictator of France.

NEVER had a state more need of a dictator.

When Danton shut his eyes he could see the long hostile columns pouring over the defenseless country. On August 19 the army of invasion crossed the frontier at Redingen. In accordance with contemporary strategy the commander in chief, the Duke of Brunswick, had no intention of crushing the French in open battle, but hoped to maneuver them out of their position with a minimum of bloodshed. On the other hand, Frederick William II had been itching to reach Paris ever since the events of August 10. The fat monarch of Prussia already saw himself in the rôle of savior and knight of the Bourbons and relished in advance the gratitude of Louis and the grateful tears of Marie-Antoinette.

Foot, horse, and artillery came, regiment on regiment, along the roads of Lorraine. Grenadiers, musketeers, and fusiliers marching with heavy flintlocks shouldered. Mounted dragoons, cuirassiers, hussars in all colors. Trundling batteries of six-pounders, of mortars, of big twelve-pounders. Sappers and pontoniers with supply trains were followed by the commanders' coaches, staff carriages, bread wagons, pack animals with tents and baggage; the roads were teeming with staff officers, judge advocates, chaplains, regimental and company surgeons, provost-marshals, gunsmiths, grooms, equerries, riding masters, sutlers. All of forty-two thousand Prussians were on the march, moving toward the Temple in Paris, where the royal family were kept prisoners. With them were six thousand men from Hesse-Cassel; fifteen thousand Austrians were operating further north with the aim of joining the Prussians later. In addition fourteen thousand Austrians were pushing on to the Rhine, to say nothing of the band of emigrants who, with their companies of nobles, volunteers mounted and on foot, Uhlans, and field police made a swaggering show, but, weak in numbers and inefficient, remained in the background. They were looked down upon by the Prussian officers, and such of Frederick William's mercenaries as were capable of thought, like Master Laukhard, private of the Von Thadden Third Regiment of Infantry, spat upon this "scum of the human race," these "vile and abominable vermin."

It was in these days that Danton confirmed the decree of the Executive Council which, on a resolution of the Convention, promoted *"sieur Gille, publiciste allemand,"* also known as Schiller, to the rank of French citizen. But he was not aware of another German writer in the entourage of the Prussian army: a handsome gentleman of middle age, probably more than an ordinary foreign correspondent, for he had a servant who addressed him as "Herr Geheimbderat" (Privy Councillor), and the aristocratic officers of the regiment of cuirassiers to which he had attached himself—bright brick-red facings and collar, in other words the "Number Six Duke of Saxe-Weimar" Regiment— Messrs. v. Schiebelstein, v. Weyrach, v. Werthern, v. Schierstedt, v. Wedell, treated him almost as their equal. Sometimes he traveled in a light open carriage in a gap in the marching column, at other times he rode on horseback, trotting along with the cuirassiers. Occasionally he rode to the advance posts and studied the French through powerful field glasses; once he got hold of a copy of the Paris *Moniteur* and thoughtfully read the threat: The Prussians may get into Paris, but they'll never get out again! One day he met in the field the Austrian ambassador to Berlin, an old acquaintance, Prince Reuss the Nth, and told him rather excitedly of new findings in the science of colors; and when they parted the Nth called back a friendly: "Au revoir, Herr von Goethe!"

Again and again the emigrants had sworn on their honor that all hearts in Royalist France would welcome the invaders, that every fortress would open its gates, and the troops of the line would join them; the rest were a rabble, not worth considering. Great was the disappointment of the Prussian aristocrats when the deception became apparent and even the weather god seemed to have adopted the Revolution. Rain poured day and night from gray skies. The roads turned into morasses. Wearily, with blasphemous barrack-room curses, the troops fought their way against cold wind and lashing rain, their wet uniforms clinging to their bodies. Boots stuck in the deep mud of the roads, even the tent ropes rotted, the baggage was bogged somewhere, and provisioning along the line of communication from Berge on the Moselle became daily more unreliable.

Still, they struggled forward. Longwy, "the iron gate of France," was invested on August 20 and capitulated three days later. On the thirtieth the Prussian guns were turned on the redoubts and casemates of Verdun.

In the night of September 1 a volunteer from the Maine-et-Loire Regiment spurred a weary horse over the Paris pavement; news for the Executive Council: the fortress and town of Verdun in immediate danger! The spark was set to the powder barrel.

Paris was still full of the fever of August 10. It was generally believed that thousands had fallen in the assault on the Tuileries; people were convinced that the Swiss had acted treacherously, appearing to fraternize and then firing on an unsuspecting crowd. Revenge! Revenge! The revolutionary Commune posted on the walls curt advice and prophecy:

> Sovereign People! Stay your Revenge!
>
> Justice has been sleeping;
>
> Today it will resume its strength!
>
> The guilty will die on the scaffold.

Under pressure from the Commune an Extraordinary Tribunal was appointed on the seventeenth to deal with all crimes in connection with August 10. There was no appeal from its sentences, which were to be executed immediately. Four days later the modern machine of execution rose in front of the Tuileries on the former Place du Carrousel, now known as the Square of Fraternity. It had been tried on a poor wretch for the first time in April; by torchlight, at ten at night, the knife cut the neck of a writing master who had been condemned as a Royalist conspirator.

To intimidate some as well as encourage others, the Commune decreed that the guillotine should remain in place "until further orders." Many who, ignorant of the decree, were going home in the mild air of the Paris autumn night, jumped back terrified at sight of the menacing shape of the instrument of death cutting a large rectangle in the starry sky.

But the tribunal worked too slowly, too carefully and considerately to satisfy the long pent-up fury of the populace. Deliberations for twenty-seven or even thirty-six hours; day before yesterday a timid sentence of death, day after tomorrow another; next an acquittal, then another one—the streets roared their betrayal and bellowed for revenge.

"Had the tyrant been victorious, twelve hundred scaffolds would have been erected in the capital, and more than three thousand citizens would have paid with their heads for having aspired to liberty, a hideous crime in the eyes of the tyrant. The French people, after defeating the most horrible conspiracy and overcoming the blackest treachery, have not yet been avenged." Thus the Commune.

August 27 there were funeral rites for the patriots who had

been "murdered by order of the tyrants" at the storming of the Tuileries. In the middle of the Gardens a gigantic obelisk was erected with the inscription:

Silence! Ils reposent!

Oxen drew the sarcophagus, and behind it were borne the statues of Law and Liberty; then came the widows and orphans of the fallen in white robes with black ribbons. Marie-Joseph Chénier delivered the funeral oration; banners inscribed "Wives, mothers, sisters, weep for the victims of traitors. We, we swear to avenge them!" stirred in the wind.

Add to this fear, alarm, desperation, and panic—and the lust for revenge. Once more Paris buzzed with rumors: Lafayette was advancing against the capital; the Vendée had risen for the King! And once the Royalists arrived with Prussian and Austrian bayonets, woe to liberty! Woe to France! Woe to patriots! The army of invasion, which indeed did not move gently, but devastated, looted, mistreated, was preceded by a cloud of atrocity stories. The Prussian hordes were content with fire and murder, but the Uhlans—did this mean those of the Austrians or the emigrants?—the Uhlans cut off the ears of every municipal official they could seize and nailed them fast to his skull!

There was treachery within and without. Had not a battalion of volunteers been handed over to the Austrians by their own officers at Thionville and compelled to fight against their country? Were not the Paris prisons stuffed with Royalists who were only waiting for the departure of the patriots to plunge a dagger into the back of the Revolution? Leave wives and children at the mercy of these murderers? By God, no! A pamphlet went from hand to hand: "Great treachery of Louis Capet. Exposure of a plot of the aristocrats and nonjuring priests, with the help of the robbers and criminals in the prisons of Paris, to murder all good citizens of the capital on the night of the second of this month." Where was the man who did not believe in this devilish conspiracy in the prisons?

And now Verdun was on the point of falling, the road to Paris lay open. Already men thought they heard the neighing of the Prussian horse.

In the evening of September 2 Royalist windows at Verdun were brilliantly illuminated to celebrate fittingly the entry of the Prussians.

The evening of September 2 the booths in the Tuileries Gardens were brightly lighted, and the avenues as usual full of strollers, coquettish women, and children at their games.

The evening of September 2 bloodstained corpses lay heaped before the Paris prisons.

It began at the Abbaye in the afternoon at the instigation of the section of the faubourg Poissonière, and it went on for days and nights in all the prisons with terrible monotony. At the Conciergerie and the Châtelet, at La Force and Bicêtre, at Carmes and the Salpêtrière, the slaughter continued matter-of-factly, soberly, almost dispassionately. The prisoners were taken to the entrance hall. At a table with candles, papers, pipes, and bottles sat a committee whose self-imposed authority nobody disputed. A brief hearing, a nod, and the door was opened. Outside the victim fell under pike and sword thrusts.

There were also acquittals, with embracings and honest shouts of: *"Vive la nation!"* Monsieur de Saint-Méard, who was spared, was astonished at the attentiveness of his judges; Mademoiselle de Cazotte covered her aged father with her own body and the people did not cry mercy in vain to the slayers; and the Marquise de Tourzel was surprised, when conversing with the voluntary executioners, to find them neither brutish nor vicious, but ready to listen to just and reasonable objections.

After all, the executioners did not come from the galleys, they were neither pimps nor professional murderers, but decent small citizens: shopkeepers, greengrocers, butchers, hatters, tailors, cobblers, goldsmiths, and barbers; they were wild with fear for themselves and their families, and they believed they were serving their country. Between whiles they would go home to have a dish of soup or to fortify themselves with a bottle of wine. But when the wife of the engraver Cortay saw her husband come in this way, with clots of wet blood on his clothes, a bloody saber in his hand, the expectant mother died of the shock.

And the bestial task roused the bestial element in men. In the end they murdered indiscriminately, innocent suspects, political prisoners and nonpolitical, the sick and the old, women and children; they killed with zest and a ribald joke. At La Force the Princesse de Lamballe—a princess by birth and marriage—was flung into the street and fell reeling. The Lamballe, it was said, was more than the Queen's friend—Marie-Antoinette indulged with her in "the German vice." In a moment the clothes were torn from the corpse; the body lay white and naked and someone thrust a pike between the legs: "This was fondled by a Queen!" Another tore the heart from the breast, and the severed head was carried off on a pike to be shown to the prisoner at the Temple.

There were more than a thousand victims. The tumbrils which carried them to cemeteries and quarries left a sticky red trail on the pavement.

For these atrocities Europe held Danton, Robespierre, and Marat responsible; since August 10 they had been for the world the three flaming stars in the revolutionary sky.

Regarding the *"Ami du peuple,"* Europe was perhaps not wholly wrong. Although he was true to his convictions, devoted to his cause, and a fanatical champion of the general welfare, only an unbalanced mind could speak as he did with the matter-of-factness of an Asiatic torturer of cutting off ears and thumbs, splitting tongues, burnings, and empalements, or indulge in such bloodthirsty statements as: "Cutting off five or six hundred heads would have assured tranquillity, freedom and happiness; a misplaced humanity has restrained your arm and prevented you from striking; it will cost the lives of millions of your brothers. If your foes triumph only for a moment, rivers of blood will flow; they will strangle you without mercy, rip up your wives, and, to destroy your love of liberty forever, will grope with bloodstained hands for the heart in the entrails of your children." Every month the number of severed heads which were to pave the road to national happiness increased. When Bouillé took action at Nancy he said: "Today ten thousand heads would hardly have sufficed to save the country." A few weeks later: "To save yourselves from destruction you may yet be compelled to strike off a hundred thousand heads." And again: "Perhaps half a million heads will fall before the year is out."

Marat did not always mean such murderous fantasies literally, for he once confessed to Basire: "I would rather have my hand wither than write out orders which I felt sure the people would execute to the letter." But the masses, which Marat himself called "stupid" and "credulous," were all too ready a soil for his seed.

Immediately after August 10 he was busy again fanning suspicion against all and sundry, foaming at the mouth because Lafayette was marching on Paris, and stirring up the masses by clamoring with his paper in the streets: "The duty of the people is to press the sentence of the traitors imprisoned in the Abbaye and to keep a hand on the courts and the National Assembly, and whenever traitors are whitewashed, to slaughter them together with the new tribunal." But why wait for the Extraordinary Tribunal to fail? "It is wiser and safer to storm the Abbaye, drag the traitors out—especially the Swiss officers and their accomplices—and massacre them. To give them a trial first is folly."

The September massacres were the realization of Marat's dreams.

It was for good reasons that the Committee of Surveillance of the Commune, which in those days acted as a spur rather than as a brake, on September 2 took the "People's Friend" into its portentous midst. The circular issued by this committee to the departments, which justified "inevitable acts of justice" by the necessity of "restraining by terror the legions of traitors within the walls of Paris," and urged the entire nation to use the same "necessary means for the general welfare" was also signed with the name Marat.

Danton was not a Marat. He was easily roused but he was also kindhearted. Nothing was further from him than a cold craving for revenge. Those who knew him suspected that his rough and noisy manner was the cloak of an essentially gentle nature. Jeanbon Saint-André, a fellow student of his at the Convent, who was a strict servant of the Protestant God and no lenient judge (Lanjuinais said of him that he had more gall in his little finger than Marat in his entire body), discovered in Danton's physiognomy "attractive traits of purity and even of kindliness." Sergent, remembering him in calmer times, testified to his sensitivity: "No unfortunate ever appealed to him in vain." In these days of August and September Danton gave evidence of these qualities. When Barnave was arrested at Grenoble for alleged counterrevolutionary activities, one of his friends appealed to Danton; and Danton the apostle in private life of "live and let live" did not prove a bloodthirsty madman in politics. His first reaction was: Let the poor devil go, what great harm can he do in exile? and he promised assistance which, however, Barnave rendered useless by his obstinacy.

Again, when Adrien Duport was arrested in the Loiret, Choudieu advised Théodore de Lameth to apply to Danton who was reputed to be amenable if one played on his feelings. Danton was all the readier to do his best since he knew Duport personally; he prevented the prisoner's transfer to Paris where the massacres were raging and insisted that the Committee of Surveillance of the Commune furnish proof of guilt or acquit him. But as Fabre d'Eglantine had smuggled proofs of Duport's relations with the emigrants from the documents in the files at the Ministry of Justice into the hands of the committee, Marat addressed a sharp remonstrance to Danton. "What? Is that toad threatening me?"—and Danton rushed furiously into the meeting accompanied by Pétion.

"Marat?"

"Here."

There was a violent clash that ended with Marat's tearing up the letter. They would both forget it. And then, of course, followed the obligatory embrace.

Danton had sufficient understanding of the stirrings in the depths of the popular mind to foresee the prison massacres. The only preventive would have been the balm to the sore popular spirit of a strict administration of revolutionary justice. As early as August 11, at his first appearance before the National Assembly, he raised aloft a far-visible placard: "Where justice begins, the people's cravings for vengeance must be silent." He guaranteed the safety of the Swiss who had taken refuge in the

Manège against the fury of the mob. "I shall take my stand at their head and I make myself responsible for them." All his speeches and actions in those days had one aim: the people must have full justice, or they would create their own justice—and that with undesirable savagery. The appeal of the Executive Council to the nation on August 25, every word of which bears the glowing traces of Danton's mind, made threatening references to traitors but for whose existence the struggle would soon be at an end: "Your active vigilance will absolutely frustrate their plans." But, soothingly: "Be calm and united! Discuss your means of defense dispassionately! Use them courageously, and triumph will be assured." Three days later he compared France to a ship in distress, whose crew jettisons every potential source of disaster, and he claimed for the Commune the right to search private houses in order to confiscate arms for military purposes. But, at the same time, in order to assuage the lowering tempest at the capital, he demanded and obtained the opening of the gates whose shutting had cut off the revolutionary Commune of Paris from the rest of France. And when, on August 31, Luce de Montmorin, governor of Fontainebleau, was acquitted by the Extraordinary Tribunal despite the gravest evidence— because he had not acted with ill intent—it occurred to the Minister of Justice that this acquittal, in view of the popular fervor, was a catastrophe. Despite whatever the letter of the law might say, he ordered a fresh trial and had the prosecutor who was apparently not impartial deposed and charges brought against him.

But when the massacres raged, Danton did nothing to prevent them. If he had the will he lacked the power. The news of the butchery did not leave the authorities unmoved. Six commissars were despatched by the Commune to the prisons to remove at least the nonpolitical prisoners, and twelve deputies set out by order of the Legislative Assembly to put an end to the atrocities. Here, however, the tricolor sashes were unavailing. A man with bloody knife and blazing eyes sprang at one of the pacifiers: "Do you want to make fools of us? If those cursed villains, the Austrians and Prussians, come to Paris, do you think they will first sort out the guilty? You know very well that they will strike right and left, like the Swiss on August 10. I am no orator, I try to deceive nobody. But I tell you I am the father of a family. I have a wife and five children that I leave behind under the protection of my section while I am at the front, and I will not allow the criminals in this prison to be freed by other criminals so they can butcher my wife and children." "He is right!" the mob shouted. "No mercy! Get on with the work!" All attempts to deal with such a temper were unavailing; one of the commissars, old Dusaulx who, in other times, had spent pleasant days translating Juvenal, reported to the National Assembly with a shrug of the shoulders: "The people are so excited that they will listen to no one. They are afraid of treachery."

As the butcheries continued, the Legislative Assembly passed a decree instructing the municipality, the Council General of the Commune and the commander of the Paris National Guard "to take all steps to safeguard life and property." This resolution was announced by the commissars of the National Assembly in the forty-eight sections, and Santerre assured Mayor Pétion that he would redouble his efforts with the National Guard. "I swear that, should it remain inactive, my body shall shield the first citizen who is attacked." But the revolutionary forces remained with arms grounded and cared as little to interfere as the unarmed mob which formed a wall around the two or three hundred butchers. Danton himself was unable to break through this wall. "No power on earth," he rightly judged later, "could have stopped these happenings." All he could have done would have been to risk his popularity, but he knew only too well how easily popularity vanishes in times like these, and it was a capital which had to be carefully husbanded for more promising operations than the rescue of prisoners who were to him politically indifferent.

The question was a political one. When even well-bred, cultured, sensitive women accepted the massacres as a "terrible necessity"—"the Prussians and the kings would have done the same and a thousand times worse"—Danton was not the man to turn away his head; he looked facts calmly in the face. He probably agreed with his friend Basire who, in November, told the Jacobins: "In its details a revolution is always hideous; but a statesman must treat it in its totality and in its consequences for the entire generation. If he is moved by the sight of private suffering, the sight of the general weal will compensate him. It is idle to look for harmony and order in a time of great crisis." The September massacres were among these hideous details; Danton was not guilty of hypocrisy when he spoke of "regrettable incidents," "horrible events," and "dreadful massacres." But Danton, if anyone, was the man to see the Revolution as a whole, and the "terrible deeds" which he had neither desired nor approved could serve the cause of the Revolution as a whole. It was not that he believed the tales of the prison plots, as did Chabot, who found it unnatural "to be exposed to the daggers of prisoners who had been promised arms and freedom to murder us, while the bravest patriots were hastening to the frontiers." It was essential to have the people in a state of revolutionary enthusiasm when leading them against the foreign enemy; and the people, in their turgid fury, required and approved the massacres. Which was better? That a few hundred "aristos" should be snuffed out by its fury or that the revolutionary enthusiasm should be impaired? And could one train guns against the people in order to save the Royalists, and the next day ask the same people to charge the Prussian guns? What were the misdeeds of September, looked at as a whole, to Danton? Determinedly he answered: "The consequences of a revolution"; and added, "Individuals may have indulged their private revenge; but in the main a nation was acting which had never seen the chief culprits called to account."

But Danton took another fateful step. Perhaps some drops of Midi blood coursed in his veins, for the man from the Champagne was fond of lifting weights before admiring spectators, even if the weights were only cardboard, and preferred to frighten children rather than be their laughing stock. Therefore he took full responsibility for atrocities for which he was no more responsible than every member of the Executive Council or the Legislative Assembly. Almost deliberately he attended a meeting of the Executive Council on September 3 wearing a scarlet coat that had long ceased to be fashionable, unafraid of provoking with it an obvious association of ideas. When Fabre

P^H. FR. NAZ. FABRE - D'EGLANTINE,

Le Théâtre N'est-il qu'un passe-temps frivole :

Au jour de Liberté, qu'il devienne une École

Prologue du Philinte

d'Eglantine sent out the circular of the Committee of Surveillance with the seal of the Ministry of Justice, and thus gave an
official aspect to this incitement to fresh massacres, Danton, far
from disavowing his lieutenant, kept silence. Now and then,
when the September massacres were mentioned, he would even
boast: "They were my work."

In this way he laid himself open to the attacks of his enemies.
In the Convention they accused him of planning to build himself a throne of the September corpses, and Prudhomme thrust
at him in the *Révolutions de Paris:* "Danton, you are silent!"
But it was the silence of contempt rather than embarrassment.

———◆———

DANTON certainly had a right to laugh at such attacks. For during the decisive days he had watched the frontiers more than
the prisons and had concentrated his energies more on the foreign than on the internal danger.

His patriotism and nationalism were not the last elements
that made his mind a reservoir of strength for an entire people
in the hour of distress. His love of country was not without a
tinge of sentimentality; when he shouted *"La patrie!"* there was
an echo in his heart which said "My home"—and for a moment
he felt on his temples the cool wind which eternally blows over
the chalky plains of Champagne. "I do not belong to Paris," he
confessed in the Assembly. "I was born in a department to which
I always look back with joy"; and although the barren valley of
the Aube in no way resembled the flowering garden around the
capital, Danton felt for the land in which he was rooted physically and intellectually, for the whole country, all the tenderness
expressed in the Song of Roland:

Terre de France, mult estes dulz païs!

But the fatherland was one's native soil multiplied a million-
fold. Among the Germans, who, with their inherited servility,
had no conception of such feelings, a learned professor, Schlözer,
might define patriotism as the familiarity of the cow with the
stable in which she has always been; for Danton all the alarm
bells of a great revolution rang in the idea of patriotism. When,

her tender body cased in steel, and the oriflamme of the Bourbons in her child's hand, the Maid of Lorraine rode at the head of Charles VII's armies, a wave of nationalism swept for the first time over France, only to ooze away quickly into the ground or to be drained off into provincial channels. The stifling air of absolutism did not allow the nation to become conscious of itself. Louis XIV, speaking of the French as his people, declared: "In France the nation is not a corporation, it is embodied exclusively in the person of the king." As late as 1789 Mirabeau could remark scornfully that France was an "accidental conglomeration of distinct peoples." There was a Breton and a Provençal "nation," and when the *cahiers de doléance* were drawn up, Normandy referred to its Charter of 1315 and Burgundy to patents of 1483, which granted them privilege on privilege; while the cahier of complaint of Morlaas raised the question: "At what point do we cease to be Béarnese and become more or less French?"

But the Revolution knocked down the vertical and horizontal barriers which hindered the unifying of France and the French; it recognized only citizens with equal rights—away with the classification of nobility, clergy, and Third Estate! In 1614, when somebody compared the estates to three sons of one mother, France, the Baron de Senecey had raged at the idea of any relationship between nobility and mob. Now, fraternity complemented liberty and equality. And away with the diversity of provinces and districts! The decree of January 15, 1790, unromantically but rationally divided France into eighty-three departments, each of approximately the same size and population and named after a river, a range of hills, or a coast. Men were no longer Provençals, Béarnese, or Bretons, but Frenchmen, part of twenty-five million brothers united by a national bond. Almost all felt what Durand-Maillane, who in both the Constituent Assembly and the Convention was anything but a drastic revolutionary, described: "The Revolution came and for the first time each one of us experienced the joy of all those ties which bind citizens to their country as the center of all affections." "Since we have had a Fatherland" became a common expression and meant since July, 1789.

Danton's first words after taking his oath on August 11 before the Legislative Assembly were: "The nation!" The unity of the nation was emphasized again in his circular to the courts which referred to the Tuileries conspiracy having been stifled by "the courage of the federates of the eighty-three departments and the forty-eight sections of the capital." On his program there stood out clearly and unmistakably "the unity of the eighty-three departments." When on September 25 he exclaimed in the National Assembly: "France must be an indivisible whole. . . . I demand the death penalty for all who seek to destroy the unity of France," he created the formula of the *République une et indivisible* which the Assembly adopted at the same meeting.

———————

THIS fatherland was in the gravest danger when Danton was called upon to protect it with his broad chest. After August 10 the foreign ambassadors fled from Paris as though it were stricken with the plague. A ring of deadly hostility surrounded France: Denmark and Sweden were the only countries with which tolerable relations were maintained; the reputation of the country had fallen so low that petty potentates like the prince bishop of Liége ventured to insult it. To oppose the invasion the vast front from Dunkirk to Basle was held by only eighty-two thousand men besides the garrisons. The artillery was good, the best in Europe; but the rest of the army was in a state of confusion. Of the nine thousand officers of the line, a good two thirds had deserted and emigrated; entire regiments—the Saxon Hussars, the Berchiny Hussars, and Royal Allemand—had joined the enemy bag and baggage. There were no trained reinforcements. The volunteers of 1791 were still in process of formation, those of 1792 full of good will but without discipline or order. The Twelfth Battalion of the Haute-Saône, recruited on August 15, consisted almost entirely of boys of thirteen and fourteen. They were short of rifles, powder, lead, uniforms, hats, boots, tents, horses, forage, money—everything. And each day a glance at the map of France showed the Prussians and Austrians drawing nearer and nearer.

Perhaps there were hours when anxiety shadowed Danton's

soul; but, if so, only Gabrielle knew it, who heard him groaning in his sleep. The people learned nothing. In public he raised his head proudly, sure that he was master of fate. In the beginning was the Deed. He indulged in no idle sword-rattling. The appeal of the Executive Council, which was his work, did not treat the people as babes in arms to be pacified with lollipops. It pointed out the severe sacrifices, the accumulating dangers, the whole gravity of the position: "Once they have seized Longwy, the enemy will threaten Thionville, Metz, and Verdun, and force their way to Paris. They may get here." And the manifesto concluded, heroically facing the possibility of defeat: "Even if we were to perish in the fight for liberty, we would at least have the consolation that sooner or later the efforts of the most magnanimous of nations will overcome all obstacles and annihilate all tyrants." And three days later in his speech before the Legislative Assembly he made no extenuation, palliation, or suppression, such as: "We hold Longwy securely!" He said: "The enemy have captured Longwy." But then came words full of sap and marrow, of fire and strength: "France does not depend upon Longwy. We still have our armies" . . . "It required a mighty convulsion to destroy the native despotism in the capital, and only through national convulsions shall we succeed in driving off the foreign despots." "Up to now you have had Lafayette's mimic warfare; from now on it will be the war of the nation against the despots. The time has come to tell the people that they must hurl themselves in a body on their foes." This was the trumpet call for the *levée en masse.*

But it is on September 2 that Danton rises to his full historic stature. The legislature resembles a council of war rather than a parliament. Outside the Manège and in the galleries there are many uniforms among the plain civilian coats. At intervals a dusty horseman dismounts at the entrance and vanishes hastily inside. The deputies, pale and excited, seem to be listening for the roar of the guns at Verdun to the east.

Citizens of Saint-Cloud appear at the bar to take the oath of liberty and equality and to congratulate the Assembly on its courage and resolution; the director of the national printing press comes to report that all his men wish to volunteer for the army. A deputation suggests that the cavalry hand over their carbines to the infantry; gunners present themselves to take the oath.

A motion of the Committee of Defense: Mail horses to be used by the artillery. Carried. Decree promulgated. The military committee reports: Two well-to-do citizens are ready to furnish a volunteer corps of four hundred hussars each. Carried. Decree promulgated. Cavalry carbines to be issued to the infantry. Carried. Decree promulgated.

In the interval Hérault de Séchelles is elected president.

Gray old Rühl, the Alsatian, reads a letter from the commandant of Metz promising to be buried with his garrison and people under the ruins of his town sooner than surrender to the enemy. In the name of this brave officer the deputy swears loyalty unto death to the principles of Liberty and Equality. Two satisfactory despatches from the commissars who inspected Belfort and Besançon; the Assembly listens pacified. Report: a courier just arrived from Strasbourg has heard on his way heavy artillery fire near Verdun.

Two members of the Paris municipality, brought before the bar, convey a resolution of the Council General of the Commune: the tocsin shall be sounded, the alarm gun fired, and every patriotic citizen of Paris and the neighboring departments summoned to assemble on the Champ-de-Mars in readiness to march against the enemy.

The president, an elegant figure, bows: "The representatives of the nation, ready, like you, to die, do homage to your patriotism, thank you in the name of France and invite you to take part in the session."

But reports of timidity and discouragement, too, flutter through the hall. Lasource refers to rumors current in the departments that the search for arms is for the purpose of delivering the citizens defenseless to the enemy: "We cry in vain: Long live the nation! Long live liberty! We are saving neither. We must act, we must march, and we must speak to the people, too. We must din the assembly into the ears of the public." Vergniaud, inspired and inspiring, warns his listeners against defeatists who sow discouragement everywhere, damp patriotic ardor, make mountains of molehills, take the dust raised by a squadron of Uhlans for marching battalions, and always despair of the safety of the country. "Let Paris rouse herself today to action and resist this panic, and our efforts will soon be crowned by victory. Men of July 14 and August 10, I appeal to you. The Assembly can count on your courage!" He demands—for the time for discussion is past—that every day twelve commissars of the Legislative Assembly shall set an example by working with pick and shovel on the fortifications outside Paris. Carried. Decree promulgated.

Other deputations at the bar, other suggestions: mechanical cars for the army, reward for improvements in gunpowder; but silence and a general craning of necks while a letter from the Minister of War is presented: "Dumouriez is preparing to defend the passes of the Clermontois and the defile of Autry, and emphasizes the necessity of gathering a large force near Châlons. Ten to twelve thousand rifles are most urgently needed."

Danton has already mounted the tribune to explain this despatch in the name of the government. Two hundred and fifty pale faces are raised toward him. As he flings back his head almost defiantly he seems to some to have the sharp outline of an antique Roman, a tribune before the people, or one of the Gracchi. Even those who have no especial love for him are fascinated by his wild look, his athletic stature, his gestures—does he not fling rocks which crush his enemies?—and the iron ring of his voice which penetrates effortlessly to the farthest corner; all recall the fabled Cyclops.

Danton speaks, as usual, without notes, not clinging to a scrap of paper like the others but snatching his ideas on the spur of the moment—speaks briefly, pithily, for hardly three minutes. The first sentence is like a banner planted firmly in the ground, waving in the wind: convincing assurance that the country will be saved.

"Everything is being uprooted, everything is in motion, and everyone is on fire for battle. . . .

"Part of the people are at the frontier, part are digging trenches, a third part with pikes are defending the towns.

"In order to support and direct the noble movement of the

people, we demand the appointment of commissars to support us in these weighty measures.

"We demand the death penalty for anyone refusing either to serve in person or to surrender his arms.

"We demand the despatch of couriers to every department to announce our decrees.

"The tocsin we shall sound is no alarm bell but the signal for the attack on the enemies of the country.

"In order to conquer these enemies, gentlemen," and his fist sweeps down like a sword, "we need audacity, again audacity, forever audacity—and France will be saved!"

Danton was ugly, but under the scorching fires of his eloquence many, like Pierre-René Choudieu, felt suddenly inspired with confidence: How beautiful he is! He was never more beautiful.

Among the deputies there were some who were to live thirty or forty years longer; but even in old age, with trembling chin and tottering knees, they would experience a strange inner thrill when they remembered the gesture with which, on that September Sunday in '92, Danton flung out like shells his: *"De l'audace! Encore de l'audace! Toujours de l'audace!"*

Danton's fierce energy was an elixir of life for millions.

Already the Assembly and the Commune had been vying with each other to accelerate the process of national armament. The armories worked at night, the arsenals were under State control, and gunmakers and dealers were compelled to furnish lists of their stock. The churches provided bells to be melted down for guns and coffin lead for ammunition. Iron railings around monuments were hammered into pikes, which for a century had been the universal arm of the infantry. Young Scharnhorst at Hanover wanted to reintroduce pikes thirteen to fifteen feet long for the first rank of the infantry, while in Paris a retired major of dragoons named Scott wrote a *Manuel du citoyen armé de la pique.*

But now, as though Danton's fierce resolution were brutally driving each individual, the efforts increased threefold and tenfold. The wealthy heaped money and gold, watches, snuff boxes, chains, bracelets, earrings, and jewels on the altar of the country; the poor offered their labor and their lives. Volunteers thronged to every enlistment place. Danton's friend Delacroix was not deterred from joining the mounted Versailles Volunteers, although at the moment he was president of the National Assembly. Every day some two thousand volunteers left for the border, and everyone was full of confidence. "Gayety and carelessness," one shrewd Paris observer wrote, "march to the sound of the drum. We see nothing but federates and hear nothing but military music. The streets are full of this vast population, which always tempts one to think that the whole universe is assembled at Paris. Everywhere they shout: *'Vive la nation!'* "

But only the smallest fraction of Danton's rousing activity was carried on before the public. When Longwy had fallen and Verdun was about to fall, the cry of terror, "Paris is lost!" carried from the streets into the Legislative Assembly and from the Legislative Assembly to the cabinet. Despondency paralyzed the Executive Council. When Kersaint returned from Sedan and reported: "In a fortnight the Duke of Brunswick will be in Paris as surely as a driven wedge enters a block," the members of the cabinet stood white and aghast in the garden of the Foreign Office. Roland, in an attack of faintness, leaned his head against a tree and stammered something about transferring the Government and National Assembly to Blois or Tours; Servan gloomily agreed, and no contradiction was heard until Danton, with a suppressed "Curs!" nailed them to their posts, thundering: "You stay here!" For him Paris was France. "I have brought my seventy-year-old mother here," he roared at the others, "I have brought my two children. They came yesterday. I had rather my family perished and twenty thousand torches turned the town into a heap of ashes than that the Prussians entered Paris." It seemed to his colleagues that a malign fire blazed under his brows when he turned threateningly to Roland: "Be careful what you say about flight. The people might hear you." They cringed and stayed.

In the War Department, too, Danton ruled with a strong quick hand. The sickly Servan seemed to him too much a philosopher and too little a man of vigorous resolution. Danton was always at his heels: Get on! Get on! The Deputy Lacuée, assistant to the minister and a former captain of the Dauphin Regiment of Foot, was also suspected of being a pale theorist, since he was a member of the Academy at Metz and author of a *Handbook for Officers in the Field*. Danton gave him no rest: On! On! He called himself the real adjutant general of the Minister of War, and interfered in every question of organization and personnel in the central office. Officials with inadequate Republican zeal were replaced by others whom he recommended, and where he was convinced of a man's revolutionary dependability he was all too ready with recommendations. In sending the old guard of his Cordeliers, including Momoro and Fréron, into the departments as delegates, where they were the instruments of his actual dictatorship, he was unconcerned with the charge of "poisoning the army with Cordeliers." For this implied that by inspiring the army with the hot breath of revolution he was urging it to the top of its capacity.

The Royalist officers continued to be a source of annoyance. Before August 10, complaint was made at the Jacobins' that many officers would not allow their men to read patriotic papers but forced Royalist newspapers on them. Even after August 10 the commander of an outpost assured his Prussian opponent that he was serving a free France and the King, while the commandant of Longwy told the besiegers that he was fighting in the name of the nation and the King, and the commandant at Verdun, called on to surrender, declared that he would not break his oath to the King, the nation, and the law. Immediately after the Revolution a number of generals were removed. Lafayette, menaced with the charge of having Royalist tendencies, fell into Austrian hands while attempting to escape to Holland. It was not without satisfaction that the Minister of Justice reviewed his orders for the prosecution of his old enemy—how the wheel had turned!

But because he realized that the elimination of all officers not completely above suspicion would weaken the army excessively,

Danton made all the more sure of having them properly supervised. Thus, when it seemed imperative to keep an eye on General Montesquiou—though without disturbing his operations in Savoy by recalling him—Danton urged that the supervising commissars should be granted extended powers and admitted that he had written to a subordinate of the suspected man: "Watch his behavior and observe his movements! If he retreats a single step, put a bullet through his head!"

Since among the higher commanders Danton thought Dumouriez the best strategist, on August 18 he arranged for him to have the supreme command of the entire forces between Dunkirk and Montmédy. But even Dumouriez was not absolutely reliable and required watching. The Alsatian Westermann, who had led the attack on the Tuileries on August 10, had become a close follower of Danton. Appointed adjutant general or staff colonel in September, he was attached to Dumouriez and was required to furnish confidential reports on his behavior to the Place des Piques. Later Danton sent two more of his intimates, Billaud-Varenne and Fabre d'Eglantine, to the camp; but the general gave them no opening. As though Danton's own eloquence had descended on him, he roused his soldiers to such enthusiasm for "sacred liberty" that they sang *"Ça ira"* and laughed in the pouring rain. But at the same time he maintained strict discipline, and punished the panic of some of the troops at the attack of the enemy by cutting off the hair and eyebrows of the guilty and dismissing them from the ranks. Resolved to support the Revolution only so far as it satisfied his ambitions, Dumouriez charmed even the morose and bitter Jacobin, Billaud, by introducing himself in the rôle of a "sansculotte general" and claiming that all his generals were sansculottes. In vain the emigrants placed their hopes in the tender bonds that united Dumouriez with the Baroness d'Angelle, the sister of Rivarol, most brilliant of all the Royalist polemicists. When at the beginning of September one of their emissaries waited on him with tempting offers, the general read the letter unmoved, tore it in little pieces and said icily: "My guns shall furnish my reply."

Although Danton was ready enough to interrupt the endless

deliberations of his colleagues with: "Drivel! I only know the enemy. We have to beat the enemy," he never dreamt of poring over Guibert's *"Essai général de tactique,"* from which all the revolutionary generals learned the rules of war, or of allowing his shadow to fall across the tacticians' chart table. The army was the province of soldiers. Yet he was consulted and he approved when Servan thwarted Dumouriez' favorite plan, the annexation of the Austrian Netherlands, and instructed the general to transfer Kellermann with his army from the region of Metz in order to defend the country between the Marne and Meuse.

The forest of the Argonne, which separates the basin of the Meuse from the valley of the Aisne, and serves as a forest barrier between the plain of the three bishoprics and the "barren Champagne," thus became a strategic position. On September 14 Dumouriez decided to unite his entire forces near Sainte-Menehould, and to hold the passes of the Argonne—the "Thermopylæ of France"—near Des Islettes and La Chalade. To this end, while awaiting Kellermann's arrival, he summoned the inhabitants of the surrounding districts to the people's Revolution. "When the alarm sounds every man bearing arms must come to the edge of the forest, and the rest fell trees for barriers."

On the evening of September 19 Dumouriez' headquarters were at Sainte-Menehould, while Kellermann lay a few miles away at Dampierre. The troops, thanks in no small part to Danton's energy, were not at all what they had been four weeks ago, although already here and there the generals had begun on their own responsibility the process of so-called amalgamation, of absorbing young volunteers into the old battalions of the line. When the Prussian Major von Massenbach entered a French army camp under a flag of truce, he was not a little surprised to find, instead of confusion and undisciplined mobs, straight rows of tents and well-trained soldiers and officers, used to discipline and obviously knowing their business. Perhaps his impression was like Hardenberg's the following year: "These were not barbarous hordes, as they were at first said to be, erupting from the interior, but a democratic army adequately organized and under a unified command."

However, the very day that Dumouriez and Kellermann determined to stand and fight, the unsuspecting Frederick William was concerned for fear the enemy wanted to escape. For this reason he intended to advance to the Châlons road on September 20 and thus cut off the French retreat. But the Prussian advance was abruptly stopped by the guns of Kellermann, which, flanked by Dumouriez, occupied the heights around the village of Valmy. When the thick mist lifted at noon the Potsdam Junkers were somewhat taken aback to find themselves faced by a composed enemy in a good position. Did these—ah—sansculottes think they could face the first army in the world, the Prussians, the pupils of the great Frederick, the laurel-crowned victors of Mollwitz, Hohenfriedberg, Rossbach, and Leuthen?

But the sansculottes did not break when the Prussian infantry began to advance with shouldered arms and parade-ground precision. Kellermann, an Alsatian with an imperfect knowledge of French, who wrote *"débuté"* for *"député"* and *"relâge"* for *"relâche,"* was not only an old warrior who had smelt powder in the Seven Years' War, but also an ardent patriot whose heart leapt at the thought of freedom. Riding far in advance of his columns, he dismounted, raised his hat with its tricolor plume on the point of his sword, and shouted *"Vive la nation!"* And for a quarter of an hour the echo *"Vive la nation!"* rolled along the French front. It was not two armies or two states that faced each other at Valmy, but two epochs, two philosophies, two social systems. On the one side mercenaries from many countries, bought, pressed, and stolen, held together not by an idea but by the club, having only the principle that their officers were more to be feared than the enemy—so many firing automata; on the other, volunteers who had joined the colors at their country's call, men who understood the cause that was at stake, champions of the rights of citizens and men: *"Vive la nation!"*

Perhaps the Duke of Brunswick had some comprehension of this. He stared for a long time through his field glass at the enemy whose bands were playing *"Ça ira";* at length, lowering the glass, he turned to his staff: "Gentlemen, we shall not be victorious here." A halt was sounded, the assault stopped, and only the artillery—forty French and fifty-eight Prussian pieces

—continued to fire until 6 P.M. But most of the shells struck harmlessly in the sodden soil, and the total loss in killed and injured, amounting to less than five hundred, stamped the day as a skirmish rather than a battle.

The vast historic importance of the fact that the Prussian army had not defeated the Jacobins, that absolutism had halted before the Revolution and that the Republican army had successfully undergone the baptism of fire was appreciated neither by Dumouriez nor by Kellermann that evening when their troops separated almost unnoticed from the enemy. But there was dismay in the Prussian camp on the evening of the very day when they had hoped to spear and devour the whole French force. Were they to retreat before this Jacobin rabble? A damned mess! A circle formed in the darkness, with no camp fire, around Herr von Goethe. And this inspired civilian spoke in the bewildered silence of the guardsmen: "At this point and at this hour a new epoch in history begins, and you can say that you were present."

———————◆———————

KELLERMANN was ambitious and sensitive; intoxicated with self-admiration by the success at Valmy, he coveted Dumouriez' position, and Danton had to mediate between the two. When he was pleased with the world Danton had a genius for handling men; on this occasion he instructed Fabre d'Eglantine to flatter the vanity of the two rivals by promising Dumouriez the supreme command and Kellermann a marshal's baton.

But Valmy also confronted Danton with political problems. Immediately after August 10 he had energetically seized control at the Foreign Office. As administrator of the Department of Paris in 1791, he had had for colleague a member of one of the oldest and noblest families of France: Charles-Maurice de Talleyrand-Périgord, until recently constitutional bishop of Autun; this suave, witty, limping gentleman could not but win Danton by the pleasant cynicism with which he toyed gracefully with the more serious problems of life. With a kind of pleasurable respect Danton heard how the thirty-seven-year-old dignitary of the church had first celebrated High Mass on the

Champ-de-Mars at the Feast of Federation of 1791 and then broken the bank twice running in a gambling hell. In 1792 when Talleyrand was attached to the Marquis de Chauvelin, ambassador at St. James's, Danton remained in touch with him; and after his return in the summer had him expound the guiding ideas of foreign policy, since in early youth this scion of the aristocracy had belonged to a so-to-speak bourgeois school of philosophy which, while keeping the commercial and industrial development of France in mind, considered an understanding with England the guarantee of the much-needed peace of Europe. Later, under the influence of Mirabeau, a defensive and offensive alliance with Prussia became an article of faith for him along with the idea of a *rapprochement* with Great Britain. For Danton these principles were convincing: he too liked England, put his hope in England, and strove to avoid a breach with England.

Accordingly when the British ambassador left Paris posthaste after the events of August 10, Danton opposed the recall of the French ambassador from London. On the contrary he insisted on the need for redoubled diplomatic efforts to keep England out of the continental coalition. At the end of August the Abbé Noël, who had collaborated with Condorcet in 1789 on the *Chronique de Paris* and had been department head in the Foreign Office, went to London more or less at his order. Danton attached his own stepbrother Recordain and his twenty-year-old nephew Mergez, both from Arcis-sur-Aube, as couriers, so he could be assured of regular information on Noël's endeavors.

But at the beginning of September an acquaintance met Talleyrand himself in Danton's antechamber, dressed for traveling, booted and spurred, with leather breeches, round hat, and little queue hanging over his collar. "Where to?" The bishop winked slyly: "I leave this morning for London with an order of the Executive Council. I am waiting for my passports which Danton is bringing." Talleyrand, it is true, had won the good graces of the Republicans by his draft of a circular intended to make the events of August 10 palatable to the governments of Europe; but he was quite willing to leave the country on a diplomatic mission. He was not only uncomfortable after the fall of the Tuileries because an infamous mob had defiled the face of freedom with blood and dirt: but there was that in his past which, if brought to light, would inevitably provoke the dangerous fury of this very mob. Talleyrand, too, kept Danton continuously informed on the state of affairs in England, so that he was better instructed than the Foreign Minister himself.

If the preservation of British neutrality demanded steady farseeing effort, Valmy seemed to provide the opportunity of breaking up the coalition and thus carrying out the other part of the Talleyrand-Danton program. All the hatred in France was concentrated on the House of Hapsburg, which was charged with having undertaken the counterrevolutionary crusade for the sake of the *"Autrichienne."* There was endless amazement at the unheard-of, the incredible, the perverse alliance between Berlin and Vienna. Everywhere it was expected that the natural and manifest step for French policy would be to attempt to separate Frederick William from Francis and make an alliance with Prussia against Austria. With this end in view Dumouriez negotiated with the Duke of Brunswick, convinced that every day spent in this way was a day gained for France, since the Prussian army suffered greatly from the inclement weather and shrank pitiably from enteric fever. Westermann, an Alsatian familiar with German, who took part in these negotiations, was despatched to Paris to report and gave Danton an outline of the situation. The cabinet decided to continue negotiations and attached to the army a civil agent, Pierre-Vincent Benoît, whom Danton had recently employed in England. Westermann, poor devil, hitherto one of life's stepchildren, felt himself to be somebody now that he was suddenly associated as an equal with Prussian grandees. In a letter of October 3 he opened his heart to a friend at Strasbourg: "I dined in the Prussian camp with the King of Prussia. For the moment I am all powerful. What can I do for you?"

In the end the negotiations came to nothing, since Frederick William insisted on assurances for Louis' safety; however, the Prussians were allowed to continue the retreat begun on September 29 without much interference. Those in power were eager to leave France with all speed so as not to lose out in the partition

of Poland, and officers and men alike were thoroughly disgusted
with the "military promenade to Paris." Under an everlasting
downpour of rain the troops moved eastward in growing disorder
over muddy roads—cavalry without horses and infantry without arms; queues had lost their tapes, disheveled hair hung
around pale, dirty, and unshaven faces; the colorful rags of
their uniforms hardly covered their nakedness, their hats of
thin felt glued on cardboard were soaked and resembled anything rather than headgear—and altogether the proud soldiers
of Frederick closely resembled the image which the beer-drink-
ing gossips of Berlin had of the sansculottes.

IF Danton appreciated Dumouriez as a military leader of more
than average capacity, Dumouriez recognized in Danton a political leader of outstanding qualities. The entire will power and
energy of which the Executive Council was capable the general
found concentrated in this one man. Because of rumors he wrote
at the end of September: "My dear Danton, I have been terribly
afraid that you would resign from the ministry. I should have
been desolated because I need your brains there." When Dumouriez came to Paris on October 12 to gather the laurels which
were his due and to obtain the approval of the government for
his new plans of campaign, he knew at which door he must
knock first. The small, vivacious general, carefully dressed and
amply powdered, who talked with lively mercurial gestures and
whose black eyes sparkled, differed from the calm giant Danton
in more than externals. Yet his bold and sometimes grandilo-
quent manner, the good humor and gallic wit which seasoned
his talk, his cold assurance amid the wildest confusion, and his
gift of inspiring the masses, drew him to the people's tribune
quite as much as his readiness to study his own interests. Danton, who was fond of laying aside the solemn mask and shocking
his stiff colleagues by an exaggerated candor, must inevitably
have taken pleasure in one who was capable of self-irony and
who once, after a committee meeting of the Assembly, jarred the
grave and decorous Carnot by linking arms with him and remarking laughingly: "We really are great rogues!"

In politics, too, they had many points of agreement. The faster the Republican army under Custine advanced on the Rhine, the more swiftly the idea of a revolutionary war of propaganda and liberation spread. When on September 28 the Convention discussed a report from General Montesquiou, who, having occupied Savoy, asked whether this district was to become the eighty-fourth department of France or a republic under French protection, Danton was swayed by conflicting feelings. Propaganda was a revolutionary force; the expansion of France increased national prestige and thus served to strengthen the Republic. Peace, on the other hand, quiet development, and the increase of economic resources were equally necessary to strengthen the new system. So Danton followed his usual policy. With a flourish of trumpets, he compromised. "We have the right," he declared, "to say to the nations: 'You shall have no more kings.' France cannot allow nations that are seeking liberty to adopt a government contrary to their interests and, by the creation of kings, provide us continually with new tyrants to be combated." Then raising his voice for the benefit of the gallery: "The National Convention must be a general council of insurrection against all the kings of the globe." But at the same time he supported the thoughtful motion of Lasource that the matter be referred to a committee for thorough discussion.

A few days later, when the tricolor waved over Speyer as it was to wave over Worms on October 4, over Mainz on the twenty-first, and over Frankfurt on the twenty-third, he called for a declaration that the country was no longer in danger. This was in line with his own sense of power, and, as he explained, with the dignity of the people and the National Assembly; but at the same time the motion—which was rejected—was intended to prevent an endless continuation of the war on the pretence that the country continued to be in danger. As a realist he feared that the Revolution would exhaust itself in a too unequal struggle if it stormed along the path of world liberation from hazard to hazard, and he wanted to conserve its power. His aims were the same as those of Dumouriez, in whose company he took pains to appear at the Opera and at banquets: to defeat Austria,

come to an understanding with Prussia, keep England neutral,
assure the peace of Europe, and obtain the international recognition of the Republic. The general, who in these days tested
opinion here and there and met an alarming number of talkers,
told Westermann with satisfaction: "There is only one man
here and that is Danton."

On October 23, three days after Dumouriez had returned to
his army, three salvos on the ramparts of Longwy proclaimed
that not a single hostile soldier remained on the soil of the Republic. September 20 had been the turning point; the invasion
had been stopped at Valmy—in Danton's own country! For
chalky Champagne—"barren Champagne"—began here; "a
strange country," as Goethe said, "whose barren chalky soil
can support only poor and scattered hamlets." As the crow flies
it was less than an hour's journey from Valmy to Arcis.

Because the defense of the Revolution against the foreign
enemy stirred Danton most passionately, he spared no pains to
prevent any breach in the inner revolutionary front. France had
to be strong, and in union alone was strength. He forced himself to believe that after August 10, as he had stated in his circular to the courts, there was only one opinion in Paris, and
that soon there would be only one opinion in France. But the
truth was that a dangerous rift had already appeared. The revolutionary Commune which, to the beating of the tocsins, had
been sent to the Hôtel-de-Ville the night of August 10, considered itself the savior of the Revolution. And rightly. So long as
the decision had rested with the Legislative Assembly, things
moved lamely and half heartedly; it was not until Paris took
matters in hand that things began to happen. So the Commune
claimed the dictatorship—in the service and for the benefit of
the Revolution.

The Commune undoubtedly represented the men of pikes, the
sansculottes, the stormers of the Tuileries, the men in shirt
sleeves and sabots. Yet it was also an integral part of the whole

Revolution. There were only two workmen among its members, and these were not wage slaves from a factory but a jeweler's assistant and a cobbler. The majority of its members were justices of the peace, lawyers, magistrate-officials, writers, doctors, architects, artists, a professor of mathematics, a few teachers, and manufacturers, merchants, dealers, and craftsmen. The social force behind them, consisting of master craftsmen and shopkeepers, was the petty Paris bourgeoisie whose conditions of living naturally inclined them toward a thorough democracy. Mayor Pétion was pushed into the background by this stormy assembly because his knife was not keen-edged enough, while Robespierre was elevated to power after he had had his section (that of the Place Vendôme) make him their deputy in the Council General of the Commune.

Under the spur of Robespierre and Marat, the Commune, far from satisfied with being a municipal authority only, assumed unlimited governing power: the imprisonment of the royal family in the Temple, the suspension of Royalist newspapers and the transfer of their presses to patriotic journals, strict supervision of foreigners, censorship of letters, house searches, arrests—all these it decreed independently and of its own authority. As it daily interfered in the province of others, its conflict with the Legislative Assembly which bore the brand of an undemocratic voting system had to break out soon. The National Assembly—faugh! Taschereau suggested at the Jacobins' that, in future, petitions be brought solely before the bar of the Commune. However, when the latter body called on the journalist Girey-Dupré to justify his conduct, the Legislative Assembly on its side called on the Council General of the Commune to justify itself and declared its warrant to be null and void; while Brissot, among whose supporters Girey-Dupré was reckoned, referring to the Commune on August 28, pointed out warningly that even the briefest dictatorship might easily become the grave of freedom.

Independent of the Brissotins, the Left Wing of the Legislative Assembly, which with its revolutionary instinct recognized the need for national unity and solidarity, feared that the unrestricted simultaneous rule of the Commune might prove confusing in times of danger. Danton's friend Thuriot, trembling with noble rage, opposed the attempt of the Commune to extend its control over the Extraordinary Tribunal of August 17, and urged the Assembly to show itself resolved to die rather than allow the law to be infringed ever so slightly. It gave way, however, when Robespierre at the bar, in the name of the Commune, opposed the formation of the new directorate of the Department of Paris, which the Assembly had resolved upon on August 11. Not until August 30 did the Assembly rouse itself and decree the dissolution of the revolutionary Commune and the election of a new municipal body of ninety-six members within twenty-four hours. When Tallien, the secretary of the Commune, appeared at the bar for protest and defense, Danton's friend Delacroix as president replied emphatically: "The formation of a provisional Commune at Paris is contrary to the existing laws and is the result of an extraordinary if unavoidable crisis. However, once the danger is past, the provisional authority must cease. Gentlemen, will you dishonor our beautiful Revolution by giving the whole country the scandalous picture of a Commune revolting against the will of the majority and the law?" The Commune did not care; it was full of scorn and hate; it had saved France and the Revolution, and now those who had achieved nothing, those who had always hesitated and procrastinated, dared to dismiss it. The country was as much in danger as ever; but on this occasion no growling mob, ripe for a quarrel with the Assembly, stood behind Tallien; and consequently the revolutionary Commune's resolution not to dissolve was held in abeyance. Eventually the Assembly, too, came to reason; instead of pouring out the troubling new wine, it diluted it with water, and a new decree was passed by which the Commune as it stood was to increase its numbers to 288 by the election of additional members.

The Commune set out to govern a second time during the events of September. Its Committee of Surveillance, pushing the Assembly aside, followed Marat and seized power; in a statement signed by Panis and Sergent it took part responsibility for the massacres. But the reaction which the carnage created in public opinion damped the desire for independence within the

Commune; in its own ranks the moderates gained power and Pétion was influential again.

Danton did not doubt for a moment the importance of the capital in the revolutionary movement. Paris alone was worth a number of revolutionary army corps, mobilized and ready to strike. Early in September, Doctor Chévetel, physician, fellow Cordelier, and the accepted lover of La Fleury, appeared at the Chancellery with a secretive air and whispered to Danton about serious happenings of which he had learned more or less by accident: Brittany . . . the Marquis de la Rouarie . . . widespread plot . . . impending revolt. Danton did not make light of this warning; as insurrection or civil war at this time would have been disastrous, he empowered Chévetel to use a war ruse and reassure the conspirators in his name of the King's safety. The fact that a domestic enemy was thus undermining the provinces was an additional reason for opposing Roland's suggestion for the transfer of the government. In Paris Danton opposed the external enemy; and in Paris were set the sturdy roots of his strength in internal politics.

If Robespierre flattered the Commune in order to win it, Danton too by no means underestimated its importance. Not only was he in a way its confidential agent within the Executive Council, but his section, that of the Théâtre-Français, represented by such of his adherents as Billaud-Varenne, Fabre d'Eglantine, Robert, and Chaumette, was the revolutionary leaven within the revolutionary Commune. Immediately after August 10 this section demanded the substitution—on all public documents as well as on the buttons of the National Guard—of the words "liberty" and "equality" for "king." It was the first section to transform its battalion of National Guards into an armed force of citizens in general, and the first to issue an appeal for the defense of the country. But Danton realized that although Paris might storm the Tuileries, France could be saved only by France. Accordingly, he neither played off the Commune against the Assembly nor the Assembly against the Commune, but tried to unite both in a policy of national defense. He allowed the Commune its right of search; but when the Committee of Surveillance tried on September 4 to draw Roland and eight deputies into its net, Danton angrily tore up the warrant: So far and no farther. He must have been satisfied to observe the course of events refuting those exalted members of the Commune who had hoped from the beginning to throttle the National Convention.

———————◆———————

BETWEEN the fifth and nineteenth of September the electoral committees which had been appointed on August 26 by universal and equal vote elected the deputies to the National Convention.

On the first day, Robespierre, who headed the list, was called into the Convention with only 338 out of 525 votes. Danton, however, on September 6 received 638 out of 700 votes. No other deputy obtained so large a number. He pleaded eloquently and successfully for his followers in the Cordeliers. Being by nature buoyant, with music in his soul, and despising the militaristic precept, *"inter arma silent musæ,"* he went before the electors, a muse at each hand. He supported the poet and actor Fabre d'Eglantine as well as the painter Louis David, the recognized head of the Classicist School with its antique arrangement of folds. Prudhomme's journal accused him of favoring artists who were little suited to the function of legislators. Other Cordeliers who entered the Manège were the butcher Legendre, Camille Desmoulins, Billaud-Varenne, Collot d'Herbois, Manuel, Sergent, Robert, and Fréron. And Marat must not be forgotten. The *Révolutions de Paris* recommended electing him as the leaven to leaven the lump.

The departments, still in the dark about the conflict which had broken out in the capital, simply confirmed August 10 by sending followers of Brissot and Robespierre indiscriminately to the Convention. Danton, anxious to preserve an unbroken revolutionary front, attempted to obtain the same result in Paris. In accord with his intentions and probably on his instructions, his friend Delacroix endeavored to achieve the election of Pétion and Robespierre on the same ballot—in order "to establish lib-

erty and equality irrevocably." But Paris rejected this policy
of reconciliation: among its twenty-four deputies there were
only two moderates. Brissot's faction took their revenge by filling the official positions of the National Convention with their
supporters: Pétion as president, and Brissot, Vergniaud, Condorcet, Rabaut Saint-Etienne, Lasource, and Camus as secre-
taries. The formal opening session took place on September 20,
and all were optimistic that a great day had dawned; but all with
the single exception of Camus were destined to die violent
deaths within eighteen months.

The galleries applauded when two deputies appeared arm in
arm in the council hall, one the former Duke of Orléans, now
Joseph-Philippe Égalité; the other the wool-carder Armonville
from the Department of the Marne. Both were foreign elements
in the Assembly. For among the 782 deputies the *ci-devants*
were scarce and Armonville had only a single proletarian colleague, Noël Pointe, a worker in the arsenal at Saint-Etienne,
who boasted: I am really one of the people! In its essence the
Assembly was the living proof, so many times repeated, that it
was the Third Estate, the bourgeoisie, that had definitely come
into its own in France. It is true that big business men and in-
dustrialists, the real beneficiaries of the new regime, remained in
the background; in this Convention the spirit of profiteering did
not show itself without a fig leaf. On the other hand, men of law
of every description abounded; for after the abrupt expulsion
of the former ruling caste they alone knew how the machinery of
state worked. There were lawyers and lawyers and more lawyers, apt custodians of the new order; and behind them a phalanx of writers, scientists, doctors, and last but not least fifty-
two clerics including sixteen bishops.

Yes, this was a bourgeoisie, but a bourgeoisie on the threshold
of its power, young, vigorous and healthy, and illuminated by
the reflected glory of its historic task; selfish, where essentials
were at stake, incapable of escaping its limitations, but neither
weak nor cowardly nor greedy; loyal to its own ideals; on the
whole able and ready to pay the price—a bourgeoisie that knew
how to live and how to die.

The Convention had only deputies, not parties. For party meant faction and faction was the result of intrigue and the forerunner of dictatorship. Each member was therefore ready to swear that he was free of all obligation and responsible only to himself. Thus Pétion: "There have been parties hitherto but now that the monarchy has been abolished what interest can exist to cause new ones to form?" And Bancal des Issarts: "No living being on earth is more independent than I." And Fonfrède: "I belong to no party; I am pledged only to my conscience and my country." And Tallien: "We form no parties and we need no leader." All agreed and Danton as well cried with courage and good faith: "I too am without party and faction. You must convince yourselves that there can be no factions within a republic!"

Accordingly Danton's greatest moments were those when his words carried away the whole Convention to the last man. Since ministers could not also be deputies, Danton, when the Convention assembled, laid down his office as member of the Executive Council, merely carrying on current business until Dominique Garat took his place at the Chancellery on October 12. From every point of view the tribune considered it more important to be a deputy—an active part of the people's will, a fraction of the sovereignty of the nation which, to his mind, was the supreme power and the source of everything new and great. Even the vigorous individual seemed to him valuable only if he drew his sap and strength from the masses and was himself a part of the people. "Remember," he urged the Convention, "that the nation is greater than you. Remember that the real genius lies in the people themselves!"

On September 21 the representatives of this sovereign people in the Manège resolved:

"THE NATIONAL CONVENTION DECREES:
THE MONARCHY IS ABOLISHED IN FRANCE."

Not a dozen words, and the proud arms of the Bourbons were flung broken into the ash barrel; and fourteen centuries followed them. In the evening the decree was proclaimed at all the

street corners to the sound of trumpets, and at a hundred thousand windows festive lights shone.

The motion to strike the last blow at the monarchy came from
Collot d'Herbois and Grégoire and not Danton, who also refrained from speaking in the brief debate. Basire, who shared
his political opinions, even attempted to postpone the decision
because an Assembly whose duty it was to safeguard the most
sacred interests of the people must not make a resolution under
the intoxicating influence of enthusiasm. Did Danton agree with
Basire? Was his mind troubled for a moment by a doubt whether
the fall of the monarchy was desired by the majority of the
people? Was the proclamation of the Republic on this special
day inopportune because it threatened to disturb the negotiations with Prussia? Had he actually received, as his enemies
claimed, those subsidies from the royal treasury? Or was he
silent simply from indolence, because the wheel turned without
effort on his part and the decree of September 21 merely sealed
the deed of August 10?

In any case, his healthy realism prevented him from interfering with the foundation of the Republic once it had been established. Ultimately the people had to give their verdict on the
Constitution evolved by the Convention. But it was a different
matter when on October 16 Manuel suddenly made the proposal
that the Constituent Committee should arrange for a plebiscite
to decide the question between monarchy and republic. Cambon
went further and urged the appointment of a committee of
eighty-three (one deputy from each department) to settle the
question, and Goupilleau suggested referring it to the Legislative
Committee. Brissot alone objected on principle to a plebiscite
which must inevitably confuse the people and make the name
Republic questionable.

Danton too frowned. These timorous souls who wanted to
hear from the "Sovereign" that their action was no sin! For
whom August 10 and the election of the Convention were not
sufficient! A member rose and objected that unless the people's
will were ascertained on the question of a republic, there was
danger of erecting a great structure on a fragile and treacherous

foundation. Danton made a contemptuous gesture: "A brilliant objection but invalid! Consider that the Republic has already been sanctioned by the people, by the army, and by the genius of liberty which condemns all kings!" Applause shook the house; the listeners in the gallery rose and cheered. "Henceforward no one may doubt that France wishes to be and will always be a republic; let us proceed then to make a constitution which is the consequence of this principle. Once you have set up this constitution—once by your lofty debate you have given official form to public opinion—then the constitution will be quickly adopted; and the unanimity of all the parts of your government will guarantee its durability." He stopped, and the Convention unanimously rejected Manuel and Cambon's motion.

———◆———

But no will, however strong, could hold together what the logic of facts tended to disintegrate. The conflict that had begun when Brissot had agitated for, and Robespierre against, a war, had continued when the Commune revolted against the Assembly, and came to a head in the Convention. The Right Wing consisted of the Brissotins, who gradually came to be grouped under the name of the Gironde. It is true that not all the members were natives of the southern department named after this river, or even of the Midi. There were a few from everywhere with the exception of the northeast—from Provence, Brittany, Normandy, Picardy, Guyenne, and Limousin. But still the majority came from the Gironde and such departments as the Somme, Seine-Inférieure, Aisne, Haute-Vienne, Ardèche, Finistère, and Jura. Three Bordeaux advocates, Vergniaud, Guadet and Gensonné, set the tone of the speeches.

Although the Girondists were coming into conflict more and more with Robespierre's and Marat's adherents who have gone down in history as the Mountain, both camps were loyal supporters of the Revolution, both were Republicans, both Democrats. But the Girondists believed the Revolution to be essentially accomplished, capable of being carried over into the quiet constitutional everyday routine, while the Mountain realized

that the Revolution must still go through a life-and-death struggle at home and abroad and demanded for these exceptional
times exceptional measures.

The difference between the two groups was most apparent in
a conflict between the departments and Paris. The departments
were so many autonomous districts, each appointing its own officials and having no representative of the central authority, each
resembling a small and almost independent republic. The Girondists appeared to desire a further federalization of the country after the American plan and the transformation of France
into a loose union of independent states. They even entertained
the idea of forming a republic of the Midi if the enemy actually
took Paris; and they absolutely refused so long as the Revolution was not secure to allow Paris that leading rôle in a revolutionary dictatorship which the Mountain was continually proposing. When the spokesman of a deputation which had come
before the Convention referred to Paris as the capital he was
roughly interrupted by Guadet, who was presiding: "Citizen, I
would have you observe that a Republic has no capital."

Behind the conflict between the departments and Paris—the
provinces and the capital—lay concealed another which was at
first scarcely recognized. The great conflict between poverty and
riches was not yet too evident, for the 50% devaluation of the
assignats in France had induced an unhealthy boom in French
industry. The foreign demand for goods purchasable with the
rapidly falling paper money enlivened factories and trades and
created a treacherous prosperity, a false flowering of trade and
industry. This made it possible for a revolutionary watchword
like "*La patrie*" to unite rich and poor; they were all patriots.
When Simond of Strasbourg at the Jacobins' talked of soldiers'
going to the front to be killed for the sake of fat capitalists, it
was unheard of! A soldier died for his country! There was little
difference in extraction, education, rank, and property between
the leading Brissotins and Robespierrists; both groups included
orators, writers, lawyers, and journalists. Nevertheless the Gironde was supported by people of property and education, the
Mountain by those who had no money and knew no Latin. The

former was backed by the bourgeoisie of the big industrial centers, the latter by the petty bourgeoisie of the teeming districts of Paris.

Among the meeting places of the deputies in Brissot's following were the Comité de la Place Vendôme, where Vergniaud presided at the table of the hospitable Madame Dodun; the Hôtel-de-Ville with Pétion, who was steadily moving toward the Gironde, and last but not least the salon of Madame Condorcet. But for some time the Roland couple had been a stronger magnet than any of these on account of the female partner. The daughter of the Paris engraver Phlipon had been devoted to things of the mind from childhood; in her own words she needed learning as much as food. She early became enthusiastic over Rousseau, the English Constitution, and all the new ideas of freedom and humanity. The Revolution of course carried her away; this extraordinary woman saw in it a magnificent opportunity for the fullest self-expression. While she was still in the provinces she sent articles to the *Patriote français,* which were published under the caption "Letters from a Roman Lady." When she moved from Lyons to Paris in 1791, her house soon came to be frequented by Brissot's supporters. Her influence increased during her husband's first ministry and by the autumn of 1792 she had become the political Egeria of those who therefore came to be called more and more frequently Rolandists.

Actually Manon Roland lacked political foresight and acumen. Without any sense of what was possible she indulged too much in heroic-sublime ideas to be tolerant of the human, all-too-human, quality of a revolution. However, the warmth of her really magnanimous spirit, with her clear intellect, her firm will, all united in a beautiful woman, had a remarkable influence on men. While he was a young medical student Lanthenas had fallen in love with the fair Manon; as a deputy of the Convention he still continued to sit at her feet. When Bancal des Issarts visited her for the first time in July, 1790, at her country place, Clos-la-Platière, near Villefranche, he burst into tears as he mounted to ride away—such was her fascination for him. Fiery young Barbaroux of Marseilles was tamed by a flick of her

Manon Roland

lashes; François Buzot, who had been a staunch supporter of
Robespierre in the Constituent Assembly, was a lost man as soon
as, having been elected to the Convention he felt her magnetism.
Manon, who confessed in old age that she had been a stranger to
passion, and Buzot who admitted that the impure breath of de-
bauchery had never defiled his senses, found each other in the
study of Plutarch. Their souls embraced; she wore a medallion
with his miniature round her neck, and he one with hers.

In order to preserve the unity of the revolutionary front, Danton made a real effort to keep on friendly footing with his colleagues. He would put in an appearance at the Rolands', at the
Ministry of the Interior in the Rue Neuve des Petit-Champs;
somewhat mistrustful, indeed, because at the gatherings the only
refreshments were apt to be a carafe of water and a sugar bowl,
but willing to act the provincial uncle, good natured, hearty, and
disarming: "Well, may I invite myself to dinner? What is there
today?"

He had no experience whatever with women of this kind. At
the age of thirty-eight Manon Roland knew that she was beautiful: tall with a stately figure, flowing hips, full bosom, an expres-
sive face, eloquent dark eyes surmounted by a helmet of black
hair, and a skin like milk and blood. Accustomed to adoration,
she whom Dumouriez had called *"vertueusement coquette"* expected the homage of men as an inevitable tribute. So she met
Danton radiant, certain of her attraction, and in the depth of
her soul where the unconscious, secret wishes stir, something
asked: "Do you want me?"

Manon was no blue stocking of the type which got on Danton's nerves. A good housewife and an indulgent mother, she
could wield the needle as well as the pen. Such a sentiment of
hers as "I should like to see my trees again after so many rogues
and fools" would have found a friendly echo in Danton. But
since in his heart of hearts he declined even the remote possibility of sleeping with women who between paroxysms of love
might perhaps begin to discuss the difference between the French
and English Constitutions, the barbed hook angled in vain. The
atmosphere around them did not become charged. Danton's

friendly smile suddenly seemed to Madame Roland the most hideous grimace. During the month of August he continued to come every day, but between him and her there was a wall of ice. Soon he began to feel uncomfortable in this strange world: an elegant lady sat at her escritoire, delicately dipping her quill with well-manicured fingers into a dainty inkwell, surrounded by elegant gentlemen of somewhat ostentatious breeding, who, despite the utmost cordiality and reserve permitted the Keeper of the Seals of France to feel that his loud voice and brusque gestures were considered a trifle plebeian.

The personal antipathy which Madame Roland felt for Danton was first curdled into the poison of deadly hate through political elements. With a little sense of proportion, a bit of penetration and just a trace of understanding, her followers and admirers could not have thought Danton the wild man he had been described as being, and could not have mentioned him as they did in the same breath with Marat and Robespierre. True, when he raged or appeared to, flashes of fire seemed to burst from dark clouds: "We must show ourselves terrible!" he thundered against the generals suspected of Royalist tendencies; and when a former minister was called before the bar of the House to justify his actions and he attempted to make a subtle distinction between a counterrevolutionary and one who did not love the Revolution, Danton put an end to such hair splitting: "In the language of liberty any official who does not love the Revolution is a traitor!"

Yet the touchstone especially for the Gironde should have been his attitude on the question of private property. The insurrection of the Paris faubourgs on August 10 had its repercussions also in the provinces: on the same day the Legislative Assembly cancelled "feudal and seignorial rights of all kinds" without compensation—if the tree of feudalism had already been stripped of its branches the ax was now laid to its very roots. Similarly, the National Assembly resolved upon the auctioning of émigré lands in small parcels with the avowed purpose of "increasing the number of small landed proprietors." The peasant received complete liberty and a piece of France as his property and from now on resolutely followed the drum which called volunteers to the defense of the country because he was very certain that under the hoofs of the Prussian and Austrian cavalry, feudal rule which had been buried for his benefit would spring to life again.

Only a couple of visionaries still hawked about the so-called agrarian law for equal distribution of land. These two were members of the Commune, Dufour and Danton's acquaintance Momoro, commissars for Normandy; they produced an outline of a new Declaration of the Rights of Man in which startled eyes could read: "The nation recognizes and guarantees the protection and inviolability of industrial property only; it recognizes landed property only pending legislation on the subject." Such chatter of independents was readily rebuked from a number of quarters; but those who had acquired national land put their heads together as uneasily as the old landed proprietors— what in the world did it mean?

In actuality, too, sanctity of property was not respected. Means and methods of communication did not allow the equal distribution of the necessary grain for bread throughout the whole of France, with the result that the price of a *setier* of wheat varied according to districts from twenty-five livres in Danton's homeland, the Aube, to sixty-three livres in the Hautes-Alpes. Although the harvest was good there were here and there shortages of grain. One reason was that more wheat was used for baking than formerly; for if white bread had hitherto been a luxury for the peasants, the Revolution made the average Frenchman a consumer of it. What Pache said in 1799 of the Ardennes, that nine tenths of the population were better housed, stocked, and nourished than ten years earlier, was true of the whole country. To place the soldiers on a level with the citizens the Assembly resolved that the army bread should be made of wheat meal in future instead of chiefly from rye meal, and this also increased consumption and demand while production and supply were diminishing. Because the number of agricultural workers had decreased as a result of conscription, and the grain producers were distrustful of the depreciated assignats, the market was inadequately supplied. There were complaints at the Jacobins' that bread had never been so dear in France under the despotism as it was under the rule of freedom. Already barges carrying grain were being stopped on the Seine by angry mobs.

As the army contractors frequently found the barn doors shut or exorbitant prices demanded, a decree was issued by the Provisional Executive Council on September 4 which compelled stubborn owners to sell their stocks to the military at a price fixed by the authorities. Roland, who had not signed the decree, although the supply of foodstuffs was in his field, attacked Danton for this measure and in doing so certainly had the backing of most owners of property who were alarmed at such interference with their rights.

But it was not Danton's policy to frighten property owners. The great upheaval which had taken place since July 14 was a Revolution supporting and not opposing property. Its aim was to assure civic property against absolutist caprice, to free the peasant's property from feudal burdens, to smooth the way for industrial and commercial property by abolishing medieval barriers, and to increase landed property by parceling out ecclesiastical and émigré possessions. At that time the bourgeois order was the only possible one, and those who supported its triumph understood the need of the hour. Those who went further and threatened property falsified the meaning of the Revolution and completely lost their bearings; without knowing or desiring it they were supporting the counterrevolution, and it was no accident that Carra stigmatized as "avowed aristocrats," "public enemies," and "criminals to be exterminated" everyone who dared to discuss the agrarian law.

Guided by an almost infallible instinct for what was possible and desirable, Danton made a part of the program in his circular to the courts "not the impossible equal distribution of property but equality of rights and happiness." And at the first meeting of the Convention on September 21 he appealed to "those excellent citizens" who feared that "ardent friends of liberty" might harm the structure of society by exaggeration of their principles. Let there be no fear, no alarm, no bewilderment. "Let us swear to refrain from every kind of exaggeration! Let us declare that we will all preserve property of every kind, whether territorial, individual, or industrial!" The Convention applauded like one man and adopted with only a slight amendment the resolution that persons and property were under the protection of the French nation.

———————◆———————

Again, on the question of the clergy Danton was no small yelping fanatic. It is true the admirer of Diderot saw in the Old and New Testament not much more than a fine collection of legends, and the suspicion of the clergy bred in him by his encyclopedist training made him put clergy and lawyers in the same category: "Both have always cheated the people." Of religious fanaticism he said that like water it always descended to lower levels, and penetrated only into servile and superstitious minds. Still more he saw in priests who refused the oath "one of the most powerful instruments of the counterrevolution"; a cleric who refused to be a citizen was a traitor "battening on the sweat of the people."

But Danton, who never attempted to turn Gabrielle's faith into disbelief, did not share the shallow wisdom of Manuel—who saw in the priests the cause of every trouble on earth—and had a poor opinion of the bitter hostility to religion which steadily spread in the Commune. In June it had opposed the Corpus Christi procession and after August 10—*écrasez l'infâme!*—it decreed the closing of all the monasteries as "hiding places of the aristocracy" and the utilization of "all bronze crucifixes, lecterns, angels, devils, seraphim, and cherubim" in the churches for the manufacture of guns. On September 10 the National Assembly followed suit, decreeing the confiscation of all the gold and silver vessels in the churches. A fortnight earlier it had decreed that all nonjuring priests must leave France within a fortnight, and thousands of them, threatened with deportation to Guiana, emigrated to neighboring countries.

The next step was the canceling of the ecclesiastical budget which amounted to one hundred million livres for 1793. Cambon made the motion in the Convention on November 13—Economy! Economy!—and further: "Workers will be paid for their work, but by those who employ them." Toward the end of the same month Lecointe-Puyraveau, Maure, and Biroteau, who had been despatched as commissars into the Eure-et-Loir, reported on their mission. They had had a bad time of it. They had found themselves in the middle of food riots; barns were plundered, angry mobs gathered, and the commissars were hemmed in, cudgeled, kicked, threatened, and eventually compelled at the points of pikes and axes to fix maximum prices for wheat and other provisions. "The grievances we were forced to hear," Lecointe reported, "frequently concerned priests and religion. . . . They did not hesitate to say that the Convention which had abolished the priests and stolen the people's pennies would have to pay for it." And Biroteau added: "If the mere suggestion of canceling the priests' stipends causes such a ferment, what unrest will a decree to that effect cause!" The grumbling of a few deputies was shouted down by Danton: "Silence! Let them finish! You will hear the same thing from me."

He followed Pétion on the tribune—not only a man from Arcis-sur-Aube who knew the country people as he knew himself, but also an aware mind that reckoned with realities and did not confuse politics with philosophy. He foresaw something of what had been anxiously expressed by the wife of the deputy Jullien in one of her letters from Paris: "I see a Republic without Republicans"; he understood that the Convention had been elected by a resolute minority. Even the universal and equal franchise brought at most only a fifth of the voters to the polls; on the very day of this debate but 11,400 Paris voters out of a total of 190,000 took the trouble to vote in the mayoral election. Why then frighten away the hesitant who were just coming around to the Revolution, by resolutions without inner necessities? "France is thrown into confusion by the too hasty application of philosophical principles which are dear to me but for which the people, especially in the provinces, are not yet ripe."

Another time he spoke of some principles of his favorite philosophy. "When fortune's stepchildren see the rich indulging all their inclinations and gratifying all their wishes, while they must restrict their own needs to a minimum, they believe and find consolation in the belief that their joys in the other world will be multiplied in proportion to their privation in this. Leave them this illusion! Before we talk to them of ethics and philosophy, let us wait until, enlightened and convinced, they are able to appraise religious ideas at their real value. . . . Until then it is a crime, it is high treason against the nation, to rob the people of their ideas and their illusions. Personally, I know only the universal God of liberty and justice. The country people believe in the God-Man, the Savior whom they consider holy because they owe him a few moments of happiness in youth, maturity, and old age. . . . Leave the people their illusions but enlighten them!" More urgently: "Tell the people plainly and without circumlocution—Keep your priests as long as you need them for your happiness!" More urgently still: "Have confidence, wisdom, and steadfastness, and you will save the Republic!"

———————

Although a hundred bridges led the Brissotins to the man whose political impetuosity was always checked by his political circumspection, Danton had one capital fault which for them was ineradicable: the very fact of his existence. It did not seem undeserved luck to the Gironde but the result of human and divine justice that the fruit of August 10 fell into their lap. Had not the course of events which ended with the storming of the Tuileries started with the dismissal of their ministers? And had not the Marseilles battalion which, in their opinion, had decided the issue of that storming day been led to Paris by the youthful, exuberant Barbaroux? And young Barbaroux answered loudly, "Present!" when the confidants of Madame Roland were called up.

The elections for the Convention, too, assured the Brissotins of their popularity. Carra was elected in seven departments, Brissot in three, and several others in two, while on the Left Robespierre alone succeeded in being twice elected. Yet in the Convention they had no more of a majority than their opponents. Both were extremists, and between them lay the center, the so-called "Plain," the hundreds of deputies whose votes had to be won on every occasion. But already the first ballots gave the upper hand to the Gironde and in the Executive Council they were certainly on top: Roland, Servan, and Clavières, all ministers in Brissot's first cabinet, had been appointed by the Assembly to their respective offices by unanimous acclamation; and Lebrun and Monge were carried along. The electorate was Girondist, the Convention Girondist, the Executive Council Girondist; the whole of France Girondist if one ignored one exception.

But this exception could not be ignored—it was DANTON.

But for Danton the Brissotins could consider themselves all powerful; except for Danton Madame Roland could fancy herself Regent of France. But Danton was not captivated by the eyes of the lovely Manon, Danton was not to be deluded by the smooth phrases of the others, Danton was not to be outvoted in the Council of Ministers. On the contrary! While Danton was able to command the street and while he had the ear of the Convention, he dominated the Executive Council.

To hell with Danton!

Each time the Rolands were exasperated when a community, a corporation, or an official authority appealed to Danton—yes, to Danton—in some affair which clearly concerned Roland, and the Minister of Justice politely passed the petition to his colleague of the Interior: "I have the honor to transmit to you the attached letter the purport of which concerns your department." It seemed plain, cunning derision; they could imagine Danton grinning as he wrote the words, and for the thousandth time Madame sighed: "It is this wild tribune who rules, and we who are oppressed."

So when the Rolandists came to deliver their attack on the Left its chief object was Danton. Hear, people! The triumvirate of Robespierre, Marat, and Danton is aiming at a dictatorship! Robespierre, Marat, Danton! A cunning scheme to couple him with the *"Ami du peuple"*; for the name of Marat was like a red rag to thousands. Brissot wrote with poison instead of ink in the *Patriote français:* "The enemy of all good citizens, the friend of disorder and slaughter, who has published the lists of his proscriptions under the blasphemous name of the 'People's Friend,' has included all the ministers in his lists with the sole exception of M. Danton."

On the evening of September 2, while swords and pikes, truncheons and daggers were doing their work at the prison gates, Billaud-Varenne had reported to the Commune a plot of

Brissot and his adherents to put the Duke of Brunswick, the leader of the army advancing on Paris, on the throne of France! Nobody laughed, although the sole ground of the accusation was an article by Carra written during the early days of the war, in which the duke was described as a friend of liberal philosophic principles. Robespierre must have known the truth; he surely knew that such a denunciation at such a time inevitably meant delivering its victims to the knives of a bloodthirsty and blood-drunk mob. Yet he had supported the maneuver; the urge to destroy whoever threatened to hinder the progress of the Revolution swept aside every inhibition of this cold calculator. As it happened, the plot failed; a search of Brissot's house revealed no incriminating evidence. The plan to arrest Roland and a number of deputies was foiled by Danton's positive "No."

But hate and vengeance smoldered, and on September 24 and 25 they flared up in the Convention in a frontal attack of the Rolandists on the Robespierrists. Restive men in restive times— feelings were boiling over whether for good or for ill. Grégoire, bishop and deputy, was unable to eat or sleep for days for joy of hearing the Republic proclaimed; even the writing sand trickling over documents and papers dried genuine manly tears beside the official ink. The district Council General of Lille reported the self-sacrifice of the population under the Austrian siege: "A number of workmen declined monetary assistance and said they had enough to live on for four or five days; they would apply to us later. We wept." The administrators of the Department of the North replied: "We, too, wept tears of admiration and compassion over your letter."

The days of these debates were times of throbbing pulses and hectic cheeks.

Suddenly Kersaint exploded over a trifle—Roland's report that a courier had been illegally stopped. For the first time the guillotine was appealed to for use against other deputies. "The time has come," the former naval officer called, as if from the bridge of his ship, "to erect scaffolds for the murderers; the time has come to erect them for those who instigate murders." Vergniaud lent his support: "Yes, crimes are committed in the Republic and the laws do not suffice." "Yes," Lanjuinais repeated, "we have laws against murderers, but we need laws against the instigators to murder."

Who was it ascending the tribune now? What was the citizen's name? Lively eyes, lips contemptuously curled, traces of melancholy on his brow. By God! In his blue coat, red waistcoat with lapels, neatly ruffled muslin jabot, and powdered hair, he was more a "monsieur" than a "citizen." Instead of drawling as usual, François Buzot was fiery and eloquent like a man who feels the warm breath of his mistress on his neck, and he revealed his position by asking for a parliamentary guard drawn from the eighty-three departments: "I ask that the National Convention be surrounded by such an impressive force that we shall have nothing to fear and the departments may be assured for our safety!" Marat's paper had demanded precisely the opposite: a meeting place for the Convention with galleries for three thousand citizens, completely unprotected and unguarded, "so that the deputies shall be permanently in the hands of the people and have no protection but their civic sense and their virtue." Kersaint and Buzot were opposed by Basire, Tallien, Fabre d'Eglantine, Collot, Sergent: "Hitherto the sword of the law has struck only at the most unfortunate class of the people." But in vain; the Convention resolved practically unanimously to appoint six commissars to report on the situation in the country and in Paris, to bring in a bill against the instigators of murder and slaughter, and to consider the formation of a parliamentary force drawn from the eighty-three departments.

Soon after the Mountain delivered its counterattack. A motion to cancel the decree relating to the Convention guard; a charge by Merlin of Thionville that Lasource had given him private information yesterday about a party that aimed at dictatorship. Who was it? Put your cards on the table! "I am ready to stab the first usurper of dictatorial powers." Lasource, a Protestant pastor from Castres, young, cultured, cosmopolitan, hotheaded, rhetorical, easily roused, wandered a little from the subject and enunciated carefully: "I here proclaim that I shall vote that all the departments contribute to the guard for the legislative body. I am afraid of the despotism of Paris. . . . The influence of Paris must be reduced to one eighty-third like that of every other department. . . . I believe that there is a party desirous of alienating the Convention from the people, of dominating and destroying it, a party that wants to rule under another name by uniting the entire power of the nation in the hands of a few individuals."

The shades of the September victims seemed to haunt the chamber; the name of Robespierre was mentioned. Straightway the advocate from Arras began to plead his own cause; lengthy, discursive, and exhausting. Those who listened to his harsh voice, saw his mechanical gestures, and heard the complacent catalogue of his virtues and merits—I . . . I . . . I—could believe the story that his rooms in the Rue Saint-Honoré, where he was pampered by the prosperous cabinetmaker Duplay as if he were a son of the house, were full of painted, engraved, and sculptured Robespierres.

But what an uproar when Marat appeared! The storm of shouts and threats almost overwhelmed him. "I have a large number of personal enemies in this meeting," he began coolly. The Convention was on its feet, fists clenched, shouting "All, all!" But the "People's Friend" faced the raging indignation, and calmly explained that he alone—differing with Robespierre and with Danton—had thought a dictatorship necessary, and why. The wrath against him grew, a decree against him was demanded; he took the speaker's stand again, drew a pistol from his pocket and put it to his temple: "I will put a bullet through my brains if the decree is passed." "Down!" the House yelled. "Down!"

Robespierre, too, disavowed the "thoughtless words of a hyper-patriot." And Danton dissociated himself from the "People's Friend" in even plainer, more drastic terms, describing him as being for the Republicans what the Royalist hotspur Royou was for the aristocrats. He was fair, though, even to Marat: "I ascribe this extravagance to the torments he has undergone. I believe that the subterranean life he has been compelled to lead has eaten into his soul." At the same time Danton did not fail to emphasize the fundamental distinction between himself and the other Paris deputies, and Marat. Already the friends of order began to look more content. Four days previously, Danton had already seized the first opportunity to dissipate "the vain phantoms of a dictatorship and the extravagant notions of a triumvirate" by proclaiming his belief in democracy and the sovereignty of the people. He who for weeks exercised a practical dictatorship, though it was in order to save the democratic Revolution, now repeated and underlined this confession: "If there is any man so vile as to want to rule despotically over the representatives of the people, his head will fall the moment he is unmasked." New laws are wanted? Good! "Let us bring in a law providing the death penalty for anyone who expresses himself in favor of a dictatorship or triumvirate."

A quick turn to the other wing where those who feared federalism were sitting: "We are told that there are men among us who believe in the necessity of splitting up the country. Let us put an end to such absurd notions by proclaiming the death penalty against their authors! France must become an indivisible whole. . . . Anyone who tries to destroy the unity of France must die." The suggestion was music in the ears of the Robespierrists.

Having thus disposed either party in his favor by telling it what it wished to hear, Danton made a vigorous manly appeal to both, a call for unity against the foe who still occupied Verdun and Longwy. "Let us destroy the spirit of faction which would dash us to destruction. Once we have sacred harmony, our enemies will be crushed."

Those who believed that the newcomer would slip on the floor of the Manège gaped. Here was a master of parliamentary tactics, using no petty tricks, dodges, and wiles, which were alien to Danton's character, but having the perspicacity and generosity to stress what was needed, what would bind, what would unite.

The Revolution itself spoke through his mouth to those of its sons who were one another's deadly enemies.

On October 29 feeling ran high again because Roland, that tearful Jeremiah, glibly recited the chief article of the shorter catechism of the Gironde, and in order to stir up the departments against the capital cursed Paris as a robbers' den. He, the honest man, said it: "The administrative body is impotent, the Commune despotic, the people loyal but misled, the armed forces ex-

cellent but inefficiently commanded—such is Paris!" Robespierre, whose name had been mentioned in the minister's report,
turned to the president with upraised arm. Immediate grumbling and interruptions—a preconcerted game of the Brissotins
to cut that hated man short, if possible. Then Danton's powerful
voice threatened: "Mr. President, it is your duty to see that the
speaker keeps the floor. I, too, shall ask for it presently. The
time has come to throw light on all this."

Today again the cry for revolutionary unity vibrated in every
sentence of his speech: there must be no more mistrust between
deputies; if anyone was guilty of causing it, out with him! Once
more Marat was solemnly disavowed: "I frankly declare that I
have learned to understand his character; it is not only volcanic and quarrelsome but also unsociable." Then the moving
assurance: "I am resolved to die rather than be the cause of dis-
union within the Republic." As for the September massacres:
"No throne was ever smashed without a few good citizens being
injured by the splinters. There was never yet a perfect revolution without the farreaching destruction of the old order being
fatal to someone or other." But if you must be everlastingly
imagining plots and would-be dictators, name names. Speak
out! "I declare that all those who speak of a Robespierre faction
are in my eyes either prejudiced or bad citizens." He moved a
debate on Roland's report next Monday, so that accuser and accused might have time to prepare themselves. "Then the good
citizens who seek only enlightenment and want to know facts
and men will soon know whom they should hate and for whom
they should feel that fraternity which alone can give the Convention the noble bearing destined to characterize it."

A voice had already asked permission to bring an accusation
against Robespierre. Former members of the Legislative Assembly knew the speaker. In earlier days he had appeared at the bar
of the House to demand a decree against the émigré princes in
the name of the section of the Lombards, and everybody had
stretched their necks to look at him. For Jean-Baptiste Louvet
was the author of a more than famous novel, *Les Aventures du
Chevalier Faublas,* in which philosophical meditations alternated with bedroom scenes, and the heroine possessed a name—

Lodoiska—which every mother of refined feelings bestowed upon her daughter. They expected to see a radiant and victorious Casanova, and were disappointed to find a meagre, thin, short-sighted, bald little man with unkempt clothes and clumsy gestures. Today this same little man drew a carefully prepared philippic from his pocket: Robespierre, I accuse you—long list of accusations—I accuse you, Robespierre.

Nor was Danton spared. First a few general thrusts at his arguments without mentioning names; then astonishment "that Danton whom nobody has attacked jumps up to declare that he is above attack"; surprise at Danton's disavowal of Marat "as though he had made no use of him in this great plot"; and the conclusion that one who had become acquainted with Marat's unpleasant character "could not clear himself entirely by pretending now to give him up." Danton turned phlegmatically in his seat, and, since the speaker was apparently reluctant to mention the Jacobins by name, called out good naturedly, "I ask that Louvet be permitted to touch the sore and even place his finger on the wound; it is an important point." This time, however, the laugh was with the novelist: "Very well, Danton, I will touch it; but don't cry out first."

Again, in trying to fix on the Mountain the responsibility for the September massacres, Louvet attacked Danton. Pétion had been powerless to interfere. "Why? Because the Paris authorities were fettered, because Roland spoke in vain—and because the Minister of Justice did not speak." A third time, talking of Marat's incendiary pamphlets and taking up Brissot's reproach, he turned directly on Danton: "In these pamphlets all the ministers were described as traitors with one exception, only one and always the same. A pity, Danton, that you cannot clear yourself before posterity of having been this exception!" However, Louvet's shafts all fell short. The Convention did not decide to accuse Marat or to institute investigations against Robespierre, and Danton merely gazed with mild surprise at the novelist, who parodied Cicero's accusation against Catiline with a somewhat light and careless eloquence. He really felt himself unassailable. The fact that a few days ago, at the presidential elections, he had received 207 votes as the nominee of the Mountain—only eleven less than the Gironde nominee Guadet—assured him of his authority in the Convention.

With the Jacobins, whose soil was more favorable than the Convention for anti-Brissotin attacks, Danton was equally restrained. August 10 had brought an abundance of power to the "Society of the Friends of the Constitution." It was compelled to close its doors to new members in order not to be swamped by opportunists, time servers, political vicars of Bray and "August Republicans." The club, which since September 21 had called itself the *Société des Jacobins, amis de l'égalité et de la liberté,* was well aware of its significance as an "advance post of the Republic." "Here," Couthon exclaimed, "the Revolution was prepared, here it was achieved; here all great events were fostered."

To outsiders this society perhaps seemed less important. Its members had occupied the outposts of the government, and transferred the center of gravity to the Convention and the Commune. But, if Danton called the club a branch of the Constitutional Committee of the Convention of which he was himself a member together with eight Rolandists, the *Société des Jacobins* considered itself a court of appeal and a supervisory body for all departments. Jeanbon Saint-André, it is true, once made an attempt to disclaim legal authority for the society; but soon after Danton's friend Robert remarked: "People are always talking of the Jacobin party, Jacobin despotism, and Jacobin power. Certainly the Jacobins are a party, certainly they are a power, certainly they are despotic. But this party is the party of the people who prepared and carried out the Revolution of August 10; this power in its turn is the power of the people who wish to preserve their work; this despotism is the despotism of public reason which will never suffer a handful of ambitious plotters and thinly disguised intriguers to monopolize the benefits of the Revolution."

And when Dumouriez, who had a keen sense for the real seat

of power, came to Paris victorious and crowned with the laurels of Valmy, where did he go? Politely, with his cocked hat under his arm, to the Jacobins'.

Indeed the variety of figures before the bar of the society continued to be a reflection of the National Assembly. A company of volunteers appeared to the roll of drums, swearing to die for liberty and equality. Next came a company of negroes to another roll of drums, and the president of the Jacobins spoke: "Hitherto a barbarous prejudice has created a bar between you and other citizens. Now the French people have won back their rights and given you back yours. . . . Go, friends and brethren, to strengthen the phalanx of liberty. Defend your rights, which are ours, for we are all brothers."

On another occasion a bright little man recited by heart the rights of men and citizens to the melting smiles of the Jacobins. Gendarmes complained of their officers, and a deputation of the "Hussars of Liberty" complained of the Convention, which had refused to accept a petition of theirs.

Again, an actress, a cute young lady of the Théâtre-Molière, appealed for protection against her manager's breach of contract. The president, all gallantry, replied that the oppressed had always found protectors in this society and that the Jacobins would assuredly fight for the pleasure of championing Mademoiselle. Again, an outraged cuckold spluttered his grievance against his unfaithful wife at the bar; a wave of horror passed through the assembly when he revealed that it was a Jacobin who had helped to cuckold him. But then brows were knit suspiciously: this must be a Brissotin, wanting to unmask the society with his denunciation!

Much scandal and laughter were also caused by the members themselves. Immediately after the fall of the Tuileries the journalist Guiraut, editor of the *Logotachygraphe,* and inventor of the "art of writing as fast as the spoken word," boasted—being apparently not quite sober—of the courage he had displayed the day before. The devil! He would like to see the man who could rival him with a gun! Violent uproar. He grasped the speaker's desk, the president was compelled to cover himself and suspend the meeting.

A few weeks later a representative of the affiliated society of Périgueux mounted the tribune without uncovering. Some shouted in chorus: "Hat off! Hat off!" and others, "No! Keep it on!" The man from Périgueux replied that he did not know the rule, but was only following the impulse of nature and liberty which permitted a man to do anything that did not harm others. The president had to shrug his shoulders and admit that there was no rule for this case.

Another day one Maure, a grocer from Auxerre and one of the big guns of the Jacobins, related an adventure—his hair was still on end from it. It happened this way. Last night on leaving the Café Mirabeau he was stopped near the Rue Saint-Honoré by a prostitute who made him proposals. You know the sort. "But," and here Maure threw out his chest, "you are well enough acquainted with me, citizens, to realize that I knew how to resist her blandishments. A representative of the people respects himself too much to debase his character." Laughter, calls of "All right! Come to the point!" "When the wench saw that I rejected her advances she asked me in a hard, cutting voice: 'Are you a patriot?' I replied, 'Yes.' 'Very well,' she said, 'then you will soon be hanged.' 'Why?' 'Because all patriots are criminals!' " And raising an admonitory finger before his astounded audience, Maure concluded: "There's more in this than meets the eye."

Did the Brissotins really feel like carps among the pikes at the Jacobin Club, and destined to be devoured? In any case they succeeded for the time being in having Pétion elected president; but the fact that Danton succeeded him in the middle of October indicated a movement toward the Left. Danton, who was restless and without any sense for time-tables, and who was temporarily laying by the honor and trouble of a secretaryship in the Convention because it involved too much clerical work, was an extraordinary president. One of the members grumbled that he had occupied the president's chair only once since his election; that when present yesterday and called to preside, he had declined. However, Legendre immediately cut the critic short: "Danton is a good citizen; he loves the people and he will always be at the post where the people place him." In other respects, too, Danton's prestige among the Jacobins was considerable. When the society published a circular giving honorable mention to those who had contributed most to save the common cause on August 10, Danton's name headed it, coming before Robespierre's; and indeed whenever great patriots were cited, the name of Danton was the first or among the first. The assertion that Danton had moderated his principles in order to please public opinion was refuted by Chabot as a Brissotin slander.

Although Danton occasionally referred to the sacred duty of opposing the plotters who tried to "feuillantize" the Republic, he took no part in the persecution of those whom Chabot called the *"intrigaillons"* of the Gironde. Fauchet was expelled from the society, Brissot was expelled, Roland, Louvet, and Lanthenas were expelled—all without Danton's assistance.

———————◆———————

BUT all Danton's services in the cause of unity did not help him with the Gironde a hundred thousandth as much as a single outburst of irritation harmed him. When on September 29 Roland, Servan, and Danton, having been elected deputies, laid down their portfolios, Buzot replied with the motion that Roland and Servan be requested to retain their posts until the deputies should have become sufficiently acquainted with the various candidates to be able to appoint worthy successors; the omission of Danton's name was intended to be a slap in the face. But Danton instinctively knew Buzot's weak points and riposted: "No one is more ready to do Roland justice than I; but I say if Roland is invited Madame Roland should not be forgotten; it is common knowledge that Roland was not alone in charge of his portfolio. I for my part was alone." Some smiled, others muttered; there were some cries of indignation, but he at whom the blow was aimed sat white to the eyes and trembling: My goddess, and the dog dares . . . !

Each new day fed the hate of Buzot's goddess against the "criminal" Danton. She had a set mental picture of him; in her waking dreams she saw him as the "leader of the horde," a dagger in his fist, inciting his band of murderers with voice and gestures; but she who set her teeth and was chaste because she willed to be chaste, also heated her imagination with pictures of the vices in which this licentious man must surely be wallowing.

Danton himself did his part to spread the rumors of his dissipation outside the boudoir of the beautiful Manon, too. He had no intention of turning that lively flesh and blood of his into a wooden saint of the Republican Church. He laughed at locusts and wild honey and a hair shirt. They were not for him.

His bearing made him a "grand seigneur of sansculottism." He, in whose mouth "little son of a bitch" was a term of endearment, disdained now as ever to use the stilted language of Robespierre among friends. He talked naturally, he let himself go, and enjoyed compelling his companions by daring and still more daring assertions to put on a mask of virtue. When a few deputies were dining together, and the food and wine were good, Danton would begin to give rein to his fancy: Now your turn has come to enjoy life—yes, expensive restaurants, choice dishes, gold and silk brocades, and not least the women of your dreams—clicking his tongue—all these are by right the property of those who have seized power. Isn't that so? A Revolution after all is simply a battle with a division of the spoils among the victors after the victory! And he gloated over their embarrassment, their bewilderment, their trying to shrink away from him. Romme, who as former tutor of a Russian grand duke at the court of the Tzarina had not abandoned his principles of rigid morality, even in the proximity of the libertine Catherine, took the least trouble to conceal his disapproval: this was going too far! Then Danton, smacking his knee, burst out: "So you think I couldn't be a sansculotte with the rest if I chose to join the mob? Do you think I couldn't show my backside to the passers-by with the rest of them?" His companions preserved a confused silence.

Thus a belief in Danton's dissipation was harbored even by the well disposed. Those who had no measure for his greatness and were frightened by the demon in his breast confidently believed the gossip about his vices. Was it not natural that so vigorous a man should have to whore whole nights outside the marital bed? Perhaps the rumors were true; but, in spite of all the gossip, nobody knew what the true facts were and this fact in itself refuted the rumors.

Of many of those who were in the limelight something was
known, of some everything. Robespierre was inclosed in such a
magic circle of aloofness as far as women were concerned that
malicious rumor had it that he shared the principal characteristic of the oriental eunuch. He was satisfied with the adoration
of his landlady's daughter, the somewhat dull Eléonore Duplay,
and with the fulsome incense offered him by those hypocritical
revolutionary ladies, his *"dévotes."* Not everyone had the chiv-
alry of Danton's friend Merlin who, having wooed Mademoiselle
Charpentier of Metz in vain, married her after she had been
cruelly disfigured and blinded by smallpox. Marat lived in perfect bourgeois respectability with Simone Evrard, a peasant
girl from Saône-et-Loire who looked up to him with admiration,
although no registrar had sanctioned the union. Of all the passions that had inflamed the Duke of Orléans in a long and empty
life of dissipation, the one that consumed citizen Philippe Egalité for the brilliant and amiable Madame de Buffon was perhaps
the purest. The deputy Choudieu, on the other hand, a former
cadet of the Metz School of Artillery and now in his handsome
thirties, was in the bondage of the semi-professional Etta Palm,
who masqueraded under the name of "Baroness of Aelder," and
with her fine, tall figure had no difficulty in disguising her forty-
eight summers. She was probably a spy in Dutch pay but her
chief occupation was unquestionably catching men. Basire, too,
was at her feet as soon as he had entered her salon in the Rue
Favart; during the September massacres he wrote to her: "If
there is any consolation for your absence it is the thought that
the hideous scenes whose heartrending performance we had to
witness these last days did not offend your lovely eyes." And
later he begged her, "Strew a few flowers in my path." In the
Rue de Richelieu, Barère's mistress, the actress Demailli, lived
in a palace the magnificence of which was as much common talk
as the amorous adventures that Hérault de Séchelles continued
to pursue. Hérault, of whom André Chénier wrote mockingly,

> *Réputé Cicéron chez toute la basoche*
> *Et bel esprit chez les catins,*

would accompany his "favorite Sultana," Madame de Sainte-

Amaranthe, to the public gallery of the National Assembly un-
deterred by the fact that her apartment at 50 Palais-Egalité was
practically a disorderly house. Her husband, a lieutenant of
cavalry who had married the Marquise de Saint-Simon when
she was thirteen, had quickly run through her money, deserted
her and her two children, and eventually become a cab driver in
Madrid. Having been the mistress first of the Prince de Conti and
then of the Vicomte de Pons, at forty Madame de Sainte-Ama-
ranthe attracted the young and seductive Hérault, although it is
not known whether he enjoyed the favors of the mother only or
included those of her brilliant daughter Emilie. In any case Suzanne de Morancy, the wife of a provincial advocate, who had
run away from her husband disguised as a boy, also had claims
upon his heart and purse.

Vergniaud delighted in the blonde Julie Candeille, who sang at
the Opera and strove not without success for dramatic laurels,
while Marie-Joseph Chénier, poet and member of the Convention, allowed Madame de la Bouchardie to maltreat him at pleasure, although to all appearance she was stupid and unattractive;
very often the noise of blows and scolding in the bedroom of
these two drew the neighbors to the windows. More ardent were
the relations between Louvet and the "Lodoiska" of his novel,
who had married the jeweler Cholet of the Palais-Royal but
again flung herself passionately at the neck of her youthful admirer now that he had become famous.

Fabre d'Eglantine remained as inconstant as he had been during his strolling days, and continued to write sentimental lyrics
as well as exceedingly intimate love songs.

> *J'ai perdu ma brunette!*
> *J'ai perdu mon trésor!*
> *J'ai perdu ma Laurette!*
> *Et je respire encore!*

It was common knowledge that in spite of his fickle fancies he
lived with the citoyenne Caroline Rémy of the Théâtre-Mon-
tansier. Grim Vadier shared his bed and board with Jeanne Fer-
rand—a tall, strapping Provençal with dark and sparkling eyes;

but there were also times when the grayheaded disciple of
Voltaire joined his colleagues of the Convention, Voulland,
Amar, and Jullien as guest at Barère's secluded country house at
Clichy, where frivolous beauties enlivened the company the
more as the hours drew on.

Even of one of the youngest deputies, who was as noted for
the almost girlish grace of his features as for his close connection
with Robespierre—Louis-Antoine de Saint-Just—it was whispered that the attractive Madame Thorin, the wife of a notary
of Blérancourt, had followed him to Paris. Too intent on preserving the appearance of virtue to share his home with her, he
had settled her in the Rue Saint-Honoré at the Hotel des Tuileries, opposite the Jacobins', where he dined with her each evening in company with his secretary, Gateau.

But Danton—what was known of Danton? Nothing. What
woman's name was ever coupled with Danton's? None. The rumor that the Duke of Orléans had sent his mistress, the young,
blonde, slim, graceful Marguerite-Françoise de Buffon, to the
Minister of Justice to win with glances, whispers, and yet more,
if necessary, his support of her lover's ambitions, was a rumor
and nothing more.

———————◆———————

DANTON's financial methods as minister laid his morals more
open to the attack of his opponents than anything else. On August 28 the Legislative Assembly had placed two million livres
at the disposal of the Executive Council for extraordinary and
secret expenditure, so that each minister was responsible for
four hundred thousand livres. On October 6, before leaving office, Danton rendered an account of his *dépenses extraordi-
naires,* but Cambon, who was no supporter of Brissot and
counted every penny merely because he was honorary Treasurer
of the Republic, observed four days later in the Convention that
while twenty thousand livres had been paid to the Minister of
Finance, 65,882 to the Minister of War, twenty-three thousand
to the Minister of the Interior, and nothing to the Minister of
Marine, "the Minister of Justice has made three drafts of one

Saint-Just

hundred thousand livres—three hundred thousand livres in all—
so that this minister has spent about one sixth of the secret
fund." Cambon added morosely that the bookkeeping methods
of the Minister of Justice were completely unsystematic, that it
had been foolish to grant two million livres to the Executive
Council, that no further sums should be voted, and that each
minister should give an account of his secret expenditure to the
Council.

In his reply Danton commended Cambon's zeal for economy,
but pointed out that his suggestion had been anticipated in the
Executive Council. Extraordinary expenditure? Certainly, but
the circumstances had been extraordinary too: "The country
was in danger, and as I have often said in the council we were
responsible for freedom and we gave you a good account of this
freedom." But the expected applause failed to come. So he continued: "I claim that I have given a detailed account of my activities to the Executive Council; I do not believe that any one
questions my political actions." But the Assembly continued
silent, and Danton, remarking, "For the rest, I support Cambon's motion," left the tribune. A resolution was passed accordingly.

Certainly the Minister of Justice had been compelled during
the critical weeks to make heavier drafts on the Treasury than
all his colleagues together. That he outdid all five of them in activity did not help him now. For his enemies perceived in this the
unprotected spot the size of a limeleaf between his shoulder-
blades where their spears could enter. And how complacently
Roland presented his own accounts to the Assembly on October
18—every livre, every sou, every penny duly entered, and not
an "i" without its dot. His supporter Rebecqui significantly remarked: "I move that all ministers render their accounts in the
same form," while Monge, without mentioning Danton's name,
marked the difference between himself and the Minister of Justice: "I declare that I for my part have made no extraordinary or
secret expenditures."

Danton repressed his disgust at such hypocrisy and explained
that by a decree of the Legislative Assembly the Executive Coun-

cil was only responsible for the expenditures as a whole and that the public could not possibly be informed of a number of secret disbursements. "When the enemy took Verdun and dismay spread among the best and bravest citizens, the Assembly told us to spare nothing, and if necessary to fling money away in order to win back confidence and stimulate the whole of France! That is what we did. We were compelled to make extraordinary disbursements and I freely admit that for most of them we have no proper receipts. Everything was done in haste, everything happened precipitately; you wished the ministers to act jointly; we did, and that is our account." Hostile murmurings accompanied his words and did not cease even when he exclaimed: "If ten million more had been spent not one enemy would have escaped from French soil!"

Cambon supported him by holding that a public account could not be asked for secret expenditures; Roland somewhat edgedly asserted that he was far from deprecating the secret expenditure of his colleagues in the common cause; on the contrary, he approved it. Only he knew nothing about the report at the cabinet meeting because he had not been present. However, the meeting was about to pass to the order of the day when fresh oil was poured on the flames. Henri-Larivière, who concealed his hate of the Revolution under a thin Republican guise, spoke of waste of the people's money; Camus proposed a public prosecution of the ministers who had squandered the finances of the State; and the Convention resolved that the Executive Council must report within twenty-four hours on the accounts of its members.

The Council did not hurry. So it happened that when Danton on October 26 interfered on behalf of a spokesman of the Commune who had appeared at the bar and was called to order—who had interrupted? Danton?—one of the Brissotins snapped out: "I demand a statement from the Executive Council as to whether each minister has rendered an account of the sums disbursed for secret and extraordinary purposes, as recently decreed." Annoyed, Danton tried to strike at the hornets that buzzed maliciously around his head. He faced the meeting: "I support this motion and if necessary will account for my whole life. But I see that good citizens are being ruthlessly persecuted." Grumbling in the Assembly, applause in the galleries, cries of "This is a plot!" uproar, and the Convention cut Danton short by passing to the order of the day.

On November 7, however, Lebrun, Clavières, and Monge, as colleagues of Danton's, stated positively in a letter to the Assembly that two ministers had anticipated the decree of October 10. "The Ministers of Justice and of War, when about to relinquish their posts, suggested reporting on their secret expenditures to the Provisional Executive Council at the meeting of October 6. Both reported in detail on the utilization of funds and produced receipts and vouchers for the inspection of the members present."

Still this did not help much toward Danton's exoneration. Desmoulin's former private secretary, the corruptible Roch Marcandier, either at Roland's order or with his support scribbled a pamphlet called the *Histoire des hommes de proie*, in which Danton appeared as the leader of the September massacres, his pockets well filled with stolen wealth. Whenever Danton appeared on the tribune the deputies of the Gironde greeted their colleague with a loud chorus of "The account! The account!" His enemies were the more convinced that he had embezzled public monies and that large sums had found their way into his and his friends' pockets, because among the items enumerated by Danton there were thirty thousand livres paid to Santerre for pikes; what had the Minister of Justice to do with pikes?

But how about the incontrovertible testimony of Lebrun, Clavières, and Monge? Given under pressure of fear of Danton. The majority of the Assembly followed the lead of the Gironde. By November in a Paris which had witnessed during these weeks the abolition of the Extraordinary Court of August 17 and had long ago seen the guillotine again disappear from the Place du Carrousel, other people than Rolandist ministers had cause to feel themselves in danger. Buzot's appeal for a parliamentary militia, even unsupported by a resolution of the Convention, had drawn to the capital thousands and thousands of federates who

by no means favored a triumvirate; they ranged the streets—
mounted dragoons grasping their swords, headed by trumpeters
—Girondists of Marseilles and National Guards—and roared
their bloodthirsty "Off with their heads!"

> *La tête de Marat, Robespierre, et Danton*
> *Et de tous ceux qui les défendront—*
> *O gué!*

Yes, the heads of Marat, Robespierre, and Danton—and hurrah!

Danton was the less concerned over this persecution because
this winter he spent many weeks away from Paris.

When Dumouriez finally received a free hand for his favorite
plan, the campaign against the Austrian Netherlands, he carried
it through with determination and good fortune. On November 6
the Austrians took up a position before the gates of Mons and
were defeated near the village of Jemappes after seven hours of
desperate fighting; the general himself attacked at the head of
hussars and chasseurs to the sound of the *Marseillaise;* a true
Republican victory with singing of *"Ça ira"* and shouts of
"Vive la liberté!" opened Belgium to the French as far as the
Meuse. A week later Dumouriez entered Brussels in triumph.
Ghent, Liége, Namur, and Antwerp fell like ripe fruits.

But while Paris was jubilant and Minister Lebrun baptized
his youngest daughter Jemappes-Dumouriez, dissension arose
between the victorious general and the new Minister of War.
When Servan, ill and weak, resigned in October, Roland's protégé Jean-Nicolas Pache succeeded him on Roland's recom-
mendation. No sooner was he in office than he sided with the
Mountain. Taciturn, cold, unemotional, and aloof, this ex-tutor
exacted respect and proceeded first of all to thoroughly repub-
licanize his department. Any officials whose hatred for the new
conditions had led them to sabotage the system and who had

made the war ministry a stronghold of the counterrevolution were dismissed without notice. In their place efficient officers devoted to the Revolution and tried Jacobins took office. If Brigadier General Meusnier was the minister's right hand in military affairs, Jean-Henri Hassenfratz, the quartermaster general, was only second to him in influence; a distinguished chemist and member of the revolutionary Commune of August 10, he took pleasure in sansculotte manners. On the door of his office hung a sign: *"Ici on se tutoie!"*

The chief objection the new men had to Dumouriez was based on his method of provisioning the army. A private company, the Société de Masson-d'Espagnac, supplied the army with horses, saddles, transport, forage, rations, shirts, boots, and uniforms— the profits ran into millions and the chief beneficiary was the Abbé Marc-René Sahuguet d'Espagnac, who had long read the Stock Exchange lists more proficiently and with more pleasure than his breviary. Having sided with the Third Estate before the fall of the Bastille, become a zealous member of the Jacobin Club and a welcome guest at the banquets of Hérault de Séchelles, and gotten acquainted through the latter, or possibly through Desmoulins, with Danton, too, he had the necessary connections to make war a profitable undertaking. Dumouriez was satisfied with him; the firm took the money but it delivered the goods, and the general was furious when on November 5 a purchasing board was set up by the gentlemen in Paris which in the future was to have entire charge of army supplies—a conflict between the free play of economic forces and the principle of regulation. When the Convention called the Abbé, together with the intendant general and the paymaster general of Dumouriez' army, to account, a letter of Westermann's was read in the Assembly on November 30 openly accusing the War Office of the delay in the advance, since supplies were falling off and even the men's pay did not arrive on time. Uncertain whom to believe, the meeting resolved on the immediate despatch to Belgium of five of its members—Camus, Danton, Dubois-Crancé, Gossuin, and Delacroix.

Dubois never left Paris; Camus and Gossuin set out on the

thirtieth, while Danton and Delacroix took the road to Saint-Quentin on the evening of December 1, joining their colleagues in Belgium. A countryman of Danton's from Arcis, the jurist Ludot, deputy delegate for the Department of the Aube, was secretary of the commission.

Although abuses in the army supplies with their evil consequences did not allow the commissioners much leisure, they were nevertheless soon compelled to attend to political problems as well. The conquest of Belgium brought France face to face with the difficult question of what to do next. Jemappes had given a new impetus to the idea of a war of liberation, a war for the overthrow of all the tyrants of the earth, a war for a world republic and lasting peace! Grégoire passionately shouted the dawn of a new age: "Europe will know no more fortresses, frontiers, or foreign nations." Hérault de Séchelles saw in a vision the throne of freedom erected on Mont Blanc, and Brissot rejoiced over a "life-and-death war between freedom and tyranny": *Novus rerum nascitur ordo!* On November 19 the Convention unanimously resolved in the name of the French nation to render brotherly help to all nations wishing to win back their liberty. This decree was to be translated into every language.

Yet when General Dumouriez informed the Belgians by proclamation from the frontier: "We are entering your territory to assist you in planting the tree of freedom," he got but slight response. No other spot on earth had a clergy nearly as powerful and opulent as the Austrian Netherlands; the cathedral chapters, the abbeys, and monasteries were the real masters of the country. The bulk of the population was wrapped in ignorance and pietism and under the guiding clerical influence held unswervingly to the old forms, the old customs, and the old privileges; the slogans of liberty, equality, and fraternity failed utterly to penetrate their thick skulls. True, a movement of independence against the House of Hapsburg had recently stirred the country; but this struggle had been directed against the anticlerical reforms of Joseph II and was a revolution aimed at preserving the status quo. The Belgians were content to have the Austrians swept from the country by the French broom; but they would have nothing to do with the French Constitution and became altogether unruly when the liberators started to urge their assignats upon the liberated at their face value and to permit them to share the war costs by making contributions. The restless and the open-minded in the population might unite in societies and clubs of liberty after the Paris fashion, but the vast majority declared at the elections their preference for autonomous bodies: the supremacy of the Church, undemocratic constitutions for towns and provinces: this was their tradition and they declined to surrender it.

Such resistance demanded resolute measures. To keep the Belgians under French control against their will meant an infraction of one of the most sacred principles of the Constituent Assembly: No conquests! To leave the Belgians to themselves would certainly mean that Belgium would not be a bulwark of liberty at the gates of France. But the Republic needed above everything security for its development; so since necessity knows no law, why not model Belgium after the French system even without the consent of its inhabitants? As always the war followed its own laws, and, once started, things developed automatically. It was only fair that the war should be self-supporting, that the population of a liberated country should pay for its liberation. And why should the fabulous possessions of the Belgian clergy escape the fate which overtook church property in France?

The fact that the watchword of a crusade for liberty stirred up street and camp alike made Danton adopt it. Presiding at the Jacobins', he welcomed Dumouriez on October 14 with the words: "May the people's pike break the scepter of kings, and crowns fall before the red cap with which the society has decorated you." When at the end of October a deputation from Savoy paraded in the same hall with warlike music and a banner inscribed "World Republic" and "To the French people, the liberators of the nations, from the grateful people of Savoy," Danton received them with the hope that the two nations would soon be one. Four weeks later the Convention resolved on the union of Savoy with France and Danton exclaimed with delight: "Assuredly the French people will always support us, if we make similar conquests for them." When someone interrupted "No conquests!" he caught himself quickly: "Conquests of reason; my meaning was clear."

Once arrived in Belgium Danton was overcome by a kind of ecstasy. Externally the representatives of the Convention appeared in the army as citizens among citizens, and had not yet adopted the costume designed for them by David, consisting of blue coat, yellow leather breeches, riding boots, round hat with tricolor cockade, tricolor sash, and sword with black hangings. Yet they were endowed with the highest powers. Danton and his colleagues had the right of deposing, replacing, and arresting at will, and even the commander in chief was nothing compared with them.

And what a wealth of new impressions they got! The first were unpleasant: the roads over which they drove were thronged with volunteers who, their terms expired, were hastening home without concerning themselves about the rest of the war. There was a serious shortage of uniforms and rations for the troops, but at the same time much confidence and optimism. At Liége Danton saw ragged soldiers—genuinely barefoot and pantless—kiss the muzzle of a twenty-four-pounder which had just arrived because they saw in it a pledge of victory. To be in the midst of this ferment, under the shadow of the victorious tricolor, conversing with Republican generals, and surrounded by the soldiers of liberty—and he himself the first! Way! Way for the commissioner of the Convention! Danton seemed to breathe the air of a new day. His lungs expanded and his chest swelled more aggressively than before.

Did he prize those days, when he felt as if he could seize the spirit of history itself by the coat tails, as much as Paris did —Paris which celebrated through the nights while women's screams drowned the gurgling of wine into glasses? At any rate his thoughts often turned homeward. A letter from the Cour du Commerce arrived, and he seized a pen: "The courier who brought word from you, dearest Gabrielle, is leaving this moment, and I have only a second to let you know"—his heart grew warm—"what a joy it was to receive your letter." Gabrielle, and by a quick association of thoughts: Arcis, home, garden, meadow, refuge! "Don't forget to see to sending my trees to Arcis"—he heard the elms rustling and saw the trees around old Charpentier's country home near Paris—"and to have your father hasten the furnishing of his house at Sèvres." When could he stretch out in the grass again, relaxed and lazy, with Gabrielle and the children? "Kiss my little Danton a thousand times! Tell him that his father will try not to be away long."

There were occasions, too, when he showed himself generous like a sated lion. In one of the towns of occupied Belgium an émigré who had neglected to escape in time awaited with trepidation the moment of discovery: I am Rouget de l'Isle, you know me; help me! As head of the army you have influence! The captain was willing and appealed to Camus; but the rigid Jansenist shook his head angrily. As a last resource Danton was appealed to. Rouget de l'Isle? Danton gazed reflectively, while the other talked, at the lips which first formed the words of the *Marseillaise* and now perhaps were forming a blessing on Louis Capet; he guessed the struggle it must cost the young idealist to come as a petitioner before the ill-reputed tribune. At length: "Very well; but why did you go to the priests first? Why not go directly to the Septembrists?" And he wrote out the passport.

Meanwhile at Namur, Danton's friend Delacroix, likewise in cheerful mood, knocked at the bishop's door and greeted the venerable dotard with a matter of fact: "Monsieur, we have come to give you permission to marry." Liége and Aix were also in Danton and Delacroix' sphere of activity. Liége was a royal bishopric belonging to the Holy Roman Empire, not to the Austrian Netherlands, while Aix was a free city of the Empire. Here an ancient, fossilized patrician rule had persisted through the centuries, yet when the French entered on December 16, the burgomaster pointed—albeit in vain—to the *"gouvernement libre, purement démocratique et populaire"* of the city. On January 3, 1793, General Dampierre took away the old powers, grand and petty council, and all the rest.

The same day the coaches with the four commissioners of the Convention jolted over the last section of the narrow, rutted road from Liége to Aix and rolled through the city gates. Danton's keen eyes noted the signs of economic decay—crowds of frightened yet insolent beggars hanging around, and piles of winter refuse before the doors. He stood reflectively in the square where the pillar of shame had once stood—a monument of disgrace for the Protestant leader in the municipal religious wars two hundred years earlier and hence for every Protestant. The French had overturned it and planted a tree of freedom on the spot, surmounted by a red Jacobin cap. He went into the cathedral, too, and perhaps plumped himself down irreverently on the clumsy marble throne on which so many German emperors had received crown, scepter, and orb.

When he ran across young Franz Dautzenberg, editor of the *Aachener Zuschauer* and one of the Rhenish revolutionary enthusiasts and friends of France, Danton tested his political pulse with the brusque remark: "This must be no milk and honey revolution, but blood, damn it, as in Paris." Dautzenberg, not at a loss, answered: "But Aix has a different climate." Whereat Danton replied: "Then the temperature must be raised."

Things seemed easier to the citizens of Aix when the Convention granted them sixty thousand livres in compensation for plundering by the French troops.

When Danton had the first issue of the *Aachener Zuschauer* for the new year translated, he learned from it of the public jubilation which greeted the erection of a bigger tree of freedom on the Market Square on New Year's Eve, and a speech by General Dampierre. He also saw tricolor cockades on hats, and on January 8 witnessed the foundation of a Jacobin Club. If he was pleasantly stirred by the inclination of the people of Aix for the French Republic, the friendship of the people of Liége for France delighted him still more. The citizens of this great industrial city of the Meuse and the coal-mining region—and indeed those of the entire bishopric—differed fundamentally from the rest of the Belgians; they were liberal and progressive and conscious of their French blood.

The report of the commissioners on the Belgian question handed in at Paris by Camus on December 11 was partly a reflection of Danton's impressions at Liége. After four days' deliberation the Executive Council allowed itself to be convinced; and on December 15, Cambon, holding Belgium up as an example, expressed to the Convention the principles of the inexorable revolutionary war and the revolutionary tutelage of France over the nations not yet ripe for liberty. "If the nations to whom the armies of the Republic carry liberty lack the experience necessary to conquer their rights, we must act as a revolutionary power and destroy the old regime holding them in slavery." And more. "It must be our first care to confiscate as indemnity for the costs of war the property of our enemies, of the Government and rulers, their supporters and partisans, their voluntary satellites, lay communities, and all the servants of tyranny." And again: "The nations who want to retain their privileged castes must be told, 'You are our enemies!' They will be treated as enemies if they do not desire liberty and equality." Volleys of applause greeted these decisive sentences.

Salvos of applause saluted the decree—unanimously adopted —which gave teeth and claws to the resolution of November 19.

In the countries occupied by the armies of the French Republic the generals will forthwith proclaim, in the name of the French nation:

The abolition of the existing taxes and dues, tithes, feudal rights, forced labor, serfdom, hunting privileges, aristocracy, and all privileges in general.

They will explain to the people that they are bringing peace, help, fraternity, liberty, and equality.

They will proclaim the sovereignty of the people and the abolition of all existing authorities and will forthwith summon the people to elect and establish a provisional administration by caucus.

But there was visible the cloven hoof of the revolutionary dictatorship:

The Executive Council will appoint national commissioners who will forthwith proceed abroad to come to an agreement with the provisional administrations, elected by the people, on the regulations for common defense, and the means for clothing and rationing the armies of the Republic, and for meeting the expenses of the troops.

No one perceived more clearly than Danton, author of this decree, that it encompassed the annexation of Belgium as neatly as the shell incloses a nut.

W<small>HAT</small> France did with Belgium concerned a third power—England.

The Court of St. James's, as always, watched the Revolution attentively but inactively. The country whose capitalism was just reaching its adolescent stage required peace in order to quietly capture the markets of the world; and from this point of view the Revolution in Paris seemed a providential gift in two respects. The more France was weakened, paralyzed, and bled by internal disorders, the healthier became the economic power of England. "When I look at the map of Europe," an honorable member of the House of Commons gloated, "I see an empty spot which was once called France." For the first time faces grew longer in London when the Republic rebounded from its defeats; the guns of Jemappes awakened no pleasant echo on the Thames.

Dissatisfaction grew when the Revolution took more powerful strides and unfolded the banner of a war of propaganda: What was the meaning of all this? Burke who, like a prophet of old, had for years been calling down fire and brimstone on revolutionary Paris, began to grumble: "Paris will not rest until she has made a republic of the universe. Sword in hand she is attempting to convert the nations by force to the Declaration of the Rights of Man as Mohammed converted to the Koran." An insular position was no protection against infectious ideas.

It was the French designs on Belgium which produced the radical change in the British attitude. Ever since the extinction of the House of Burgundy, three hundred years before, it had been a fundamental article of British policy never to allow the French to seize Brabant, and never to suffer a rival on the other side of the Channel; the French ambassador at St. James's, Chauvelin, showed keen judgment when he remarked in October, 1792: "Pitt seems resolved to declare war sooner than allow us to complete the annexation of Brabant without interference. He believes that we intend some day to annex Belgium to the French Republic. He further believes that we intend to foment a revolution in Holland and, by expansion, to get a control over the sea which would condemn England forever to impotence or at least to a very decided inferiority." The French fleet in Antwerp Harbor? Unthinkable for any Englishman! So when the Convention opened the Schelde which had been closed to shipping since the peace of Utrecht and began to think of revolutionizing Belgium, England cocked the pistol, expecting that the next stroke would be dealt at Holland. The decree of December 15, by paving the way for the annexation of Belgium, made war with England inevitable.

The war that Danton hoped to avoid! In 1791 he had visited London; he spoke English and his library contained twenty-three volumes of Adam Smith, Shakespeare in eight volumes, Johnson in seven, Pope in six, eight years of the *Spectator*, Richardson's *Clarissa*, and Robertson's *History of America* and *History of Scotland* in the original, and even English translations of Don Quixote, Plutarch, and Virgil. But Danton was too thorough, too full-blooded a Frenchman, to be able to understand what appeared to the British nation the vital question on the Continent. Still less could he comprehend that with the problem of Belgium, Antwerp, and Holland, there began the great combat between the two bourgeois states of Europe, with the markets of the world for stake.

But above all, he overestimated the forces in England favorable to France. At times easily inclined to believe what suited his plans, he heard with satisfaction the report of his London agent that England was on the eve of a revolution and that the storming of the Bastille would soon be followed by the storming of the Tower. Certainly the French Revolution had been welcomed by the English democrats. In London, Manchester, Birmingham, Dublin, and Belfast, everywhere, societies, unions, and clubs were formed which repeatedly expressed their sympathy with the new order in France by toasts at banquets, addresses to the National Assembly at Paris, and by sending deputations to the bar of the Convention. Toward the end of November, indeed, the Constitutional Society of London pledged itself to provide a thousand pairs of shoes weekly for the soldiers of liberty at Calais.

As a living example of such generous sentiments Danton had Thomas Paine in mind. Although Paine could not speak even the worst French, he was a member of the Convention; as he had once defended American independence against his countrymen, so now he championed the French Revolution amongst them; his *Rights of Man* was a salute to the present, to the epoch when mankind was reaching man's estate and putting on the *toga virilis*. It was an appeal for a future of disarmament and world peace. Danton failed to appreciate the fact that Paine was speaking for only a minority of his countrymen. He did not grasp how deeply wounded was the national pride of even the British Left when Grégoire, the president of the Convention, portrayed to a deputation of British democrats the possibility that when the French phalanxes were victorious on the Rhine, the Schelde, the Var, and the Isère, they might cross the Channel to champion British democracy! He even built air castles and imagined how, if war did break out in spite of everything, the people of England would revolt against their Government.

But the King's fate, too, affected the relations between France and England.

Around the Temple where the Bourbon family were kept imprisoned, the people raged, clamoring to see the fallen rulers brought to justice. The papers discovered after the fall of the Tuileries and those found in the so-called "Iron Safe" left no shadow of doubt of Louis' guilt. In 1790, 1791, and 1792 he had continuously instigated foreign governments to bring the French to reason by force of arms; and during the war he had attempted to paralyze the national defense and to bring about the defeat of France; if ever there had been a case of high treason, it was this.

Since the question of law did not matter, the question of Louis Capet's fate was a purely political one. Before the end of August the Jacobins voiced the desire that the royal couple should stand trial before the Convention met—if it was the aim of the Revolution to give a great example, to intimidate the Royalists, and to stagger Europe, then the first weeks after the Second Revolution were indeed the most favorable for the trial. As instead the Gironde irresolutely and perplexedly postponed the trial again and again, Louis' adherents had food for many hopes of rescue.

At the end of October Théodore de Lameth ventured back to Paris from exile, mounted the two storeys in the Cour du Commerce and rang the bell. Madame Gabrielle—young, pretty, sweet mannered, as he noted hurriedly—conducted him to Danton. "Oh, where have you come from?" "From London." "You must be mad. Don't you know the penalty is death?" "I know," Lameth smiled, and he plunged directly into the attempt to soften Danton's heart for the King, his virtue, his kindness. . . . Danton interrupted him roughly. "Often weakness seems to be virtue and kindness." But Lameth would not give up and dared to propose the abduction of the King from the Temple. Danton, preferring not to hear this suggestion, went on to say that he thought it wise to remove the King from his present position. "I shall use my best skill and courage to do what I can to this end; I will run the risk if I see any chance of success; but if I see that there is no hope, then, I tell you candidly, I shall be among those who cast their vote against him, for I do not wish my head to fall with his." Lameth, surprised, asked: "Why the last?" "In order to be frank," Danton concluded with emphasis, and Lameth disappeared.

If this dialogue, as Lameth recorded it word for word and sentence for sentence decades later, corresponded even approximately to the facts, then Danton did not allow himself to be so carried away by compassion for a guilty man as to make rash promises in this important political question. Political considerations alone weighed with him: considerations that included the question of England's attitude. In September Chauvelin addressed a report to Lebrun, which Danton doubtless read, saying that even the warmest adherents of the Revolution would regard the execution of the King as disastrous to the cause of freedom. Miles, an Englishman who was very much in favor of an understanding with France, made it clear that the safety of Louis and his family must be assured before Great Britain could recognize the French Republic. Danton's agent Noël, too, reported: "There is no chance of resuming relations with England unless the royal family is spared," and he considered recognition of this so important that he despatched Benoît to Paris with the sole object of emphatically informing those in power of it. This was at the end of October. It may well be that on that day Benoît handed the doorknob to Lameth at Danton's, so that the émigré found the tribune in a reflective and responsive mood as far as the fate of the Bourbons was concerned.

Whether Danton acted in accord with his promise, and what he did Lameth never discovered. When on November 6 Valazé reported to the Convention on Louis' misdeeds, and opinions were divided as to whether the report was to be printed immediately or first supplemented by further documents, Danton expressed himself in favor of printing, and made some general observations. If kings were infallible the people were, too. Every contract must be reciprocal. If the former King had wished to violate, betray, and destroy the French nation, eternal justice demanded his condemnation. Justice, yes; but as to the political expediency, Danton remained silent. But the Convention applauded the vigor of his speech.

When the commissioners at Aix were instructed to despatch one of their number to report at Paris, and when on January 12 Danton left Liége accompanied by Delacroix, a year of momentous decisions had begun. The course of events in Belgium necessitated a policy which meant war with England. Therewith considerations for Louis' safety ended, and Danton, on the road, reading hastily through the Capet trial in the latest issues of the *Moniteur,* once more became fully conscious of the gravity of sending the last King to the scaffold. It meant digging a ditch filled with blood over which no bridge led back to the past; it also meant driving the nation forward relentlessly, always forward! A great example, Delacroix, an historic hour, an event of European importance!

But when on Wednesday, January 16, Danton entered the Manège, it was no vote on the King's sentence that he broke in on, but a lively discussion of a question concerning the theater. He could hardly believe his ears. The Commune had banned Laya's *Ami des lois* because, for the last fortnight, its counter-revolutionary sallies had been applauded by a Royalist pit at the Théâtre de la Nation. Yesterday, however, the public had shouted for the play; when Santerre appeared at the head of armed forces he was jeered at and ridiculed as "General Beer-froth." At the moment the Assembly was debating that subject, with the old conflict between Commune and National Assembly in the background. It was Guadet who belled the cat: "The Commune has arrogated to itself the power of legislating, it has got to be stopped at the beginning. Today it bans plays, to-morrow it will ban pamphlets." Such were the trivialities and petty quarrels which exercised the Assembly at this hour! And Danton sneered: "I thought, citizens, that you were about to enact a tragedy with the whole of Europe as spectator; I thought that today you would have made a tyrant's head fall, and I find you busy with a wretched farce."

People lean forward in the galleries. Look, Danton is back! The private spectators' gallery in the body of the hall is filled with ladies in their finest clothes, wearing tricolor ribbons and thirsting for excitement. Their friends among the deputies send them ices, oranges, and liqueurs from the members' buffet; these ladies too murmur contentedly: Ah, Danton!

The discussion continues in circles. Have any deputies been threatened? Is the Convention debating with the knife at its throat? Have the town barriers been closed? What of the guns at Saint-Denis? The Gironde and the Mountain come to blows, the ladies in the gallery, it seems, will get their money's worth—until Danton calls the Assembly back to the one matter of vital importance.

The Gironde, still unhappy about the King's trial, makes a new attack. During the last sessions the King's guilt has been admitted, and the appeal to the people rejected. Now Lanjuinais demands a two-thirds majority for the verdict. Danton briefly overrules the appeal: "If a simple majority vote is enough to decide the fate of the entire nation and to establish the Republic, I am surprised that other forms are demanded to settle the fate of a single person and a conspirator at that."

At eight in the evening the vote is taken by roll call on the question: which penalty has Louis, formerly King of France, incurred? The voting begins with the Department of the Haute-Garonne. Mailhe: Death; Delmas: Death; Projean: Death; other suggestions: imprisonment, banishment; some give elaborate explanations, others speak but two monosyllables: *La mort!*

Robespierre, heading the Paris deputies, introduces a long speech by deprecating many words on a plain issue and winds up: "I vote for death." Danton is short and concise as usual: "I am not one of those statesmen who are ignorant that there can be no negotiating with tyrants, who do not know that kings must be hit over the head, that the kings of Europe will make concessions only at the point of the sword. I vote for the death of the tyrant."

Collot d'Herbois, Billaud-Varenne, Desmoulins, Legendre, Sergent, Robert, Fréron, and Fabre d'Eglantine—all follow his lead. Attention increases when the citizen Egalité, former Duke of Orléans, begins to speak. "Following only the call of duty, and convinced that all those who have infringed or shall infringe the sovereignty of the people deserve the death penalty, I vote for death."

Thursday evening, after an exhausting sitting of thirty-six hours, Vergniaud, amid profound silence, announces the result: 387 in favor of death, 334 for imprisonment, banishment, or a conditional death penalty. "I declare in the name of the National Convention that Louis Capet is sentenced to death!"

On the evening of the nineteenth another vote by name is taken on the question of postponing execution. Three hundred and ten deputies are for it; Danton's "No" lands like lead on the scale which dips with 380 "No's."

On Monday, January 21, 1793, a misty, rainy morning, the guillotine is erected for the first time in the Place de la Révolution close to the base on which until now the statue of Louis XV has proudly stood. Here, at 10: 24, while the drums beat and ten thousand throats shout a fanatical *"Vive la République!"* the anointed head of His Majesty King Louis XVI falls.

NONE realized more clearly than Danton the momentous significance of this act, when he cried ten days later to the Convention: "You have declared war on the kings; you have flung down your gage and this gage was the head of a tyrant!"

There were results. They poured forth like water through opened sluices. England expelled the French ambassador; Naples, ruled by a sister of Marie-Antoinette, joined the coalition; in Spain Godoy, fresh from the Queen's bed and hating the Revolution, took the reins of government.

Republic, the ring is closing! Republic defend yourself!

War, war, war has become the element of the Revolution.

Only this was needed to call up in Danton all that nationalist energy which drove the country forward in September. He felt himself as never before at the height of his energy and intellectual power. He shook his revolutionary lion's name.

What would have been braggadocio at another time in any other man was sincerity here and in Danton. On January 16 the president had reported the receipt of a letter from the Spanish ambassador; Danton sensed interference in the King's trial—in the private affairs of the nation. "If every one were of my opinion war would at once be declared on Spain. . . . It is an outrage to refuse to recognize our Republic and to attempt to dictate its laws! . . . There is perhaps no harm in listening to this ambassador, but I trust that the president's answer may be worthy of the people whose instrument he is. I trust he will reply that the victors of Jemappes will not betray the glory they have won and that the strength which has given them victory before will aid them to stamp out all the kings of Europe who conspire against us!"

Five days later he was speaking on the Belgian question in the Convention: "Fear nothing from the world! We have seen the soldiers of France; each one thinks himself worth two hundred

slaves. Such is the resolution and the Republican spirit of the
army that if we told three hundred men, 'You must perish or
march on Vienna!' they would reply, 'We will march to death
or to Vienna.' "

On January 22 Delacroix read his report on Belgium; and a
deputation from Mons asked in the name of the Province of
Hainaut for admission into the Republic as the eighty-fifth department. The meeting of the last day of January began with
the reading of a letter from the mayor of Liége to General Mi-
randa. At the name of Liége, Danton pricked up his ears; aha,
9,660 out of 9,700 voters had declared for union with France;
in the whole district of Liége, in the cities of Verviers, Visé,
Dinant, Waremme, and in the country parishes similar votes
would be recorded without French interference. But in other
districts only the clubs clamored for incorporation, although
under the threatening eyes of the French authorities nobody
ventured to vote against it. A bad farce.

Danton, however, thinking only of the Liégois' genuine
friendship for the French and firmly resolved that the annexation of Belgium was a political necessity, was induced to act
more rapidly by the letter he had heard read. He at once demanded "in the name of the commissioners of the Convention in
Belgium" a decree on the union of the former bishopric with
France similar to that on the "former duchy of Nice"—"I ask
nothing of your enthusiasm, but everything of your reflection,
all in the interest of the French Republic." It was an impossible
policy for a great nation to present liberty to another nation, together with the necessary constitution and organization, and
then leave it to its own devices! Justice and humanity demanded
this union; the man in the street and the Belgian peasantry
wished it. . . . On it depended the triumph of freedom in Belgium proper; for the supporters of the old regime were cunning
enough to pretend that France did not want annexation. The
Austrian faction found adherents in Brussels only because the
defeatists doubted that annexation would come about. . . . The
news of the annexation of Liége would evoke similar petitions
from every part of Belgium. . . . "Then French laws will be in-

troduced, then the soil of liberty will be purged of malcontent priests and aristocrats, and after this purge we shall be richer in men and richer in resources; we shall be true Republicans, Europe will see that our principles are not illusions."

England? Danton made a vague gesture. In England things must take their own course; nothing more could be lost there. Only ten minutes earlier Lasource had spoken of "our impending war with England" as though it were a mathematical certainty, and after all, with her eleven million inhabitants and a navy hardly superior to the French, England was not yet a world power. Perhaps Danton shared Brissot's opinion that England intended to pursue the policy Austria had attempted the year before; a policy of postponement, to gain time to complete her armaments and declare war at the psychological moment. Better to get in the first blow. He trusted in the possibility of intimidating Britain by a series of rapid blows—the occupation of Holland, and the seizure of the Dutch navy. He believed in the magic force of accomplished facts; and a simple phrase about England—"liberty will rule in that country, too"—revealed the hope that the people of the United Kingdom would refuse to follow their rulers.

Danton did not despair when the next day the Convention declared war on England. This was inevitable. Who suspected that this war would rage twenty years, who suspected what it would devour!

But as always when Danton appeared to be moved only by wild passion, he was curbed by cool deliberation. Almost a year ago, in February, 1792, Dumouriez, in working out his plan of campaign, had assigned to France a defensive position wherever mountains, seas, or great rivers formed natural barriers, and had planned attacks as far as the Rhine to the north and as far as the Alps to the south. In November, however, Talleyrand in a memorandum to Lebrun from London cautioned him against a policy of annexation and desires for hegemony which were more suitable for an absolute monarchy than a republic. The territory of France was big enough for its population and for the great economic rise which must inevitably be stimulated by

the genius of freedom. Accordingly he recommended an alliance
with Savoy, Belgium, and Liége for mutual defense, and concentration chiefly on the development of economic resources:
"After a political revolution, there must be an economic revolution."

Danton had in mind the advice of both Dumouriez and Talleyrand when, on January 31, he outlined his doctrine of natural
frontiers: "The frontiers of France are marked by nature; we
shall reach them at four points; the Rhine, the Ocean, the Alps,
and the Pyrenees. These must be the borders of our Republic,
and no power on earth shall prevent us from reaching them."

But these words were more than a trumpet call and signal to
attack. They were the definite surrender of the mirage of an
endless war of propaganda. The word "frontier" was emphasized at least as much as the word "natural." Wise limitation
would prevent stabbing the air and wasting the resources of the
Republic.

The natural frontiers and stop! A French Republic in the
European system of states, strong, flourishing, and peacefully
devoting her forces to the exploitation of her internal wealth—
such was Danton's dream.

———————◆———————

UNITY at home was more necessary than ever. The King's
execution had been a challenge to the world. Soon all Europe
would be in arms against the Republic. A feeling of overwhelming responsibility drew from the leaders the command: Close
the ranks! Not only did a mystical misanthrope of the Gironde
like Bancal des Issarts preach that the time had come to forget
selfishness, hate, and every form of discord—"A general call
of friendship and fraternity must resound throughout the length
and breadth of France!"—but Saint-Just, that reservoir of revolutionary energy, recognized the necessity of solidarity: "Forget
yourselves! The Revolution stands between a triumphal arch
and a rock which would wreck us all. You must remain undi-
vided, in your own interest, in spite of all differences of opinion.
The tyrants permit no differences between us. We must conquer
or perish together."

Still more Danton felt it his duty to achieve harmony between opponents and create an unbroken revolutionary front. The task was the more attractive because during the King's trial the Gironde had demonstrated its lack of internal cohesion. Many had voted first for imprisonment and then for postponement of the death sentence; some of the leaders, like Buzot, Brissot, Vergniaud, Pétion, and Lanthenas had been for a conditional death sentence; others like Barbaroux, Boyer-Fonfrède, Carra, Chambon, Gensonné, Isnard, Lasource, and Rebecqui had joined the Mountain and voted simply for death.

On the afternoon of January 20 a former member of the King's guard, Deparis, ran his sword through a deputy in a restaurant of the Palais-Egalité, exclaiming: You voted for the death of the King! The murderer escaped, and the wounded man, Lepelletier de Saint-Fargeau, died within a few hours. The descendant of one of the wealthiest and most respected families of magistrates, himself elected president of the Paris Court of Justice in 1785, he had slipped into the revolutionary movement together with his friend, Hérault de Séchelles. He was a pure and selfless character; only envy attributed to him the words: "With an income of six hundred thousand livres, a man must be either at Coblenz or at the summit of the Mountain."

A most impressive funeral was prepared by the Republic for its martyr. David had charge of this day, January 24. The base of the statue of Louis XIV on the Place des Piques was draped in black; a scaffolding was erected on it, on which the body was laid out, naked to the loins, with the mortal wound visible to all. At noon the whole Convention approached under a pall of deep silence; Vergniaud ascended the structure and pressed a wreath of oak leaves and immortelles on the brow of the murdered man. Muffled trumpets sounded and a long procession moved to the Pantheon where by resolution of the Convention, Lepelletier was to be buried with honor. Fabre d'Eglantine alone broke from the ranks once on the way to ask a promising-looking lady for her address.

Three days previously this murder had caused the wildest excitement in the Convention. The blood rushed to the deputies' heads faster than usual; the air was full of accusations, charges, and denunciations; plots were scented; there was clamor for extraordinary measures, for reconstituting the Committee of Defense, and for searches, searches.

Meanwhile Barère poured oil on the troubled waters. At the grave of the victim passion must be stilled. Here, if anywhere, men should be friends and brothers. Solidarity! Robespierre said, too, but behind his glasses his eyes remained cold: "The harmony which is our right is not that of individuals, but of principles." Pétion complained: "How many men there are in this Assembly who suspect and detest each other and yet would feel nothing but esteem if they only knew each other better. I venture to assert that men who appear entirely opposed to each other are equally desirous of Freedom."

Pétion's very act of speaking was like a wind driving on fire. But then Danton began; and his love for the Republic found expression in words like these: "Let us swear upon this grave to serve the cause of freedom, not to desert our posts until we have given the people a constitution, or die under the daggers of the assassins."

After the emotional exordium there came some skilled strategy. In order to assure himself of firm support, Danton sided clearly and unequivocally with the Mountain. While admitting Roland's good intentions, he questioned the possibility of his continuing to be minister; for ever since the Commune had wished to arrest Roland, he had taken a purely pessimistic view of things in Paris, and stirred up against it the hate of the departments. "But Paris is the city of all the departments; it is the City of Light."

Next came an appeal to the hearts of the Gironde: "I am free of all passion; I know how to combine recklessness with the equanimity proper in a legislator, elected by the people. . . . I do not thirst for revenge, because I do not need it." He added immediate proof, declining absolutely to entertain the idea of the right of search, which sent cold shivers down the backs of many Girondists. The Committee of Defense might be granted increased powers, nothing more!

The keynote of his speech: "Let us direct all our resolution

and all our energies to the war! We want to wage war against
Europe, not against ourselves." As minister he had always
worked for the cause of unity: "I beseech you, Pétion, I beseech
you, Brissot, I beseech you all, for I would finally have you know
me; I beseech you all for I wish finally to be known as I am."

And the conclusion was powerful, sincere, convincing: "I shall
always have only one passion, to die for my country. May
Heaven grant me the fate of the citizen whose loss we deplore
today!"

Since Roland unexpectedly resigned the next day, one obstacle
in the way of a reconciliation seemed to have been removed.
Danton put out a feeler and began to negotiate with Vergniaud.
The latter knew that some of his friends agreed with the opinion
of Danton held by young Géraud who wrote from Paris, where
he was studying, to his people, a wealthy family at Bordeaux:
"Danton is accused of domestic vices, a disreputable private
life, and numerous debts, but on the other hand he is admired
as a statesman of great political ability, possessing a strong,
courageous mind, irresistible eloquence, prudence, and far-
sightedness. . . . His ability as minister has won him universal
esteem." Further, Danton and Vergniaud had several qualities
in common which drew them together. Both were lawyers, both
ugly, both pockmarked; both lazy at times, both fond of enjoying life, both careless in money matters, both powerful speakers,
although of different types. Moreover Vergniaud was as unpopular with Madame Roland as Danton. With Dumouriez' advice still in his ears—"Peace with Danton"—he showed considerable understanding of the demands of the hour. But Madame
Roland had anathematized Danton; between Manon, who
loathed Paris, and Danton, who relied on the capital, there was
no link.

Danton shrugged his shoulders, and following instructions of
the Convention, left for Belgium.

———————◆———————

IN the little fortress of Condé a message from his brother-in-law
Charpentier overtakes him: Gabrielle is seriously ill! Danton
has scarcely dropped the letter before he is racing by express

coach for Paris, day and night, as in a fever, his breath stifled, his heart oppressed.

How the horses fly! Oh, how the horses creep!

Finally Paris, and the Cour du Commerce, and up the stairs, and he stands as if lost in an empty apartment. The blow strikes to his very heart: Gabrielle dead, and days under the soil!

The baker downstairs steps out horrified before his door, passers-by halt their steps white faced, such a roaring issues from the second floor. Danton is on his knees before Gabrielle's wardrobe, fumbling among clothes, gauze, and ribbons to which her fragrance clings. . . . A felt hat, a little lace bonnet, a flower-printed morning wrapper, a fur jacket of marten lined with blue silk, a Pierrot collar—how well he knows all this! And he roars and roars, a wild beast threatened by death.

Never again the consolation of this clear face, when, his blood poisoned with contempt of man, he returns home from a disorderly session—never! And that the meanness of fate should dare such a blow against him, the inviolable! He bites his lips, howls, weeps.

The news of his grief shakes Paris. Letters of sympathy arrive —one: "If the knowledge of having an affectionate and devoted friend can afford you some consolation, I offer it to you. I love you more than ever and until death. . . . Let us make the tyrants feel the force of our deep grief, those tyrants who are the cause of our public and private suffering. . . . Embrace your friend!" Signed: Robespierre. At the Jacobins' Collot d'Herbois eulogizes *"la généreuse femme du citoyen Danton"*: the Girondists, with their continuous slander of her husband, have her on their conscience!

But Danton raves. Tyrants, Gironde, politics—all nonsense! Dirt! *Merde!* He thinks only of Gabrielle! He wants only Gabrielle! He shakes the gates of Hades wildly, demands Gabrielle back!

To the cemetery, where the *requiescat in pace* has died away above her grave! Get shovels! How to oppose this maniac, these bloodshot eyes, this sunken face, these clenched fists—and this is the almighty Danton, yesterday a dictator, tomorrow a dictator!

Antoinette-Gabrielle Danton

The shovels turn up the ground. And Danton throws himself on the beloved body, kisses, kisses in madness, what already is half the worms'. And is suddenly overwhelmed by a feeling of great, of utter futility.

He beckons, and at his order an awkward individual approaches, emitting gurgling sounds, struggling to make himself understood with gestures. The sculptor Claude-André Deseine, a deaf mute from birth, has sometimes sold busts of Mirabeau, Robespierre, Pétion, with the help of the Jacobins; because of this Danton knows him.

Now, deaf mute, immortalize in a death mask the face that among all human faces on earth was dearest to Danton!

Deseine, equal to his task, is not satisfied with the mechanical work, the making of the mask. He forms, molds, creates: not death but glowing life is born under his hands.

One who looks at the works of Deseine in the art exhibition of 1793 in the Louvre may discover next to a bust of Lepelletier de Saint-Fargeau that of a woman in her prime whose features have a curious resemblance to those of Danton. The catalogue lists it as Number 78, *"Portrait de la citoyenne Danton, exhumée et moulée sept jours après sa mort."*

IV

Entanglement and Fall

1793—1794

WAR was, and war decided the fate of the Revolution.
Intent on barter on a grand scale—the Electorate of
Bavaria for the Austrian Netherlands—the House of
Hapsburg sent a strong force under the command of Prince
Friedrich Josias von Coburg-Saalfeld to recover Belgium. The
French troops, widely scattered and wretchedly equipped—infantry without boots, cavalry without saddles, artillery without
teams—could not withstand them. In early March an avalanche
of disastrous reports reached Paris: Aix had been hastily evacu-
ated, Liége was in the enemy's hands, the siege of Maestricht
had been abandoned, there had been reverses everywhere and
the Belgian people had risen against the retreating French, maliciously felling the trees of freedom. There was panic in the
army and panic in Paris; once more the frontiers seemed threatened and the black flag was hoisted over the Hôtel-de-Ville: *La
patrie en danger!* Everywhere there was rage and despair; the
campaign was hampered by lack of the barest necessities; in
Liége Coburg had seized a hundred guns and forty thousand
rifles, and sixteen guns and two flags had been lost at Aix.

Was Danton still alive? Whenever the heart of France began
beating more feebly and needed a camphor injection the call
arose not for Robespierre or Marat but for Danton.

He was back in Belgium and was despatched to Liége with
Delacroix, on March 5, at the first danger signal, to supervise
organizing and equipping the local National Guards. But there
was no time for this; a report at Paris was more urgent. So Danton proceeded to Paris.

March 8 found the Convention in a state of anxiety over the
turn of events in Belgium. At the opening of the session the new
Minister of War Beurnonville, a countryman of Danton's from
the Aube and a former marquis, read letters from Generals Mi-
randa, Valence, and Darson, each more meaningless and more
optimistic than the last. Delacroix had to ascend the tribune and
tell how affairs actually were going. Robespierre accompanied
his report with a studied speech in which he emphasized (a) the

divine mission of the French nation to bring liberty to mankind,
(b) the necessity of eliminating the aristocratic spirit among
the generals, (c) the possibility of crushing the traitors like in-
sects. But nobody was carried away by this speech, nobody was
spurred to action—until Danton put his clenched fists on the
rails before him and flung back his head. He roused, heartened,
inspired, stirred the meeting; he was a goad and a whip, he was
no man for gentle means, for hushing and for sleeping draughts
and "bye and byes." He pulled back the curtain brutally and the
Convention saw fortresses surrendering to the enemy, cities entered by the Austrians, and country roads thronging with defeated French battalions in confused retreat.

Danton felt as he had in September of '92 that he was the man
to give the nation its rallying cry and signal for attack. If the
French character requires danger before it is capable of resolute action—"Well, this moment has come. We must proclaim to
the whole of France: If you do not succor your brothers in Belgium, if Dumouriez is surrounded in Holland, and his army
compelled to lay down its arms, incalculable disasters may follow. The destruction of the national welfare and the death of
six hundred thousand Frenchmen may be the consequence. Citizens, not a minute is to be lost."

The blood began to pulse more swiftly in his listeners' veins
and confidence shone in their eyes.

In February a new method of organizing the army had been
resolved on independently of Danton: one battalion of troops of
the line was to be brigaded with two battalions of National
Guards into an "amalgam"—Dubois-Crancé's famous half bri-
gade. The "Whitetails" and "Cornflowers," nicknamed for the
color of their uniforms, were to vanish in an army of homo-
geneous blue. But for the time being this decree remained on
paper in that issue of the *Moniteur* which announced: "The National Convention calls to the colors three hundred thousand
men who are to join the armies of the Republic with the minimum of delay." There were gaps everywhere; in Belgium there
were battalions of sixty and companies of five to six men.

The problem was how to translate the decrees into reality
without any delay. Just as in the previous summer, so now Dan-

ton thought of Paris as the center of the national resources:
"Once again this famous and much maligned city is destined to
give that drive to France which led to our last year's triumphs."
On his motion the Convention decreed the despatch of deputies
to the forty-eight sections to call the citizens to arms and pledge
them to defend Belgium. In the departments, too, the Convention had to sow the dragon's teeth from which armed men were
to spring. On March 9 a resolution was presented asking the appointment of eighty-two members as commissars to conduct a
propaganda campaign throughout France and accelerate the
conscription of the three hundred thousand. "Say to every
Frenchman," Danton exclaimed, "that the great debate between
freedom and despotism is now to be decided."

He added fuel to the flames on March 10: We need deeds, not
words. The commissars must leave this very night! Not a moment must be lost in deploying all the forces of the nation! "Do
we really want freedom? If not, let us die now; if we do, let us
all march if need be!" It was an historic hour and Danton knew
it. "The eyes of Europe are on us"; the Convention "has the
entire globe for its gallery." With an imperious gesture: "You
have the nation for lever, and liberty and reason for fulcrum;
how can you fail to move the world?"

The hot draught of Danton's energy flowed from the speaker
to the Convention, from the Convention to Paris, and from Paris
to France.

But Danton's practical sense showed him the chief source of
weakness—the duality and lack of coöperation of the Executive
Council and the Convention. Deputies should not be ministers;
in that lay the cause of the slackness and carelessness in the administration. It was true that the Committee of Defense had
been in existence since the beginning of the year; but this body,
composed of delegates from other committees, was divided in debate instead of being united for action. It was a kind of miniature Convention, at best an investigating committee unsuited
for action if only because every deputy had access to its deliberations. Danton therefore saw the only salvation in a centralization
of power which would unite all the resolution of the Convention
and of the nation. Hence his bold suggestion of eliminating the

ministers from the Convention: "Who among you does not feel
the necessity of cohesion, of direct daily contact between the
ministers of the revolutionary executive power who are the
champions of liberty against the united forces of Europe, and
yourselves who are in supreme charge of the civic legislature and
the external protection of the Republic?"

If the Convention abandoned Montesquieu's doctrine of the
division of power in its exaggerated form in favor of Danton's
counsel, the cabinet would become a supreme committee of the
Convention. Brain and hand would be united, and this union
was all that was needed!

———————————

IN order to heighten popular confidence and because of the
manifest danger, Danton stressed the merits and capacities of
the commander in chief: "With military genius Dumouriez
combines the art of arousing enthusiasm and courage in the
troops. We have heard a whipped army crying for him." He did
not vouch for his character, leaving it to history to pass judgment on his talents, passions, and vices. "But one thing is certain: he is interested in the glory of the Republic."

Some voices, indeed, blamed Dumouriez for the defeats; but
among the important municipal and national authorities they
met with no response. Danton was certainly not alone in his
view that now when the faltering army needed to be bound with
hoops of steel, it was a most unpropitious moment to remove a
popular leader: no crisis within a crisis! In the Convention
Barère proclaimed: "Dumouriez alone is worth an army." And
Robespierre, too, agreed with Danton. "I trust Dumouriez . . .
I trust him because the success of our arms means safety and
glory to him personally." Even Marat, who had for months been
accusing the "false intriguer" of "criminal plots," and as recently as February 12 had represented him as a hireling of the
King of Prussia, was now of the opinion that unless Dumouriez
retained supreme command the army would fall to pieces. On
the evening of March 12 Billaud-Varenne too, cold and unsentimental as he was, defended the general at the Jacobins', urging
that he could no longer retreat and must either conquer or die;

while conversely that same day an uproar arose in the Convention when the section Poissonière sent a deputation whose speaker demanded the accusation of Dumouriez and his staff. There were cries of: Slanderer! He has been bought by the enemy! To prison with him! Aristocrat! Criminal!—it was Marat who called "Criminal!"

But while his ears ought to have been ringing with the praises heaped upon him, Dumouriez himself took a decisive step off the path of duty and honor on this very March 12. Restless and thirsting for power, he realized that in such a time a victorious sword could easily become a magic wand; he had often seen himself in the rôle of dictator of France and had longed for the great hour to come. Today he was convinced that the European powers would entertain no such plan. But another object lured him: As Constable of a restored monarchy, he would be the first man beside and behind the throne. The internal and external position of the country encouraged him to venture on the project.

He returned from Holland to Belgium and boldly and deliberately abandoned the policy prescribed by the Convention, based on the decree of December 15. When the commissars demanded an explanation he replied on March 12 with a letter to the president of the National Convention. A letter? A declaration of war! He blamed the late Minister of War, Pache, for the recent defeats and for the bad morale of the army; he condemned the whole system favored by the Paris government in Belgium, charged that the Belgians had been mistreated and their churches plundered, and he struck at Danton: "You have been deceived with regard to the annexation of several parts of Belgium. You believed that it was voluntarily accomplished only because you were misinformed." And the rebellious general concluded by appealing to history as the world's court: "We conquered so long as our cause was just. Now that we are guided by greed and injustice, we have destroyed ourselves to the advantage of our enemies."

Two days later Bréard's hands trembled as he scanned this manifesto. A catastrophe! A double, triple catastrophe if the Convention or the people or the army heard of it. He could not be responsible. In the Hôtel d'Elbeuf the Committee of Defense, too, was greatly alarmed and hastily summoned Danton and Delacroix, who, coming from Belgium, should be best informed. It was plain to all that Dumouriez' action was antirevolutionary mutiny, to be met by immediate arrest. But now counterarguments were advanced. Precipitate action might perhaps drive the hesitating general to high treason. Danton was among the most eloquent advocates of a last attempt to persuade the rebel. Perhaps a deputation to Dumouriez, including such thorough Girondins as Guadet and Gensonné, to show him that regardless of political conviction the whole Convention was against him, might make him change his mind. Eventually Danton and Delacroix were sent alone. "We shall either bring him to reason," the former promised on leaving, "or put him in a strait-jacket."

So once again Danton and Delacroix took the road to the northeast, but this time with feelings of despondency and dejection very different from their mood in December. They were not even roused by the rumor that Dumouriez intended to seize them and hand them over to the Austrians to be exchanged for Marie-Antoinette and the Dauphin.

The further they advanced into Belgium, the more single fugitives or disordered bands of retreating troops they met. They first learned now that on March 18 Dumouriez had faced Coburg on the plain of Neerwinden and been defeated.

On March 20 the emissaries met the commander in chief in the open field, near Louvain. There was a skirmish in progress, bullets were flying, and they could smell powder. The general requested them to present themselves late in the evening at headquarters in Louvain.

The doors were guarded by the First Regiment of Hussars, the former Berchiny, the bulk of which had gone over to the émigrés. Plaits of hair hung down their faces from under their high Tartar caps; and their wide shining swords rested carelessly in the crooks of their arms. They were too indifferent to the commissars' entrance to be patriots; no doubt they were Germans who did not care either way about the Revolution so long as they were paid. About the aides-de-camp in the antechamber there was an intangible air of the old regime, and they showed no excessive haste to announce the citizens from Paris.

JEAN FRANÇOIS DELACROIX,

Citoyen du Village d'Anet, Député du Département d'Eure
et Loir, Président de l'Assemblée Nationale le 21 Aout
1792, et de la Convention le 5 Octobre suivant.

In the commander's room, the general's hat, flung hastily on the table, lay on one side so that only the white feathers in the tricolor plume were visible—a symbol; and the sword lay beside it—a menace. Dumouriez received the two politely but nervously. His resolve had been taken. Once assured of the benevolent neutrality of the Prince of Coburg he would advance on Paris with his battalions, on whose absolute devotion he reckoned, disperse the Convention, restore the Constitution of 1791, and proclaim Louis XVII King. So why talk?

Nor could Danton recapture the easy conversational tone of their Paris discussions. This dark, tempestuous March night the representatives of two hostile forces stood face to face: the Revolution and the military Condottieri; and the conversation was heavy, embarrassing, full of pauses. Danton wished to leave no stone unturned; he recalled past military laurels, and more still to be won in the service of the Republic. The other's face showed no esteem for the Republic. Danton talked of the Convention; the general spoke with hard contempt: "Three hundred fools who let themselves be led by the nose by four hundred knaves." Danton quoted a decree; the general: "It will soon have no importance outside the precincts of Paris." Danton, choking with anger, dared the word "arrest"; the general shrugged his shoulders pityingly: Indeed! Where was there anyone far or near to execute the warrant? The aides-de-camp in the anteroom? They would laugh uproariously. The hussars at the gates? They did not even understand French! And indeed Danton had learned from his colleague Gossuin that the soldiers had kissed the general's hands and boots in the commissar's presence with shouts of: Our little father Dumouriez! We will follow him wherever he wishes!

All that Danton and Delacroix obtained after much debate was six lines from Dumouriez to the president of the Convention asking him not to act on the letter of March 12 until further explanations had been received. At best time had been gained, nothing else. On leaving headquarters, the two friends exchanged a look of understanding: the general must go overboard! This Dumouriez was lost to them, to the Revolution, to the Republic.

While Delacroix stayed in Belgium and forcefully urged Dumouriez' immediate arrest on a hesitating council of commissioners, Danton hastened to Paris to report on March 26 to the Committee of Defense on the subject of their greatest worry. On the twenty-eighth four commissioners of the Convention were despatched by the committee together with the Minister of War, Beurnonville, to the Belgian headquarters to depose the mutinous general and arrest him. Instead of which the general seized them and gave them to the Austrians as hostages. His attempt to draw the entire army with him was foiled by the attitude of the artillery—*Vive la république!* and the volunteers—*Vive la république!* The Third Battalion of the Yonne under Lieutenant Colonel Davout, who thirteen years later was to acquire a dukedom on the field of Auerstadt in Thuringia, took up arms against Dumouriez. And the traitor escaped with difficulty to Coburg, miserably followed by a few hundred men—a gambler who had lost the great game of his life.

DUMOURIEZ' treason, a terrible blow that dazed many weaker men, did not knock down a fellow of Danton's build. On the contrary, the heightened danger increased his powers. He urged the formation of a powerful reserve army and the construction of a fortified camp twenty miles from the capital. Knowing that the enemy sought to stab France in the heart by an assault on Paris, he thought this the time to proclaim to the universe that "Paris will always be the center of liberty or will perish." "The enemy will enter Paris only through a heap of ashes," he flung at the Convention, and no one thought it empty boasting when he continued, glowering: "I will set fire to the city with my own hand, supported by every good citizen, before I will allow it to be surrendered to the enemy."

Another idea that Danton had sowed—a concentration of powers, union of the Convention and the Government and an action committee—bore fruit. On March 18 Barère demanded the appointment of a Committee of Defense to keep in immediate and frequent contact with the Executive Council and to urge it to action; but even this new committee, which contained twenty-five members including Danton, and deliberated in public, did not meet Danton's idea. It was not until Dumouriez' treachery seemed to take away the ground from under people's feet, until the Austrians blockaded the northern fortresses, until Custine's army of the Rhine left beleaguered Mainz and was driven into Alsace, and the Spaniards in the Pyrenees and the Piedmontese in the Alps were preparing to advance, that—in these feverish days when the Convention was in perpetual session—necessity found the solution.

Because the ministers were inefficient, uncoöperative, and acting each for himself, Garnier of Saintes on April 3 suggested the formation of a Commission of Twelve to be selected from the Convention and to divide all the work of the Revolution among themselves with the help of twelve assistants. "And these twenty-four men shall say to you: Either the country shall be free or our heads shall fall." The next day Isnard, speaking in the name of the clumsy and inefficient new Committee of Defense, and taking the motto "More action, more energy, more unity," moved the appointment of a *Comité d'exécution* to consist of nine members. This committee was to fulfil the functions of the Executive Council and to enact all measures necessary for national defense: "Let us at last seize the reins of government with a bold, firm, clean hand. Questions of form do not matter; what matters is the safety of the country."

At last a new authority was to be formed to create armies and discover leaders. Danton nodded approval: "I believe that a Republic, even if it rejects the idea of dictators and triumvirs, has none the less the capacity and even the duty to call into being a power which will inspire terror." Together with Barère, Isnard, Thuriot, and Mathieu, Danton drafted the regulations of the new authority, and on April 6 the Convention baptized the Committee of Public Safety. It was to have nine members, secret deliberations, and extensive powers; while it had the right to disregard ministerial instructions, ministers were obliged to execute its orders immediately. This meant that the Executive Council was driven against the wall and the Convention, too, began to lose much of its prestige. Soon there was no higher or more influential post than that of a member of the Committee of Public Safety. If one of the nine showed himself in the halls of the Convention he was immediately surrounded by a circle of attentive listeners, and if he shook hands with one of these the little man could be seen visibly swelling as he marched back to his place. Marat welcomed the formation of the committee as an instrument for the destruction of royal despotism and the erection of a "despotism of liberty." And indeed, the committee became more thoroughly identified with this Republican despotism every day.

When the appointments to the Committee of Public Safety were made, Barère, that smooth time server, got the most votes —360; Danton was fifth with 223, his friend Delacroix last with 151. Besides Cambon the other members of the committee were Delmas of Toulouse, who under the old regime had been a militia officer in the so-called provincial infantry which admitted members of the bourgeoisie to commissioned rank, and was still an expert in military matters; Bréard, Canadian born, the son of a naval officer, and himself a naval expert; Lindet, a lawyer, capable, extremely industrious, but apt to lose his nerve; Guyton-Morveau, for twenty-one years avocat général at the parliamentary court of Burgundy, author of verses, something more than a dabbler in chemistry, and above all an investigator and supporter of the newborn science of aeronautics, who was just then preparing to employ the "Montgolfière" and the "Aérostat" for military purposes; and finally Treilhard of the Paris bar, with whom Danton had become better acquainted as commissioner of the Convention in Belgium. They were all men of character and action; Cambon especially stood out. Yet none of them had Danton's stature. Danton towered above them, Danton dominated and guided them, the more so in that he attended the meeting of the committee with unwonted diligence. Indeed, it was not easy to sit in the Hôtel d'Elbeuf from nine until two and again from eight until past midnight behind a table covered with green cloth which sometimes called to mind the fresher, lusher green of the valley of the Aube in summer; but it was necessary and it brought results.

Soon people spoke only of the Danton Committee, and indeed

in these months the Committee of Public Safety was no more than Danton's ministry.

————◆————

A PRECARIOUS venture to interfere with every branch of the administration while the ship of state was tossing in a heavy gale. But spurred by Danton's "forward" the committee went at their task with a will.

Starting as a war committee they expedited conscriptions, appointed a new Minister of Marine, deposed generals or called them to Paris to give an account of themselves, reorganized the army, instructed the new Minister of War—Bouchotte of Metz, a former officer in the Royal-Cravates and Esterhazy Regiments —to direct the mass production of cavalry pistols; ordered the building of corvettes, despatched commissars to the army, sent agents to Switzerland to buy rifles, ordered the erection of foundries to melt down bells for guns; limited the number of married women with the troops in the field; collected information about Royalist sentiment in the Fourteenth Regiment of Dragoons, arranged for experiments with mountain guns and mule transport; procured field water bottles and canteens for an army; saw to the rationing, the coast defense, the increase in cavalry, the artillery defense of Perpignan, and the supplying of gunpowder to all fortified towns from Dunkirk to Rocroy—all in conformity with the demand that Danton thrust at the Convention on March 10 that the country must be mobilized! Danton himself was not only influential in these matters through Delacroix, who was devoted to him and who, with Delmas, was in charge of the War Department; but he was also intrusted on June 29 by the committee with the control of the activities of the Minister of War and supervising of the execution of all decrees and regulations. This was necessary in the interest of increased activity in the War Department.

Much as Danton desired to be the controlling force of the national defense, he did not see the revolutionary power of war as a panacea. The loss of Belgium and the treachery of Dumouriez had given him cause for thought. A single battle, at Jemappes, had won the Austrian Netherlands. A single battle, at Neerwinden, had lost them. And if defeats meant the destruction of the Republic, victories, too, threatened its existence. A series of defeats must end with the old regime and the gallows for the champions of liberty, a series of victories would end in military despotism: there was not much to choose. And this war that had to be waged against England, Prussia, Austria, the Holy Roman Empire, Spain, Piedmont, and Naples was like a gaping wound through which the best strength of the country was rapidly draining away! Keeping twelve armies in the field cost three hundred million livres a month; and the losses in men were more serious for the Republic than for the coalition. According to Saint-Just the former lost free men in each battle, the latter only slaves. Things could not go on indefinitely like this. Robespierre, too, had told the Convention very seriously: "The war cannot last long; there is a limit to the vast expenditures of a generous nation." And was not this limit almost reached?

The Republic was fighting for its existence—a struggle illumined by the steely light of antique heroism, a struggle that seized the soul. When on June 18 the Convention debated whether the Constitution was to include the statement that the French nation concludes no peace with an enemy on its soil, Mercier objected that such articles were written or canceled with the point of the sword: "Do you really flatter yourselves that you will always be victorious? Have you concluded a treaty with victory?" Basire interrupted him amid the applause of the Convention: "Our treaty has been concluded with death!"

Bravo! Bravo! But if France was to emerge unharmed from these dangers antique heroism must be companioned by modern diplomacy. Danton felt not only that he had in him the capacity to pursue such a diplomacy, but that since the committee had intrusted him with the conduct of foreign affairs, he had also the power. He was supposed to move conjointly with Barère, it is true, but his colleague from the Department of the Pyrenees was of too southern a pliability to resist Danton's domineering will.

As the committee resolved at the outset to "pursue plans of campaign and of negotiations simultaneously," Danton immediately began to test the enemy front in order to discover the most suitable point for launching a peace offensive. That he was compelled in this to rely entirely on the men and in part on the methods of the old school, did not distress him. He had never been overfastidious in personal relations—it was repeated in every public house that Fabre d'Eglantine had shamelessly made a fortune in the autumn by supplying worthless boots to the army —and in politics Danton was even more ready to adopt the unpuritanical principle that men must be taken as one found them. Strength interested him more than virtue. During a revolution a fullblooded man whose passions could be utilized by a skilful hand to heat the revolutionary caldron was more valuable, even without a certificate of good behavior, than a righteous milksop who could only bleat. Danton had boldly intended to exploit the evil ambition of Dumouriez in the service of the Republic and he had as little compunction in employing a number of suspicious figures with dark histories provided they were conversant with the underground ways of diplomacy. You had only to watch out that they did not cheat you and to keep a tight rein. Danton was just the man to do this. And so, while waiting for their secret missions in his antechamber, the Belgian banker Proli (the alleged illegitimate son of the Austrian chancellor Kaunitz), who successfully played the rabid Jacobin, rubbed shoulders with the Abbé Soulavie who was composing a "Politics of All the Cabinets of Europe under Louis XV and Louis XVI," based on the secret papers seized in the Tuileries on August 10; and with the former Marquis de Poterat, who had profited from many a dirty deal; and with Sémonville, a marquis too, who had been in charge of the King's secret fund in the days of the Constituent and Legislative Assemblies.

However shady might be the antecedents of these individuals, the peace which Danton achieved through their instrumentality was distinctly a peace with honor, calculated to safeguard the dignity of France and to promote the revolutionary cause. The foreign ministry in the Rue Cerutty with Danton's sanction drafted a memorandum "On a Plan to Bring About Peace," which in the plainest terms instructed the "representatives of the people on special mission to the armies," as the commissars of the Convention had recently come to be called, that no foreign power could hope to enter into negotiations with Paris unless it recognized the Republic, gave up interfering with France's internal affairs, and promised to surrender the émigrés with the "Regent," the Comte d'Artois, at their head. Other questions, territorial questions, were left open for discussion.

Danton soon realized that the propaganda war for which he himself had recently broken a lance was a serious obstacle in the way of negotiations. Therefore, overnight he once again adjusted his tactics to a new situation; for he was contemptuous of routine, systems, and formulæ and a passionate lover of the essential realities of life. He did not hesitate to admit in the Convention that he had given up the illusion of a conquest of Belgium, although a few weeks ago there had been no more ardent champion of this idea. At the moment the decrees of November 19 and December 15, 1792, which made the Convention a "general committee of insurrection against all the kings of the world," were also a thorn in his flesh—away with them! When Robespierre on April 13 demanded the death penalty for anyone who suggested any understanding whatsoever with the enemy, Danton fell in with this idea, but cleverly twisted the motion to his own use; he agreed with the death penalty "for everybody who proposes to the Republic an understanding with any enemy not recognizing the sovereignty of the French people." This was changing not only the key but the melody. Nor did he miss this opportunity to unburden himself of other matters on his mind: "Citizens, the time has come to let Europe know that the National Convention understands how to combine diplomacy with the republican virtues." In a moment of exaltation a decree had been passed promising protection to all peoples desirous of casting off the yoke of tyranny. No doubt the motives were beautiful; but it was a piece of biting irony that this decree would oblige the nation to support a few enthusiasts who might perhaps wish to start a revolution in China. "Citizens, it is our duty above all to consider the preservation of the State, and to establish the greatness of France. Once the Republic is assured, a strong and enlightened France will in itself exert sufficient attraction on all the nations."

The meeting resolved unanimously:

The National Convention declares in the name of the French

people that it will in no way interfere with the governments of other powers, but it simultaneously declares that it will sooner be buried under its own ruins than allow any foreign power to interfere with the internal administration of the Republic or modify the Constitution which it is about to adopt.

The Convention decrees that any person who proposes negotiations with enemy powers which have not solemnly recognized the independence and sovereignty of the French nation and the indivisibility and unity of the Republic based on liberty and equality shall suffer the death penalty.

A retreat from the world republic to the French Republic: an advance from Utopia to reality.

Anacharsis Clootz, the intoxicated prophet of the universal republic, it is true, unconcernedly continued to blow soap bubbles in the air; a few days after Danton's speech and the adoption of the decree he took the opportunity afforded by a debate on the Constitution to pronounce it the duty of the French nation to perpetuate liberty in the universe. He saw in the Convention so many deputies of the human race, and in the human race the basis of sovereignty—*"une, indivisible, imprescriptible, immuable, inaliénable, impérissable, illimitée, sans bornes, absolue et toute puissante"*; he pictured the globe inhabited by a single nation, and with the stars of future centuries above his head, he exclaimed in ecstasy: "The Republic of the human race will never have war with anyone, for the planets have no intercourse with each other." Robespierre, too, on this day was another Clootz, without the sweet intoxication. He proposed articles for the Constitution which he himself admitted implied endless dissension between France and any monarchy. He still retained Danton's belief of last September in the revolutionary power of a war of propaganda, and so he suggested the following for the first paragraph: "The men of all countries are brothers and the different peoples must support each other to the best of their ability as if they were citizens of the same state."

On heads growing hot with enthusiasm for the world republic, Robert, at one in this with Danton, poured a shower of ice cold water: "We are not the representatives of the human race; I wish that the legislators of France would forget the universe for a moment and concern themselves exclusively with their own country." He even dared to speak of "national egotism" and explained, "I love all men, especially all free men; but I love the free men of France more than all the others in the universe." France! France before everything in the world! Danton's watchword was chiseled on the marble tablets of the new Constitution and Section XXV, Articles 1 and 2, read: "The French people declare themselves the natural friends and allies of free peoples. They do not interfere with the government of other nations; they do not suffer other nations to interfere with their government."

The decree of April 13 amounted to a cancellation of the decrees of November 19 and December 15, a fact of which Thomas Paine highly approved: "I entirely agree," he wrote Danton on May 16, "with your proposal to abstain from interference with foreign governments, and not to allow foreign governments to interfere with the administration of France. The decree to this effect was a necessary condition of peace." And in fact the recantation of April 13 was aimed chiefly at Paine's country. England had become the most resolute and dangerous of all the enemies of the tricolor Republic and she pursued wholly selfish ends. On February 11 Prime Minister Pitt proclaimed the beginning of a war of extermination, and Lord Auckland, British Ambassador to Holland, explained with calm assurance at a conference of the allies on April 8 that England not only desired to make France a "complete political nonentity" but that she also intended to make conquests and hold them. The British leopard's mouth watered for Dunkirk as well as for the French possessions overseas. It was only now under British leadership that something like unity of will began to prevail among the members of the coalition—Austria, Prussia, the Holy Roman Empire, Sardinia, Spain, Portugal, and Naples; pursuing its ancient policy London subsidized the smaller and poorer states in order to use them as mercenaries on the Continent.

Danton was among the first to recognize that the British Cabinet was "the center of enemy activities." If he did not define matters with the happy accuracy of his friend Desmoulins, who said that England had taken up the sword solely from commercial rivalry with France, whose industry had been unfettered by the Revolution, still he had a suspicion that it was the markets of the world which were at issue. A memorandum from the Rue Cerutty in February or March of 1793, with which Danton was probably acquainted, bluntly stated that public opinion in England had never been as unanimously in favor of war with France as now; yet it reckoned, too, with the effect of a French declaration of peace on British public opinion. Danton was led even further by the hopes he placed in Fox, Sheridan, and Grey, despite the fact that the sponsors of liberty had only a quarter of the votes that Pitt had in the House of Commons. He calculated that the strangulation of British trade would entail the fall of the ministry and then the Republicans on the Thames would make peace with the Republicans on the Seine.

Before Danton took over the conduct of foreign affairs Minister Lebrun had bought the services of a certain James Tilly Matthews, an Englishman with a French mother, who was on friendly terms with the opposition and the peace party in England and who undertook to prepare the ground for negotiations. He went to London in April, only to return in June with a curt refusal from the British Foreign Minister. The Committee of Public Safety resolved to continue these efforts. George Forster, a Republican of Polish parentage from the Rhine, and Citizen Petry were sent to General Murray, commander of the British division in the army of Coburg, to learn Pitt's intentions and to sound out the possibilities of peace. But because Danton had meanwhile left the Committee of Public Safety the two emissaries did not make much progress; and for the same reason when Matthews returned from London to Paris in August he found his position radically changed. He was curtly dismissed by the department head in the Foreign Office whom he assured of the high esteem which Danton enjoyed in England and soon after he was placed under police supervision in his room as a suspicious foreigner. He appealed to Danton in vain for a passport. Nevertheless gossips ferreted out that Danton had dined with the Englishman at the latter's hotel, at 26 Rue Grange Batelière, with no less a caterer than the famous Rose and—words fail me, citizen—at a hundred thalers a cover!

Baron Ludwig von Esebeck, Minister of the Duke of Pfalz-Zweibrücken, offered his services in attempting to reach an understanding with Berlin. A political prisoner in the military prison at Metz, the baron had been waiting for his release since February, and losing patience, wrote to Danton: "My hopes and confidence will not be disappointed when I turn to the greatest man in the French Republic. If I can trust my instinct he is also the most generous." After Desportes, who had been appointed French Minister at the court of the Duke of Württemberg, had tested Esebeck, it was not long before Frederick William II, eager for prey and scenting it, despatched his Chamberlain, the Baron Luxburg, to Metz. All hail! It must be from this direction that the dove of peace would arrive. Was it not a moral gain, implying recognition of the new French form of government, that a letter, in itself unimportant, dealing only with an exchange of prisoners, bore the superscription, "The King of Prussia to the French Republic"? But things never got beyond this stage.

It was Danton's policy at the same time to sound out the House of Hapsburg, which was supposed to be the most implacable enemy of the Revolution on the Continent, even though after Dumouriez' disastrous treason these attempts could do no more than delay the Austrian advance. Colonel Chérin who bore a letter from the commissars of the Convention to Imperial headquarters concluded from a conversation with the Prince of Coburg on April 13 that Austria was inclined toward peace and recognition of the Republic. At the same time Custine learned from his opponent General Wurmser that the Emperor Franz was not averse to peace. But nothing binding was undertaken, and the mysterious mission on which the deputy Cusset was despatched to the army of the Moselle with extraordinary powers, "the success of which would have had great influence on the war," never bore fruit. Whether it concerned Austria or Prussia was never disclosed.

Peace feelers were also put out in Spain—where the monks were preaching the "holy war" against the Revolution—in Sardinia, and in the kingdom of the two Sicilies. The Queen of Naples was a sister of Marie-Antoinette, so that at this court the fate of the Widow Capet was not a matter of indifference. Danton was wholly out of sympathy with an emotional policy which would have sent the deposed Queen without ado to the scaffold, and nothing could have been more welcome to him than the prospect of buying a separate peace or even an alliance by setting free the "Autrichienne." Accordingly when Sémonville, accompanied by Danton's nephew Mergez as his Secretary of Legation, was about to take up his duties as Ambassador to the Grand Duke of Tuscany, a prince of the Hapsburg family, he received oral instructions.

This very unsentimental policy did not disdain territorial jobbery as a means to an end. It was hoped that Prussia and Bavaria could be baited by scraps of the clerical electorate of Cologne, Trèves, and Mainz that were to be secularized, and an attempt was made to direct the attention of Victor Amadeus of Sardinia to Genoa and those parts of Italy which he might seize from Austria with French assistance. Finally, in dealing with Poland and Turkey the policy of the first Committee of Public Safety reached the acme of cold, matter-of-fact political cynicism. If any nation had a claim on the passionate support of the French Republic of liberty it was Poland, whose inhabitants had been brutally divided like a herd of slaves among three neighboring states. Instead Frederick William II was promised at least the tacit approval of France in the partition. And if there was any potentate who deserved the bitter hostility of the Republic of Liberty, it was the Grand Turk whose power was based on the unspeakable misery of the enslaved Christian rayahs in the Balkans. Yet every effort was made to obtain at any price the alliance of the Ottoman Empire. Before Danton took over foreign affairs the Rue Cerutty had started to worm its way into Constantinople; and Danton, to whom Dumouriez had probably pointed out occasionally that Turkey as well as Sweden was one of France's natural allies, continued this policy —in order to attack Austria in the rear—although it represented a tradition burdened with Royalist associations and could be traced back as far as the marriage between Mary of Burgundy and Maximilian of Austria.

All these intrigues behind the scenes eventually harmed Danton; the gossamer threads of diplomacy turned into cords in which his feet became entangled. And to the nation the policy of peace brought no visible good; it was broken off prematurely and it ran counter to events within France which again and again destroyed the belief of other powers in the stability of the Paris government.

CONTRARY to the custom of a time when wars generally involved only professional soldiers and left civilians in peace as far as possible, Pitt resolved to beat down the enemy across the Channel by blockade and starvation. As early as the end of 1792 England had placed an embargo on grain exports to France; now, on declaring war, she seized all French vessels in British ports and enforced a rigorous blockade against the Republic. The British Cabinet succeeded in inducing its allies and even neutrals to adopt similar methods with the result that France came more and more, as Philippeaux said, to resemble a beleaguered city.

The spring of the year I of the Republic found Paris joyous, lively, and colorful. The promenades were thronged with ladies gracefully attired, moving in clouds of perfume, and with well-groomed gentlemen; and night after night the amusement places were packed—the Académie de Musique, the Théâtre de la Nation, de l'Opéra-Comique, de la République, de la Rue Féydeau, du Marais, de la Citoyenne Montansier, du Vaudeville, du Palais, du Lycée, des Arts, and the Théâtre-Français, Comique et Lyrique. But in the less elegant sections careworn women were not aware that the latest creations of fashion were called *Robes à la Psyché, à la Ménagère,* or *à la Turque,* and shirt-sleeved men had no idea that white batiste cravats were now being worn like a belt round the neck, the essential point being to leave both ends loose.

In the faubourgs, the workers' quarters, and the slums the polonaise of misery never ceased before the bakeries. Although the municipality contributed twelve thousand livres a day to keep the price three sous a pound for the benefit of the destitute, bread continued to deteriorate in quality and quantity, and the blockade also made itself felt by a shortage of other foodstuffs and necessities. Hunger hurt. The wives and mothers who were in line before dawn and stood from four in the morning until late in the forenoon to bring back a wretched two-pound loaf for the many hungry mouths at home did not experience the kindliest of human feelings—but only hate for those who could fill their bellies and envy of those who wore decent coats—and when the wives plodded home weary and with nerves on edge, the men joined them in abuse of the cursed profiteers.

From this time the progress of the Revolution was accompanied by a universal chorus of hunger.

Soon spokesmen of the starving millions arose, stirred by sympathy or seized by ambition or both. While the Mountain and the Gironde fought for power, dangerous groups appeared on the Left of both and their entire political program was summed up in the cry: "We are hungry, we want bread!" For the benefit of the street at the point where it became the gutter, Jacques-René Hébert published *Père Duchesne*, which put all its rivals in the shade with the obscenity of its language, the vulgarity of its tone, and the vileness of its insinuations; beside it Marat's *Ami du peuple* was academic. But he who wrote this paper in the slang of the faubourgs, spiced with curses, in no way resembled his "Père Duchesne," that stovemaker who smoked his pipe—damme!—and gave vent to his *grandes colères*—his fits of fury; on the contrary, he was a studiously polite, well-dressed young dandy with an insipid face and a taste for self-indulgence, and a wife who had been a nun in a Carmelite convent.

Anaxagoras Chaumette, the procurator of the Commune for whom Hébert substituted, followed the same movement. His motto was *"Acheronta movebo!"* and his followers were artisans, tradesmen, all small people who had to starve because of the blockade and who were infuriated by the increasing devaluation of assignats.

Chaumette, again, had a protégé, Jean Varlet, a youthful official in the postal service, who, being an enthusiastic champion of the poor and having no mean opinion of himself, vigorously played the same tune. He in turn was almost drowned out by the Abbé Jacques Roux, a man in his late forties with a somewhat

shady past. Lured by the Revolution from Angoulême to Paris
as a constitutional clergyman, he soon won himself a following
as a public speaker in the densely populated section of the Gravilliers. He had been elected to the jury of the Extraordinary
Court of August 17, but had been refused on account of his
cloth, and the elaborate flatteries he addressed to Danton were
unavailing. Later he became a member of the Commune and
was one of the two commissars who accompanied Louis Capet in
his final journey. When the Bourbon requested him to hear his
last wishes he refused icily: "My function is merely to conduct
you to the scaffold." The part he had played on January 21 gave
him another claim to leadership among the most embittered
classes of the people; but his greatest success was due to his influence over women, whom he had learned to deal with in the
confessional. When he spoke his listeners scented along with the
odor of the fresh bread which he promised an exciting mixture
of blood and incense.

But the masses who greeted the attacks on the rich by Hébert,
Chaumette, Varlet, and Roux with calls of "Go on!" "Give it to
them!" had the same ideas and ideals as the bourgeosie; only
they were hungrier. They did not want a new form of society,
they took off their hats to prosperity, they only wanted enough
to eat. The horizon of the vague interpreters of their vague demands was no wider. At the moment Hébert advocated the partition of large landed estates, and Chaumette wanted to give the
poor the hope of sometime becoming landed proprietors themselves; but Varlet deprecated any suggestion of an attack on
honestly acquired wealth, and Roux did not dream of overturn-
ing the laws of property. They all attributed the destitution of
the country not so much to the faulty structure of society as to
the wickedness of the selfish rich. It was only because usurers,
hoarders, monopolists, middlemen, profiteers, and speculators,
did not respect holy equality, but shamelessly kept on grabbing,
that the poor had to go hungry. The solution and salvation lay
not in changing the laws of property, but in penalizing the
profiteers—hang the scoundrels!—and in exceptional measures
for an exceptional time—fixing a maximum price for grain.

Roux told the deputies of the Mountain to climb up from the

third floor to the ninth in this revolutionary city and see the "tears and lamentations of the vast population without bread and clothes which has sunk into this state of misery and misfortune as the result of usury and speculation, because the laws, which were made by the rich for the rich, are cruel to the poor." But the Mountain was as much out of sympathy with such endeavors as the Gironde. A movement which glorified the regulation of the grain trade under the old regime had a very outspoken counterrevolutionary flavor for the Mountain which considered the food riots and the shop raidings of the early spring of 1793 the machinations of foreign countries. Surely Pitt's gold and Coburg's agents were at work here, and Robespierre loftily remarked: "Have the people no worthier target for their attack than paltry grocers?"

The Mountain was as averse as the Gironde to the establishment of maximum prices; freedom of trade was one of the most glorious acquisitions of July 14; to touch it meant to shake the confidence of the proprietors in the new order, a dangerous game, since the sale of national lands was the financial basis of the Revolution. So the Convention on March 18 passed a decree that was curt and sharp and severe—making death the penalty for undertaking "to introduce the agrarian law or any other law tending to destroy landed, mercantile, or industrial property." It was only to prevent the masses from becoming estranged from the Revolution that the Convention—partly against its will, pressed by the man in the street—on May 4 set a maximum price for grain, varying from department to department. Soon however the Enragés, the Extremists, began to clamor for similar measures applied to all the necessities of life, and Jacques Roux as spokesman of a deputation from the faubourg Saint-Antoine fumed at the bar of the Convention because the death penalty against profiteers and usurers was not "anchored" in the Constitution: "How long will you suffer wealthy egoists to drink the purest blood of the people in golden goblets?" On this occasion, however, he was not only driven from the bar with cries of execration, but Robespierre saw to it that the Jacobins cast him off and even the Cordeliers renounced him. Sadly the visionary retired to his lodging with the seamstress Widow Petit in the

Rue Aumaire and locked himself in his poor chamber, where his soothing harp leaned against the wall and his dog welcomed him.

Danton lacked the keen sense for economic processes of Barnave and Saint-Just. Barnave, intuitively getting to the root of the thing, traced the Revolution to a series of economic causes, seeing in the "increase of movable property in Europe the democratic element and the cement of unity between States." And Saint-Just, in one of his first speeches at the Convention, attributed the distress of the country to the "uncontrolled issue of paper money." But Danton still remembered, from the days when the Encyclopedia had been his Book of Revelations, Diderot's definition of the word worker: "Wage earner paid by the day. This class of men is the majority in a nation. A good government must concern itself first of all with their welfare. If the worker is badly off the nation is badly off." Danton admitted that he was no expert in financial questions but he claimed to be an expert on the welfare of the people.

But neither Danton nor any of his contemporaries suspected that the host marching behind the flag of hunger were the forerunners of a new class, destined some day to shake to the foundations the new gloriously established order. For him the poor, the have-nots, the laborers and all those who lived from hand to mouth, were simply "citizens whom fortune had not favored." Like most of his contemporaries he recognized that it was a duty of the community to support them; even a moderate Girondin like Bancal des Issarts declared: "To the poor society owes work when they are strong and support when they are incapable of work." It was on Danton's proposal that Article XXIV of the new version of the Rights of Man was given that wording which Vergniaud admired: "The guarantee of society consists in the effectiveness of the group in assuring to the individual the enjoyment and pursuit of his rights. It is based on the sovereignty of the nation."

Danton was all the more in favor of the State's supporting the needy in that it was the broad masses who bore the Revolution on their shoulders. When, toward the end of July, an effort was being made to withdraw the assignats bearing the King's portrait from circulation, because they were treasured by those with secret aristocratic leanings who hoped to redeem them on the re-establishment of the monarchy, Danton exclaimed: "Who bears the burden of the public misery? Who sheds his blood in the cause of freedom? Who fights against the aristocracy of the bourgeoisie and the financiers? Those who have not a hundred-livre note in their pocket."

But how to remedy matters? On March 9 Danton prefaced with the resounding proclamation: "I shall demand the destruc-tion of the tyranny of riches over misery," a minor regulation—the abolition of imprisonment for debts—certainly onerous and degrading for individuals but of no importance to the masses. Essentially it was a symbolic measure. "It is a disgrace to hu-manity, law, and philosophy, that a citizen who has borrowed money has to answer for it with his person." Later he pointed to the "disproportion between the wages of the poor and the cost of living." On April 5 a deputation of the section of the Quatre Na-tions appeared at the bar of the National Assembly, asking for additional taxation of the rich "to allow all the departments to eat bread at three sous a pound like Paris." Danton was the one who had suggested to the spokesman, Sébastien Lacroix, the idea of making such a demand; forthwith he made it part of his program: "In all France the price of bread must bear a reason-able relation to the wages of the poor, and the excess costs must be borne by the rich! Only through this decree will you assure the people of a decent livelihood, bind them to the Revolution, and win their respect and love. Then the people will say: Our representatives have given us bread; they have done more for us than any of our former kings." This was clearly a reply to the Abbé Roux who always harped on the regulation of the grain trade under the old regime; and an equally obvious rebuff to the Enragés who clamored for a fixed maximum price; the decree as he eventually formulated it emphatically stated that neither agriculture nor the grain trade must be harmed. A free play of forces was necessary for the benefit of the individual and the nation.

Danton turned against the rich in so far as they were luke-warm Republicans and cowardly citizens. The commissars of the Convention should say to them: "The people have only their blood which they give lavishly. Go on, you scoundrels, give your riches as lavishly." He was fond, too, of the argument: "The rich man is often not worthy to fight for freedom, let him pay what is needed and let the man of the people go to war." Each citizen was to be equipped with a pike at the expense of well-to-do citizens and Danton advocated the graduated scale of income tax, which had been so often demanded, on the ground that it met the requirements of eternal justice and reason. When the Convention voted for a forced loan to be subscribed by the wealthy, proposed by the Department of Hérault, Danton's voice sounded like the trump of doom in the ears of many a plutocrat: "Paris possesses incalculable riches. Your decree will squeeze the sponge."

But much as he wanted to squeeze the sponge and to make the rich bear their share of public burdens, Danton waged no war against wealth, still less against the property system which was in fact the firm basis of his own existence. Indeed he reassured the rich by striking yet another blow at the notorious "agrarian law." He explained to them that sacrifices were necessary in their own interests because they would suffer most from a foreign invasion; he pointed out that property would be sacred and respected in proportion to the size of the sacrifices they were ready to bear; he flirted—here, too, a unifier—with the idea of binding the rich as well as the poor to the Revolution. His motto was "Respect misery, and misery will respect the rich." All regulations were exceptional measures, necessary in a state of siege. "So long as the ship of state is in danger, the property of the individual is the property of all." But only so long. And for what purpose? "For the preservation of the whole of society."

Foreign war led to civil war.

The defeats suffered by the armies of the Republic caused its enemies everywhere to become arrogant, and hostility, south of the Loire, burst into open flames in March. Although the peasants here had welcomed the year 1789 with its abolition of tithes and feudal dues, once satisfied, they turned a cold shoulder when the Republic asked for taxes and recruits. Having little to do with the political problems of finance and being the victims of isolation in those regions of scant traffic and few roads where each farm was a separate entity, they were more dependent intellectually on the priests than peasants elsewhere. The conscription of the 300,000 made no great demands on these regions; the two Departments of the Vendée and the Loire-Inférieure, with 735,000 inhabitants, had to find no more than 11,524 men. But the population, already roused, replied with open resistance. In this way a conspiracy which had long been working underground, in which the aristocracy and clergy placed all their hopes, came to a head. Long live Louis XVII! Long live religion!

Among the leaders of the movement there were obscure men from the masses like Stoflet, a gamekeeper who had emigrated from the region of Lunéville, and Cathelineau, a cloth peddler and others; but the guiding spirits were former aristocrats and officers. The leading ideas were Elbée's. The cleverest plans of campaign were devised by the Marquis de l'Escure, and Charette de la Contrie provided ample material for legend with his train of Amazons on horseback and his aura of amorous adventures. The higher ranks of the clergy were represented among the insurgents by the ex-Curé Guillot who by his own wits and swindling had promoted himself to be bishop of Agra in India and apostolic vicar for the west of France. Since he did nothing to prevent it the fomenters of the revolt could freely inflame religious superstition. At Somloire a milkmaid who claimed that she could live without food had a large following, because she fell into trances in which she had visions and prophesied. In other places the Virgin appeared in person. The peasantry blindly believed their spiritual shepherds who assured them of resurrection within three days if they fell for the good of the cause on the field of battle. Evidence was provided which might have convinced the most doubting Thomas; three old men were produced with blood-red scars around their necks. Who would suspect that the scar was only a welt made by a cord tightly tied? Who was not ready to swear that by divine miracle and the grace

of God each of the three old men had grown a new head in place
of the one cut off by the guillotine?

The insurgents in the Vendée, in Anjou, and in Poitou did not
form military units but were grouped according to parishes. In
place of a uniform they wore a red cloth heart of Jesus sewn on
their waistcoats, and the officers, following the example of young
Henri de la Rochejaquelin, wore a red handkerchief around
their heads as a badge of rank. Being hunters and poachers, the
people of the Vendée were sure shots and well acquainted with
their wooded country and they excelled in guerrilla warfare: a
volley from an ambush—and the attackers vanished without a
trace. If they advanced in the open they drove Republican prisoners as a living screen before them; the women behind the
fighting line urged the men on with shrill cries. And after a victory they behaved like savages. The set formula of the émigrés
that the Revolution could only be tamed by terror seemed to
have been deeply engrained in these champions of throne and
altar. Drunken hordes were unleashed for pillage and rape on
any cities that had dared to remain faithful to the Republic, and
woe to anyone who so much as went to hear mass celebrated by
a constitutional priest; he was put to the sword without mercy.
There were rumors of prisoners whose wrists had been sawed
through by the insurgents and of others who had been buried
alive. In the small village of Machecoul 542 men, women, old
people, and children were butchered.

The west of France was without troops, and the insurgents
soon obtained the upper hand in eight departments; a proclamation issued by the *armées catholiques et royales* at the end of
May claimed that the cross and the royal standard were everywhere victorious over the bloody flags of anarchy. At first the
Republic relied on its weak reserve force, but in May the coast
defense corps of La Rochelle and Brest were drawn upon, and
when the movement began to spread farther and farther thirty
thousand men from the armies of the Rhine and the north were
hastily brought on the scene of the revolt. Having at length
grasped the danger, the Convention was eager to master the insurrection; for the rebels, with their ties to the émigrés and the
British, sought as their strategic aim the seizure of a port like

Pornic or Les Sables where the British fleet could anchor and land troops.

———————

THE defeats in Belgium, Dumouriez' treachery, and the insurrection in the Vendée, all coming on top of the scarcity of food, necessarily caused the sea of Revolution to run high in Paris. On March 9 and 10 good citizens barred their doors; it looked as though a riot was in the air. The Enragés, headed by Varlet, called out the sections, but only three or four followed, among them the Théâtre-Français; and the whole movement accomplished nothing more than smashing the printing plants of a few unpopular papers.

In the provinces there was a different spirit. Jeanbon Saint-André, who was sent into the Departments of Lot and Dordogne as a "representative of the people on special mission," reported that the "sacred enthusiasm for liberty is stifled in all hearts" —"Everywhere men are tired of the Revolution."

And now when there were dangers within and without, civil war, restlessness, and despondency, Danton took a deep breath in order to fan the flames of Revolution. They were watery souls who thought the Revolution finished! He felt the gale of passion in the sails. The fine thing about a revolution was that it unloosed every passion—in other words every power. Danton simultaneously exulted and gave warning: "A great nation in revolution is like ore seething in the furnace. The statue of liberty has not yet been cast, the ore is liquid; unless you know how to mind the furnace the fire will consume you all." The news from the Vendée made him bitter; the counterrevolution was raising its head more insolently than ever. Danton clenched his fists: "Those who dare to argue in my presence for a counterrevolution and to challenge the men who are carrying on the Revolution—as some have—will receive their reward at my hands. My head may fall later, but at least I shall have given an example to posterity."

No one who saw the flashing eyes, the massive chest, the hammering arm, doubted the seriousness of the threat. Thunderous applause rolled through the Convention. Riding the wave of

enthusiasm, Danton exclaimed: "I ask the Convention to declare
not only to the people of France but to the entire globe that it is
a revolutionary institution, that it will champion freedom, and
that it is resolved to strangle the serpents that gnaw its bosom
and to crush all monsters—by means, if need be, of a law that
will go to the extreme of revolutionary severity." He sounded
the tocsin: "Show yourselves terrible! Show that you are the
people, and you will save the people!"

Again and again he referred to the people. He himself came
from the people; they were the soil in which every strong thing
grew: "Those who wish to prove themselves Frenchmen must
not become estranged from the people; the people have brought
us forth; we are not their fathers but their sons." But while
Danton was ever ready to sing their praises: The people are
great, the people are just, all honor to you, people elect!—
Robespierre's relation to the people was something different.
For the model pupil of the Lycée Louis-le-Grand, who con-
structed the Revolution with compass and protractor, and never
by a lusty oath or an obscene gesture completed his identification
with the street, the people were a *vis mystica*—an entity half
belonging to metaphysics, with an astral body; and when he appealed to the people it seemed like an inverted appeal to Divine
Right. But the people to whom Danton appealed were creatures
of flesh and blood, breathing, eating, drinking, toiling, sweating, laughing, dancing, singing songs, and begetting children.
Robespierre, the disciple of Rousseau, fervently believed in the
goodness and virtue of this people; Danton had a different and
firmer conviction: the people in the mass possessed more revolutionary instinct than all those who gave themselves the airs of
great men.

In spite of their classical masquerade these people did not
possess the stoic equanimity of the Romans. They were subject
to panic, and once terrified, called for the Reign of Terror to
terrify their enemies. Saint Guillotine, help! As early as February the Jacobins had longed to "run the razor of the nation
over France," and the March panic gave additional support to
the belief that the Republic could keep its head erect only by
cutting off the heads of its enemies. The street called for a

thoroughgoing Revolutionary Tribunal, and the Convention echoed its cry. On March 9, Carrier, a jurist and hitherto obscure deputy from Auvergne, took up the demand of several sections for the establishment of a Revolutionary Tribunal; Bourdon asked for the reinstitution of the Extraordinary Court of August 17, and Levasseur, a surgeon and obstetrician from Le Mans, evolved a decree to this effect, which was accepted and passed on for drafting to the Legislative Committee.

When the Convention met the following day it found the streets in no state of Sunday quiet; men armed with pikes were abroad, and the more timid souls in the Manège were listening for the tocsin's sound. Garrau rose to point out that the organization of the Revolutionary Tribunal was due for consideration. But the Convention had first to deal with the Belgian question; Dumouriez' letters were read out, reports heard, and the hours passed. Garrau rose again, and Cambacérès said with decision: "I object to the meeting being closed before the formation of the Revolutionary Tribunal has been resolved on." Delacroix supported him, Lesage and Lindet produced two drafts, and a discussion arose as to whether the Tribunal was to have a jury or not and if so how it was to be appointed. Meanwhile, six o'clock struck and President Gensonné rose: "The meeting is adjourned!"

A resounding voice rang above the talk of the dispersing members: "I ask all good citizens not to leave their seats." Noise and chatter died away into complete silence. Dusk had fallen. The hall was dimly lit by a few lamps, and the tribune from which the call to stay had come was in semidarkness. But everyone knew the voice.

With pounding words like hammer strokes Danton drove in the idea of the Revolutionary Tribunal. Not because the street clamored for it, or because Danton, not easily frightened himself, believed in the power of terror, but because the function of the Tribunal would be to convince the people that steps were being taken against the traitors, and so to charge them with energy and restrain them from excesses. He made no secret of these political considerations: the purpose of the Tribunal was to prevent the people from taking justice into their own hands in dealing with the counterrevolutionaries: "Humanity demands that you should save the enemies of liberty from the people's vengeance."

From the lips of a deputy who was swallowed up in the twilight of the hall—was it Lanjuinais?—fell the single word: September!

Ghostly shadows flitted along the walls; calls for order came from every side.

But Danton, no whit annoyed, took up the interruption: "Since somebody has dared to recall those bloody days which every good citizen deplores, I claim that if such a Tribunal had existed then, the people who have been so often and so cruelly blamed for those days would not have stained them with blood." And since the safety of the people demanded great and terrible measures: "Let us make good the omissions of the Legislative Assembly. Let us be terrible to save the people from being terrible! Let us erect a Tribunal so that the people may know that the sword of justice is suspended above the heads of their enemies!"

Three weeks later Danton urged that the prosecuting attorney of the Revolutionary Tribunal be empowered to prosecute on his own account. Here again he acted not only in order to set the new Tribunal going but also "to avoid sanguinary scenes such as popular vengeance would bring with it" if the intervention of the Convention in each individual case were to delay the course of swift justice.

Danton knew that his contemporaries as well as posterity would misinterpret his motives; that the part played by Carrier, Bourdon, Levasseur, and Garrau, and the sections would be forgotten, while he alone would be considered the creator of the Revolutionary Tribunal and would be remembered as the bloodhound. Yet he took on himself the great historical responsibility at the command of history.

The Extraordinary Court began to function on April 6. Danton could say that every means of defense was provided for the accused. The procedure of the Tribunal in examination of the accused and of witnesses, and the speeches of prosecution and defense did not differ from those of the ordinary courts, but it

confined itself almost entirely to crimes connected with emigration and to counterrevolutionary activities, and admitted no
possibility of appeal. As time went on Danton continued to exer-
cise an influence on the Tribunal not only because he soon
became almighty in the Committee of Public Safety, but also because the public prosecutor, Fouquier-Tinville, formerly a lawyer at the Paris bar, had been appointed to office during Danton's term as Minister of Justice on the strength of a letter addressed to Desmoulins, who was a distant relative. He was not
Danton's only supporter in the court; the most devoted of all
was the clerk Fabricius Pâris.

During the three months of the supremacy of Danton's Cabinet the knife of the guillotine fell thirty-one times, or only once
every third day; in twenty-two cases the Tribunal granted swift
acquittals.

FEARING the competition of the Enragés in courting the favor
of the street, the Mountain sought to turn the people's fury on
the Girondists. Traitors who had voted against the death of the
tyrant! As early as March 1 the Jacobins excluded from their
number the "Appelants," those who had favored the appeal to
the people on January 15; and three days later they showed no
sign of disapproval when the Society of the "Defenders of the
One and Indivisible Republic" produced an address which demanded not only the dismissal of the faithless deputies but their
execution. And on March 24 the Jacobins asked in a circular to
the affiliated societies that the departments pass sentence on
Brissot, Gensonné, Vergniaud, Guadet, and others; the ther-
mometer hardly ever fell below fever point.

Neither Robespierre nor Marat intended to use force against
the Gironde. The former hoped that Brissot's adherents would
be fatally compromised by the latest events and would be swept
out of politics, although because of his rigid devotion to consti-
tutionalism the "inviolability of deputies" remained sacred; it
would be the most disastrous of all measures if the representa-

tives of the people were interfered with. Marat continued to see in the Convention itself, "in the party of Roland, in the statesmen who want to destroy the Republic," the hotbed of conspiracy. But on March 12 he protested against a petition of the section Poissonière, which shouted for the heads of Gensonné, Vergniaud, and Guadet: "An abominable crime aiming at the dissolution of the Convention and the destruction of the country!"

As usual it was Danton who took a long step toward safeguarding the Gironde. Unity was his hope, his faith, and his aim.

He was no rhapsodist who could not bear the thought of splitting with the Gironde, no unctuous admonisher—"Brethren, love one another!"—no orator who greeted with swimming eyes the day of harmony. Danton was only a man awake to political facts when he denied to the last the necessity for civil war. The Mountain and the Gironde were not the representatives of two different classes of society, so that the defeat of one and the victory of the other fulfilled the logic of historical development; the two opposing parties were only two different expressions of one and the same movement which extended from Buzot to Marat. The Gironde represented the urge for economic development, the Mountain the political vigor of the Revolution. The vital difference between the two was voiced by Barère in the Convention on March 18: "One part of the meeting rightly believes that we are still in the midst of a revolution; the other part does not." Doom lay in the fact that each party had eyes only for itself; the Mountain failed to see that without the urge for economic development represented by the Gironde the Revolution must become meaningless and sterile, and the Gironde did not perceive that without the political power of the Mountain the Revolution had no ground under its feet and must succumb to foreign attacks. Danton alone recognized both and attempted to unite Mountain and Gironde.

The story went that in the middle of March Danton tried to come to an understanding with the Girondist leaders. Bancal and Vergniaud were well disposed but Guadet, taking his cue from the Salon Roland, proved obdurate. "There must be war!" he exclaimed. "One of us two must perish." Danton sadly took the zealot's hand and looked fixedly in that face flushed with anger: "Guadet, Guadet, you want war and your part will be death." And he dropped the hand that lay grudgingly in his.

Whether this actually happened or not, Danton appealed to the Gironde from the tribune of the Convention. He was aware of the dissatisfaction on the other side caused by Marat's extremism, so he took care to stress his own deliberation. He knew the cold political and personal hate Robespierre felt for the Brissotins and he emphasized his own freedom from such feelings. He was well aware that the others accused him of aiming at dictatorship, so when discussing the appointment of deputies as ministers, he vowed that he would never take a portfolio while he had the honor to be a member of the National Convention.

But it was to no avail. The *Patriote français* was already giving out that the new cabinet had been drawn up and that Danton would be Minister of Foreign Affairs: "No one doubted that Danton wanted to be first among these ministers; one felt sure of it, when one heard him swear in the name of the country. . . . Danton swearing by his country! The country of an ambitious man! It was like hearing an atheist swear by the Supreme Being."

In those years of malicious polemics slanders flourished with tropical exuberance. It was a common accusation against those of a different political complexion that they were plotting with the enemy. In his *"Secret History of the Revolution"* Camille Desmoulins not only accused the Gironde of intending to divide France into twenty or thirty federated republics but represented Brissot as an agent of Orléans and the Girondins as Royalists, and wanted them thrown out of the Convention for being in the pay of Pitt. In return floods of Girondin calumnies poured over Danton; the federates of Brittany sang:

> *Quoi! sur cette place fameuse*
> *Qui fume encore du sang breton,*
> *On verrait la troupe hideuse*
> *Et des Cobourgs et des Dantons.*

Salle, deputy of the Meurthe, and Doctor of Philosophy from

the University of Pont-à-Mousson, did not scruple to confide to Garat, the Minister of the Interior, that the Cordeliers were negotiating with all the governments that were intent on destroying French liberty. As a result of these conspiracies the Duke of York would come to the throne and would be murdered by the Duke of Orléans; Orléans in turn would be assassinated by Marat, Danton, and Robespierre; the triumvirate would divide France among them until the most skilful of the three, Danton, assassinated the other two and governed alone, first as dictator and presently openly as king. This utter nonsense was believed by otherwise quite reasonable men, and it was as a result of such feelings that a Girondist called out at the meeting of March 10, "You behave like a king!"

Although Danton retorted, "And you speak like a coward!" he carefully avoided slandering others and shook off vituperations as a poodle shakes off raindrops. With the revolutionary thunderbolt in one hand and the olive branch in the other, he never wearied of urging: We all desire the welfare of the people, we all have one aim. On March 27 he published a letter of Roland's enticing Dumouriez to join the Gironde in order to "crush the Paris party—and especially this Danton." But no more of that: "Let us form a sacred league for the salvation of liberty. Let us clear away all points of difference. There need be no embraces, for private enmities are insuperable. But the safety of all is at stake; let us cease to hate each other and do away with misunderstandings and animosities."

On March 30 the above-mentioned Salle was the center of excitement in the Manège. He was supposed to have written a letter to the vice-president of the administration of the Department of the Meurthe, Piquelet, in which he attempted to prejudice him against the commissars of the Convention. It was moved that this letter be produced for examination. Danton, by asking for the production of Piquelet's letters to Salle, too, called up with this harmless demand the violent indignation of the Right. As though they had been waiting an occasion, his enemies burst out: "Why don't you ask for the Inquisition!" Someone called insolently, "The account! The account!" And someone else, "What about the four millions in the secret fund?"

Danton, mounting the tribune to report on Belgian affairs, did not break out like an infuriated bull. He straightened up, ready to account for everything. Let whoever had or knew something against him speak out without subterfuge. He needed neither mercy nor consideration, and would answer every charge. Accusations, not insinuations; speak up, speak up! Accordingly he suggested for the next day a report of the Executive Council on the activities of the commissars, and then his own defense, to be followed by a general debate. In this way all the obscurities would be cleared up at the eleventh hour. With all Europe in arms against France, there was no more time for domestic strife. Once more he urged unity: "May danger at last unite you! Remember that we are in the midst of the most terrible crisis." Unity and mutual confidence are essential. "And have not certain authorities called for my head? My head is still firm on my shoulders and it will stay there! Let each man use his own head not to give way to petty passions but to serve the Republic."

A large part of the meeting was stirred, but Lasource's voice rose disagreeably: "I move that Danton's motion be postponed until Dumouriez has appeared at the bar. I accuse nobody; but I consider the disaffection of the army in Belgium the result of a conspiracy, and I wish to have an account of these matters." The motion was accepted.

And Danton knew where he stood.

Ever since the bomb had burst in Belgium the Gironde had trembled lest Dumouriez should cause their destruction: for Dumouriez was their man; the Gironde had flattered him, had defended him against Pache, the Minister of War, and, jealous that Danton and Robespierre praised him, claimed him as theirs. So now, partly to cry "Stop thief!" and partly in order to defeat a hated enemy, they made this treacherous attack on Danton, whose relations with the insurgent general were open to the eyes of everybody.

But Danton parried the blow in good time. On the evening of March 31 at the Jacobins', he was like a man who draws his sword against a pressing crowd and puts his back to the wall. Challenged by Marat, he explained his conduct in the Dumouriez affair, vowed his loyalty to the people, recalled his struggle against Lafayette, referred to the Mountain, which was as indivisible as the Jacobins and the Republic, and suggested appealing to the departments for the withdrawal of those deputies who had not voted for the death of the tyrant. "The Convention is infested with former members of the Constituent Assembly and with aristocrats; let us take care that it purges itself without causing fresh dissensions."

The Jacobins and the galleries shouted approval. Marat, pleased, turned his yellow face to the speaker: "Danton, I never meant to attack your Republicanism, only your lack of prudence . . . Danton, I ask you to ascend the tribune of the Convention and rend the veil." And Danton: "I have undertaken the obligation and I shall fulfil it."

At the meeting of the Convention the next day Marat continued his campaign by blaming the Brissot faction for the war and the inadequate defense of the fortresses. There was a tumult and calls for order; the ruffled surface grew smooth again; letters and reports were read; Pénières attacked Danton because of Dumouriez' letter of March 12, which had been kept from the Convention for several days; Danton replied matter-of-factly, once more challenging his accusers to take the tribune, certain that his head "instead of falling, would prove the Gorgon's head that would cause all aristocrats to tremble."

But the attacks were redoubled and Danton had need of all his firmness.

As yesterday, it was Lasource, the priest from the Cevennes, who coupled Danton's name with Dumouriez'. Dumouriez and Danton! Dumouriez wanted to restore the monarchy, Danton was his accomplice. Danton had kept Dumouriez at the head of the army, Danton had kept up the people's confidence in Dumouriez, Danton had exaggerated the dangers to the country in order to cause riots and to provide Dumouriez with reason for taking action. Lasource demanded the immediate appointment of a committee of investigation: "Finally, in order to prove to the nation that we shall never have dealings with a tyrant, I insist that each of us swear to slay the man who attempts to make himself king or dictator." The Assembly rose as one man to swear; the whole Gironde swore against Danton.

And he sat during this speech with crossed arms, head flung back, the veins on his forehead swelling. But this rage was caused by more than personal feeling. He was more than ever convinced that the Gironde was worthless to the great cause. The Girondists had made light of the defeats in Belgium and shut their eyes to the insurrection in the Vendée, had raised shouts of indignation over the demand for a unified executive power, objected violently to the Revolutionary Tribunal as "the most terrible of inquisitions," and in short had rejected every vigorous measure for the defense of the country. They were the destroyers of the Revolution. The Gironde was a dead limb on the body of the movement.

Those who knew Danton and saw him sitting there immovable on his bench, knew the meaning of that contemptuous lift of the lip. His looks expressed scorn and contempt: The idiots! Now and then his face twitched and as he walked toward the tribune he growled to himself, "These criminals want to fasten their crimes on me."

His first sentences were drowned by a surge of excited calls. His voice rose above the sea of voices and was drowned again: Speak before the committee, not here! Refer the matter to the committee!

The suggestion was adopted and Danton was muzzled, but no sooner had he returned to his seat than the Mountain burst out with: Back to the tribune! Go on! Go on! The galleries applauded and the applause swelled when he stood again on the speakers' stand—the staunch Republican Danton, as Collot d'Herbois had just called him at the Jacobins'.

The president covered himself, and interrupted the meeting to ask the House whether they wished to hear Danton; Lasource observed loftily: "You may as well hear him."

Danton drew a deep breath—and for two hours the fury of his words lashed the Gironde.

He was not one of those sages who are always right and when they are wrong cling to the semblance of right. He freely admitted that his policy of moderation had been a mistake. He turned to the Mountain: "You have charged me with being weak, and you are right; I admit it before France." Again he explained the Belgian affair and briefly referred to Lasource's "fairy tale" about his relations to Dumouriez: "Why did I give up the system of silence and moderation? Because there is a limit to deliberation and because when I am attacked by those who ought to be thankful for my restraint, I have a right to attack and fling aside caution."

Applause from the Mountain and the galleries. Danton's voice boomed like an alarm gun calling the soldiers to the breach.

He launched on a merciless attack on the Gironde: Only those who wanted to spare the King must have really wanted a king. "Yes, they alone are the tools of the conspiracy! Yet they accuse me! Me! I am not afraid of Dumouriez or of any of those with whom I have been in touch. If Dumouriez can produce a single line of mine warranting the shadow of an accusation, I will forfeit my head."

A storm of applause.

Then he cut through the last chain. "I do not believe there can be any more truce between those patriots who voted for the death of the tyrant and the cowards who wanted to save him and so calumniated us before the whole of France."

For minutes on end roars of applause echoed along the walls of the chamber.

"I therefore appeal to you who sat in judgment on the tyrant to close your ranks. Call the people to take arms against the foreign foe and crush the domestic foe, and by your immutable strength of character destroy all the aristocrats, all the moderates, all those who have cast aspersions on you in the departments. With these there can be no more compromise."

He held the whole Assembly hypnotized and enthralled until the last sentence: "You will see whether I am afraid of my accusers. I have entrenched myself in the citadel of right; I shall sally forth with the artillery of truth to grind my enemies to dust."

The Mountain had long followed Danton's policy of national union with surprise and disappointment, had considered him a moderate, a leader of the "Plain." So this irrevocable declaration of war against the Gironde intoxicated them with triumph. They now felt themselves on the summits, sure of victory; their emotion broke its bounds and the speaker was smothered in their embraces.

From this hour the Girondins were lost; not so much because Danton had turned against them as because he had hitched Dumouriez to their coat tails. As early as April 5 the Jacobins had sent a circular to their affiliated societies denouncing the horde of despots whose patricidal hands were tearing the vitals of France, and had called for a swarm of petitions from the departments to drive the "faithless deputies" out of the Convention. But the Gironde were undaunted. The fortnightly elections of presidents continued to confirm their majority in the National Assembly: Lasource on April 18, Boyer-Fonfrède on May 2, and Isnard on May 16. Attack was therefore the best defense and on April 12 Pétion called for a policy of ruthlessness; no weakness toward these criminals! And Guadet, a lean, lanky, dark, black-haired Southerner aimed a shot at Danton, whom he described as a kingmaker in the service of the Duke of Orléans, and at Marat who, because he had signed the Jacobin circular of April 5, ought to be brought before the public prosecutor. Philippe Egalité was behind lock and key because his son, the Duke of Chartres, had followed Dumouriez into the camp of Coburg; Orléanism was now a fluttering ghost—it had never amounted to much—and it was easy for Danton to dispose of the charges against him by demanding that citizen Egalité be brought before the Revolutionary Tribunal of Marseilles and that a price be put on the heads of the émigré Bourbons and of General Dumouriez. It was in vain, however, that he pointed out the gravity of prosecuting a member of the House and how serious might be the consequences, especially when the evidence was not completely convincing: Hands off the National Convention! Marat was sent before the Revolutionary Tribunal by 226 against 92 votes. Twelve days later the "People's Friend" was acquitted and carried back to the Manège in triumph by cheering throngs, with a civil crown on his brow. Danton praised this "edifying spectacle," not because of the accused, whose assumption of infallibility he disliked as much as his coquettish air of martyrdom, but because of the accusers, because the acquittal was a defeat for the Gironde!

Yet it seemed as though Danton could not entirely break away from his policy of reconciliation; he was incapable of a radical breach with the Gironde. He no longer tried to save the handful of leaders who, blinded by passion, obstinately swayed toward the abyss; but he repeatedly appealed to the bulk of deputies backing Brissot and Buzot, whom he considered amenable to reason: "Let us draw together, let us have a brotherly union. Our safety is at stake." When Philippeaux pleaded for unity on April 16 and pointed to the foreign dangers, everyone suspected that the speech had been inspired by Danton who, a little later, spoke to the same effect: "When all Europe swarms in on us, why do we not form a united phalanx, since we must either die together or save the Republic together?" Louvet, however, wrote a pamphlet in which he attributed to the Left the intention to destroy, plunder, proscribe, and massacre in order finally to rule under a puppet king. "Shall we keep peace with them? Never. No armistice is possible between proud Republicans who are devoted to freedom, and faithless Royalists who are resolved on tyranny. Between virtue and crime there must be implacable war, everlasting war!" This was the Gironde's answer to Danton.

Since the beginning of May it had been growing plainer every day that the sections, driven by hunger, were fomenting a revolt against the unpopular deputies. This, too, the Gironde met firmly. They required their adherents to attend the meetings of the sections, which suddenly were swamped by a crowd of domestic servants, pampered mother's darlings, houseowners, well-fed bourgeois, dandies with two watch-chains, and rentiers with heavy sticks who intended to crush the lower middle-class Enragés by force of numbers. A keener weapon in the hands of the Gironde, if only because of its composition, was the Commission of Twelve, elected by the Convention on May 18, whose powers were roughly the same as those of the Committee of General Security.

A week previously the Assembly had moved from the Manège to the Tuileries into a remodeled theatrical hall on the first floor, where once the Corps de Ballet had floated up and down before the *Roi Soleil,* and where old Voltaire had been crowned in 1778. The deputies had ten semicircular rows of seats. The speaker's stand faced them, with the president's seat above it. From a box hung three huge tricolor flags which were set on an altar with the inscription *"La Loi."* Colossal statues of Solon and Lycurgus stared into the room and the walls were decorated everywhere with the Roman fasces and the lictor's ax.

The Convention brought its morbid irritability with it to its new home. In fact it grew worse, for in the absence of proper ventilation the deputies breathed too much dust and not enough oxygen, and as the sound waves were caught in innumerable niches, one had to shout to be heard. The deputies would have shouted in any case; they shouted at each other; they shouted each other down. Also the street could interfere in these meetings to a much greater extent than at the Manège. The two thousand spectators in the twenty-four galleries—many of them wearing, as one deputy said, "the livery of misery"—shouted, too, in moments of excitement, and threatened and shook their fists and drew their weapons.

Nor was the president able to prevent unpleasant scenes between the deputies. When Gensonné, climbing the nine steep steps to the speaker's stand, stumbled and exclaimed angrily: "They're like the steps of a scaffold!" Carrier called with bitter sarcasm, "You might as well practice." Marat was fond of waving his pistol in the air, and others carried weapons in the back pockets of their tail coats or displayed sword canes. When the hunchback Larevellière-Lépeaux, an otherwise upright man, screeched at Danton, the latter laughed: "What, do you think you can touch me? I will twist you around my thumb and if that is not enough for you, I will throw you down from the tribune as your presumption deserves."

Marat was no longer hiding his desire to bring that "group of statesmen" who had haled him before the Revolutionary Tribunal to the scaffold—and to do so by getting the street to put pressure on the reluctant Convention. But Robespierre, with his restraining "lawfulness above all," disappointed the Jacobins and still more the Enragés. Danton observed with even more

mixed feelings the deliberate preparations for a new August 10,
hunger being not the least impulse for it. The final incentive,
however, came again from the Gironde, which became more
boisterous as its adherents at Lyons, Marseilles, Bordeaux, and
Nantes became more lively.

The gun was aimed and fired in one motion: On May 24 the
Commission of Twelve ordered the arrest of Hébert and Varlet
for sedition. As Hébert was deputy procurator of the Commune,
the next day a deputation of that body attested his innocence
and requested his release. Isnard was presiding, and suspecting
a threat from the street, he lost his nerve: "If ever the dignity
of the Convention were to be insulted; if ever by one of these
revolts which have been perpetually occurring since March
10 . . ." Interruptions. Lively dissent on the Left, applause on
the Right, and calls from the Mountain: "That is no answer!"
Fabre d'Eglantine lowered his lorgnette: "I request the floor
against the president!" But Isnard refused to be silenced: "If
these continually recurring disorders were to interfere with the
representatives of the people, then I declare, in the name of all
France . . ." No, no! on the Left. Yes! yes! on the Right. Speak
in the name of France! Isnard: "I declare in the name of all
France that Paris would be destroyed . . ." Confusion and
hubbub and Marat's shrill voice: "Get down from your seat, you
disgrace the Assembly!" But Isnard: ". . . and men would
search the banks of the Seine to see whether there ever was a
city of Paris." Tumult, shouting, Danton's appeal to be heard
and calls of: Danton has the floor!

But Danton did not bludgeon down Isnard and did not label
his threats, as others did later, "desecrations" and "monstrosi-
ties." It is true, he censured the "bitter answer"—a president
should not talk like that. He poured sarcasm over the felt-shod
moderates, and asked what would have become of the Revolution if there had been no hotheads, if the people had never become violent? True, he presented those who were overcautious
with the "great truth" that, if the choice must be made between
two excesses, it was better to take freedom than to return to
slavery. True, he proclaimed the glory of Paris, "this vast city
which renews its youth each day." But the aim of his impetuous

and confident words was to scare the street away from the Convention: "Would Paris touch the National Assembly? Would Paris, that first broke the iron scepter, injure the Ark of the Covenant intrusted to it? No, Paris is loyal to the Revolution, and, by its sacrifices in the cause of Freedom, it has deserved the embrace of every Frenchman."

Among the masses, however, Isnard's threats acted as a vigorous ferment. Was Paris to be leveled to the ground? Was there to be a second Duke of Brunswick? To arms!

Unfortunately, the Gironde, too, had arms. On May 27 several companies from the moderate section Butte-des-Moulins were summoned by the Commission of Twelve and set up their cannon on the Place du Carrousel.

The next day the spokesman of a deputation from the section of the Gardes Françaises assured the Gironde: "You have but to say one word, and you will be surrounded by defenders! Then the courage of good citizens will be seen on this side and, on the other, the cowardice and treachery of a handful of brigands." Such a provocation was too much for Danton, who called to the Mountain: "Don't be afraid; you have behind you the vast majority of the Republic. Look at Paris!" And he unfurled a banner: "The time has come for the people to quit the defensive and to attack all the supporters of the principle of moderation."

This was declaring civil war in the Convention.

Things now began to happen at headlong speed: Hébert's acquittal, the abolition and reinstitution of the Commission of Twelve—and amid all the tumult, shaken by fever, the Convention still despatched current business. On May 29 Barère reported in the name of the Committee of Public Safety on the question of Public Instruction and the Constitution, with golden words of conciliation: "Nobody has the monopoly of patriotism; let us march united." When the Gironde applauded these sentences, Cambon exclaimed: "The words you cheer are the words of a man you calumniate—Danton." But Barère's report was already some days old and had been overtaken by the precipitate course of events.

On the day when the report was submitted the representatives of the sections met at the bishop's palace; an insurrectionary committee of nine was elected; the Hôtel-de-Ville was packed, a revolutionary Council General of the Commune formed, and, Santerre having left for the Vendée as general, Hanriot, a former clerk of the *octroi*, was appointed commander of the National Guard.

For hours the tocsin had been hammering and the assembly sounding, and mobs armed with pikes had thronged around the Tuileries when, in the cool of the morning of May 31, the deputies entered the hall. Danton was sitting, almost alone and reflective, on his bench. Louvet remarked to Guadet: "Do you see the horrid hope illuminating those ugly features?" And the man of classical education replied: "Doubtless today Clodius is driving Cicero into exile."

Indeed, having hesitated like Robespierre until the last moment to make the cause of insurrection his own, Danton had finally become convinced that the popular movement could no longer be stopped. So he too threw himself into it head first. He had already taken steps on the previous day to cut short the deliberations of the Committee of Public Safety and of the Convention; the night was needed for preparations for the insurrection.

Even though Danton lent his name and his driving force to the insurrection, and so turned the revolt of a party into the revolution of a people, he hated unnecessary bloodshed. No September massacres! Soon a young idiot, Leclerc d'Oze, the idol of the Society of Republican Women and especially of its president, Claire Lacombe, the actress, would report indignantly to the Jacobins that the criminal resistance of Danton and Legendre had compelled the insurrectionaries to moderation on May 31: "Legendre and Danton opposed the revolutionary measures which we had taken in those great days to destroy all the aristocrats of Paris." And on the evening of May 31 Chabot had showed signs of nervousness at the Jacobins' because Danton seemed to have lost his old energy.

But to what did Danton owe these criticisms? When during the session of May 31 the majority resolved to call Hanriot before the bar for having had the alarm gun fired, and the Mountain was somewhat frightened and embarrassed, it was Danton

who showed the way to satisfy the people without humiliating
the Convention. He appealed to the people, to this "advance post
of the Republic," and to the city of Paris which had deserved so
well of the country; his suggestion was simply to abolish the
Commission of Twelve, an attempt to turn the fury of the street
away from the bulk of the Gironde onto the smallest possible
fraction. It was again at the instigation of Danton, who ruled
the Committee of Public Safety, that Barère brought forward
the same motion in the name of the committee. The Convention
accepted it and the day, which had begun with threatening gestures, ended with some laughter and a torchlight procession.

Two days later Hanriot had surrounded the Tuileries with
five or six thousand men drawn from the most determined of the
sections. The Convention deliberated under the muzzles of the
cannon, and beside each piece stood an iron grate with a coal
fire to heat incendiary shot. Lanjuinais, a tenacious Breton who
was not to be intimidated, accused the criminals who had seized
authority. Legendre, the butcher, screamed furiously: "Down
from the tribune, or I'll slaughter you." And Lanjuinais answered contemptuously: "First let the House resolve that I am
an ox."

But the street for the last time demanded the decree for the
accusation of the Gironde deputies. The committee devised still
another means of escape, perhaps thought out by Danton, and
proposed by Barère: the deputies who were particularly hated
by the street, twenty-two in number, should resign voluntarily
—yes, voluntarily—in order to preserve the dignity of the Convention. Isnard, Lanthenas, and Fauchet were ready; but Lanjuinais said coldly "No," and Barbaroux passionately "Never!"

Indeed the dignity of the Convention had gone up in smoke
long ago! Sentries posted at the doors prevented the deputies
from leaving the chamber. Danton protested: "Who gave these
orders? The committee will avenge the injured majesty of the
nation."

In order to demonstrate the freedom of the Convention to
everybody, Barère suggested a walk. Headed by the president,
Hérault de Séchelles, the Assembly moved through the anteroom, the Hall of Liberty, and down the great, broad staircase

into the sunny warmth of the spring day. Outside were guns, rifles, pikes, National Guards, crowds, black two-cornered hats with tricolor cockades, red Jacobin caps, blue uniforms, and bare muscular arms. Hanriot, no giant physically, but clattering his sword, brisk and very important under his brand new general's plume, barred the president's way. A few polite words of protest from Hérault; a curt, harsh, contemptuous reply from Hanriot, another attempt at protest, and Danton could see the commandant's eyes flashing like powder in the pan, and hear the thunderous command:

"Stand to your guns!"

The gunners with lighted fuses took their posts.

No God helped here!

Moving along the railings of the Tuileries gardens, the humiliated Convention returned to the hall, doing the inevitable with a shrug. Couthon, whose legs had been paralyzed for many years, rolled his mechanical wheel chair up to the tribune, and in his slightly whining voice demanded a decree for the arrest of Gensonné, Vergniaud, Brissot, Guadet, Pétion, Buzot, Barbaroux, Lasource, Lanjuinais, Louvet, and a dozen other deputies, besides the members of the Commission of Twelve and the ministers Clavières and Lebrun, and their being kept under surveillance at their respective homes.

Resolved!

The Gironde had ceased to exist.

Even the most convinced adherents of the Mountain did not feel quite comfortable about their own victory. It was one thing to decapitate the king anointed by the Lord, but a very different matter to villainously mutilate the parliament elected by the people and solemnly appointed to bring salvation to the world. None of those present forgot this meeting of June 2 with its frightening pauses: the Assembly sat mute before a silent president for minutes on end. Only from outside there came the noise of arms and the murmur of the crowd.

And to Danton it seemed at times as though, deprived of the Gironde, he had lost something solid; as though the air of the Revolution was heavier to breathe and the new region afforded him no opportunity of using his full skill in maneuver. But Danton never denied facts and he boldly confessed his adherence to the insurrection: without May 31 there could be no liberty in France!

THE essential difference between the Gironde and the Mountain was that the former favored a constitutional, that is a peaceful and orderly government which took it for granted that all was settled and definitive inside and outside of France, while the latter was in favor of a revolutionary government, a provisional government using extraordinary means, because the Republic was still struggling for its existence along the whole line. No man was more profoundly convinced of the necessity of a revolutionary government than Danton, the creator of the Revolutionary Tribunal and the instigator of the revolutionary dictatorship, the man who had wanted to put the aristocrats "under the pike of the sansculottes"; yet at the same time no man felt a greater longing for a permanent constitutional regime and no one, at least in the Mountain, more wholeheartedly championed the opinion that this structure must be built immediately. The French needed only to follow that ancient people who "wielded the trowel in one hand and the sword in the other."

Because the work of constructing a constitution did not progress, Danton's impatience grew. A constitution for the Republic seemed to him of paramount importance: it ought to be based on the most democratic principles that were possible, assuring the maintenance of the people's rights down to the last detail, opening the best road for legislation and allowing the government a maximum of force without permitting it to assume absolute power. It would be an immortal work that would banish at once the dangers at home and abroad. And after the events of May 31 and June 2 Danton was not the only one to call for a constitution as a bulwark for the Republic.

The Constitutional Committee of the Convention to which Danton, too, belonged at times had been dawdling long enough. The debates on Condorcet's draft of February 15 dragged on for weeks and months. Finally Hérault de Séchelles had to sit at the same table with Couthon, Saint-Just, Ramel, and Matthieu in order to get a swift, thorough job done. Then the dust began to fly, but still the amiable epicurean found time to make fun of his intellectually slower colleagues, Couthon as well as Saint-Just. The name of Minos, the judge of the dead in classical legend, was mentioned; since the others did not follow the allusion, Hérault promptly sent to the Bibliothèque National for "the laws of Minos which must be in some of the Greek law compendia." But on June 10 he was able to read the completed draft of the Constitution to the Convention.

Danton took part in the debate on only two occasions. On June 12 the question of secret or public ballot at elections was debated. Ducos, a lawyer from Bordeaux who had only just missed proscription as a Girondist, got at the nub of the matter when he explained that a public vote would permit factory owners or large farmers to exert pressure on their workers or laborers. Danton, on the other hand, as the spokesman of a time which showed a tendency toward heroism in every field, held that truth and frankness were the daily bread of freedom and spoke in favor of the undisguised expression of the political will of the voters. Perhaps he also felt some anxiety lest otherwise the counterrevolution muster strong battalions at the polls. But his common sense led him to grant the secret ballot to those who preferred it. The Convention agreed with his view.

When four days later the Assembly was debating whether a declaration of war should be effected by decree, that is, whether a resolution of the legislative body would be sufficient or whether a law that expressed the will of the whole people was necessary, healthy common sense was again Danton's adviser. His friend Thuriot, with the peaceful attitude of the prosperous French bourgeois, objected to giving the right to declare war to the people's representatives instead of to the people themselves. A parliament might be swayed by questions of prestige or imaginary vital interests of the nation, whereas the people might be more ready to give up a disputed right rather than lose their happiness and repose. To this Ducos objected that it might be necessary to anticipate the attack of an enemy threatening the frontier; it would be absurd to spend weeks and weeks taking a plebiscite. Into the tablet of new values to be drawn up by the Convention Danton chiseled first of all the sentence: The French people will never wage an aggressive war! But he agreed with Ducos in declaring: "If I see an enemy aiming at me I shall shoot first if I can, but only in self-defense." Likewise if the safety of the State should be in danger the Legislative Assembly, too, must attack in self-defense. However, he was at one with Thuriot when he added: "But even after hostilities have broken out there is nothing to prevent a plebiscite to decide whether the war shall be continued or not." The Convention resolved that with this reservation of Danton's a law was necessary before war could be declared.

On June 24, 1793, the Constitution of the French Republic was adopted, bearing a new Declaration of the Rights of Men and Citizens: "The happiness of all is the aim of society." Built on the broad foundation of popular sovereignty, originating in the people who were the source of every power, with a plebiscite for keystone and a solemn affirmation of the right to insurrection, the Constitution was erected, a proud temple of political freedom, the like of which the earth had never seen. This Magna Charta of democracy was adopted by plebiscite by 1,801,918 against 11,610 votes.

On August 10—the anniversary of the taking of the Tuileries —the Constitution was solemnly proclaimed. David had placed and divided the crowds with his painter's eye and planned the celebrations, which cost more than a million livres. Danton walked in the procession with the other deputies, each bearing a sheaf of wheat spears and branches.

On the square where once the Bastille had darkened the sky, a mighty statue of Nature had been erected—a giant figure of a woman holding her full breasts so that jets of water spurted from them, silver in the sunlight. Hérault de Séchelles, like a figure cut from a revolutionary fashion magazine with his tricolor-plumed hat and big sword at his side, a heathen and a scoffer but moved in spite of himself, stepped out before the goddess: "O Nature; accept the eternal homage of the French nation to your laws! May the fruitful water that flows from your breast, this pure draught that quenched the thirst of the first human beings, stream into this cup of equality and fraternity, there to sanctify the oath which France offers you today. Since first the sun moved through the universe it has witnessed no more glorious day than this." Holding out an agate goblet, he filled it at the gleaming stream and carried it to his lips, then filled it again and again and handed it in turn to each of the eighty-six venerable representatives of the departments. A gentle breeze fanned their white hair; the *Chant du départ,* with words by Marie-Joseph de Chénier set to music by Méhul, was sung, and the guns thundered.

Danton, too, was stirred. Very different had been the thunder of the guns a year ago, and much had passed since that other August 10! It was promise and fulfilment—sowing and reaping.

To Danton the Constitution was also a battery for firing shells to confound the enemies of freedom.

Keen eyes like his perceived that the arrest of the Girondins which the street had enforced would lead to harm. In order to avoid the worst disaster the Committee of Public Safety first endeavored to satisfy the provinces as to the safety of the arrested deputies. At Danton's suggestion Barère proposed on behalf of the committee that deputies of the Mountain should offer themselves as hostages to the departments. When Danton warmly supported the motion in the Convention, Couthon was the first to offer himself.

But it was too late! Twenty of the arrested deputies had evaded the lax surveillance of their homes. Hastening into their constituencies, they carried the fuel of discontent into the towns and provinces. Caen, Lyons, and Marseilles blazed up as the three great centers of the resistance against Paris. Soon the flames of civil war were leaping from department to department. Eure, Calvados, Finistère, Ille-et-Vilaine, Côtes-du Nord, Morbihan, and Mayenne broke away from the Convention and raised armed levies of their own. The whole of the Midi was ablaze. By the middle of June only some twenty departments were absolutely loyal to the Jacobin Republic, while behind the Girondin insurrection of the others the Royalist counterrevolution was lying in wait.

But this accumulation of new danger could not intimidate Danton either. At the Pavillon de Flore in the Tuileries, now known as the Pavillon d'Egalité, where the Committee of Public Safety was now meeting among Gobelin tapestries, mirrors, marbles, and gilded bronzes, with a well-stocked buffet close at hand, he was still the source of power and courage. He continued to think of Paris as the focus of French patriotism and he maintained that the insurrection in the provinces was the work of a handful of agitators and was not supported by the bulk of the inhabitants. Were the departments in a state of insurrection? Certainly not! It was only a matter of a few scoundrelly officials. But he was ready to take vigorous steps. His plan was to bring help quickly to the threatened points by creating a central reserve corps to which each of the primary electoral bodies was to contribute two armed men.

First came the Vendée: "Strangle the insurrection in that part of France and you will have peace." With his usual political wisdom he intended to apply the death penalty, once the insurrection was quelled, to the ring leaders only, allowing the masses to return home without hindrance. But in order to crush the insurrection first, he also made it his business to appoint commanders in the disaffected districts. He had to shut his eyes to a good deal in supporting General Gontaut-Biron for better or for worse; since both by background and descent, as former Duke of Lauzun, friend of the Queen, and author of salacious tales, this commander in chief was not the man to inspire the genuine Jacobin die-hards with confidence.

Danton had more cordial relations with Westermann, who acquired in the Vendée the reputation of a fearless sabreur. When the dashing Alsatian charged at the head of his Norman legion, wildly spurring his horse and brandishing his curved broadsword, hatless and coatless, with shirtsleeves rolled up, the pious peasantry scattered as if they had come face to face with Beelzebub. In this way he took Châtillon, the center of the insurrection, on July 3; but two days later he was caught napping, was severely defeated, and lost both baggage and artillery.

Many people laid the troubles in the field and at home to the Committee of Public Safety and since Danton was the soul of the committee, much of the dissatisfaction centered on him. When Marat, who had been bedridden for many weeks, sarcastically asked the Convention: "Is the committee asleep or does it refuse to act?" when he blamed the "dawdlers of the committee" for "supporting aristocrats like Biron, Custine, Menou, and Westermann," when he recalled how six months ago he had sounded the alarm against Dumouriez and none of the patriots of the Mountain had heard it, he did not name Danton, but everyone thought of Danton. A direct attack was made on June 4 at the Cordeliers', and four days later a Jacobin who vaunted his Republicanism gave as his opinion that "this deputy is not as revolutionary as he used to be; he no longer comes to the Jacobin Club; once he turned his back on me in order to talk to a general." Desmoulins, it is true, praised his friend's civic sense, and eight days later Danton himself assured the Jacobins that he could never lag behind them in revolutionary spirit and courage, and would die a Jacobin; Robespierre too, at the same meeting, praised the committee and pointed out that though it might err occasionally, it had the welfare of the Republic genuinely at heart. But all words were vain: the impression grew that as at present constituted the Committee of Public Safety was finished.

On May 10 and June 10 the Danton Committee had been renewed without opposition; but on July 10 the clouds of wrath gathered over Westermann. Commissars Goupilleau and Bourdon sent in a report on his culpable negligence; a motion was brought for his recall and court martial; and old Rühl of Strasbourg fulminated against his countryman from Molsheim: "He is a traitor; his place is before the Revolutionary Tribunal; his head must fall under the sword of the law." Chabot's plea persuaded the Convention merely to summon the general before its bar to account for himself.

While the storm was raging, however, one of its bolts struck the Committee of Public Safety. The committee was openly blamed for the defeats; even Desmoulins, annoyed for personal reasons, grumbled about its incapacity, and Drouet, the postmaster who had prevented the King's flight in 1791, dared to assert openly that certain members of the committee had ceased to enjoy the confidence of the patriots. Perhaps he had Barère in mind—the weathercock who was always on the side of power and of the victors, and whom Marat with his last breath called "the most dangerous enemy of the country." But when the new committee was elected, Barère and Jeanbon Saint-André headed the list with 192 votes apiece. Danton and Delacroix were not reëlected. Their views in the new committee were represented by Thuriot and in a measure by Hérault de Séchelles; but the election of Saint-André, Couthon, and Saint-Just gave the preponderance to the devoted adherents of Robespierre; and as their lord and master took the place of a retiring member on July 27, it was from that day the Robespierre Committee and Robespierre's government.

———————◆———————

THE fact that he had been jettisoned from the Committee of Public Safety neither displeased nor discouraged Danton. Ambition and a desire for power were strong springs of action in his character; but he laughed at those who believed themselves necessary and must always be on top. Every now and then he was overcome by a yearning to be lazy, as powerful as the craving for a drug. And from the point of view, too, of politics, he liked intervals during which others toiled and wore themselves out until the masses remembered that Danton was indispensable.

Although he had been exiled from the Pavillon d'Egalité, Danton by no means stood in the background.

When he was attacked at the Jacobins' for having recommended a certain Peyron, whose Republican dependability was doubtful, to Dalbarade, the new Minister of Marine, even Robespierre testified for Danton. Angered by these vague denunciations, which served only the enemy, he bitterly remarked that it was vain to devote one's life to the cause of Freedom "when a quarter of an hour suffices for any malcontent to destroy the confidence that is your due and to deprive you of the fruit of your toil." Two days later, on July 12, Danton defended himself rather casually at the Jacobins', remarking that he knew the Peyron in question slightly, but always as a patriot and that he had recommended him, but given no guarantee for him; the only sensible thing was to let persons of this sort watch each other. Neither indignant nor surprised that people took this opportunity to spread all sorts of gossipy little stories about him to wake the suspicions of his fellow citizens, he barely shrugged his shoulders: "Calumnies—those who are afraid of them are not fit for public life."

He was proudly conscious of his historic part: convinced that he was working for posterity, assured of his place in the eyes of the world and certain that whenever death should come, he would leave behind him a great name.

On July 25 he had the satisfaction of being elected by 161 out of 186 votes to preside for the customary fortnight at the National Convention.

Before and after, however, he was more than merely one of 700-odd deputies, and could trust in the force of his personality and the power of his eloquence. Desmoulins justly compared his friend's eloquence to the Nile, "which is never more beautiful than when it overflows its banks." And Danton still felt that he had in him the steel, the fire, and the tension to drive the Revolution forward.

The changes in the Committee of Public Safety did not put an immediate end to the national misfortunes—one alarming report followed another. Condé fell on July 12, Mainz July 22, and Valenciennes July 28; but the dismay reached its height when the domestic foes joined the enemy at the gate and an important port of France was opened to the antagonist. On August 28 Toulon sided with Louis XVII against the Convention and surrendered to the British and Spanish forces.

But defeats and disasters kindled afresh in Danton the flame of September, 1792—"No tarrying, Patriots, to work!" Once again the powerful lungs in that broad chest became the bellows which fanned confidence in victory; "The French Constitution must be announced to the rulers of Europe with gunfire." Carnot, a member of the Robespierre Committee who called up hosts by stamping on the ground and was putting young Republican generals like Kléber and Marceau in the right place and so insuring victory, must have found Danton a vigorous supporter. "The enemy," Danton exclaimed "has hitherto only seen the advance guard of the nation. May he finally feel the full weight of the united efforts of this glorious people." Therefore, on August 12 he demanded the conscription of four hundred thousand men, exhorted, "Let us fight like lions!" and asked for one hundred thousand livres for the manufacture of guns, rifles, and pikes. "In all towns of any importance the hammer has only to strike the anvil to forge iron for use against the foe!"

Since again and again, when their terms of enlistment had expired, individuals or whole units cheerfully turned their backs on the front, Danton succeeded in having the death penalty imposed for this kind of desertion. But he did not pound the table; as always he united energy with circumspection: "Farreaching plans are devised by energy and executed by reflection." Because soldiers without bread and arms were no soldiers at all, Danton pointed out what many overlooked, namely, that the conscripted troops ought to be called to arms only in such measure as rations and equipment were available. He attached great importance to both; for the French soldiers who fought out of patriotism could not be treated like the Austrian mercenaries who were flogged for a spot on their uniforms: "The man who serves his country well has a right to good equipment and food." Danton promised to strip all the *Muscadins,* all the scented fops and dandies who were suspected of Royalist tendencies, in order to clothe the army, and Saint-Just may have had this in mind when, eight weeks later, as commissar of the Convention, he had proclamations posted on the walls of Strasbourg: "Ten thousand men in the army are barefoot. The aristocrats of the town will be deprived of their shoes today, and by 10 A.M. tomorrow the ten thousand pairs of shoes must be on the way to headquarters."

Nor was the ship of the Revolution tossed only by news of disaster from the front. On July 13 a fanatic who had become unbalanced by the destruction of the Gironde—Charlotte Corday of Caen—plunged a knife into Marat's heart while the sick man was sitting in his bath correcting the proofs of the *Ami du peuple.* A wave of genuine grief swept over all the slums of Paris; fists were clenched, teeth bared, and hoarse oaths of revenge sworn. The dead man was all but deified; children, mountains, and parishes were named after Marat; and the Marseilles section itself (formerly the Théâtre-Français) in which Danton lived, adopted the name of the "People's Friend."

It was during Danton's term as president that a deputation of the Cordeliers announced to the Convention on July 26 that an altar would be erected to Marat in their debating chamber the following Sunday. An urn containing the embalmed heart of the deceased was to be solemnly suspended from the ceiling. Danton was still presiding on August 3 when the National Assembly was invited by the Revolutionary Society to attend the unveiling of a bust of Marat. He said: "Marat was obsessed by the Revolution as by a fever, and this was justified, for he knew the criminal disposition of the enemies of the Revolution. In his death he served the cause of freedom even more than in life, for his death showed his murderers in their true colors." Although in its lack of rhetoric this obituary differed considerably from the usual dithyrambs with which the memory of the "People's Friend" was celebrated elsewhere, an anti-Jacobin lampoon loudly proclaimed:

> *Danton, ce mufle de damné,*
> *Par la nature condamné*
> *A porter ce masque effroyable*
> *Que n'oserait porter le diable,*
> *Est seul digne de louanger*
> *Ce héros qu'on vient d'égorger.*

To the end Marat had opposed the Enragés. Varlet was a "harmless intriguer," Leclerc "a cunning customer." Now, however, although Varlet and Leclerc remained in the background, Roux and Hébert vied for the privilege of carrying on Marat's work and name. The strangling of France by the British blockade assisted them in their designs. The queues before the bakeries grew longer and longer and the mood of the people more and more sulky; at the hours when bread was distributed sentries of the National Guard were posted at the bakeries and the streets were patrolled. The adoption of meat cards was already under discussion, and meatless days and weeks, a kind of *Carême civique* or extra-ecclesiastical Lent, were suggested.

Men with empty stomachs listened only too readily to the incendiary speeches of the Enragés. Roux demanded the arrest of all bankers and the choking of "all those bad citizens who have acquired vast properties during the past four years." Bravo! Leclerc toyed with the idea of "coldbloodedly sacrificing 100,000 criminals to the cause of the Revolution." Both suggestions met with applause. Massacres were in the air. Why not? Hébert, who had originally opposed Roux and Varlet, now with Chaumette's support played the same game in order not to lose his own followers. His *Père Duchesne* grossly attacked the "vile shopkeepers" who were supposed to be hoarding their wares in order to create a famine and thus doing Pitt's work for him. Beat them! It was easy to arouse the street: Bread! Bread! The news of Toulon's desertion infuriated the mob; the sections shook their pikes threateningly. As their spokesmen, the Enragés presented their political demands: the trial of Marie-Antoinette and the Girondins, the arrest of all suspects, the removal of all former nobles from public offices, and the formation of a revolutionary fighting force in Paris. At the bar of the Convention Chaumette adjured the "Holy Mountain" to become the Sinai of France, to change into a volcano and bury under its glowing lava all the enemies of liberty; he was followed by a fierce speaker from the Jacobins' Club who announced: "The time has come for the scythe of equality to sweep over the heads of all. Now is the moment to inspire terror in all conspirators. *Eh bien, législateurs, placez la terreur à l'ordre du jour!*"

In order to deal with hunger riots and to prevent the Royalists from turning the scarcity of food to their advantage, the Convention as early as July decreed the death penalty for hoarding the necessities of life in order to raise their price. In August public storehouses for food were established in all the districts, while Danton's suggestion of a fixed price of three sous a pound for bread and additional taxation of the rich for purposes of subsidy was dropped, although Chabot had taken it up. Finally, on September 4, the Assembly adopted the principle of general maximum prices, while on September 29 wages and the prices of all necessities were definitely settled according to an index dating back as far as 1790.

The Hébertists took the credit for this triumph of the street and waxed insolent in proportion. They were a power, they had the favor of the street and noisy adherents among the Jacobins, and at the Ministry of War they had the firm support of Bouchotte. In the Vendée General Rossignol, a former goldsmith's apprentice, Ronsin, a former playwright and dramatist and present head of the food Commissariat, as well as the publisher Momoro and the writer Robert (two friends of Danton's from the days of the Cordeliers) who were now commissars, were Hébertists. The election to the Committee of Public Safety of Billaud-Varenne and Collot d'Herbois, who had considerable leanings toward the Hébertists, was a fresh sign of their triumph. On the other hand the fist of the rulers struck all the more vigorously at the other wing of the Enragés. Varlet was imprisoned, Leclerc vanished from Paris, and Jacques Roux, arrested, killed himself with his pocketknife.

If Robespierre suspected Royalist agents in every queue before a bakery, Danton regarded the Enragés with deep suspicion, if only because he was repelled by the disproportion between their talk and their thinking. He particularly objected to the rough feminine following of Claire Lacombe who burned alternately to lock up all the "priestesses of Venus" and to compel all women to wear the red cap. Fabre d'Eglantine mocked at the "ladies errant," the "emancipated maidens," and the "female grenadiers" who ran to the club instead of caring for their children and kitchens, and Danton could not help being pleased with these sarcasms.

Before this, when Danton had supported the insurrection of May 21, he had uttered a warning: "Should a number of really dangerous persons be desirous of prolonging a movement which becomes superfluous, as soon as you have obtained your rights Paris will thrust them back into the void." He did not differ from these blindly furious and aimless agitators in his desire to strike and strike hard at the counterrevolutionaries. Like them he refused amnesty to traitors; but he had no use for the craving to drag guilty persons to punishment at any price and wished to see locked up only the genuine suspects, the great criminals, and the actual conspirators. The present policy of attacking poor nobodies was ridiculous. When on September 5 the street was seething, he, too, threatened a third revolution, and agreed that the Revolutionary Tribunal might well operate more swiftly. But if his call for one aristocrat's head per day sounded bloodthirsty, since at that time an execution took place only every third day, Danton's measure was surely the essence of moderation compared with that outlined by the Hébertists and what was still to come. On the same occasion Drouet fulminated: "Our virtues, our wisdom, our moderation, have availed us nothing; for the sake of the people we must become ruffians." And Thuriot called him to order: "France does not thirst for blood but for justice!" These words, which saved the honor of the Convention, were quite in accord with Danton's sentiments.

Danton not only revealed to the Convention that the secret of every government consists in just rewards and punishments, but also taught them the "great truth" that every government unable to assure the livelihood of the people is in danger of collapse. At an early period he advocated a census of the entire grain resources of the country, and on August 17 a decree of which he was the spiritual author fixed a penalty of ten years' imprisonment for all those who concealed grain stores. On September 3 the Food Committee of the Convention proposed a maximum uniform price of grain for the whole Republic. Since, however, even the Mountain was convinced of the blessings of free trade, the objection was made that a fixed price for grain would mean starvation in the midst of plenty; a maximum price was not only useless, but also unfair and dangerous. But after Thuriot had attacked the peasantry, who had never been conspicuous for their zeal in supplying the towns and fortified places, Danton said the decisive word: "The Convention must decide whether it favors the profiteers or the people: it must decide today. . . . Let whoever desires to speak against the fixing of a maximum price come to the tribune! I myself will oppose him." But nobody came and the Convention prohibited unrestricted trade in grain and decreed a uniform maximum price.

September 5 was a day of sultry commotion; deputations crowded the bar of the Tuileries and the quays were black with excited throngs. All eyes were anxiously turned toward the Committee of Public Safety, then in session at the Pavillon d'Egalité.

The *rapporteur* was expected at any moment—and the House was requested to wait another half hour. But patience at such a time!—for half an hour! Danton seized the opportunity by the forelock. After a speech which brought ringing applause from the House and the galleries that carried him again to proud heights, he struck the Hébertists a blow which was intended to make them reel. This group controlled the sections because the meetings of the sections were usually attended by only a small number of citizens, most of them professional claquers. Danton smiled: all that was necessary was to limit the meetings to two a week, on Sundays and Thursdays, and to pay a compensation for lost earnings of forty sous to all who attended! If this was done, the mass of Republican-minded and reliable citizens would soon outnumber the wild men.

Danton did not reveal the purpose of his suggestion, but it was easily guessed by the others. Romme vainly opposed the motion because it implied a doubt of the Republican zeal of the citizens; and when a fortnight later Varlet spoke against the decree "in the name of the forty-eight sections," Robespierre put the young man in his place, pointing out that the rejection of the motion would be to the advantage of "the rich, the plotters, and the Muscadins" only, but not of the "artisans and the respectable class of laborers." The two weekly assemblies and the payment of forty sous were adopted.

But now as ever Danton believed that to keep the car of state from swerving right and left the reins of government must be held in one hand. Instead there was still a fatal division of authority or at any rate the form of it. "We shall not meet with success," he told the Convention, "until we remember that the Committee of Public Safety is one of the achievements of liberty and permit it to act and develop as fully as possible." Accordingly he moved that the Committee of Public Safety be constituted a provisional government and that fifty thousand livres be put at its disposal. In vain. Again after the fall of Toulon he urged the committee not to be afraid of expenses for secret purposes. A week later the Convention accepted his proposal that all committees be supplemented from lists to be drawn up by the Committee of Public Safety, which thus became a committee of committees, superior to the others which had hitherto ranked with it at least on paper. Power became centralized to a terrifying degree in the Pavillon d'Egalité.

Who held all this power? Robespierre! In the committee Saint-Just was his right, and Couthon his left hand. This revolutionary trinity managed the entire conduct of government, dictated policy, and controlled the whole, while Billaud-Varenne and Collot d'Herbois kept in touch with the Convention, the authorities, and the "representatives of the people on special missions," and Carnot and Prieur were the experts in the War Office, Jeanbon Saint-André had the Navy, and Lindet was in charge of food supplies. Convention? Commissars? Revolutionary Tribunal? Attention! The Committee of Public Safety comes! The committee was the brain of France, executing swift justice through the instrumentality of the Committee of General Security, which consisted almost exclusively of followers of Robespierre, with the dry, tenacious, inexorable Vadier at the head as grand inquisitor, and included the "Tiger of the Committee"—the cold and inscrutable Amar—the painter David, the pious Jansenist Voulland, and Lebas, a friend of Saint-Just.

But Robespierre's power was not anchored in the committee or in his popularity, which put that of all others in the shade— for his name was on every tongue, his picture in every shop-window, and he was venerated by all the women who, at other times, would have thronged to the confessional. What was more important was that a vigorous Republican blast swept once more through the public offices, carrying away all those who were unable to provide a certificate from their section vouching for the genuineness of their Republicanism. The older generation of civil servants who were secret adherents of the old regime and in their hearts had no sympathy for the new order was replaced to the last man by a sansculotte bureaucracy for whom the Republic was at once an ideal and a source of income. The revolutionary Committees of Surveillance alone, forty thousand of them which formed an iron network over the whole of France, cost half a million livres a year, and as the Committee of Public Safety could appoint, dismiss, accuse, arrest, and execute at will, Robespierre had only to press a button and the whole enormous apparatus began to function. He controlled the machine, the machine explained his power.

For the moment, however, Robespierre was still afraid to appear in his true light. Danton's suggestion of identifying the committee with the government he declined with a few embarrassed phrases. He suspected a trap; perhaps Danton was aiming at unmasking the committee by forcing on it the whole responsibility and the control of millions that could not be accounted for. This suspicion grew when on September 25, after fresh defeats on the northeast front, a concentrated attack on the committee started in the Convention, with the aim of bringing about its fall. Danton, himself, it is true, remained in the background, but Robespierre, who just succeeded in mastering the revolt, did not forget that the movement had been guided by Danton's special favorite, Fabre d'Eglantine.

Later, when Danton made a formal attempt to transfer the entire executive power to the committee, he deprecated any suggestion that he was indulging private ambitions. "I swear by the freedom of the country that I shall never accept any office in this committee." However, when his speech of September 5 carried away the Convention, Gaston exclaimed: "Danton has the head of a revolutionary! He alone knows how to execute his ideas. I move that he be taken into the Committee of Public Safety, even against his will." There was applause and the motion was adopted; but Danton protested that he had given his oath and insisted: "I shall belong to no one committee but shall spur them all." Indolence? Reluctance? Calculation? Perhaps all three. It may be that he wished to wait until Robespierre's hour had passed in order to seize power again at the right moment. If such was his aim, he was much in error. The Republic gave its leaders no rest. In the France of 1793 there was no room for a Cincinnatus, and the name of Danton was too important and active an asset to the Revolution for its bearer to be allowed to withdraw unpunished.

Perhaps he was only weary, physically and spiritually. The Revolution used its servants up swiftly, put furrows in their faces, and made their bearing nervous. Robespierre sighed that he had been "exhausted by four years of Revolution." Danton,

31 Vandémiaire N° 77.—

C II

697

Citoyen président

Delivré d'une maladie grave, d'après l'avis des gens de l'art, j'ai besoin pour abreger le temps de ma convalescence d'aller respirer mon air natal, Je prie en consequence la convention de m'autoriser à me rendre a arcis sur aube, il inutile que je lui proteste que je reviendrai avec empressement à mon poste aussitot que mes forces me permettront de prendre part à ses travaux

Danton

21e ... mois de l'an 2 de la republique

Danton's Request for a Leave of Absence

too, was pumped empty, and he fell ill. As soon as he was missed in public life, there were whispers: Have you heard the news? Danton has emigrated! The committee intrusted him with diplomatic negotiations abroad and he has escaped into Austria.

If such rumors reached Danton at all, he disregarded them. His fever was cooled by dreams of a wind-ruffled river, a green garden, and a sunny square with a white house: his river, his garden, his square, his house. As soon as he was out of bed he asked the Convention for a furlough: "In order to hasten my convalescence, I must breathe the air of my own country."

AT Arcis-sur-Aube the neighbors were telling each other across the fence: He is back. He came yesterday. He brought his young wife with him. Everybody knew who "he" was, and everybody knew that he had married again.

Danton had felt chilled and lonely in the Cour du Commerce, and when he looked at his motherless boys, the idea of a new marriage occurred to him, struck roots, grew, and soon filled his mind. The choice was made easy because he did not have to search long; he had only to stretch out his hand. One of the regular customers of the Café du Parnasse was Marc-Antoine Gély, a former Admiralty official. A friendship had grown between the Charpentier and Gély families and Danton's marriage drew him also into this circle. Gabrielle was fond of the Gély's little daughter, Sébastienne-Louise, and Danton, too, took pleasure in watching the graceful child blossom. Now that he wanted to leave the double bed empty no longer a thousand voices in him called out: "This is she."

There was only one difficulty. Both Mère Gély and her daughter were pious and considered marriage without the blessing of a "genuine" and not a constitutional priest a deadly sin. The disciple of Diderot smiled; but if he was tolerant anywhere it was in matters of faith. *Louise vaut bien une messe!* On June 12 the Abbé de Kéravenant, a recusant priest whom by rights Danton ought to have denounced to the Revolutionary Tribunal, se-

cretly married him to Demoiselle Gély. The bride brought a
dowry of ten thousand livres; Danton himself contributed
thirty thousand, pretending that they were the gift of a certain
Aunt Lenoir.

And Louise was his! Sixteen! A child! Like a downy feather,
like a nosegay of violets!

Had Danton taken this wife as one takes a drug? There were
times when he felt giddy: he was drifting with a swift current in
a rudderless boat over rapids, between reefs, without a chance
of steering or of landing: with nothing to do but shut his eyes or
drug himself. Danton knew many intoxicants: the wine of Auvergne, the wind of his home land, the loneliness of the deserted
fields on a Sunday, the applause of the masses, the consciousness
of making history, and the feeling of building the future; but
there was no draught of oblivion like the fragrance of his wife.

Sébastienne-Louise! Sébastienne-Louise!

His restlessness and fever vanished as he lifted little Antoine
and Georges from the carriage and stretched out his hand to help
his wife alight in the sleepy little town on the Aube that fine
warm October day.

October, however, was no longer the right word. A new Republican calendar was in force, the invention of the effervescent
Fabre d'Eglantine. Fabre d'Eglantine, the poet! Look at these
names—Floréal, lilacs in bloom; Fructidor, appletrees bending
under their load of fruit; Brumaire, wisps of mist clinging to
blackthorn hedges; Nivôse, an endless glittering expanse of
snow. This was still Vendémiaire, and Brumaire was about to
begin; Danton's birthday was now on the 5th Brumaire.

The people of Arcis stared when Citoyenne Danton jumped to
the ground. A charming brunette indeed, with delicate features,
fresh complexion, smiling mouth, radiant eyes, and a slender
waist. Danton embraced his mother and sister, his brother-in-law
Pierre, and the old nurse Marguerite Hariot—so the good old
girl was still alive!

Little cared Danton whether it was October or Brumaire; he
turned resolutely to his own countryside.

Paris? Paris was on a different planet. What hummed around
him now was not the Convention in stormy session, but the bees

buzzing around the hive; the distant roar was not the street rioting, but the weir of the Aube; and instead of the hasty arrival of panting couriers from the front, only the pigeons hurried home to their loft.

Danton, the happy landlord, was beyond the reach of Paris. True, it was not so long ago that he had heard the report delivered before the Convention by a committee that was inquiring into a new invention for the transmission of messages called the telegraph, an upright post with two movable arms—the work of a certain Chappe. A message could be sent thirty or forty miles in a few minutes; a good thing that there was no telegraph as yet at Arcis. When the Paris papers arrived they were at least two or three days old, and in any case Danton hardly looked at them. If anyone began to talk of politics, he was stopped firmly.

He derived more pleasure from a wild sow and her two young which he kept behind a fence than from all the nonsense in the Tuileries. He showed her proudly to the boys who little suspected that they had entered world history before their teens: the other day their father had mentioned them at the Convention!

He smacked the four dappled cows on the rump; he went into the kitchen garden and picked caterpillars; he fed the chickens. He had two of the three black mares in the stable put to the *tape-cul,* the "bonebreaker," and went around to call on acquaintances.

He played trictrac.

He went hunting with friends.

He spent entire days in his boat on the Aube with the net streamed.

Or he did nothing at all; he reveled in just being alive, and at ease, and though the outer world pictured a fierce Danton with a red Jacobin cap, the people of Arcis saw a peaceable Danton lounging before his door in a cotton nightcap.

Sometimes they looked through the window into his paneled dining room and smiled to see him enjoying his food.

Those were blessed weeks, free from restless hours. Each moment of life between sunrise and sunset was like the quiet breath of a man who knows no care.

Meanwhile, outcast, pursued, devoured by hate, Buzot sat in

his retreat at Saint-Emilion and in his bitter defense of his actions wrote: "Where would humanity, morals, and virtue be if Robespierre, Barère, and Danton were to die peacefully in their beds?"

In these days Danton indulged with almost passionate fervor in the dream of ending his days at Arcis after a long leisurely earthly pilgrimage and surrounded by grandchildren and great-grandchildren; he discussed with his friends the idea of settling permanently in his enchanted home town and bought additional property for four hundred, two thousand, and three thousand livres, well knowing that all this was imagination, self-deception, and a fantasy from which some morning there would be a rude awakening.

And Paris did catch the happy landowner Danton.

The new rulers, to convince themselves of their own courage, found work for the guillotine which had been operating on the Place de la Révolution since May 10. On October 16 Marie-Antoinette of Austria-Lorraine, the Widow Capet, was executed, and on the thirty-first the turn of the Girondists came. There were twenty of them; up to the very foot of the scaffold they sang the *Marseillaise;* the rain poured, and in thirty-eight minutes it was all over. Brissot, Gensonné, Lasource who had attacked Danton so bitterly, and Vergniaud with whom he had sometimes laughed so heartily—all met their doom. A pity about Vergniaud; a pity about them all. Danton's eyes grew misty at the bad news, and when a neighbor expressed surprise at such sympathy for rebels, he flared up: "Such rebels are we all; if they deserve death, so do we."

Brumaire ended and Frimaire came. The weather grew raw, the north wind swept the dry leaves along. One such day Danton's nephew Mergez burst into the room excited and covered with dust. He brought letters from friends in Paris. Danton, beware; plots are being hatched, slanders are finding credence; Robespierre is busily making a net to throw over your head. Make haste, Danton!

For the last time he leaned over the bridge railing, gazed long into the moving waters of the Aube, and drank in as though forever the purling of the weir.

Louise and Antoine Danton

A quick farewell. The family were packed into the traveling coach; Antoine sat on his stepmother's lap, nurse took the youngest on hers, the servant mounted the box, and last of all Danton took his place. The journey began.

The night of November 18 was spent at Troyes at the "Petite Louve," and on the nineteenth the coach was rolling once more over Paris streets. Compared with other days the lighting seemed poor and the streets themselves ill kept.

DURING Danton's absence Robespierre had taken a still firmer grip on affairs. The ministers, the president of the Committee of General Security, the commander of the National Guard, and the public prosecutor of the Revolutionary Tribunal made their reports to him every day as if to a king.

In his notebook he entered this formula: "Unity of will is necessary, be the will Royalist or Republican. A Republican unity of will requires Republican ministers, a Republican press, Republican deputies and a Republican government." He did everything in his power to create such unity, like Danton who used every opportunity to increase the powers of the Committee of Public Safety and insisted: "All power must emanate from the center; this is the only means to tie the departments more closely together and to destroy the federalist system." No one emphasized more strongly that "the spirit of centralization must be the nerve and basis of the government." The "representatives of the people on special mission" were so many beams radiating from the central sun at Paris, not only illuminating every corner, but also fusing the independent departments. The law of December 12 abolished the autonomy of the departments and, following a suggestion of Danton's, attached to the provincial authorities national agents whose function it was to execute the wishes of the capital; in this matter the supremacy of the Committee of Public Safety was finally established.

Robespierre guarded this supremacy jealously; it was to him the basis of the salvation of France. Woe to those who should kick against the pricks of the committee; and woe to those who should rise against Robespierre, who was the Revolution and the Republic. Madame Jullien might describe him "abstract as a thinker, dry as a bookworm, but gentle as a lamb"; but in reality he was by no means so abstract. He endeavored to be "revolutionary" and "politic," to unite vigor and wisdom in his person, and he had a definite plan: the defense of the Constitution (which, however, was kept in the china closet until quieter times should prevail), of the Convention, and of the Committee of Public Safety; the crushing of the insurgents and the taming of all conspirators through terror, and forbearance for the prejudices and foibles of the masses.

His great strength consisted in the fact that he knew how to direct all endeavor firmly and unswervingly toward one point. There was, however, something measured and mechanical about him, something dry and brittle, and nothing whatever to remind one of sappy birch trees in spring; mistrust and suspicion blighted all his more fruitful qualities. His inner uncertainty prevented his ever finding objective reasons for any failures of the Revolution. Again and again it was human wickedness that he blamed. If there was a defeat at the front, it was the result of treason; if a fort was surrendered, Pitt's gold had been at work; a hunger riot in Paris was the work of foreign agents; an attack on Robespierre's policy was perpetrated by criminals. He looked with the worried and reproachful eyes of a schoolmaster through his green spectacles upon a rather mediocre world and it seemed as though the disciple of Rousseau had inherited some of the persecution mania that had darkened his master's mind.

Robespierre saw two cliffs past which he must steer the ship of the Republic; *exagération* and *modérantisme*. There was danger both in going too far and in not going far enough.

The former tendency found its advocates in Hébert and his followers. If Robespierre was inclined to "support patriotism even in its aberrations," Hébert's group went too far. In the War Office Vincent, Bouchotte's second, dealt the cards, and the Hébertists did much as they liked in the army, which was supposed to be combating the insurrection in the west. A brand-new general like Rossignol, undoubtedly a seasoned Republican, who was admittedly courageous, frank, and not too much of a braggart, was out of place in a high position of command; and the others, Ronsin, Momoro—well! The deputy Philippeaux, the strict and pious author of a *Catéchisme moral et religieux,* whose guiding rule was "Respect the law," was terrified when he went into the Vendée as commissar of the Convention and witnessed the behavior in the general staffs where the Hébertists set the style. His judgment was somewhat severe, yet the fact remained that the revolutionary officers whom he met swaggered in gold and silver braid, rattled their sabers and twirled their moustaches, and altogether gave themselves airs as though they had spent all their lives leading dashing cavalry charges. They broke the neck of many a bottle, and hugged the neck of many a wench; Philippeaux accused Ronsin of taking four courtesans in a costly barouche with a guard of honor of fifty hussars to attend a review, and this was not the only instance reported of "whore-mongering" in the staffs.

These soldiers were in no hurry to see the pleasant life in the field come to an end. France had an army of one million, two hundred thousand men under arms, which meant that lads with the connections of the Hébertists had innumerable opportunities of obtaining snug berths, promotion, salaries, contracts, and other means of making money. Golden epaulets and golden ducats! Long live the war! Pacifist agitation was a crime, for it struck at the root of their existence: Down with peace!

Internal affairs did not move swiftly enough to please them. The Convention and the Committee of Public Safety were far too sleepy and the guillotine too slow. Two heads on the 28th Brumaire; then a pause of three days; on the 2d Frimaire two more heads; then a day's pause; the 4th Frimaire only two more —this was nothing. Weaklings! And all this thoughtfulness! Chaumette complained in the Commune that the condemned men were given a sip of brandy before their last journey, with the result that they were firm and impudent when what was wanted was trembling victims to serve as an appalling example.

The Hébertists waxed fat on the hunger of the masses. It soon appeared that the system of regulating the necessities of life was a failure; there was too much resistance and not enough authority to enforce half the regulations. The fixing of maximum prices,

the registration of supplies, the establishing of rationing committees, bread, meat, and sugar cards, standard bread, and the
prohibition against baking cakes did nothing to diminish the
famine. Potato starch was sold for sugar, wood ash for pepper,
beetroot oil for olive oil, and colored cider for wine—and everywhere there were substitutes and adulterations. And the queues
still stood before the bakers' shops.

The promises of the Hébertists, vague, hollow, and bombastically exaggerated, provided no bread for the masses, but only
material for Samson's knife. If there was a shortage of food it
was merely necessary to make the Girondins "sneeze into the
bag" and, so *Père Duchesne* asserted, "silver, gold, and flour
would be abundant." But the execution of Vergniaud and his
associates did not produce a single ounce of flour, and now Hébert fulminated against "the league which the sellers were forming against the consumers," and threatened to have no more
mercy for the smallest greengrocer than for the fattest wholesaler. Lady Guillotine, "most high, powerful, and swift Lady
Guillotine," help!

Not only were the Hébertists unable to fill the poor man's
hungry belly, but they deprived him of his spiritual consolation.
For Hébert, Jesus was the "most radical Jacobin of Judea"; but
with Heaven the husband of the ex-nun would have nothing to
do. Once Gobel, the constitutional bishop of Paris, had been
dragged before the bar of the Convention, and he and his vicars-
general and his curés had solemnly "unfrocked themselves," it
became quite fashionable for clerics to renounce their God and
their faith there. The Commune decreed the closing of the
churches. Notre Dame became the "Temple of Reason," and
amid the applause of the members of the Commune and of the
people's representatives, the "Goddess of Reason," arrayed in a
long white robe and azure cloak, with a Phrygian cap on her
flowing locks and an ebony pike in her right hand—she was none
other than the Citoyenne Aubry of the Opera, and a damned
handsome wench at that—descended from her throne in the nave
of the cathedral, and to the sound of music and song, bestowed
an official kiss on ugly old one-eyed Laloy, the president of the
Convention.

Robespierre had no use for the crude excesses of the free thinkers. He was something of a mystic, and was himself preparing the way for a cult of the Supreme Being; and he was also a politician who feared that such needless antireligious demonstrations would shock the insufficiently enlightened masses. Danton was equally out of sympathy with the movement. At the Jacobins' Robespierre launched an attack on those who wanted to "make Atheism into a sort of religion"; there was a threat in his statement, "Atheism is aristocratic." What the people needed was the belief in some great Being watching over oppressed innocence and punishing triumphant crime. Five days later, on November 26, Danton in the Convention attacked the "priests of unbelief" and the "antireligious masquerades," for which, in his opinion, the bar of the National Assembly was not the place. Robespierre adopted the term and described Gobel's pompous renunciation of his priesthood as a "philosophical masquerade." In this sphere Danton and Robespierre were wholly one.

Again, in the conduct of the war, there were moments when Robespierre seemed to be closer to Danton than to Hébert. Danton had read in Diderot that war is "a violent disease of society, associated with convulsions," and similarly Robespierre saw in it a "deadly disease." On the other hand, while Danton hoped that the coalition of the kings would offer "peace with honor," provided that force were allied to subtlety, the more rigid and less nimble Robespierre saw only the coffin lid of a system over his head and never dreamt of other means than force for bringing the war to a successful conclusion. Danton was in favor of a peace by conciliation, Robespierre of a victorious peace. While Sheridan, the leader of the opposition in the House of Commons, advocated a peace with France, Robespierre vented his hatred not only against Pitt's government but against the British people in general. "God punish England!" It was music in his ears when Barère in the Convention called for the destruction of London and the extermination of the English people, or when Bontemps at the Jacobins' shouted: "We shall never grant peace to the nations allied against us until they ask for it on bended knees." Danton's lip curled sarcastically at such verbiage; Danton wanted to fight with the arms of diplomacy as well as with the diplomacy of arms.

Danton must be a defeatist!

And did he not also stand for moderation in internal politics? The longer Danton watched the Reign of Terror, the more clearly he perceived it to be the reign of those who were themselves paralyzed by terror. The dull thud of the ax was a reassuring note for the unsteady nerves of insecure rulers. Late in the autumn a wild Reign of Terror descended on Lyons; the guillotine worked much too slowly and in the Plain of Brotteaux hundreds of the guilty and innocent were mowed down by salvos of grapeshot. Who was in charge here? None other than Fouché, the cowardly, the stealthy. In Toulon again mass executions took place; the knife ran up and down unweariedly in the guides; a woman taken from childbed, a man of ninety-one were dragged to the scaffold. And who was it here who gorged himself with blood? The womanish Fréron, whom Danton remembered as the "Lapin." The rabbit had become a tiger; it was enough to make one laugh—and weep!

Danton suspected vacillation, weakness and fear even, behind Robespierre's rigid mask.

He himself neither wavered nor hesitated, and he felt no fear. Looking around with an unclouded eye, he saw no reason for despair. The sansculotte battalions had inflicted severe defeats on the Prince of Coburg at Hondschoote in September and at Wattignies in October; the Piedmontese had been driven from the valley of the Arc and the Spaniards from Roussillon and the Basque districts; new, young, and ardent Republican generals like Jourdan, Pichegru, and Hoche were guarantors of victory. Since the October night which had witnessed the confused retreat of the vanquished Royalist army to the right bank of the Loire, the Vendée had ceased to be a danger. Marseilles and Lyons had been brought to heel and had long since reacknowledged the Convention; and in December the recovery of Toulon was celebrated in Paris. The chief merit for this feat belonged to a young officer of artillery who had just reached his twenty-fourth year; a man with an Italian name, Buonarotti, or something like that; no, it was Buonaparte.

Altogether things were not in a bad way. Danton inquired of the Convention: "Is not the Republic terrible to all its foes? Does it not stand victorious and triumphant? Have you not taken farreaching and terrible measures to crush inner and outer foes? And have they not all met with the success that might fairly be looked for? . . . Are you not conscious of your strength?" Danton was. "The counterrevolutionaries may wish to extinguish the flame of freedom on its most glowing altar; but the vast mass of true patriots, the sansculottes who have overwhelmed their enemies a hundred times, are still with us." On these Danton relied, and he himself was ready to sound the tocsin, if necessary, to rally them.

The creator of the Revolutionary Tribunal would have been the last man to say that the Terror could be dispensed with. He could read in the people's faces that they wanted "the Terror to be the order of the day." But according to the interpretation of the feelings of the masses which he gave the Convention on November 26, "the people wish the Terror to be directed against the real enemies of the Republic and against them only; they do not wish a man to be treated as guilty simply because he was not born bursting with revolutionary energy." These words were inspired by the latest decree which classed as suspects those "who, while not guilty of any action against the cause of liberty, had done nothing for it." It was a short step from suspicion to condemnation.

The people wanted justice. Danton could not impress urgently enough on those who wielded power over life and death how necessary it was to "be just to all who are not your enemies." But a decree which permitted juries to declare that sufficient information had been placed before them as soon as any case had lasted three days—a decree passed for the special purpose of accelerating proceedings against the Girondins, a decree polished by Robespierre—such a decree had nothing to do with justice.

The execution of women was particularly agonizing. On November 8, Madame Roland had ridden to the Place de la Révolution, head erect, unshaken—a Roman. Danton knew that she had hated him, and yet poor Manon! About the same time Marie-Olympe de Gouges died on the scaffold—a feminist who months ago had bequeathed to Danton the task of carrying out her principles.

But after all these were political women who were destroyed by politics. It was not an edifying spectacle when Louis XV's ex-mistress, *"Jeanne Vaubernier, femme Du Barry, ci-devant courtisane,"* struggled for life with the executioner, screaming, scratching, and biting; yet her end was not unearned. But what sense was there in dragging to the scaffold a decent fifty-six-year-old serving maid like Catherine Clère of Valenciennes, because she had shouted: *"Vive le roi!"* when not quite sober? Or in executing a drunken prostitute who, when arrested by the police, cheered for Louis XVII? And beside the few great, there was a whole host of poor devils, locksmith apprentices, gunners, vintners, and clerks who were anything but aristocrats and who, having babbled some rebellious words in their cups, were promptly denounced to the Revolutionary Tribunal and guillotined. Insignificant transgressions of insignificant people; it was a sorry Republic that trembled before such as these.

It was not primarily humanitarianism that induced Danton to protest against this abuse of the Terror. Robespierre, "gentle as a lamb," was certainly not more bloodthirsty than he; but Danton had a clearer head. He realized that it was a better policy to spare the innocent and small fry; for blood spilt senselessly poisoned the blood of a number of the living and created new deadly enemies for the Republic. His views were faithfully reflected in the *Vieux Cordelier* which his old friend Camille Desmoulins started to publish on December 5, in deliberate opposition to the present Cordeliers, where the Hébertists daily indulged in more extravagant excesses. Danton expected more of the "guillotine of public opinion" than of Samson's steel triangle, and similarly Desmoulins made himself the champion of a press that was mercilessly censored, demanding that freedom for it which he declared to be the terror of all ruffians and counterrevolutionaries. The talented journalist had never written with more dash or spirit or warmth than in this sheet which stigmatized the Terror as the former instrument of despotism, appealed to the rulers to "set free the two hundred thousand citizens whom you call suspect," and demanded the appointment of "Committees of Mercy." Robespierre, whom Desmoulins addressed as "my old schoolmate," approved of the first two issues; and because neither the *Vieux Cordelier* nor Danton dreamt of attempting to check the headlong course of the Revolution, Desmoulins' publication rejected a general amnesty as counterrevolutionary. Indeed, the "Committees of Mercy" seemed to Desmoulins to be the most efficacious measure in the service of the Revolution.

Soon however, suspicion grew lively again within Robespierre: These attempts to deprive the guillotine of heads must be directed against himself—in other words, against the Revolution! With a mechanical, ominous movement he turned his pale face toward the bench where Danton and Desmoulins sat; and one of his satellites, the young and ardent Fayau, who had just returned wounded from the Vendée, interrupted a speech of Danton's with: "When the people should be terrible, he calls for mercy." Unheard of!

Were not the serious consequences of such tactics already apparent? The wine merchant Pierre Gaudon had been condemned to death by the Paris criminal court solely because, although his stock of wine had been reported as required by law, his son had neglected to publish the list. The sentence seemed barbarous even to the Minister of Justice. The day of the execution drew near and Danton loudly asked the Convention for a postponement. Numerous deputies supported him, and eventually postponement was resolved on; Danton commented: "We honor ourselves by saving an innocent man. I hasten to inform him myself of the decree on which you have resolved." Loud applause followed; the case was perfectly clear, and the resolution had been adopted unanimously. But still was it not astonishing that Danton displayed such zeal on behalf of a profiteer?

In his endeavor to put an end to the wild Terror Danton was moved also by his longing to reconstruct the Republic. He was impatient and would have been best pleased to see the community cared for and growing like his own trees. Having wielded the sword he was anxious to use the trowel: "The pike destroys but the compass of reason is required to erect the structure of society on a firm base." Accordingly he carefully turned in his mind the problem of education and instruction which more than any other question occupied this generation that had been so influenced by Rousseau's *Emile*. The plan which the murdered Lepelletier de Saint-Fargeau left behind him, for the education of the young in boarding schools at the public charge, led to a violent division of opinion as to whether children belonged to their parents or to the State. Danton strenuously asserted the right of the masses to be educated: "Next to bread, education is the first need of the populace." He emphasized that "in private education everything is narrowed; under public education every-thing is broadened." He called his Gallic humor to his aid. Yes, he too was a father and more so than the aristocrats "who object to education in common because they are uncertain of their paternity; nevertheless my son does not belong to me, he belongs to the Republic." In this way he succeeded in putting over a sug-gestion which led to one of his favorite compromises: the found-ing of State schools, where children might receive free education, food, and lodging; together with day classes for those boys and girls whose parents wanted them to live at home. Personally he favored the boarding school. Although he was a family man through and through, he pointed out "the dangerous influence of the home," and heaped his praise on State education. "All the sentiments of the child and all his thoughts must be fused in one sentiment and one thought—love for his country and his fellow citizens; he must learn while young to love them and to be pre-pared for every sacrifice, even for that of life; and he must imbibe these principles with his mother's milk." Individualist though he was, no man felt more deeply that all were bound to all.

Up to this point Danton and Robespierre were practically at one, but they differed fundamentally in their view of the func-tion of the State. Danton had another mental picture of society at heart. The spokesmen of the Revolution talked the language of future centuries in basing the State on the sovereignty of the people, but to achieve this end they attempted to set back economic development to a stage that had been left behind. Politically they looked into the future; economically their eyes were fixed on the past. The majority were under the influence of Rousseau, who had formed his idea of the world in a miniature republic of petty bourgeois and peasants, and whether they were Girondins or Montagnards they believed democracy incompatible with great differences of wealth. Louvet spoke for all when he said: "Political equality and the Constitution have no enemy more greatly to be feared than exceptional inequality of wealth."

In the Convention and in the Constituent and Legislative Assemblies only a few believed in the rise of large-scale industry; for they considered monopolies and privileges a preliminary requisite to this, and monopolies and privileges were abolished in 1789. But where they thought such a rise possible, they tried to oppose it. Rousseau had not appealed in vain to the State to repress by legislation the trend toward an increasing inequality of wealth. Rousseau had condemned luxury as a corrupter of morals; Marat cursed abundance. His ideal was a return to the system of small peasant proprietors, artisans, and barter. Again Rousseau—always Rousseau—had given the palm to agriculture before all other pursuits, and similarly Billaud-Varenne held a society based on agriculture the best because it set a limit to wealth. According to him no man should own more than a certain number of acres, and settling the division of inherited estates by law might also insure some equality of wealth.

For Robespierre's followers, who had to rely on the support of the poorer classes, the economic world would be balanced only if it were based on agriculture, with a preponderance of small proprietors, and neither rich nor poor; what they wanted was a moderate temperature, economic calm, and reasonable comfort. Saint-Just, the political and social philosopher of Robespierrism, saw salvation in a France shut off as far as possible from the rest of the world and practically entirely composed of small landed proprietors; each man possessing his few acres, his wife, his children; no rich or poor, silver and gold prohibited, and luxury a crime. "A plough, a field, a cottage, safe from the interference of the State, a family secure from the lust of robbers—*voila le bonheur.*" Such a doctrine appeared to make a virtue of the ne-

cessities of the country in a state of siege, and therefore Saint-
Just's plan of an ideal society provided for nine meatless days
per month. Robespierre shared these views; if his master Rousseau had fallen on his knees before the savage, that quintessence
of purity and goodness, Robespierre swung the censer before the
poor man; the poor were innately virtuous, the rich innately
vicious. Couthon explained the source of this cult: "Virtue ever
made the people her favored dwelling place, because the people
always remained closer to nature." While English caricatures
showed the Jacobins as ragged cannibals, an engraving widely
circulated in France entitled *"Le bon sansculotte"* showed a good
man with a tricolor ribbon on his hat eating his bourgeois soup
and feeding his dog. This honest creature in whose beard virtue
had made her nest, and whose earthen cup and wooden spoon
bespoke frugality and content, was the Republican after Robespierre's heart.

Danton's picture of the Republic was no lean hag whose aspect counseled self-control, all skin and bones, with every rib
showing; but a comely woman, with full bosom and generous
hips, a painting by Rubens, the symbol of fruitfulness and
prosperity.

Of all the details which became known of Saint-Just's plan
for the State, only one rule met with the approval of Danton,
that practiced swimmer of the Aube and Seine, namely, that lads
of sixteen must give proof of virility by swimming across a river.
But for the rest? Good God! "Saint-Just," he remarked ironically, "wants a Spartan Republic, but what we need is Utopia."
As though foreseeing that the economic forces of the bourgeois
epoch would create works to outdistance the Egyptian pyramids,
the Roman aqueducts, and the Gothic cathedrals, he urged full
expansion rather than repression and the swift-flowing stream
rather than the trickling gutter.

The dawn of the new era gave no sign as yet of the icy chill of
selfishness which was destined to be its chief characteristic;
Danton was never unmoved by the misery of the poor. His ire
was roused because war invalids were compelled to beg at the
bar of the Convention for what was their due; and he suggested
that land and cattle in the neighborhood of Paris might be al-

lotted to them, thus founding "a colony of patriots who suffered for their country." But it was folly to fix economic development at a point which had long been passed and to reduce the standard of living to an almost unendurable penury. Diderot had taught that those who despised property and luxury were enemies of human progress; was it not written in the book of books, in the Encyclopedia, that the great modern States require wealth in order to maintain their power and greatness and that, accordingly, the man who works in order to grow rich is useful to the State, and a rich man who enjoys life shows good sense?

Danton's ideas on this point, in fact, were much less like those of the Mountain, with its puritanical limitations, than those of the Gironde who, through their seaports, could get a clear view of the oceans and ocean-borne trade. On May 8 Vergniaud had poured sarcasm on the fanatics who asked for a poor, moral, and warlike Republic, a second Sparta; and Danton listened with approval to his colleague from Bordeaux who explained that the industry of the people must be used to increase the sources of wealth, the geographical position of France to extend her trade, and the gifts of the French to create masterpieces of art and glorious inventions.

Desmoulins, too, in his *Fragment de l'histoire secrète de la Révolution,* eloquently developed Danton's theme: Paris, situated halfway between the mouths of the Rhine and the Rhone and connected with the sea by canal and harbor; France at the height of her prosperity, laws developing, arts, trade, and industry free from restrictions, France reviving to the amazement of England, grammar schools everywhere, in place of priests Republican-minded schoolmasters in each village explaining to the children the Rights of Man and the *Almanach du Père Gérard;* free schools of arts and crafts, everything to show that the Republican Government was fostering trade, which of course could flourish only in republics, growing as freedom grew within, and as foreign nations became more enslaved. Athens the watchword!—The rich fitting out triremes, the poor serving as rowers but honoring the rich and elevating them to high office; a Republic fulfilling what the monarchy promised in vain two centuries ago: a chicken in the pot of every citizen.

These were Danton's own ideals: the union of freedom and beauty, and freedom no enemy of pleasure; the rich, too, had reasons for joining the new State: "We did not found a republic of barbarians." The French were cheerful, laughed, drank, and danced, and when Robespierre attempted to force the thin soup of equality down their throats, Danton felt like Crudell in Diderot's *Entretien d'un philosophe avec la Maréchale de . . .*: it would not do to force on an entire people a way of life that suited a few kill-joys. Danton was no kill-joy; in his eyes it was a sign of the decay of the times when the Committee of Public Safety had potatoes planted in the flower beds of the Tuileries and the Luxembourg, and overzealous commissars of the Convention uprooted vines and made cornfields out of vineyards. No, the people were entitled to flowers and wine and games. Danton summoned artists to erect a festival hall where national games could be celebrated on certain days; the Greeks had their Olympic games, France would celebrate her Sansculottides.

Danton's laughing view of life made Robespierre look gloomy. How could Robespierre, reading edifying passages from Rousseau at supper to the assembled family Duplay, compare in warmbloodedness with Danton who spent the hours in the privacy of his chamber enjoying the juiciest passages of Rabelais. In Robespierre's eyes Danton was wholly devoid of virtue. For virtue was a continually recurring topic in the Committee of Public Safety, and though virtue meant primarily devotion to the Republic, this continual reference to the word ended by producing the atmosphere of a nunnery. Day after day the police searched for amorous engravings, obscene books, and ladies of easy morals—to save this threatened virtue. Couthon stated that a virtuous government was the very definition of democracy; Saint-Just with raised eyebrows remarked: "A Republican government has virtue as its guiding principle, and, in default of virtue, terror"; and Robespierre complacently pointed out: "The virtuous have ever been a minority." Virtue, virtue, virtue—one day when these descants were too much for Danton he flung in Robespierre's face the laughing blasphemy: There is no better virtue than that which I practice every night with my wife. The worshiper of virtue à la Rousseau was chilled with horror every time he recalled the remark. Could a politician so utterly devoid of morals really be a champion of liberty?

Above all, Robespierre and his adherents were ignorant of the meaning of compromise, they were dogmatic, worshipers at the shrine of the Absolute, who did not know and did not want to know that every earthly thing depends on something else; they could see only black or white, and no intermediate shade, they believed themselves infallible, the executors of Nature itself; they marched their straight and narrow path with the security of sleepwalkers. But Danton had a feeling for shadings and transitions and a sense of the relativity of things as well. The world would always be imperfect, it was impossible to do anything absolutely well and it was much to do a minimum of evil. At the end of December the Jacobins sat in judgment on Philippeaux, who had placed the responsibility for the defeats in the Vendée on Rossignol and his fellows. The case was somewhat obscure; it was one man's word against another's. Danton esteemed the "sansculotte general," and indeed his influence had obtained Rossignol the supreme command; on the other hand he knew that while Philippeaux might be vain he would never make a statement without being firmly convinced of its accuracy. Just as a few weeks later he blamed the Convention for adopting decrees without investigating for itself, without knowledge of the facts, simply because a committee chose to recommend them, he now refrained from any judgment on this case, and only remarked thoughtfully: "Perhaps the sole fault here rests with circumstances." But anyone who came to the conclusion that the only fault was in circumstances differed—as much as fire differs from water—from Robespierre, who looked for and found guilt in men only and never in things.

THE Danton persecution was begun by the Hébertists. As early as the beginning of August, Vincent attempted to prejudice the Jacobins and Cordeliers against him: "However noisy his words, and however great his insistence on his patriotism, we shall

never be deceived by Danton." Far from turning the other
cheek, Danton riposted vigorously. In December his friend
Fabre d'Eglantine succeeded in having Vincent and Ronsin arrested, although they were soon set free again, and in the *Vieux
Cordelier* his other friend Desmoulins did some deadly rapier
work against Hébert. Danton himself dealt with the "ultra-
revolutionaries" in the Convention, urging that such men might
become as dangerous as the most rabid counterrevolutionist. He
knew himself surrounded by gossip and by slander. While he
was recuperating at Arcis, it was rumored that he had fled into
Switzerland. There were fools who believed him ready to proclaim a Regency in the name of Louis XVII, and even the émigrés spread a saying, supposed to have originated with him: "I
shall let loose the little tiger," meaning the Dauphin. In spite of
this he opposed a suggestion made in the Convention for imposing the death penalty for libel: No! The Revolution admitted the
right of individuals to commit such errors of taste. "It is better
for public functionaries to be libeled than to have no critic arise
for fear of being punished as a libeler."

But on December 3 he finally proceeded to a counterattack at
the Jacobins. He proved that the enormous wealth with which
his enemies credited him was actually only the modest fortune
he had possessed for a long time, and appealed to the ghost of
Marat whose intrepid defender he had always been. No longer
fully certain of his response, he exclaimed: "Has my face lost
the characteristic features of a man of freedom?" Murmurs of
disapproval greeted the once popular Danton; but now Robespierre rose. He began by counting over like the beads of a rosary
the various rumors attached to Danton's name. Then he turned
to him: "Danton! Surely you know that the more courage and
patriotism a man has, the more intent are the enemies of the
common weal on his destruction. Do you not know—and do you
not all know, citizens—that this method is infallible? . . . If
the champions of liberty were no longer calumniated, it would
prove that there were no more priests or nobles to be combated."
In a final tableau the president of the Jacobins solemnly embraced Danton amid unanimous applause; and the Cordeliers,
whom the Hébertists frequently succeeded in antagonizing

against him, gave out three days later that "Danton remains as firm as at the beginning of the Revolution."

Robespierre still needed Danton and his followers in his campaign against the Hébertists. When Billaud-Varenne—still the beau of the sansculottes in his puce coat and his little red wig—rose at the green table of the Committee of Public Safety and, hardly opening his bloodless lips, moved the prosecution of Danton and his friends, Robespierre's glasses began to sparkle with rage and a shrill excited voice protested against the destruction of the best of patriots. Others, however, continued to dig at him —Billaud and Collot, the head of the Secret Service, and Vadier, the embodiment of suspicion, and the gloomy, sinister Amar, whose rosy, highly polished finger nails so little resembled a tiger's claws, and the painter David as well, whom, all too trustfully, Danton still considered a friend.

Their reasons, arguments, and suspicions began at length to take root in Robespierre. Walking in the quiet of the evening in the Champs-Elysées with his Great Dane, Brount, he began to suspect that possibly Billaud and the others might be right after all. Danton's criticism of the system was becoming dangerous to the Revolution and the Republic—indeed was already dangerous.

Although he neither knew nor wished it, Danton had become the hope of the bitterest enemies of the new order; the *Vieux Cordelier* passed from hand to hand among all those who were Royalists at heart. True, a policy of reason and moderation such as Danton recommended appeared to be perilous only so long as it was the motto of the opposition; once adopted by the Government it became a guarantee of strength. But this fact Robespierre, by reason of his intellectual blinkers, was unable to perceive.

Instead he considered a different course—here, Brount! To strike at the Hébertists it would be necessary to have a counterweight in order to avoid appearing reactionary to the masses; to defeat the Left one must also defeat the Right if only to prevent Billaud, Collot, Vadier, Amar, and the rest from becoming recalcitrant. It was as clear to Robespierre as that two times two is four that to destroy Hébertism Dantonism must be destroyed.

Chance disclosed an unsavory affair which spattered the Dantonists. In the Rue Anjou Saint-Honoré in Paris there were two brothers, converted Moravian Jews who had made fortunes in the Austrian wars against the Turks by obtaining orders for the army and had been made Barons of Schönfeld by Joseph II. They had been living for some time in the most impressive style. When they entered the "sacred soil of liberty" at Strasbourg with their secretary, the Danish lawyer Diederichsen, they took the simple name of Frey. They were the most ardent of Jacobins; the elder, Junius, invariably wore a "Carmagnole" coat and an enormous tricolor cockade as big as a cartwheel on his red cap. In the summer of 1793 he had a *Philosophie sociale* printed at his own expense, a book fraught with lofty sentiments and full of references to the speeches of Socrates, the Gospels, and the works of the "Immortal Kant." The brothers Frey dined well—they spent forty to fifty thousand livres a year—and the notables of the Revolution, deputies among them, were frequent guests at their house. But a confidential report in German stated: "They are so cunning that they succeed in pumping their guests without their knowing it." To the political police they were known as spies, profiteers, or both.

This, however, did not prevent Chabot from maintaining increasingly friendly relations with them and finally marrying their sixteen-year-old sister Léopoldine, who brought him a dowry of two hundred thousand livres and adoringly lisped: "You are the greatest Frenchman next to Robespierre." Chabot, on his part—he had recently taken to wearing sabots to exhibit his increased patriotism—was hand in glove with two colleagues, Basire and Delaunay, with whom he had formed a plan to fleece the India Company which was being liquidated, through parliamentary maneuvers. The plan was to spread alarming rumors until the shares of the company fell, and to buy in as many as possible in order to sell them at an enormous profit as soon as they had been allowed to go up again. But Chabot, tormented by fear of discovery, reported the business to the Committee of Public Safety in the middle of November and presently found himself under lock and key in company with Basire and Delaunay. They were soon followed by the brothers Frey. From the

Luxembourg the former Capuchin friar besought Danton to defend his innocence. "Dear colleague," he wrote, "I know your genius and your indolence as well; I am afraid that you would not read to the end if I wrote in detail." Whether Danton read to the end or not, he certainly disappointed the prisoner's hope for getting energetic help.

On January 13, 1794, a dull, rainy Monday, Amar, smoothing his lace ruffles, informed the Convention in the name of the Committee of General Security that Fabre d'Eglantine had been arrested during the night for forging a decree in connection with the Chabot affair. Danton jumped up to move that Fabre and the other accused be allowed to plead at the bar of the Convention although the order of arrest be permitted to stand. This aroused the bitterness of all those who had hoped to strike at Danton through Fabre. Vadier, launching an indirect charge of pro-Royalist sympathy against Danton, loosed a poisoned arrow: "The principles of the last speaker would carry us back to the Constitution of 1791, which guaranteed the unconditional inviolability of deputies." And Billaud-Varenne had no need to mention names; everyone knew whom he meant when he said coldly, slowly, with deliberate emphasis: "Woe to the man who sat by the side of Fabre d'Eglantine and still remains his dupe."

About the same time Robespierre dealt with Desmoulins at the Jacobins'. At first he was tolerant, treating him like a spoilt child corrupted by bad company. Then when Desmoulins rejected the suggestion for burning the *Vieux Cordelier* on the spot with Rousseau's words that burning was no argument, he attacked more vigorously and with a very sullen face. As a result, the society, which purged itself daily, excluded Camille, too, from its number. Lucile trembled with terror when she heard of this scene. Before her husband she showed a cheerful face, but she wrote secretly to Fréron at Toulon with a trembling pen: "Come back, Fréron, come as quickly as possible; there is no time to lose. Bring with you all the old Cordeliers you can find. We need them most urgently . . . You have no notion of what is going on here . . . Come back! Come back quickly, we await you impatiently."

Camille in turn, remembering how at the Jacobins' somebody had cried "To the scaffold!" and that elsewhere he had been threatened with "This Desmoulins is already grazing the guillotine," quoted to his friends with a somewhat forced smile the words of the Corinthian letter: "Eat, drink, and be merry, for tomorrow we die."

Haunted by a similar premonition, Hérault de Séchelles spent his strength in the white arms of blonde Suzanne or brunette Adèle; he kissed with a purpose and a furious desire, trying to cram ten years into one day: "When they tear me away, they will think they are slaying a man of thirty-two, but I shall be eighty." On March 15—good-by Suzanne, good-by Adèle—he too was imprisoned in the Luxembourg on the charge of having harbored an émigré!

In her letter to Fréron poor Lucile had despaired: "No one listens to Marius any more; he is losing courage and growing weak." Marius was the nickname for Danton in the circle. Was it true that he was losing his strength, courage, and vigor? Certainly there were moments when he loathed mankind if not life. When Garat met him he spoke only of the country and of fresh air; he must get away from men in order not to choke. Power seemed to him an insipid draught; he almost longed for the time when he had to scribble away half a bottle of ink a week in order to earn his living.

But, like all strong men, Danton thought little of the danger threatening him. Robespierre? Bah! Yet the man with the green glasses was a terrible opponent because he was never indolent, because he did not love the pleasures of the table, because he knew nothing of fishing, because he had in his heart no quiet longing for Arcis, and because he was worlds removed from Danton's frank confession, "I must have women."

There were still times when Danton felt the urge to mount the tribune at the Convention. He pleaded the need for convincing proof before charging warm friends of liberty with counter-revolutionary tendencies, and it was as though he were pleading his own cause. Once more the applause of the Assembly inter-

M. M. J. ROBERSPIERRE

*Chef du Committé
du Salut public*

rupted him when, with his old proud bearing, his left hand on his hip and his right hand outstretched, he flung at the chamber: "Do not be alarmed, Frenchmen, if liberty in its early stages is frothy! It is like a strong young wine that ferments violently until it is clear of scum. Never have the representatives of the nation seemed to me greater than today. This is the new age whose characteristic is the triumph of freedom!" At the close of the speech President Rühl and Danton embraced effusively and the chamber rang with joyous applause as in his best days.

Radiant with confidence, Danton descended the nine steps of the tribune. Day after tomorrow, he reflected, on the first Germinal of the year II, March 21, 1794, Tallien, a close friend, would be president of the Convention, and Legendre, the most faithful of the faithful would be president of the Jacobins; and, what was more, six days ago the committee had taken a serious step against the Hébertists.

The latter had just been planning a *coup de main,* a "sacred insurrection" against the Committee of Public Safety and the Convention, including massacres of prisoners and God knows what else. But they had scarcely draped the table of the Rights of Man at the Cordeliers' with black crape, to indicate a state of anarchy, when Robespierre struck. On March 13 Hébert, Ronsin, Vincent, Momoro, and others were arrested; on the twenty-first they appeared before the Revolutionary Tribunal, and on the twenty-fourth the tumbrils carried them to the scaffold. While Anacharsis Clootz, the spokesman of the human race and philosopher of the universe, remained serene to the end—a Socrates before the hemlock cup—Hébert writhed in mad terror of death. After he was strapped down on the board, the executioner's assistant wiped his nose for him with his red cap. The bloodthirsty mob yelled with joy and shouted the obscenities which Père Duchesne had strewn so lavishly.

But the relief of the Dantonists was premature; their destruction had been resolved on at the same time as that of the Hébertists. The triumvirate of the committee required a free hand; as early as February 5 Robespierre's gaunt index finger had pointed at the "internal foes of the French people," two parties with one aim—"the destruction of the people's government, the overthrow of the Convention and the triumph of tyranny"—although their banners and their method of approach were different. "One party is urging us in the direction of weakness, the other toward excesses; one wants to transform liberty into a bacchante, the other into a prostitute." This became still more plain, when three weeks later Saint-Just took the tribune, arrayed in a light blue coat with gold buttons, white waistcoat and white stock and looking like a cherub of the Terror with his pale, soft, delicate features; he played with a carnation, but there was a cold light in his blue eyes and the cold words he spoke tasted of blood and terror. . . . Sympathy with the guilty is a crime. . . . A Republic must be inflexible. . . . Justice is not mildness but severity. . . . "There is a group of politicians in France who wish to be happy and enjoy life." A plain hit at Danton. "Those who are most guilty wish to break the scaffold because they are afraid of mounting it." Another hit at Danton. "I imagine the French nation bound by an enormous chain, one end of which is held by the tyrants and the other by the moderates; between them they are strangling us." Danton, always Danton!

And again it was Danton against whom Saint-Just directed his long report on "foreign conspiracy" on the 23d Ventôse, which immediately preceded the arrest of the Hébertists. "The moderate faction, with its eagerness to save criminals, and the turbulent foreign faction are drawing together in order finally to strangle liberty between two crimes. . . . A patriot is a man who supports the whole Republic; those who combat it in details are traitors. . . ." He ended by proposing a decree declaring all those traitors who "attempt to open the prisons" and who "aim at the overthrow of the revolutionary government."

Yet plain as such language was, it apparently was not plain enough for Danton.

Although he was moved when he heard of threats like Vadier's malevolent, "We will soon clean out that fat porpoise!" and cried to David, "Tell the scoundrel that if I felt my life in danger I would be more cruel than a cannibal. I would eat his brains and spit into his skull!" he was not roused to action.

His friends, all sensing the impending disaster, attempted to bring about a compromise between him and Robespierre. The dramatist Laignelot, whose tragedies *Agis et Cléomène* and *Rienzi* had earned their author his seat in the Convention, succeeded in persuading Danton to call at 366 Rue Saint-Honoré. The two passed through the gateway, with a restaurant on the left and a jeweler's on the right, and crossed the court; saws were screaming in the workshop, and there was a smell of fresh wood. Robespierre's nephew Duplay, who had lost his left leg at Valmy, limped up the stairs to announce them. Robespierre received them in the small antechamber outside his living room and study; the hairdresser who called every morning to curl and powder his hair had just left.

Danton began without preface: "Let us reach an understanding and save liberty! It has dangerous foes, betraying the people who believe them to be friends." Robespierre, slowly buttoning his striped blue waistcoat, was evasive and icily polite. When Danton and Laignelot smelt the fresh wood in the court again they knew their walk had been in vain.

Another time, on leaving the Convention, a violent altercation arose between Danton and Vadier, Amar, Voulland, and Barère on the subject of Philippeaux. Danton threatened them, but when a friend urged him to return at once to the hall and strike —because otherwise he might be arrested that very night, he shook his head contemptuously: "They would not dare!" He took the other gayly by the lapel and exclaimed: "Come on home and have dinner."

There was never a spring like the spring of 1794. Day after day the tumbrils rolled to the Place de la Révolution; there was no pause now. All sorts and conditions met their end here in this month of Germinal: postmasters, abbés, students, wine merchants, rentiers, generals, sergeant majors, bishops, public prosecutors, tradesmen, printers, a Carmelite nun, and a Benedictine monk of seventy-nine. Light spring breezes carried the pink chestnut blossoms from the gardens of the Tuileries to the scaffold, and every meadow around Paris was yellow with buttercups. Danton had rented a country house at Choisy, a refuge, a harbor of love. Soon he would escape there or to the green solitude of his first father-in-law's estate at Sèvres. The spring was like wine. Your lips, Louise!

Again and again friends came with warnings. Danton alternated between passive resignation and an illusory sense of security. To one friend he replied, "Better to be guillotined than to guillotine," and to another, "Look at my head. It is still firm on my shoulders." And he repeatedly consoled himself, half weary, half convinced, with "They will not dare." Delacroix and Desmoulins pleaded with him to seek safety, to escape abroad; he brushed the suggestion aside: "I cannot take my country abroad with me."

The evening of March 30 the two so-called governing committees—the Committee of Public Safety and the Committee of General Security were convoked in the Pavillon d'Egalité—the usual preliminary to important decisions. A fire was flickering in the grate; Couthon had his little whippet on his paralyzed knees. Most of those present did not know what was in hand until Saint-Just, supplied with data by Robespierre, read his report, cold as ice, keen as a knife—the measured dose of poison.

He asked for Danton's head.

The others listened mutely; Carnot had scruples: "Consider it carefully; a head like Danton's will draw many others along with it." Lindet also refused his coöperation. "My function is to provide food for citizens and not to kill good patriots." And old Rühl, mindful of the recent embrace, likewise refused. The others, headed by the triumphant Billaud-Varenne, signed the warrant Barère had drawn up ordering the arrest of Danton, Delacroix, Camille Desmoulins, and Philippeaux. Among the other signatures, hidden in a tiny script, as if ashamed, was the name that had stood under the declaration: "I love you more than ever and until death."

Danton had been warned once more, and this night he was haunted by black forebodings. He was tired, so tired. But it was no use now going to bed. While Louise sat anxiously watching over him, he stretched out in an easy chair to wait with closed eyes until they came. Sometimes he murmured, "They will not dare." Five o'clock struck, then half past, soon it would begin to grow light above the roofs of the Cour du Commerce.

And then the easy chair was empty; the heavy steps of the gendarmes grew faint on the pavement outside. In the silent, deserted house Louise crouched full of a terror which had rarely left her since that man of terror had first looked on her with favor.

V

The End

1794

THE great clock of the Pavillon d'Egalité in the Tuileries struck ten; ten o'clock in the morning of the 11th Germinal of the year II of the Republic. The Convention was about to sit.

The usual crowds thronged around the booths in the gardens. Besides wine, coffee, tobacco, meat patties, and fruit, there were books and pamphlets on questions of the day for sale, as well as pictures of Robespierre, engravings showing the execution of Marie-Antoinette and plaster of Paris casts of Marat and Lepelletier de Saint-Fargeau. Those who had booths under the trees had to be in good standing in their sections, for the ground was official ground, the forecourt of the Temple of the Republic. At each gate and at the entrance to every building the grenadier-gendarmes of the Convention stood on guard, grave figures, their rifles with fixed bayonets at their side: Their uniforms were bright—yellow leather equipment, blue tunics with red facings and red epaulettes, yellow breeches and waistcoats, black leggings reaching to the knees, and tall bearskin caps with red plumes.

This day the Tuileries were humming with unusual activity. Rumors were abroad: during the night something extraordinary, unheard of, had happened. Details were unknown; but people hardly dared to whisper the name of Danton. Even the grenadiers-gendarmes were affected by the excitement. From beneath their caps they looked questioningly at each deputy as he arrived: What has happened? What's going on? What's in the air?

In these days of supreme suspense the Convention, without will, force, or authority, was like a flock of sheep crowding together during a thunderstorm. It had handed over its power to the Committee of Public Safety; to everything the committee proposed the deputies nodded mechanically. Watched over by the secret police at every step, each member was in continual fear that the terrible eye of the Committee of General Security might fall on him—that its terrible arm might be stretched out to seize him. They were cowards deliberately, and had only one wish—to live.

But on this day the feeling of mute resignation, of the mean-
inglessness of their entire function, of boredom and shame, had
given place to restiveness—for the first time in many months.
Instead of indifference, alarm could be read in many faces. Here
and there groups were conversing with animation; a watchword
appeared to have been passed among the benches. The committee had gone too far; it was time to show the committee. . . .

Tallien rang his bell; the meeting opened.

Delmas began to speak. In the list of suspicious persons kept
by Robespierre with methodical exactness, he was entered as a
"ci-devant noble," an "infamous plotter," and an accomplice of
Danton. He moved the recall of all members of committees into
the plenary meeting, a motion which was harmless in appearance, but behind which Robespierre's adherents rightly suspected an attempt to use the committees of records, of decrees,
of markets, assignats, currency, war, finance, legislation, education, marine, and colonies—in short all the other nineteen committees—as a makeweight against the two omnipotent governing
committees. A zealous deputy hastened to report to the Master.

The others started to interrupt, but the huge figure of the
butcher Legendre, Danton's lieutenant, hastened up the steps
of the tribune. He had sat at Danton's table so often that now,
when his friend was in danger, he could not but remain loyal.
That Delmas' motion had passed so easily encouraged him.
Feeling all eyes resting on himself with unaccustomed interest,
he began: "Citizens, last night four members of this House were
arrested: I know that Danton is one of them; the names of the
others I do not know . . . Citizens, I consider Danton as pure
and honest as myself—and I do not think that I can be charged
with any action capable of shocking the tenderest Republican
sensibilities."

He was met with disapproval; but Clauzel called on the president to protect the freedom of speech. Tallien replied—and
there was no doubt at whom his words were directed—"Yes, I
will maintain freedom of speech; everyone shall express his
thoughts freely, and we shall remain assembled here to protect
the cause of liberty."

Encouraged by Tallien's reply, Legendre recalled the part

Danton played in 1792: "In those days the enemy was at the gates of Paris. Danton came and his plans saved the country. . . . I repeat, I believe Danton to be as pure as myself." He closed with a motion to call Danton and his fellow prisoners before the bar so that the Convention itself might examine, accuse, or acquit them.

There was applause and cries of "Down with the dictatorship!" A gust of revolt swept through the hall.

There was a minor panic in the Committee of Public Safety when the news was heard and Robespierre's henchmen were alarmed. Obviously this was a preconcerted action; it was easy to imagine what would happen if Danton were allowed to thunder before the house, sweeping the timorous and vacillating deputies with him by the magnetism of his will to the destruction of the committee. If this were allowed to occur, it would be the turn of Robespierre, Couthon, and Saint-Just to spend the night in a dark cell.

Delay was dangerous. Robespierre gathered up his papers and hastened to the Convention. Tallien gave him the floor.

Moving like an automaton Robespierre mounted the tribune; he turned his head mechanically right and left, staring through his glittering spectacles at the rows of faces and letting his eyes rest for two heart beats on those he mistrusted. It was like the hypnotic act of a snake charmer; the murmurs and interruptions were frozen into a deathly stillness. He exchanged the glasses which his myopic eyes had required for this scrutiny for another pair to examine the papers before him on the desk and began, sure of being listened to with attention, with respect, with fear.

His address was harsh, dry, and arrogant; the text—No privileges for deputies! "Legendre has mentioned Danton, no doubt because he believes that a privilege attaches to his name. But we will have no more privileges and no more idols." The Robespierrists applauded. "We shall see today whether the Convention has the power to break an idol long rotten or whether the idol is to stand until it falls and in its fall crushes the Convention and the French nation. . . . Has Danton any claim to privilege? Is he in any respect superior to Chabot and Fabre d'Eglantine, his colleagues and intimate friends whom he so ardently defended? Is he in any respect better than his fellow citizens?" Friends of Danton, he continued, had attempted to put pressure on himself, Robespierre, had thought to prevail on him by recalling their ancient friendship; but all this had no weight with him. "I, too, was a friend of Pétion; when he threw off his mask I left him. I, too, had relations with Roland; he became a traitor, and I denounced him. Now Danton is trying to take their place; in my eyes he is simply an enemy of the country. . . ." The arguments used against his arrest betokened the destruction of freedom and the decay of fixed principles. Was there anyone in this hall who dared to sacrifice the interests of his country for personal reasons —perhaps from fear? "It has been said that the arrest was an arbitrary act; such criticism implies mistrust of the justice of the people—of the men who enjoy the confidence of the Convention; it implies mistrust of the Convention itself, which gave them its confidence and of public opinion which confirmed it. I repeat," and here the voice grew cold and threatening, "I repeat that those who tremble at this moment are guilty; for innocence has never yet feared public scrutiny."

There was a pause. While applause burst round him, Robespierre once more deliberately changed his glasses and Legendre felt the cold glance resting on him. The man of brawn shuddered: the knife of the guillotine was no great distance from his own neck. Down, Legendre: to heel. You are not destined to grow old, but still, pleasant nights await you in the bed of the famous Louise Contat of the Comédie-Française where you will be the successor of marquises, counts, and the King's own brother.

Legendre was not content with obsequious silence. He stammered an embarrassed retraction; nothing was further from his thoughts than to sacrifice liberty for the sake of an individual. Next Barère, copying Robespierre's style, produced a few conventional phrases containing comparisons with the senates of Venice and Genoa and an attack on the "new aristocracy" of those who wished to appear before the bar of the Convention to meet their accusation; and finally the whole Convention was overawed; Danton and his associates would get no hearing.

Again there was silence, as though the Angel of Destruction were sweeping through the Chamber; and now Saint-Just minced up to the tribune, in his blue coat with the gold buttons and high white batiste stock, prepared to report in the name of both committees—remote and cold as marble in spite of his pure brow, his delicate lips, and his innocent almost feminine face.

Many inner voices might have called to him, "Stop, you have no right to be unmerciful." He might have thought of the prison he lodged in eight years ago because he took the family silver with him when he ran away from home. He might have remembered his endless epic *Organt*, an amateurish performance which, however, by the standards of the Committee of Public Safety, was immoral and salacious and incited to libertine pleasures:

> *Dans une tendre et pétillante orgie,*
> *Oh! qu'il est doux de presser tour à tour,*
> *Contre son sein sa bouteille et sa mie*
> *Ivre à la fois et de vin et de l'amour.*

Did he not know that no one was beyond the shafts of slander? That only last year a broadside of the Enragés had charged him with dining luxuriously every day while the people starved? That Couthon, who lived most modestly, was alleged to have bought a farm near Clermont and paid for it in gold?

Did he not suspect that even Robespierre, that spinsterly image of correctness and respectability, would be accused of being a drunkard, a roué, and the lover of Eléonore Duplay? Did none of this prevent Saint-Just from exaggerating the human frailties of his political opponents until they became dire treason?

No, the fanatic of twenty-six remembered nothing, knew nothing, suspected nothing, and had ears only for that inner voice which peremptorily cried, "The Republic is in danger! Destroy its enemies!"

Saint-Just's first report had been rendered before the Committee of Public Safety and the Committee of General Security. Robespierre had supplemented it from his secret archives, dipping the ready arrow in deadly poison. Line by line, and often word for word, Saint-Just followed the details of this report as he began to read, in a low and deliberately affected yet firm voice, the manuscript in his left hand, mechanically raising and lowering his right until it seemed to his hearers that they were watching the knife of the guillotine at work.

After a few introductory generalizations, Saint-Just attacked those "men who have long been betraying the popular cause, who have waged war against you in alliance with all the conspirators, Orléans, Brissot, Hébert, Hérault, and their accomplices, and who at this moment are conspiring against the Republic with the allied kings."

Did no one of those who knew better leap up to say, "Saint-Just, you are raving"? Did not one of Danton's friends flush red with indignation?

Not one. The Convention trembled and was silent.

And Saint-Just denounced "those last adherents of Royalism who have been stalking liberty for five years as a tiger stalks his prey." The monotonous, dispassionate voice went on to speak of England whose money bought men, of the party of the Duke of Orléans, of Dumouriez, of Clootz "who loved all the universe but France," of the foreigners whose hands were at work everywhere, of the clique of Fabre d'Eglantine, this "Cardinal de Retz of our days," of Hébert, and Chaumette who had denied the immortality of the soul.

Next came a trowelful of flattery for the Convention. "Is there on earth a body so loyally devoted to the people, so useful to the people, as you?"

And finally, it was Danton's turn. Saint-Just addressed him as though he were sitting before him in his accustomed place. Vadier had been shrewd enough to oppose the delicate experiment of allowing the Convention to decide the accused men's fate in their presence. Saint-Just's apostrophes were directed at a vacant seat; no one was there to fling back his head, to curl his lip in scorn, to frown in anger, and to fling in the accuser's face in a voice which shook the windows, "Dog, you lie!"

So, there was no danger at all in mentioning Mirabeau, or the Duke of Orléans, or Dumouriez. "Do you dare deny, Danton, that you sold yourself to these three men who were the most

deadly conspirators against freedom? . . . Do you dare deny
that at times of crisis you always deserted the common cause?
. . . While you were minister you made Fabre rich. . . . The
Brissotins brought accusations against Marat; you declared
that you were his enemy. You deserted the Mountain when it
was in danger, and you are proud of never having denounced
Gensonné, Guadet, and Brissot; you even held the olive branch
out to them—a proof that you were allied with them against the
people and against the strict Republicans. . . . You sent Fabre
to Dumouriez under pretense of bringing about a reconciliation
with Kellermann. The result was a guarantee of the safety of
the Prussian army on secret conditions which were explained
by your later conduct. . . . You said that you could harbor no
hate; is it not a crime not to hate the enemies of your country?"

Yet Danton had rendered the country enormous services. He
had inspired the national resistance in September, 1792, and in
March, 1793. Saint-Just turned these merits into so many
crimes: "On returning from Belgium you suggested the *levée en
masse* of patriots to protect the frontier." A cunning move to
clear Paris of revolutionary elements. "Had your attempts been
successful, who would have been left to resist the aristocrats
who would have risen in insurrection again and again?"

Still not a man rose in indignation. No peal of shrill, scornful
laughter greeted these monstrous misrepresentations; the Convention crouched and was dumb.

No matter that the speaker craftily picked to pieces a great
career, that he made the silliest accusations of the Girondins and
the Hébertists against Danton seem terrible, and dispensed with
proofs as superfluous. For the Convention the argument sufficed
that it would be a peaceful and happy world once the remnants
of the Orléans faction had been exterminated! It obeyed the
order: Be adamant! Without a note of protest the Convention
swallowed the decree accusing Danton and his associates of
Royalist conspiracy; and the deputies, breathing again as
though they had escaped disaster, applauded their own decree.

The great clock of the Pavillon d'Egalité in the Tuileries
struck four; four o'clock in the afternoon of the 11th Germinal

of the year II of the Republic. The session of the Convention closed.

At the moment of Danton's arrest Paris contained more than seven thousand political prisoners, whose papers were in the hands of the Committee of General Security awaiting transfer to the Revolutionary Tribunal. The old prisons of the Conciergerie, La Force, L'Abbaye, Saint Lazare, Bicêtre and Salpétrière could no longer cope with such numbers; monasteries, hospitals, barracks, colleges, and the Luxembourg Palace were used as temporary quarters. Among the *"Prisons muscadines,"* this former palace of Marie de Médicis ranked first—the Luxembourg was the most eligible for dukes, duchesses, counts, marquises and vicountesses, and lesser nobles, and was thronged with them; and as the prisoners were allowed to mingle freely during the day, the good form and elegant tone of the old regime prevailed. The address of "citoyen" elsewhere universally in vogue was in the worst taste here. In this fashionable prison those who had money did not brood over a diet of bread and water: Arthur Dillon, count, general, and friend of Desmoulins, who had been sent by the Martinique planters to the Constituent Assembly and had first commanded the Army of the North and later a division under Dumouriez, drank himself under the table every day with good red wine. Why not? There was nothing more intelligent to do. Others spent the time playing cards or music, gossiping, or composing songs and verses. In the shadow of the scaffold many a sentimental, many a frivolous love affair budded; each evening the head turnkey, Vernet, read out the names of those who were to come before the Revolutionary Tribunal next morning; and many a lady, hitherto unapproachable, lost her timidity and made up with hasty and passionate embraces what she had missed during years of enforced abstinence while she was free.

The *ci-devants* did not hide their derisive joy when Danton and his friends were brought in. They stood and stared and smiled. When Delacroix, tall, well built and erect, was led past, one of them said appreciatively: "He would have made an excellent coachman." To show the damned "aristos" that he and his companions were not weak and that their arrest would not improve the fate of the mockers, Danton turned casually to the onlookers: "If men make blunders they are laughed at . . . But you have my sympathy, all of you, because if reason does not soon return, your present state will seem like a bed of roses compared with the future." Then suddenly he saw Thomas Paine, who had been imprisoned in the Luxembourg since January for being a friend of the Girondins and was engaged in writing a book, *The Age of Reason*. To his questioning look Danton said in English: "What you have done for the happiness and freedom of your country, I have tried in vain to do for mine. I have been less lucky. But that does not make me culpable." The next was meant for the aristocrats, too: "They are sending us to the scaffold; I shall go serenely."

In the courtyard Hérault de Séchelles was playing *la galoche,* a game which consisted in knocking a coin off a cork with another coin; he hastened up in amazement and flung himself into his friends' arms.

Since the warrant for Danton and his companions ordered separate and secret confinement, they were put in different cells. Philippeaux, the grave and austere, all but turned Epicurean and sent his wife a note asking for half a pound of tobacco: "I have had none since last night, and as the good Swiss said, it is almost as bad as being without bread."

From a neighboring cell Desmoulins heard groans; he called his own name, and then heard clearly the voice of Fabre d'Eglantine: "My God, you here? So the counterrevolution has been victorious?" But Desmoulins did not dare to talk, nor was he in the mood for it or for losing himself in Young's *Night Thoughts* which he had put in his pocket at the moment of arrest—that book in which the black flower of melancholy bloomed on the edge of the abyss of all earthly vanity. His head and heart were full of other things. He cursed politics, the man-eating witch, and sadly confessed that he was born to write verses. He knew that apart from some taunts at vindictive colleagues in the Convention, he was being sacrificed for his friendship with Danton, and yet he was half grateful to his assassins for sending him to death with Danton and Philippeaux. One could not have better company. Yet how repugnant was death itself while there was Lucile!

Poor, poor Lucile! She brought soup for her Camille without being allowed to see him; she wandered under the trees of the Luxembourg Gardens where notices admonished passers-by to move on and not look up at the prison windows! But she paid no more heed to the stern injunction than an old lady in veils who sat there every day on a bench, the mother of Hérault de Séchelles. As though he felt the presence of his beloved wife, Desmoulins opened his arms, longing to press her to his heart. He feverishly covered sheet after sheet with his delicate writing: *"Adieu, ma Lolotte, mon bon Loup!"* He felt himself drifting away from the shores of existence and driving out to sea. "Farewell, Loulou, my life, my soul, my goddess on earth!"

No pair of tender poets, Danton and Delacroix remained unshaken. By raising their voices they could talk from cell to cell; they shouted to each other their fury and rage without any respect for those in power. Delacroix: "If only I had known that they were going to arrest me!" Danton, half regretful and angry with himself: "I knew it, I was warned, but I refused to believe it."

At noon on the 12th Germinal Danton's examination took place in a hall of the palace; a tedious formality to satisfy the letter of the law and performed with the utmost possible despatch. At a little rococo table was seated Denizot, formerly judge in the Court of the Fifth Arrondissement, and now in the Revolutionary Tribunal, and beside him the recorder Girard with his inkwell at hand. The question was put: Had Danton conspired against the French people to introduce the monarchy and destroy the representative and Republican government? Denizot shrank before the flash of those dark eyes, the thunder of that rumbling voice: "I was a Republican even under the tyranny, and I shall die a Republican." Then the second question: Had he a defense counsel? Danton: "I am defense enough for myself." The proceedings were over. Girard read his sheet.

Be good enough to sign. Danton seized the quill and signed with a flourish like the sweep of a sword. This signature augured no good.

The same evening he and his friends received the indictment. The trial would be the next day. Philippeaux, on being handed the paper, laid aside the Helvetius which he had been reading for his edification and wrote to his wife Marguerite-Françoise: "If this letter should be our last kiss on earth there is another place where loving and virtuous souls may meet again." Desmoulins, watching his fate approaching irresistibly, foamed with impotent rage.

But Danton and Delacroix exchanged imprecations. The other prisoners shivered to hear Danton ask with a laugh: "Well, what do you say to that lousy paper?" "That I shall cut off my hair so Samson won't touch it." Danton's laughter had a grisly sound: "A pretty ceremony when Samson cracks our cervical vertebræ."

Next morning the prisoners were transferred to the Conciergerie. Fabre was so wretched and weak that he had to be lifted into the carriage; Desmoulins seemed dreamy, pensive, full of very painful thoughts. Hérault took his leave from his equals in misfortune and station with the politeness of a man of the world about to travel for pleasure. Danton and Delacroix left the Luxembourg noisily, laughing and shouting, as if they were going from one tavern to another.

Their road led past Danton's section, close to the Cour du Commerce; the streets, the noises, the smells, all were familiar. Unholy thoughts beset him; suddenly a verse which he had read recently in a calendar and remembered occurred to him:

> Le riant Germinal féconde les semences
> Promet, fait concevoir de douces espérances.

Yes, promising seeds and pleasant hopes—while one was being unloaded at the Conciergerie!

———————◆———————

THEY had not been locked in their cells long when a clerk of the Revolutionary Tribunal followed by gendarmes came to fetch them. Down a long echoing corridor and up a gloomy staircase, they were led into the court.

The accused looked at each other in surprise: what had they to do with these others? The prisoners fell naturally into three groups. There were political prisoners accused of high treason: Danton, Delacroix, Desmoulins, Hérault, and Philippeaux, too, on whom Robespierre was now avenging himself because he had dared to attack the majesty of the Committee of Public Safety in the matter of the Vendée campaign. What in the world had they to do with the second group: Fabre d'Eglantine, Basire, Chabot, Delaunay, criminals who had to answer for profiteering and forgery! The only man who was perhaps at home among them was the Abbé d'Espagnac, army contractor, speculator, and wholesale profiteer. There was, however, a method in the mixing; in this way bearers of great political names were linked with plain rogues and knaves and so were lowered in the public eye. Not even the prosecution could pretend that the third group had anything in common with the first or even the second. But the destruction of the Hébertists and then the Dantonists was to be a two-act tragedy entitled "The Conspiracy of the Foreigners"; and there is no better cover for a malicious attack on a political opponent than the accusation of working hand in glove with the country's foes. In order to put the people on this scent foreigners were accused with both the Dantonists and the Hébertists. The Austrian brothers Frey, their Danish secretary Diederichsen, and the Spanish Andrés Maria de Guzman, a colonel and adventurer with an unknown source of money, gave the desired color to the Danton trial.

The seat which was normally the prerogative of the chief accused was on this occasion allotted to Fabre d'Eglantine because of his ill health. Chabot, who had attempted to forestall the guillotine by swallowing corrosive sublimate, had recovered sufficiently to share with the others the primitive dock with its tiers of seats. Danton sat between a friend and a scoundrel, between Delacroix and Delaunay.

In this court Hérault had pleaded in other days when he was a young scarlet-robed avocat-général in the parlement, but the place had greatly changed since it had been renamed the "Salle de la Liberté." The ceiling with its gold and blue decorations, and the black and white marble floor remained; but the velvet tapestry with the embroidered silver lilies had vanished, and in place of Dürer's *Christ* there were plaster busts of Marat, Lepelletier, and Brutus, and a couple of cardboards with the new Constitution and the Declaration of the Rights of Man printed on them. Even this bright spring morning did not entirely banish the gloom; a dull light filtered through the windows which opened on the dark court of the Conciergerie.

Danton was less interested in the room than in the men with whom he had to deal. At one end of the long hall, on the left and at right angles to the dock, stood the judges' bench, and there sat Denizot, whom Danton knew from the previous day's examination; Bravet, formerly judge in the Department of the Hautes-Alpes; Masson, one-time assessor in the record office; and Foucault, the former manager of a stud farm—the man who was supposed to be the author of the maxim, "We need blood; the people want blood!" Herman, who presided, was a handsome, well-groomed man of thirty-four, a jurist who had had a varied legal career. He was no sadist or vampire or monster; his inclination was for books and gardening, his home, and his little son Aristide. But he was a rigid formalist and unbending Republican who was entered on Robespierre's list as "a virtuous and resolute man suitable for high office." Herman swore by Robespierre. What Robespierre ordered was right. If it were suggested that the safety of the Republic seemed to demand an undue number of heads, well—every skirmish at the front cost the lives of five or six hundred innocent patriots.

In front of the judges' bench, behind a table covered with papers, sat the public prosecutor, Fouquier-Tinville, with his pale face, black hair, bushy eyebrows, and bullet head as round as a cat's. He, too, had spent many years in the legal profession, and far from being a cannibal, was a thoroughly gentle, domestic man, married respectably to his second wife Henriette. But he was a bureaucrat, the most zealous, exacting, and conscientious bureaucrat of the Terror, who killed without passion, from a sense of duty, because it was his job. Whatever others might think, he was simply doing what his office demanded, like any other civil servant. He salved his conscience by telling himself "It is the will of the Committee of Public Safety."

Fouquier did not wear the red Jacobin cap, but, like the judges, the severe costume prescribed for magistrates: black silk gown and black hat with upturned brim and great black feathers; in spite of the medal inscribed *La Loi,* which hung on a tricolor ribbon on their chests, they had a certain unhappy resemblance to undertaker's men.

Opposite the dock were the table and easy chairs of the jury, today numbering seven: the lutemaker Renaudin, a fanatical adherent of Robespierre's; one of the bodyguard of the "Incorruptible" who invariably accompanied him on the street; the sabot manufacturer Desboisseaux, the musician Lumière, who had formerly been secretary to Fouquier; a man with the revolutionary nickname *Dix-Août,* who tried to obliterate his past as Marquis Leroy de Montflobert by a brutal zeal; the wigmaker Ganney, whom it was not easy to persuade of the innocence of anyone who came before the Tribunal; the carpenter Trinchard, a Jacobin zealot who had won his spurs in the trial of Marie-Antoinette, and, as he informed his brother, was proud of having condemned *"celle que lon califioit si deven de Raine";* and finally the surgeon Souberbielle, who lowered his eyes, ashamed, before Danton's glance.

Justice and law left the composition of the jury to chance and drawing by lot; but what had right and law to do with this trial? To be quite certain Fouquier had sifted and searched his files; the usual tendency of the jurors was to treat every accused as an enemy of the Republic, and also as a personal enemy, but today the jury was composed of even more reliable men than usual, "an ax in the hewer's hands," the hewer being the public prosecutor.

Behind the railing of the gallery a dense throng had gathered, filling lobby, corridors, staircases, and courts. Thousands packed the Quai des Morfondus, the Place Dauphine, the Pont-Neuf, and the Quai de Conti as far as the Mint, some eager to see and hear, others secretly moved; some for and others against the accused.

The buzz which filled the court ceased when the defendants

were called by name and the identification began. Chabot, Basire, Fabre d'Eglantine—Desmoulins when asked his age replied: "As old as the sansculotte Jesus when he died—a critical age for patriots." Danton was asked where he lived; he flung back his head: "Soon it will be the Beyond, and my name in the Pantheon of History."

The presiding judge leaned back in his seat and the clerk of the court droned out the indictment: first of all Amar's report to the Convention on the 20th Ventôse against Fabre d'Eglantine and his associates; an irrelevant attack, without proof, against Hérault and Desmoulins on the same charge, and the vague and general concluding remark: "Danton and Delacroix are no better than the men whose offenses have just been described."

Before any of the accused could get in a word Herman rose: "The session is closed." The intention was to give the public the impression that Danton and his friends were also implicated in crimes and profiteering.

The Conciergerie where they were kept in custody for the night was no Luxembourg, but an ancient underground dungeon with thick walls that sweated moisture whenever the Seine rose, tiny windows, perpetual gloom, sinister passages and forbidding bars. In addition there were the jailers with their frank smell of brandy and their big hounds, the sickening stench of the ordure buckets—*griaches* in prison jargon—and the nerve-shattering crash of the heavy ironbound doors; it took all one's will power to resist succumbing to such depressing surroundings.

But Danton had so much of meadow, river, and trees in his heart that he mounted unbroken the next morning to the Salle de la Liberté: "I want to see how these fellows stand up to me."

Overnight the number of the accused had grown by one. Since the opportunity was favorable, the Committee of Public Safety had had Westermann, who was generally known as the sword of the Dantonists, arrested. Fouquier simply put him in the dock without the legally prescribed preliminary examination. What? No examination? Herman smiled sweetly: it was of no moment, a superfluous formality! Danton exploded: "But we are here in order to observe formalities!" So the sitting of the court was suspended, and in an adjoining room Denizot had to ask the

general the customary two questions. Meanwhile the president
and the public prosecutor bent busily over their documents; but
they were hardly able to disguise their alarm when Danton's
voice was heard again thundering: "If we are only allowed to
speak freely I shall crush my accusers; and if the French people
are what they ought to be I shall be forced to beg mercy for
them."

But he was a simpleton if he imagined that he would be allowed to talk.

The Alsatian returned and with a grandiose gesture addressed
the people in the galleries rather than the bench: "I wish I
could undress here before everyone, so that you might look at
me. I have received seven wounds, all of them in front! Only
once have I been stabbed in the back—by this accusation!"

Next the indictment against Danton and his associates was
read; it amounted to a copy of Saint-Just's report. Cambon was
called on to give evidence on the affair of the India Company.
It was none of Danton's business; but when he saw his colleague
he called to him: "Cambon, do you believe that we are conspirators? Look, he laughs; he does not believe it. Record that he
laughed!" And indeed, the evidence of this financial expert,
while heavily damning for Jullien, Delaunay, and Espagnac,
stated plainly that Danton and Delacroix had turned against
Dumouriez as soon they had suspected him of high treason. In
April, 1793, Cambon himself had felt doubtful about the success
of the Revolution, but Danton and Delacroix had assured him
that the Republic would triumph over every crisis and would remain one and indivisible.

During the cross-examination Fabre d'Eglantine demanded
the production of the original decree so that the alleged forgery
might be proven. Delaunay, Chabot, Basire, and Espagnac tried
to take the attitude of poor sinners, but Cambon tore to shreds
their tissue of lies and effrontery.

And now people began to listen intensely behind the spectators' bar, and stand on tiptoe with excitement: Danton was
about to be cross-examined, or rather to cross-examine his opponents. Fully versed in all the tricks of the trade, he began by

handing Fouquier of the cat's head a list of defense witnesses whose examination he asked; these were members of the Convention—Simond, Gossuin, Legendre, Fréron, Panis, Lindet, Calon, Merlin of Douai, Courtois, Laignelot, Robin, Goupilleau, Lecointre of Versailles, Brival, and Merlin of Thionville. Delacroix added Pache, Jazot, Guyton-Morveau, and with Danton's vigorous approval, Rose of the Rue de la Grange-Batelière, the proprietor of the restaurant with the legendary breakfasts at a hundred écus a head.

Herman, however, was firmly resolved to muzzle Danton's attack by giving him lessons in good manners. A dozen times he pointed out that his behavior was not that of a well-brought-up defendant in court. Danton exploded with indignation; the blood hammered in his temples, and his answers were volcanic eruptions. Each time the president's bell replied, and a soft voice gently reproached him, "Danton, insolence is appropriate to the guilty and calm to the innocent. A defense should be moderate and kept within the bounds of decency." But Danton, within an inch of the guillotine, and facing merciless judges, not the polite society of a salon, burst out: "When I think of the grave and unjust accusation brought against me, I cannot control my indignation toward my calumniators. I am a revolutionary heart and soul; how can I answer calmly?" A fresh explosion, the bell again, renewed admonitions.

Seeing Vadier, Amar, and David skulking in the background, Danton longed to cross swords with his great enemies, Saint-Just, Robespierre, Couthon; to look them in the eye and to measure himself against them. "Bring them to me and I will fling them back into the oblivion from which they ought never to have emerged. . . . Miserable traitors, show yourselves, and I will tear off the mask which preserves you from the common verdict!" Again the bell and the president protesting with dignity against "unseemly attacks" on men "enjoying the public respect."

Good manners, decency, moderation, calm, and good form—when life was at stake!

But Herman's insistence on formalities was simply a matter

of tactics. For some time he had been casting an uneasy eye at the spectators' gallery and he had noted with growing disquiet how Danton's matter-of-fact replies drove home. For Danton was DANTON—the people's Danton, the hero of the Cordeliers, the man of August 10, no profiteer, no traitor, no climber, and above all no coward trembling before the scaffold; everyone believed him when he exclaimed with loathing, "I am weary of life and long to be rid of it."

At the charge of bribery, he straightened: "Men of my kind cannot be paid; their foreheads are marked with the indelible seal of freedom, the very emblem of the Republic!"

Had he plotted with Mirabeau? He shrugged his shoulders contemptously: "Everyone knows that I fought Mirabeau and crossed his plans as soon as I believed that they threatened freedom."

Had he recommended following the policy of Barnave and Lameth? His small eyes flashed: "A lie, prove it!"

Had he had an understanding with Guadet, Brissot, Barbaroux, and the entire outcast party? He brushed the suggestion aside: "Barbaroux demanded the heads of Danton, Robespierre, and Marat!"

Had he retired to Arcis with criminal indifference at crises like August 10? There was sarcasm in his voice: "Where are the men who had to put pressure on Danton to show himself that day? Where are those privileged beings from whom Danton had to borrow energy?" He half turned to the railing where people hung breathlessly: "For two days the court has known Danton! Tomorrow he hopes to fall asleep in glory. He has never whined for mercy, and you will see him going to the scaffold with that serenity of mind which comes from a good conscience."

With alarm Herman and Fouquier noted the growing applause of the audience; each of Danton's strong words was echoed outside and flashed like lightning to the farthest borders of the vast crowd that was following the proceedings on the square, the bridges, and in the streets. Woe if this mob burst through the barriers and cheered Danton and carried him on their shoulders! Then it would be all over with Robespierre and the Committee of Public Safety and Herman and Fouquier. The two jurists exchanged anxious glances and Herman sent Fouquier a reassuring note: "In half an hour I shall interrupt Danton's defense."

But applause fired Danton: "Within three months the people will tear my enemies to pieces."

Applause, cheers, and growing excitement. The president rang his bell and said with almost paternal solicitude: "You are tired, Danton, you need a rest. Tomorrow you can continue."

The session was closed—it was high time.

From his cell Danton could talk with Westermann on the other side of the wall. Some vigorous words and curses were exchanged, but when an odor recalled the water of the Aube there came a deep sigh: "Better to be a poor fisherman than to govern men."

But for all this Danton slept more peacefully that night of the 15th Germinal than Herman and Fouquier, who were beset by a nightmare. What would the next day bring? That evening the public prosecutor had hastened to the Committee of Safety, and there had been a hurried consultation; for what would happen on the morrow if Danton's indestructible lungs blew down the prosecution's house of cards? Saint-Just and Billaud-Varenne in particular were beside themselves and thought the Republic lost. Fouquier left profoundly depressed, finding no consolation in the fact that he had been instructed to prevent the production of Danton's witnesses at all costs—they would just be missing. The question was where to find the legal justification.

When the court resumed its session Danton rose immediately and asked peremptorily whether his witnesses had been summoned. Fouquier, with strong inhibitions against the truth, replied almost apologetically that he was waiting for the decision of the Committee of Public Safety. What? Danton exploded wrathfully: Were his bitterest enemies to decide on a step which was his by right of law? Robespierre? And that fop Saint-Just? And Couthon? And that old villain Vadier? While Herman's bell pleaded vainly for quiet, Danton and Delacroix stormed and raged: A pretty justice! Nice judges!

Fouquier, staring piercingly at the accused and frowning, said in his shrill voice: "It is time to put an end to an altercation which is equally scandalous to the court and to the public. I shall write to the Convention for their decision, which will be scrupulously obeyed."

Good! An agreement at last. Herman began to breathe again, and the proceedings were resumed, while the public prosecutor wrote: "There has been a storm rumbling ever since the court began to sit: The accused frantically demand the cross-examination of the witnesses for the defense and appeal to the people on the ground that it has been refused. In spite of the firmness of the president and the whole court, the frequency of their complaints disturbs the proceedings. They have loudly declared that they will not be silent unless their witnesses are examined and that without a decree. We therefore request you to instruct us definitely how to deal with this complaint. The rules of the court do not provide us with any excuse for refusing." Signed: Herman, Fouquier; and sent by special messenger to the Committee of Public Safety.

An hour passed. More and more frequently Fouquier looked uneasily toward the door expecting the saving word. He began to feel unpleasantly warm under the hat with the nodding black plumes.

Meanwhile Danton was contemptuously rejecting the "hideous calumny" that he had opposed the popular insurrection of May 31. "Once more I demand the examination of witnesses who are able to accuse me and of those whose evidence will exonerate me." Delacroix indignantly refuted the charge that he had been "the friend of the kings," and Philippeaux proudly interrupted the public prosecutor: "It is your privilege to destroy me, but I forbid you to insult me!" Westermann made a gesture of resentment when the evidence of a dead person, now beyond cross-examination, was adduced against him; Hérault was not even questioned on the charge of harboring an émigré, for which he had been arrested. Diederichsen made a decent but insignificant impression. And so the case dragged on until an usher whispered in Fouquier's ear.

He jumped up, hastened out, and in the corridor came on Amar and Voulland.

"Well?"

"Here is the decree you asked for."

"God knows it's time!" and snatching the paper, Fouquier hurried back.

It had been Saint-Just's task to force this decree from the Convention. To this end he had drawn a gloomy picture of the alleged "revolt of the guilty," and pointed to their impudence as evidence of a bad conscience, calling on the Assembly to strike the last blow "at the party which was tolerant of your enemies and is today renewing its energy in order to combat freedom." Then he played his ace of trumps: "At this very moment a conspiracy is in progress in the prisons to rescue them. . . . Dillon has stated that Desmoulins' wife has received money in order to start an insurrection culminating in the destruction of the patriots and the Revolutionary Tribunal."

The truth about the conspiracy was that for a number of days a certain Laflotte had been active in the Luxembourg. He was quite obviously what was known in prison slang as a *"mouton,"* a stool pigeon, whose function was to mingle as a prisoner with the prisoners and spy on them. In a fortunate moment for the hard-pressed ruling party the "mouton" had reported that General Dillon—the one who got drunk daily—had confidentially informed him that a plot was on foot, in view of the popular feeling, to tear the Dantonists from the Tribunal by force. He further reported that Dillon had given Lucile Desmoulins a thousand écus to hire a mob which was to congregate around the Palais de Justice. What more could be wanted? No sooner had this report been read out than the Convention was filled with rumors that the conspirators planned to massacre the Committee of Public Safety and to disperse the Convention, and that Danton was plotting to storm the Temple with shock troops and put the young Capet on the tyrant's throne. As a result the decree was unanimously adopted.

When Fouquier unfolded the paper and read the decree by which the Convention empowered the president "to use all legal means to enforce his own authority and that of the Revolutionary Tribunal and to suppress any attempt of the accused to disturb the public order or to interfere with the course of justice," and ordered that "anyone of the accused resisting or affronting the justice of the nation is to be immediately removed from court"—when the public prosecutor with a triumphant gleam under his bushy eyebrows read out this murderous decree, the accused were not alone in feeling the weight of the bludgeon.

Danton's huge figure was the first to leap up with a roar of indignation. The president's bell tinkled, the other accused, too, jumped on their benches, the spectators' gallery was in an uproar, there were threats against the tyranny, the bell clanged, Danton called judges, jury, and people to testify if he and his friends had ever resisted or attempted an insurrection. Pandemonium, shouts of "Treachery!" "Perfidy!" The bell again— and Herman with difficulty succeeded in declaring the session closed.

Fouquier wiped his low brow. It had not been done well, but it had been done. Three days of it and then the decree! The end was in sight.

THAT morning when Charles-Henry Samson visited the Conciergerie to inquire about business, one of the gendarmes clapped him on the shoulder with a laugh: "Big game today!"

This 16th Germinal of the year II, this April 5, 1794, was bright with spring. The squares, the streets, the palaces, the river, and bridges of Paris were bathed in brightness. At the Rond-Point in the Champs-Elysées sheep were grazing as usual; the queues stood before the bakeries; street singers roamed about accompanying the restless times with their songs; the famous restaurants—Beauvilliers in the Palais-Egalité, Venua in the Rue Saint-Honoré, Méot in the Rue des Bons-Enfants—offered delicacies, hot eel pastry, ragout of cockscombs and kidneys, capon with rice, artichokes in white sauce, *omelettes aux fines herbes,* and the choicest wines, Chablis, Beaune, Graves, Richebourg, l'Hermitage, Champagne Silléry; the younger Robespierre wrote to his great brother recommending reliable patriots, among them "the citizen Buonaparte, a general of artillery of quite remarkable merit"; a patriotic farmer presented twenty oxen to the Commune of Paris; Vadier met no contradiction when he told the Convention that it consisted "almost entirely" of virtuous men; a thousand women painted themselves to walk the streets; in the evening music would strike up in sixty dance halls, the theaters would play; *The Inauguration of the French Republic* would have its first performance at the opera; and the world-famous riding master Franconi would give an exhibition of horsemanship assisted by his children and pupils, including demonstrations of the High School, dancing on horseback, and "diverse scenes and laughable intermezzos" at the Amphithéâtre d'Astley in the Faubourg du Temple at half past five.

But at half past five, too, Danton would die.

When the court met that day everything moved rapidly and smoothly. Danton began by repeating his indignant question about his witnesses, and indeed he might well ask what had happened to Simond, Gossuin, Legendre, Fréron, Panis, Lindet, Calon, the two Merlins, Courtois, Laignelot, Robin, Goupilleau, Lecointre, Brival, Pache, Jazot, Guyton-Morveau, and the restaurateur Rose. Fouquier's reply was cold and assured: "The prosecution could produce numbers of witnesses if it wished; but we do not need witnesses, we have adequate written proof!"

While the accused were still gasping, the brief examination of the brothers Frey was finished, and the prosecutor, referring to the decree of the 7th Brumaire, asked the jury whether they were sufficiently instructed.

It was too much.

Danton was on his feet, bellowing, and the others were chanting in chorus with him: "Tyranny! Judicial Murder! The trial has hardly begun! Strangulation! Don't trouble to deliberate! Murderers! Take us to the scaffold!"

Fouquier had been waiting impatiently for this very outburst; he made the motion, on the strength of yesterday's decree, to have the accused removed for contempt of court. His motion was adopted and gendarmes dragged the struggling Dantonists from the benches; Desmoulins resisted most desperately.

The jury had already returned. Yes, they were sufficiently instructed. Herman put his questions like a bait: Do you find

Delacroix, Danton, Desmoulins, Philippeaux, Hérault de Séchelles, and Westermann guilty of taking part in a conspiracy
for the restoration of the monarchy?

Guilty? They had not even been properly charged with this
crime! No evidence, no facts, no witnesses—the entire procedure
was nothing but one long process of playing on feelings. Not
even this picked jury took the bait immediately, although they
had been worked on in the intervals by Vadier, Amar, and
David. In the jury room, however, in strict confidence, as a State
secret, "a letter from abroad to Danton" was shown them, a
mysterious document which appeared and vanished again as
though by magic. Its contents and authorship remain unknown,
but the jury permitted itself to be convinced, and when they filed
back to their places in the court Trinchard replied for them all
with a vehement "Guilty" on every count.

It was superfluous for the court to withdraw to determine a
sentence or to bring the accused to hear the verdict. Herman recited before an empty dock: Under the law of the 25th Ventôse
as applied to Part II, Chapter 1, Section 5, Article 7 of the Penal
Code, Fabre d'Eglantine, Delacroix, Danton, and so forth and
so on are condemned to death, and their property confiscated
for the State's Treasury; said sentence to be executed within
twenty-four hours on the Place de la Révolution in Paris and to
be published in print throughout the whole Republic.

The case was over.

WHILE Herman walked home, satisfied, and sure of a word of
praise from Robespierre, to bend tenderly over the cradle of his
little Aristide, and while on Hanriot's order the first, second, and
third legions of the Paris garrison prepared reserves for all
eventualities, the condemned were taken singly to the office of
the Conciergerie to hear the sentence. When the court clerk
Ducray found himself face to face with the giant whose name
was already half legendary he hesitated and stammered. But
Danton broke in roughly: "Don't trouble to say it. Keep your
sentence to yourself! I don't want it. They can take us to the
guillotine without it."

REQUISITION
ou *Commandant - gé-*
néral de la force armée
parisienne.

AU NOM DE LA RÉPUBLIQUE.

L'ACCUSATEUR PUBLIC , près le Tribunal criminel-révolutionnaire, établi à Paris par la loi du 10 mars 1793, en exécution du jugement du Tribunal *aujourd'huy* requiert le citoyen commandant-général de la force armée parisienne, de prêter main-forte et mettre sur pied la force publique, nécessaire à l'exécution dudit jugement rendu contre *fabré déglantine Danton et treize autres* et qui le condamne à la peine de *Mort* laquelle exécution aura lieu *ajourd'huy Seize Germinal quatre* heure, de *Relevée* sur la place publique de *La Revolution* de cette ville. Le citoyen commandant-général est requis d'envoyer ladite force publique, cour du Palais, ledit jour, à *quatre* heures précises de *Relevee*

FAIT à Paris, le *Seize Germinal* l'an *2* de la République française, une et indivisible.

ACCUSATEUR PUBLIC.

A. Q. Fouquier

The Order for Troops on the Day of the Execution

The last stage but one was the room next to the office where the condemned were accustomed to wait for the executioner. Because the wait lasted sometimes hours, sometimes a whole night, there were chairs and mattresses here and there. In this gloomy chamber, Danton's protégé General Biron, the former Duke de Lauzun, had swallowed his last hearty meal of fresh oysters, and when Samson entered had politely requested to be allowed to finish the last dozen.

Desmoulins' thoughts did not turn toward oysters. He did not even remember a former quarrel with the man who was soon to do his office on them all. This quarrel dated back more than four years; Samson had sued the editor of the *Révolutions de France* for libel because this paper had called him the "Executioner of Paris." He was no executioner, he was an official, and his proper title was "Executor of Sentences." Philosophical meditations on the late and cruel satisfaction which Samson would now obtain did not concern Camille. What thoughts and feelings were seething in him were overshadowed by the one strangling thought that everything was over. He did not want to die. When the executioner's assistant came to cut off the long black locks on his neck he resisted wildly; strong hands had to hold him down on the chair. His coat ripped at the shoulder; he cried: "Lucile, come, Lucile!" If he had had any power of reflection left, he might have foreseen how this poor woman, denounced by Saint-Just, would come to join him. The low vaults of the chamber echoed shrilly, *"Lucile! A moi, Lucile!"*

Delacroix felt depressed. Dr. Guillotin had once recommended his machine as a marvel of humanitarianism; the victim experienced only a slight sensation of cold in the neck. But could one be certain of this?

Fabre d'Eglantine had been condemned to death once before, to the gallows, at Namur in 1777, for the abduction of pretty little Catherine Deresmond, nicknamed "Catiche." Did he remember this and infer that no man escapes his predestined fate? For weeks he had been tortured by a different thought. Among his papers, which were seized and sealed when he was arrested, was a nearly finished play of which he had great hopes—*"L'Orange de Malte."* If Collot d'Herbois had discovered it that worthless scribbler and sensationalist was capable of having it produced as a work of his own and of reaping the fame which was Fabre's due. Death and damnation! While his hair was being cut, Fabre shouted wrathfully for Fouquier. Fouquier had gone home to lunch long ago. Then his substitute! He was not available either. The infuriated poet called his companions in fate, executioner, jailers, and everyone present to bear witness to his public protest "against the infamy of the criminals of the Committee . . . they have stolen my comedy and they are keeping it although it has nothing to do with my case!"

When Philippeaux felt the scissors on his neck he groaned aloud: "My wife, my wife! My son! I shall never see you again!" Then he grew calm, and remained so until the end.

Danton, too, was a prey to fierce emotions; but no outward sign revealed the turmoil within him to his companions, the executioner's assistants, the gendarmes and the gunners who stood with drawn swords before the railings. He sat almost comfortably, talked as though he were at a barber's for the usual haircut and with grim humor prophesied evil: "Everything will go to the dogs because of the Committee of Public Safety. Couthon is a cripple and Robespierre a eunuch! If I could leave my legs to the one and my virility to the other perhaps things might run for a while; as it is France will awake in a mixture of blood and filth."

From outside came the drone of a vast throng of people, the stamping of the horses before the waiting tumbrils, the rattle of the scabbards of the gendarme escort.

On the stroke of four the two tumbrils, the first bearing Danton and the political prisoners, left the court of the Palais de Justice where Danton had once planted the Maypole in company with the Basoche. How many centuries had passed since then!

Slowly they rolled over the Pont-au-Change; Danton could see the glittering Seine; with the early spring it would soon be warm enough to swim. But that was over now. The tumbrils turned clumsily left. What a crowd along the Quai de la Mégisserie! And not a soul stirred a hand to hold back the turning wheels. *Canaille!*

They reached the end of the Quai and Danton felt a tug at his heart as on that day when Gabrielle was sitting at the till of the neighboring Café du Parnasse and he came with springing step to ask for her hand.

Then a turn to the right, into the Rue de la Monnaie, with its Café de la Monnaie, the rendezvous of the true, "the pure" revolutionaries.

In the Rue du Roule Danton raised his eyes to the houses. Every window was crowded with heads, but what moved him most was a goldfinch singing in a wooden cage. Its bill was opened wide but the murmur of the crowd drowned the song.

Before the procession turned left down the Rue Saint-Honoré, Danton's look rested unthinkingly on a tall church in the distance: Saint-Eustache.

The houses in this street were tall and narrow—only one or two windows wide. The throng was dense; the procession halted. At the corner of the Rue de l'Arbre Sec there was an old fountain; the water gushed in a thick stream. Soon the blood would flow from their headless corpses like this. And indeed had not the present spot, too, once been a place of execution?

Desmoulins, holding a blond curl of Lucile's in his fettered hand, strained desperately against his bonds and tried to rouse the people around him: "I am the first apostle of liberty! Do not let them murder me! Help!" But only eyes full of a merciless curiosity were raised and Danton admonished: "Be still. Can you hope to move this *canaille?*"

Slowly though the tumbrils advanced, the Palais d'Egalité was already reached. When its owner was executed an unknown negro stood in the crowd and wept, and on the day of the execution of Louis XVI a woman jumped into the Seine and a wigmaker of Rue Culture Sainte-Catherine cut his throat; the world had come to an end for them. Danton shook his head; no throat would be cut for his sake—although there would be some to weep. His mother in Arcis would weep bitterly, and his sister Anne-Madeleine, and the other sister Marie-Nicole, the nun, would even pray for his soul—queer to think of it.

And poor Louise! A shadow crossed his face and his eyes grew misty. But weakness must be forced down; mustn't let the dogs have this triumph.

For that was what they wanted; waiting at the Café de la Régence, pad on knee and pencil in hand, was David, with his eager boyish face, his tousled head, and his observant eyes; come to draw Danton in his evil hour, wretched, helpless, broken, for the greater pleasure of the committee. Danton flung him a word that lashed: "Lackey!"

But because David the great artist remained subject to the inexorable law of truth, his hand refused to make a caricature, and he fixed on paper what his incorruptible glance read in Danton's face: pride, defiance, scorn, disgust at the pettiness of existence, shame at being so easily duped, and, since Danton was a man, a man's fear of death mastered by will power.

Having done with Robespierre's lackey, Danton turned to his companions, whispered a word of consolation to Camille, saw Hérault nod smiling to an acquaintance, and watched Westermann, who with compressed lips was again living through August 10, 1792, when he rode up to the railings of the Tuileries Gardens and in his Alsatian dialect called on the Swiss Guard to surrender. How near he had been to death in battle then and many times since! And now he was to die at the hangman's hands.

On the steps of the Church of Saint-Roch a woman in the curious throng, smiling broadly, lifted up her child so that it might enjoy the spectacle; Danton resisted a strong temptation to put out his tongue at the brat to give it something to remember.

Another halt, in front of No. 364, and next to it No. 366, shuttered tight—the house of the accursed Robespierre. A wave of fury swept over Danton; he stamped with his hobnailed boots on the floor of the tumbril, raised himself to his full height and raged: "It is useless to hide! Your turn will come! And Danton's ghost will roar for joy in the grave when you are sitting in this cart." The tumbril had begun to move again; twisting around with effort, he shouted back: "This house will be razed to the ground and salt sown where it stood."

If Danton had had the gift of second sight he might have seen

Danton

a day, not long distant, in Thermidor, in July, when Robespierre would stand, pale green, in the Convention, his words drowned by loud interruptions, and would feel everything crashing around him, and again try vainly to speak and hear Garnier of the Department of the Aube call to him: "It is Danton's blood that chokes you."

Danton flushed red to the roots of his hair as a wave of excitement passed through him; and a spectator coolly remarked, "He's as red as a lobster."

To the right a glimpse of the Place des Piques where he had worked as minister; and now the tumbrils turned irrevocably down the Rue Royale with midges dancing round the horses' heads. At the end of the street rose a gruesome silhouette, two narrow upright beams with the steel triangle between.

The guillotine was waiting.

Danton's reaction to the sight was like that of the rest; the blood rushed to his heart and his face grew pale. But he quickly drew up his upper lip and again his look was sheer contempt.

How many more turns of the wheels?

The Place de la Révolution seemed paved with heads; only around the scaffold erected between the base of the Statue of Liberty, where formerly Louis XV had stood, and the Garden of the Tuileries a space had been kept free by soldiers and gendarmes. The horses were used to it and stopped of their own accord. The prisoners climbed from the tumbril. This was the spot where it was customary to say good-by to friends—and to life.

Samson knew the list and called the condemned by name. Diederichsen came first. Of the remaining fourteen some lowered their eyes; others stared resolutely at the scaffold where a number of sturdy figures were silently doing their work. There were three parts to the process. The board fell into place, the neck iron snapped closed, and the knife struck. Hardly a second elapsed between sound and sound.

Delaunay mounted the steps, then Basire, then the elder and the younger Frey. And each time as soon as the victim reached the top, the board fell into place, the iron closed, and the knife struck. And the mob shouted *"Vive la République!"* and sang snatches of the *Marseillaise*.

Desmoulins requested the executioner to carry Lucile's lock to his father-in-law as a last consolation. Hérault smiled up at a window of the former Treasury, where, as had been arranged, a white hand waved to him.

Fourteen times Danton watched the knife fall. Last of them all he mounted the ten steps with bare neck and hands tied behind his back and stood on his final public platform, in the steaming blood of his companions.

He drew a deep breath and for the last time let his eyes linger on Paris—on his left the trees of the Tuileries, on his right the trees of the Champs-Elysées, and behind them the magic sunset of the spring day; he could almost imagine that he smelled the nearby Seine. Feeling the executioner's grasp on his shoulders and arms he turned peremptorily on Samson: "Show my head to the people, it is worth it."

The knife struck.

———————————◆———————————

ELEVEN days previously another cemetery had been opened for the victims of the Revolutionary Tribunal, the churchyard of the Madeleine being overfull. The new cemetery—*Les Errancis* —was in the Faubourg de la Petite Pologne amid the ruins of the Naumachie, in a lonely green field where birds sang in tree and bush. Thither the corpses of the 16th Germinal were carted with no more ceremonial than would be given so many dead cattle, and soon what had been Danton changed into a certain quantity of water, carbonic acid, and ammonia.

———————————◆———————————

THE guillotine had made Sébastienne-Louise a widow before her eighteenth year, but she soon married Claude-François Dupin, whose father had been a lawyer of Metz and his mother a De Corny, and who under Napoleon became prefect, officer of the Legion of Honor, and baron of the Empire. Sébastienne-Louise witnessed the 9th Thermidor, the Directoire, the 18th Brumaire, the Consulate, the First Empire, the return of the Bourbons, the Hundred Days, the Restoration, the July Revolution, the bourgeois King, the February Revolution, the Second Republic, the Second December, the Second Empire, and died at the age of eighty in the year of the Peace of Paris, 1856. But in all this time she never mentioned the man to whom she had once belonged, and whose name, tradition, history, and party struggles pronounced around her in praise or blame a thousand times. As though a cell in her brain had been paralyzed, Louise's lips remained closed for a generation to the name of Danton.

Bibliography

BIBLIOGRAPHY

UNPUBLISHED SOURCES

Cartons A F II 48, BB14 702, C 164, 242, 244, 274, W 342, 526, 554 in the Archives Nationales, Paris.

PUBLISHED SOURCES

Aachener Zuschauer, Aachen, 1793.
Aegerter, La vie de Saint-Just. Paris, 1929.
Almanach National de France. Paris, l'An II de la République.
Almanach Royal. Paris, 1792.
Alméras, Fabre d'Eglantine. Paris, 1905.
Annales Historiques de la Révolution Française. I–VI. Reims, 1924–29.
Annales Révolutionnaires. III–VI. Paris, 1910–13.
Arnaud, Le fils de Fréron. Paris, 1909.
Aulard, Études et leçons sur la Révolution Française. I–IX. Paris, 1893–1924.
—— Histoire politique de la Révolution Française. Paris, 1921.
—— La Révolution Française et le régime féodal. Paris, 1919.
—— Les orateurs de la Révolution. I–III. Paris, 1905–06.
—— (ed.) La Société des Jacobins. I–VI. Paris, 1889–97.
—— (ed.) Recueil des actes du Comité de salut public. I–VI. Paris, 1889 ff.
Avenel, Anacharsis Cloots, l'orateur du genre humain. I, II. Paris, 1865.
—— La vraie Marie-Antoinette. Paris.

Babeau, La province sous l'ancien régime. Paris, 1894.
—— Paris en 1789. Paris, 1892.
Bailly, Mémoires d'un témoin de la Révolution. I–III. Paris.
Barère, Mémoires. I–IV. Paris, 1842.
Barras, Memoiren. I. Stuttgart, 1895.
(Barrière), Bibliothèque de mémoires relatifs à l'histoire de France. VIII. Paris, 1863.
Barthou, Mirabeau. Stuttgart, 1913.
Belloni, Le Comité de sûreté générale. Paris, 1924.
Béraud, Le 14 Juillet. Paris, 1929.
—— Mon ami Robespierre. Paris, 1927.
Billaud-Varenne, Mémoires. Paris, 1893.
Biré, Journal d'un bourgeois de Paris pendant la Terreur. I–V. Paris, 1907.
Blanc, Histoire de la Révolution Française. I, II. Paris.
Bloch, Études sur l'histoire économique de la France, 1760–1789. Paris, 1900.

Boguslawski, Das Leben des Generals Dumouriez, I, II. Berlin, 1879.

Bonald, François Chabot. Paris, 1908.

Borgnet, Histoire des Belges à la fin du XVIII siècle. I, II. Bruxelles, Paris, 1861–62.

Bos, Les avocats du Conseil du Roi. Paris, 1881.

Bougeart, Danton. Paris, 1861.

—— Les Cordeliers. Caen, 1891.

—— Marat. I, II. Paris, 1865.

Bournand, L'amour sous la Révolution. Paris, 1909.

Boutiot, Histoire de la ville de Troyes. I–V. Paris, 1870–80.

Braesch, La Commune du dix août 1792. Paris, 1911.

Brewer, Geschichte der französischen Gerichtsverfassung. II. Düsseldorf, 1837.

Brissot, Mémoires. Paris, 1877.

Buchez et Roux, Histoire parlementaire de la Révolution Française. I–XXXII. Paris, 1834–1837.

Buzot, Mémoires sur la Révolution Française. Paris, 1823.

Carnot, Mémoires. I, II. Paris, 1861–63.

Casenave, Etude sur les tribunaux de Paris de 1789 à 1800. Paris, 1873.

Champion, La France d'après les cahiers de 1789. Paris, 1921.

Cheslay, La Convention nationale. Paris, 1884.

Choudieu, Mémoires et notes. Paris, 1897.

Chuquet, Dumouriez. Paris, 1914.

—— Les guerres de la Révolution. I–X. Paris, 1886–1894.

Claretie, Camille Desmoulins, Lucile Desmoulins. Paris, 1875.

Clemenceau-Jacquemaire, Vie de Madame Roland. I, II. Paris, 1929.

Compardon, Le Tribunal Révolutionnaire de Paris. I, II. Paris, 1866.

Courtois, Rapport fait au nom de la commission chargée de l'examen des papiers trouvés chez Robespierre et ses complices. Paris, An III de la République.

Couthon, Correspondance (1791–1794). Paris, 1872.

Crétineau-Joly, Histoire de la Vendée militaire. I–IV. Paris, 1865.

Cunow, Die revolutionäre Zeitungsliteratur Frankreichs während der Jahre 1789–1794. Berlin, 1908.

Danton, Discours. Édition critique par André Fribourg. Paris, 1910.

—— Discours civiques. Paris, 1920.

Dard, Hérault de Séchelles. Paris, 1907.

—— Le général Choderlos de Laclos. Paris, 1905.

Dauban, Les prisons de Paris sous la Révolution. Paris, 1870.

—— Paris en 1794 et en 1795. Paris, 1869.

Daudet, Histoire de l'Emigration. Paris, 1890.

Description des ouvrages de peinture, sculpture etc exposés au Salon du Louvre. Paris, l'an 2 de la République.

Desmoulins, Oeuvres. I, II. Paris, 1906.

Diderot, Oeuvres complètes. I–XX. Paris, 1876.
Dodu, Le parlementarisme et les parlementaires sous la Révolution (1789–1799). Paris, 1911.
—— Trois mois à Paris sous la Terreur. Paris, 1921.
Dubost, Danton et la politique contemporaine. Paris, 1880.
Dubreuil, Histoire des insurrections de l'Ouest. Paris, 1929.
Dumouriez, Mémoires. Paris, 1802.
Durand de Maillane, Histoire de la Convention nationale. Paris, 1825.
Dussane, La Célimène de Thermidor. Paris, 1929.
—— La Comédie-Française. Paris.

Fabre d'Eglantine, Oeuvres politiques. Paris, 1914.
Faguet, L'oeuvre sociale de la Révolution Française. Paris, 1910.
Fleischmann, La guillotine en 1793. Paris, 1908.
—— Les femmes et la Terreur. Paris, 1910.
—— Les pamphlets libertins contre Marie-Antoinette. Paris.
—— Robespierre et les femmes. Paris, 1909.
Fleury, Mémoires. I–VI. Paris, 1835–38.
Forster, Ansichten vom Niederrhein. Leipzig.
Fouquier-Tinville, Réquisitoires. Paris, 1911.
(Frey), Philosophie sociale. Par un citoyen de la section de la République Française ci-devant du Roule. Paris, 1793.
Funck-Brentano, L'Ancien Régime. Paris, 1926.

Gallier, La vie de province au dix-huitième siècle. Paris, 1877.
Glagau, Reformversuche und Sturz des Absolutismus in Frankreich (1774–1788). München, 1908.
Goethe, Sämtliche Werke. XIV. Leipzig.
Gomel, Histoire financière de l'Assemblée Constituante. I, II. Paris, 1896–97.
—— Histoire financière de la Législative et de la Convention. I, II. Paris, 1902–05.
Gottschalk, Jean-Paul Marat. Paris, 1929.
Guadet, Les Girondins. I, II. Paris, 1861.

Hamel, Histoire de Robespierre. I–III. Paris, 1865–67.
—— Histoire de Saint-Just. Paris, 1859.
Hauréau, La Montagne. Paris, 1834.
Hébert, Le Père Duchesne. Réimpression. Paris, 1922 ff.
Hentig, Robespierre. Stuttgart, 1924.
Hérault de Séchelles, Oeuvres littéraires. Paris, 1907.
Hérissey, François Buzot.

Jaurès, Histoire socialiste de la Révolution Française. I–VIII. Paris, 1922–27.

Jovanović, Vodji francuske revolucije. Beograd, 1920.
Jung, Dubois-Crancé. I, II. Paris, 1884.

Kautsky, Die Klassengegensätze von 1789. Stuttgart, 1889.
K. u. k. Kriegsarchiv, Krieg gegen die Französische Revolution 1792 bis
    97. Wien, 1905.
Kropotkin, Die französische Revolution 1789–1793. I, II. Leipzig.
Kuscinski, Dictionnaire des Conventionnels. Paris, 1917.
—— Les députés à l'Assemblée Législative de 1791. Paris, 1900.

Lacour, Trois femmes de la Révolution. Paris, 1900.
Lallemand, Histoire de l'éducation dans l'ancien Oratoire de France. Paris,
    1888.
Lameth, Mémoires. Paris, 1913.
Larevellière-Lépeaux, Mémoires. I–III. Paris, 1895.
La Révolution Française. Revue. I–LXXXIII. Paris, 1881–1930.
Launay, Barère. Paris, 1929.
Lecomte, La vie amoureuse de Danton. Paris, 1927.
Lennox, Danton. Paris, 1878.
Lenotre, La guillotine pendant la Révolution. Paris, 1927.
—— Le drame de Varennes. Paris, 1926.
—— Le Tribunal Révolutionnaire. Paris, 1908.
—— Les massacres de Septembre. Paris, 1928.
—— Paris Révolutionnaire. Paris, 1928.
—— Vieilles maisons, vieux papiers. VI. 1930.
(Lescure), Mémoires sur les Comités de salut public, de sûreté générale et
    sur les prisons (1793–1794). Paris, 1878.
—— Mémoires sur les journées révolutionnaires. Paris, 1875.
Lévy-Schneider, Le Conventionnel Jeanbon Saint-André. Paris, 1901.
Lichtenberger, Le socialisme et la Révolution Française. Paris, 1899.
Lintilhac, Vergniaud. Paris, 1920.
Liste des victimes du Tribunal Révolutionnaire à Paris. Paris, 1911.
(Lockroy), Journal d'une bourgeoise pendant la Révolution 1791–1793.
    Paris, 1881.

Madelin, Danton. Paris, 1914.
Marcère, Une ambassade à Constantinople. I, II. Paris, 1927.
Marion, Dictionnaire des institutions de France. Paris, 1923.
Mathiez, Autour de Danton. Paris, 1926.
—— Danton et la paix. Paris.
—— Etudes Robespierristes. I, II. Paris, 1927, 1918.
—— L'affaire de la Compagnie des Indes. Paris, 1920.
—— La Révolution et les étrangers. Paris, 1918.
—— La Révolution Française. I–III. Paris, 1927–29.
—— La vie chère et le mouvement social sous la Terreur. Paris, 1927.
—— Le Club des Cordeliers. Paris, 1910.

—— La victoire en l'An II. Paris, 1916.

—— Robespierre terroriste. Paris, 1921.

(Maugras), Journal d'un étudiant pendant la Révolution. Paris, 1890.

Mautouchet, Le Conventionnel Philippeaux. Paris, 1900.

—— Le gouvernement révolutionnaire. Paris, 1912.

Mège, Le Conventionnel Bancart des Issarts. Paris.

Mellié, Les sections de Paris pendant la Révolution Française. Paris, 1898.

Mémoires de la société académique d'agriculture, des sciences, arts et belles-lettres du département de l'Aube. XXXXV. Troyes, 1881.

Mercier, Le nouveau Paris. Paris.

—— Tableau de Paris. Paris, 1781.

Michelet, Histoire de la Révolution Française. I–IX. Paris.

Miles, Correspondence on the French Revolution. I, II. London.

Minutoli, Der Feldzug der Verbündeten in Frankreich im Jahre 1792. Berlin, 1847.

Mirabeau et La Marck, Correspondance. I–III. Paris, 1851.

Monchanin, Dumouriez. Paris, 1884.

Mortimer-Ternaux, Histoire de la Terreur, 1792–1794. I–VIII. Paris, 1868–1881.

Niessner, Zwanzig Jahre Franzosenherrschaft am Niederrhein, 1794 bis 1814. Aachen, 1907.

Notice des pièces authentiques relatives aux principaux Agents de la faction de l'Etranger, qui ont conspiré contre la souveraineté du Peuple français et contre la représentation nationale. Paris, An Deux de l'ère républicain.

Nourisson, Trois révolutionnaires: Turgot, Necker, Bailly. Paris, 1885.

Perraud, L'Oratoire de France. Paris, 1865.

Pollio et Marcel, Le bataillon du 10 août. Paris, 1881.

Pottet, La Conciergerie du Palais de Paris. Paris, 1926.

Reichardt, Vertraute Briefe über Frankreich. Berlin, 1792–93.

Réimpression de l'ancien Moniteur. I–XX. Paris, 1858–1870.

Revue de Paris. XXXIX. Paris, 1857.

Revue Historique de la Révolution Française et de l'Empire. III. Paris, 1912.

Robespierre, Discours et rapports. Paris, 1908.

Robinet, Danton. Mémoire sur sa vie privée. Paris, 1884.

—— Danton émigré. Paris, 1887.

—— Danton homme d'État. Paris, 1889.

—— Dictionnaire historique et biographique de la Révolution et de l'Empire. I, II. Paris.

—— Le procès des Dantonistes. Paris, 1879.

Rosenkranz, Diderots Leben und Werke. 1, 2. Leipzig, 1866.

Roujon, Ce bon Monsieur Danton. Paris, 1929.

Saint-Just, Oeuvres complètes. I, II. Paris, 1908.

Saunier, Louis David. Paris, 1903.

Scheiber, Die Septembermorde und Danton. Leipzig, 1912.

Scheins, Aachen vor hundert Jahren. Aachen, 1887.

Schmidt, Tableaux de la Révolution Française, I–III. Leipzig, 1867 bis 1870.

Sorel, L'Europe et la Révolution Française. I–III. Paris, 1908–13.

Stéfane-Pol, Le Conventionnel Le Bas. Paris.

Stern, Anacharsis Cloots. Berlin, 1914.

Tableau des prisons de Paris sous le règne de Robespierre. I–IV. Paris, 1795.

Talleyrand, Correspondance diplomatique. Paris, 1889.

Thénard et Guyot, Le Conventionnel Goujon. Paris, 1908.

Thévenot, Notice généalogique et biographique de Danton. Arcis-sur-Aube, 1904.

Tourneux, Bibliographie de l'histoire de Paris pendant la Révolution. I–III. Paris, 1890–1900.

Tournier, Vadier. Paris.

Tuetey, Répertoire général des sources manuscrites de l'histoire de Paris pendant la Révolution Française. XI. Paris, 1914.

Turreau, Mémoires. Paris, 1824.

Vialay, Les cahiers de doléances du Tiers-Etat. Paris, 1911.

—— La vente des biens nationaux. Paris, 1908.

Villiaumé, Histoire de la Révolution Française. I–IV. Paris, 1850.

Wallon, Histoire du Tribunal Révolutionnaire de Paris. I–VI. Paris, 1880–82.

—— La révolution du 31 Mai et le fédéralisme en 1793. I, II. Paris, 1886.

Zinkeisen, Der Jakobiner-Klub. I, II. Berlin, 1852–53.

Index

INDEX

Adelaide, 45

Aelder, *see* Palm

Aiguillon, Duke of, 33

Alembert, 16

Amar, Jean-Pierre, 23, 24, 178, 271, 293, 295, 299, 321, 324, 328

Angelle, Baroness d', 138

Annonville, 79

Anthoine, 34, 57, 97, 98, 100

Arcis-sur-Aube, 3–6, 12, 43, 47–48, 49, 83, 142, 162, 184, 186–187, 272–277, 292, 296, 322, 331

Artois, Comte d', 40, 68, 75, 86, 222

Assembly, National, *see* Constituent Assembly, Legislative Assembly, National Convention

Auckland, Lord, 224

Audu, Reine-Louise, 70

August 10, 1792, 101–105, 109, 119, 123, 124, 127, 131, 137, 138, 142, 146, 150, 153, 158, 163, 171, 174, 221, 259, 260, 322; Extraordinary Tribunal of August 17 created to deal with crimes connected with, 120

Austria, 74, 92, 98, 100, 116, 118, 121, 126, 131, 137, 143, 145, 159, 165, 184, 198, 199, 214, 216, 217, 220, 224, 226, 227, 265; invasion of France, 131–141, *see also* War with Austria

Babeuf, Gracchus, 63

Bailly, Jean-Sylvain, 52–55, 58, 59, 61, 67, 76, 81, 83

Bancal des Issarts, 152, 156, 200, 232, 242

Barbaroux, 156, 163, 201, 255, 256, 322

Barentin, de Paul de, 24

Barère, Bertrand, 22–23, 24, 110, 176, 178, 202, 212, 216, 217, 218, 220, 242, 253, 255, 260, 263, 276, 281, 299, 300, 308

—— Elizabeth (de Monde), 23

Barnave, Antoine-Pierre-Joseph-Marie, 22, 24, 33, 66, 82, 90, 125, 232, 322

Barral, Bishop Claude-Mathias-Joseph de, 9

Basire, Claude, 35, 73, 101, 124, 127–128, 153, 166, 176, 220, 294, 333; trial of, 316, 319, 320

Basoche, 11–12, 330

Bastille, 99, 259; fall of, 26, 29, 41, 50, 63, 67, 71, 183

Beauharnais, Vicomte de, 33

Beaumarchais, 44

Bécourt, 71

Belgium, 92, 139, 182–190, 197–200, 203, 209–216, 217, 218, 219, 237, 245, 247, 248, 311; Lückner's campaign (April, 1792), 92; Dumouriez' campaign in, 182; commissioners' visit to, 183–188; commissioners' report on, 188–189; decree concerning occupied countries, 189–190; question of annexation of, 191, 197–200; Talleyrand advocates alliance with, 200; Coburg's campaign to recover, and French reaction, 209–213; Dumouriez' treachery in, 213–216; second visit of Danton and Delacroix as commissioners, 214–216

Benoît, Pierre-Vincent, 143, 194

Bertin, 45

Bérulle, 8

Beurnonville, Minister of War, 209, 216

Billaud-Varenne, Jacques-Nicolas, 20–21, 34, 42, 45, 138, 149, 150, 164–165, 196, 212, 268, 271, 287, 293, 295, 300, 323

—— Mme. (Doye), 20

Biroteau, 161–162

Blignac, 68

Bontemps, 281

Bouchardie, Mme. de la, 177

Bouchotte, Minister of War, 219, 267, 278

Bouillé, Marquis de, 71, 72, 123